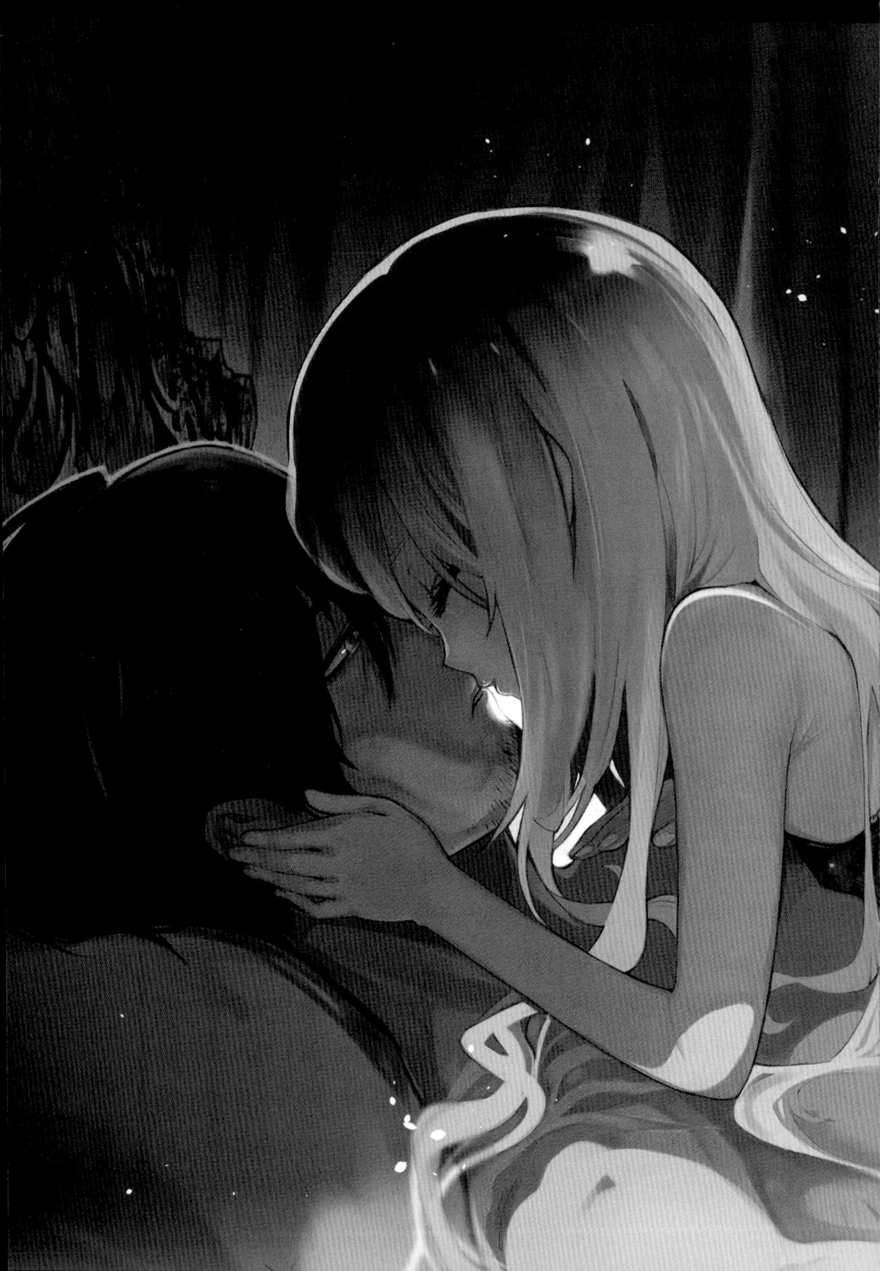

#001 “V”

MOMO
-the blood taker-
CONTENTS

1

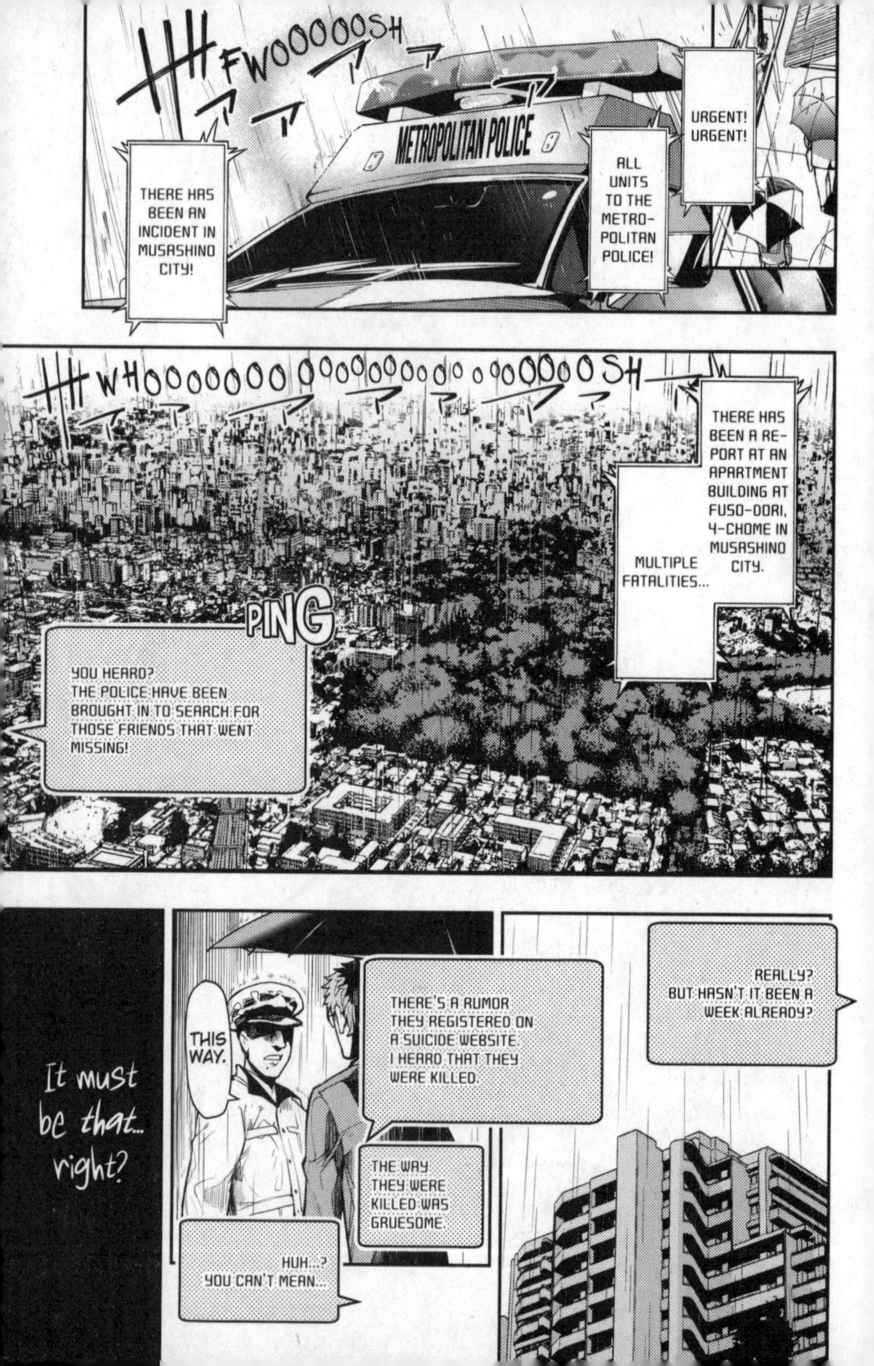
FWOOOOOSH
METROPOLITAN POLICE
URGENT! URGENT!
ALL UNITS TO THE METRO-POLITAN POLICE!
THERE HAS BEEN AN INCIDENT IN MUSASHINO CITY!
WHOOOOOOOOOOOOOOOOOOOOOOOOSH
THERE HAS BEEN A RE-PORT AT AN APARTMENT BUILDING AT FUSO-DORI, 4-CHOME IN MUSASHINO CITY.
MULTIPLE FATALITIES...
PING
YOU HEARD? THE POLICE HAVE BEEN BROUGHT IN TO SEARCH FOR THOSE FRIENDS THAT WENT MISSING!
REALLY? BUT HASN'T IT BEEN A WEEK ALREADY?
THERE'S A RUMOR THEY REGISTERED ON A SUICIDE WEBSITE. I HEARD THAT THEY WERE KILLED.
THIS WAY.
THE WAY THEY WERE KILLED WAS GRUESOME.
HUH...? YOU CAN'T MEAN...
It must be that... right?

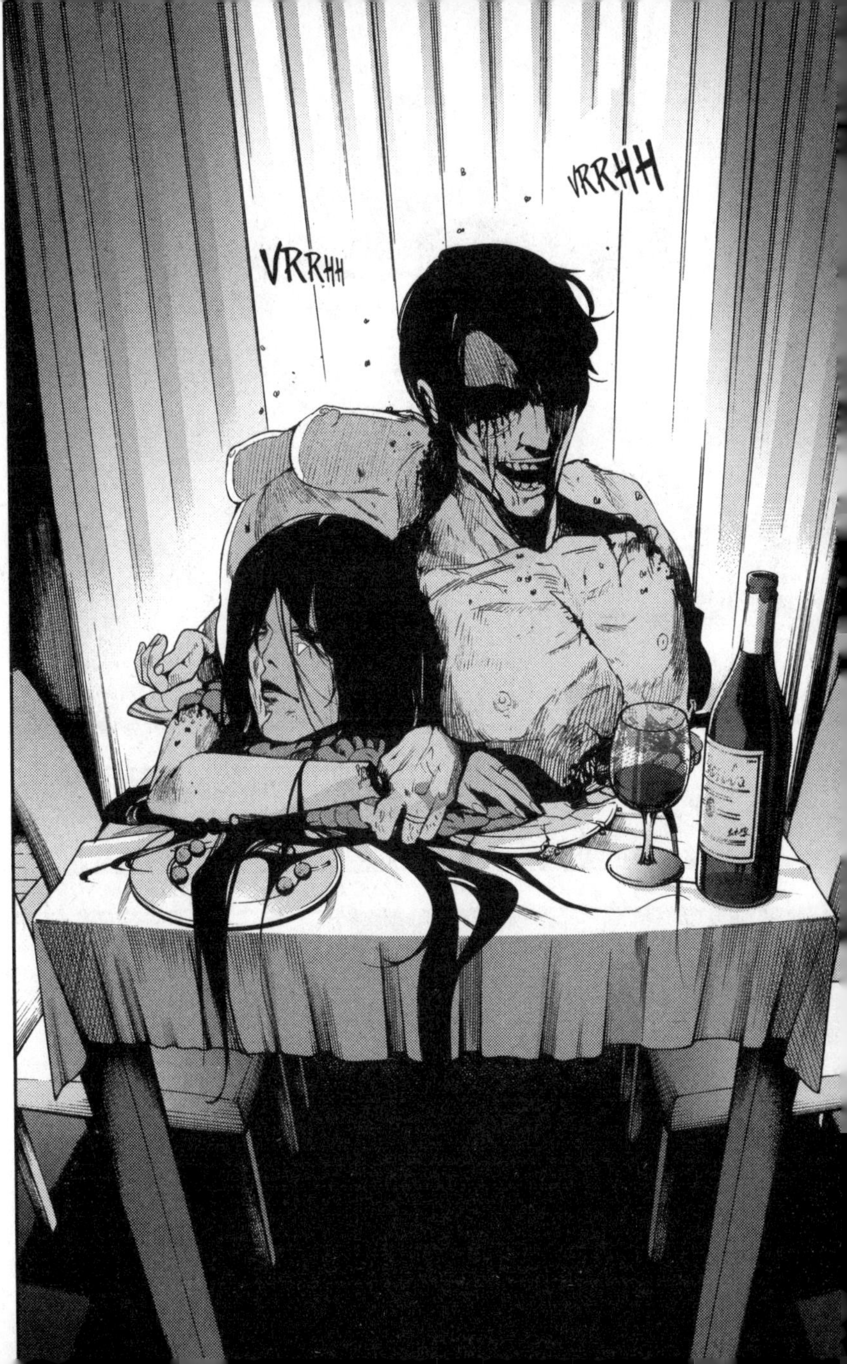
VRRHH
VRRHH

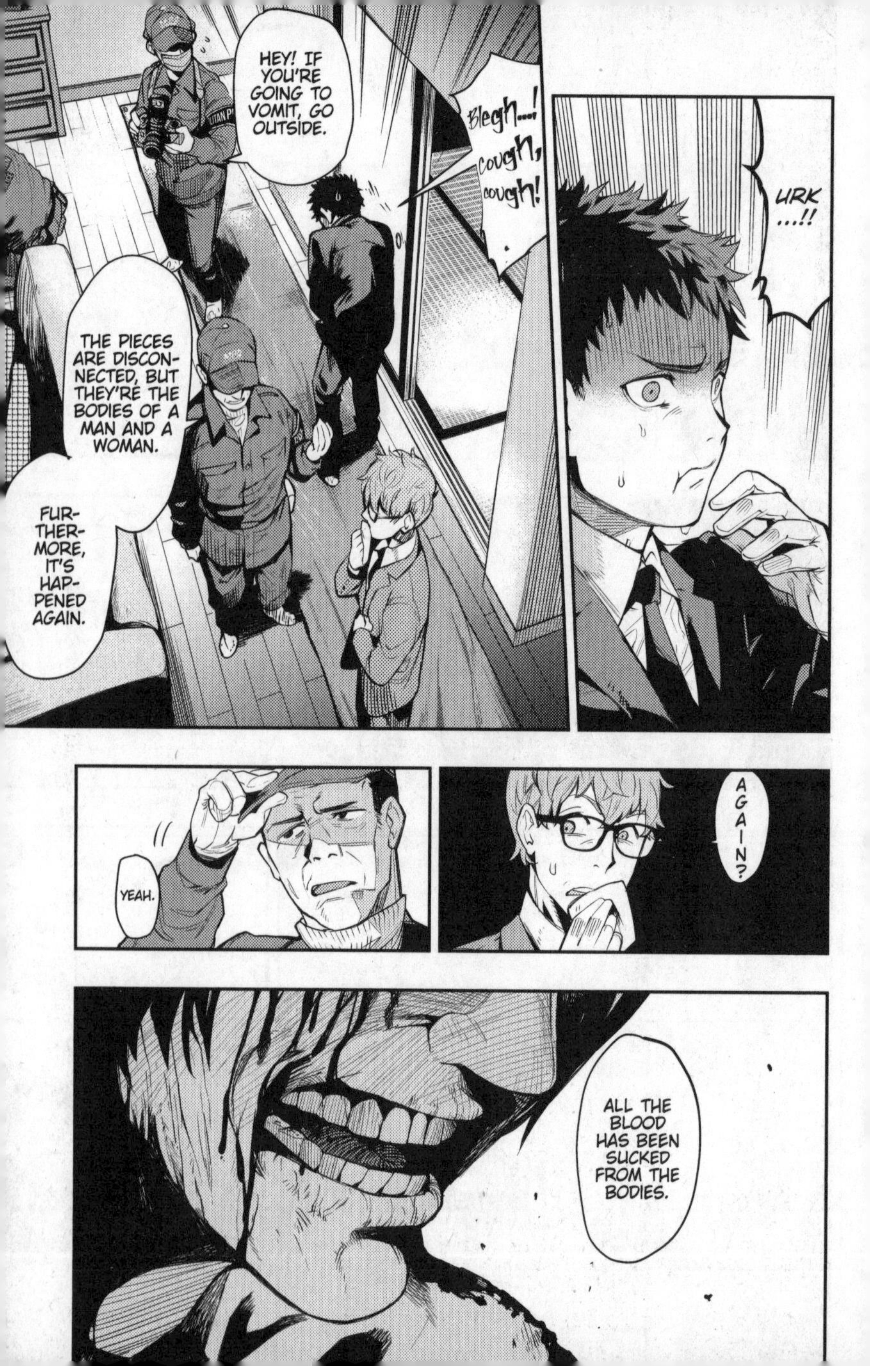
URK ...!!
Blegh...! cough, cough!
HEY! IF YOU'RE GOING TO VOMIT, GO OUTSIDE.
THE PIECES ARE DISCONNECTED, BUT THEY'RE THE BODIES OF A MAN AND A WOMAN.
FURTHERMORE, IT'S HAPPENED AGAIN.
AGAIN?
YEAH.
ALL THE BLOOD HAS BEEN SUCKED FROM THE BODIES.

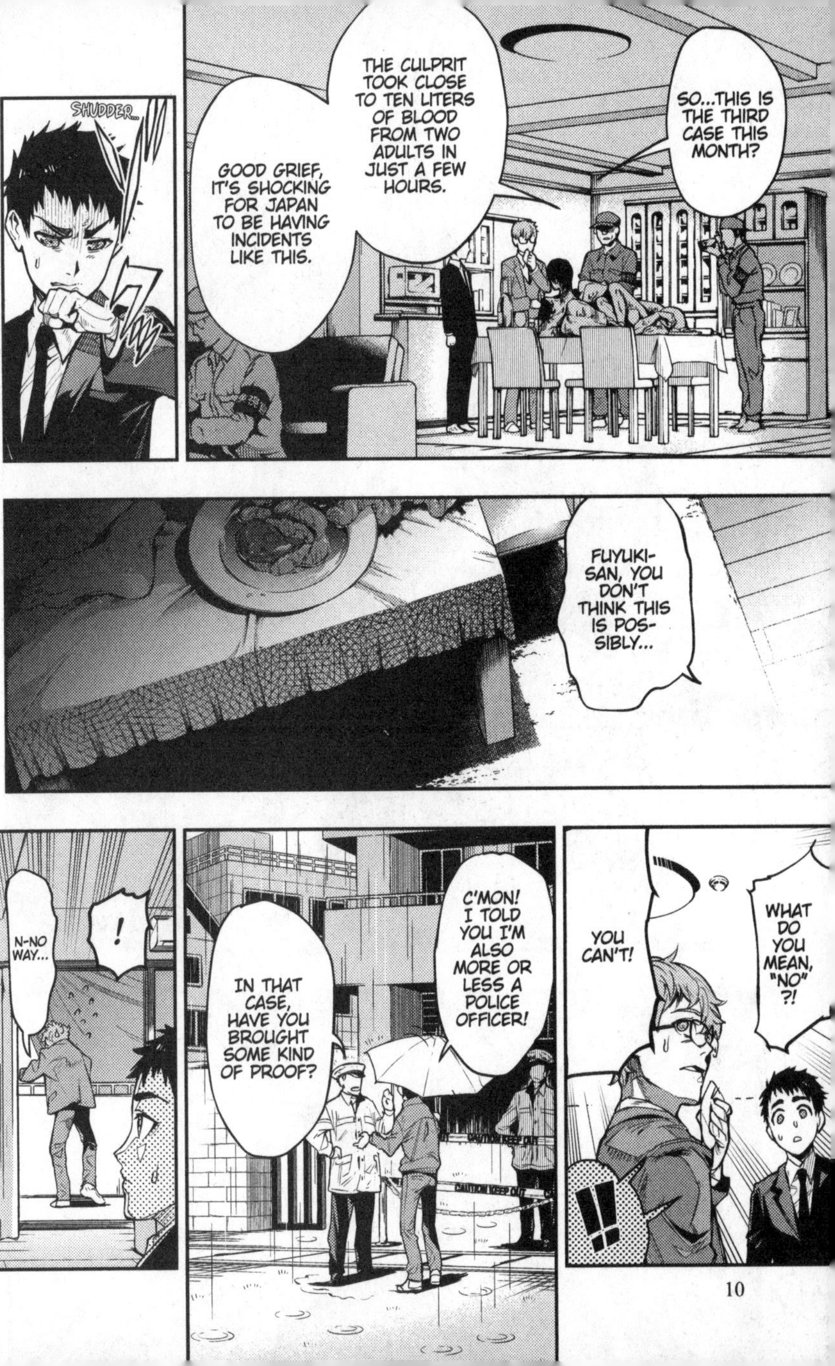
SO...THIS IS THE THIRD CASE THIS MONTH?
THE CULPRIT TOOK CLOSE TO TEN LITERS OF BLOOD FROM TWO ADULTS IN JUST A FEW HOURS.
GOOD GRIEF, IT'S SHOCKING FOR JAPAN TO BE HAVING INCIDENTS LIKE THIS.
SHUDDER...
FUYUKI-SAN, YOU DON'T THINK THIS IS POS-SIBLY...
WHAT DO YOU MEAN, "NO"?!
YOU CAN'T!
!!
C'MON! I TOLD YOU I'M ALSO MORE OR LESS A POLICE OFFICER!
IN THAT CASE, HAVE YOU BROUGHT SOME KIND OF PROOF?
CAUTION KEEP OUT
!
N-NO WAY...

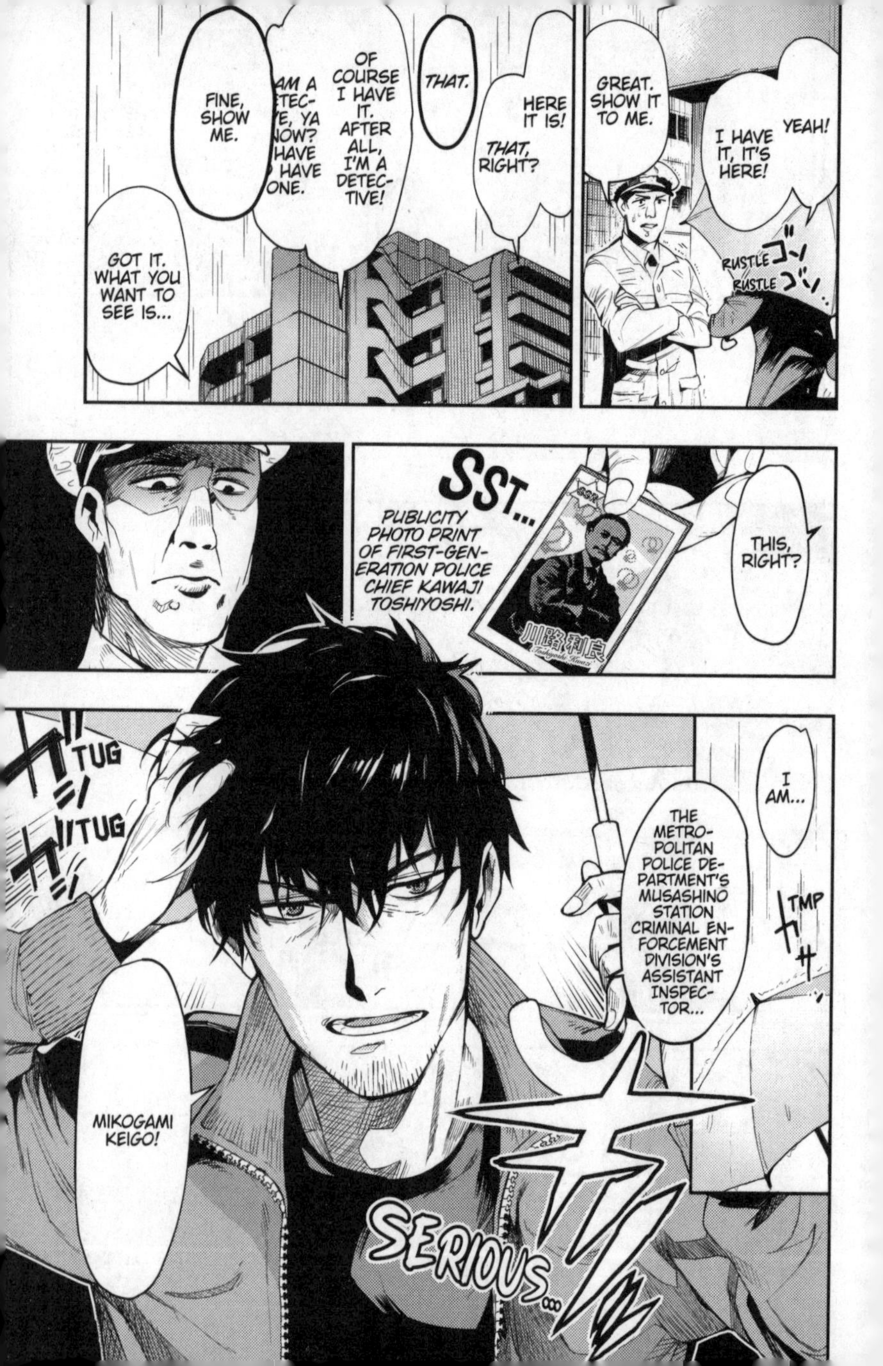
YEAH!
I HAVE IT, IT'S HERE!
RUSTLE RUSTLE
GREAT. SHOW IT TO ME.
HERE IT IS!
THAT, RIGHT?
THAT.
OF COURSE I HAVE IT. AFTER ALL, I'M A DETECTIVE!
AM A ETEC- VE, YA NOW? HAVE HAVE ONE.
FINE, SHOW ME.
GOT IT. WHAT YOU WANT TO SEE IS...
THIS, RIGHT?
SST...
SSR
川路利良
Toshiyoshi Kawazi
PUBLICITY PHOTO PRINT OF FIRST-GENERATION POLICE CHIEF KAWAJI TOSHIYOSHI.
I AM...
THE METROPOLITAN POLICE DEPARTMENT'S MUSASHINO STATION CRIMINAL ENFORCEMENT DIVISION'S ASSISTANT INSPECTOR...
TMP
TUG TUG
MIKOGAMI KEIGO!
SERIOUS...

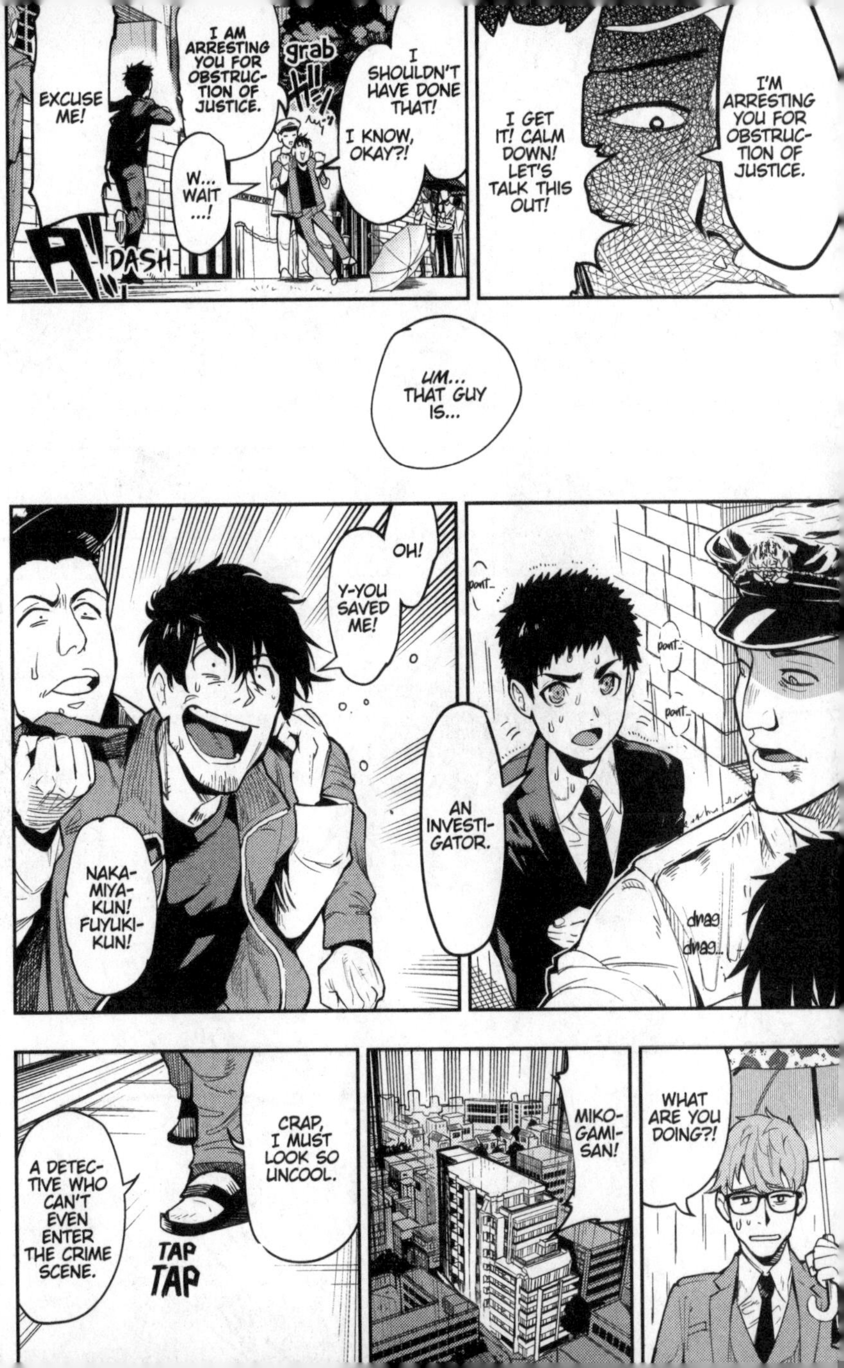
I'M ARRESTING YOU FOR OBSTRUCTION OF JUSTICE.
I GET IT! CALM DOWN! LET'S TALK THIS OUT!
I SHOULDN'T HAVE DONE THAT!
I KNOW, OKAY?!
grab
I AM ARRESTING YOU FOR OBSTRUCTION OF JUSTICE.
W... WAIT ...!
EXCUSE ME!
DASH
UM... THAT GUY IS...
pont..
pont..
pont..
AN INVESTIGATOR.
drag
drag...
OH!
Y-YOU SAVED ME!
NAKAMIYA-KUN! FUYUKI-KUN!
WHAT ARE YOU DOING?!
MIKOGAMI-SAN!
CRAP, I MUST LOOK SO UNCOOL.
A DETECTIVE WHO CAN'T EVEN ENTER THE CRIME SCENE.
TAP
TAP

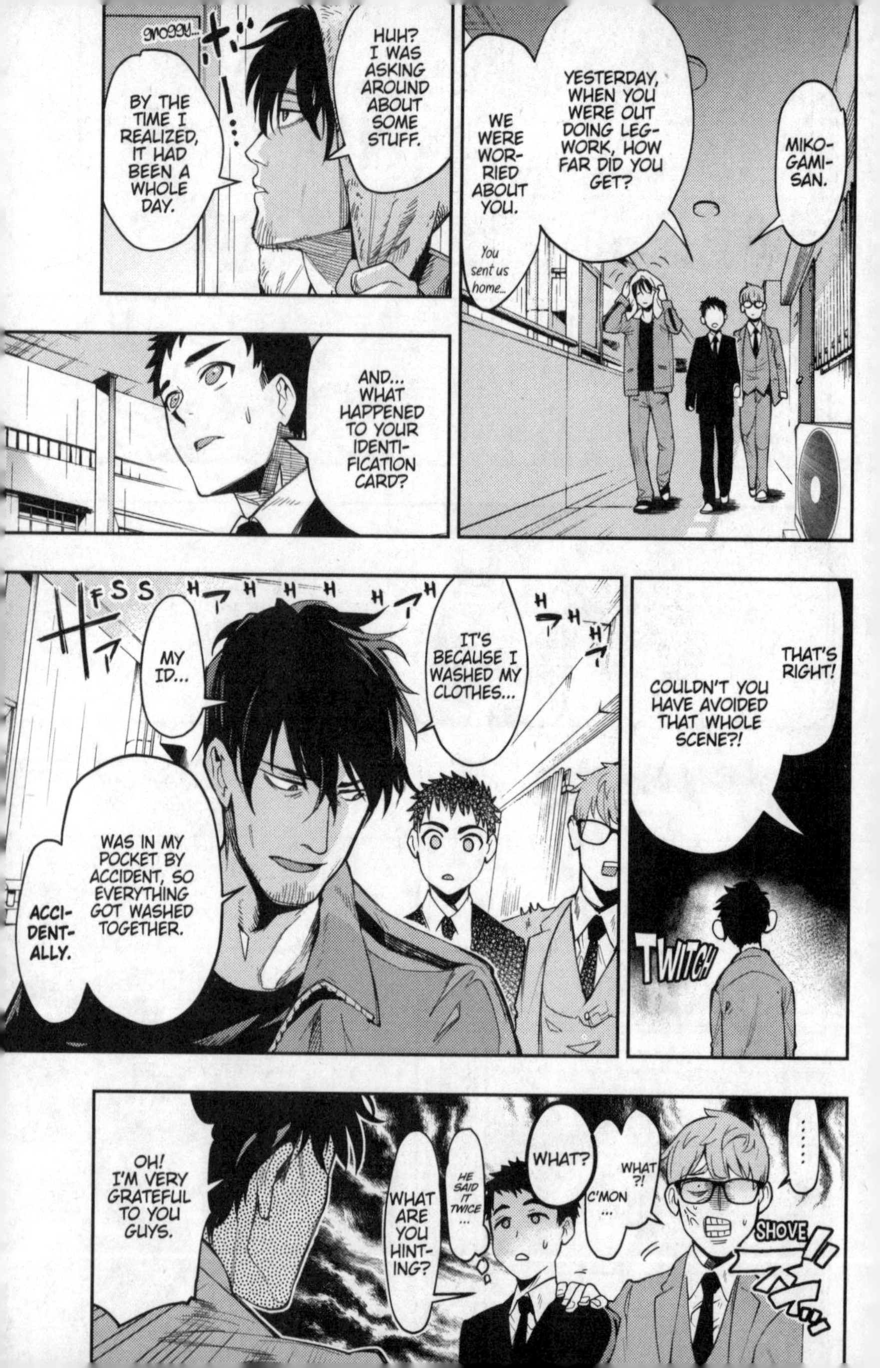
MIKO-GAMI-SAN.
YESTERDAY, WHEN YOU WERE OUT DOING LEG-WORK, HOW FAR DID YOU GET?
WE WERE WOR-RIED ABOUT YOU.
You sent us home...
groggy...
HUH? I WAS ASKING AROUND ABOUT SOME STUFF.
BY THE TIME I REALIZED, IT HAD BEEN A WHOLE DAY.
AND... WHAT HAPPENED TO YOUR IDENTI-FICATION CARD?
THAT'S RIGHT!
COULDN'T YOU HAVE AVOIDED THAT WHOLE SCENE?!
TWITCH
FSS
IT'S BECAUSE I WASHED MY CLOTHES...
MY ID...
WAS IN MY POCKET BY ACCIDENT, SO EVERYTHING GOT WASHED TOGETHER.
ACCI-DENT-ALLY.
......
WHAT?!
C'MON...
WHAT?
HE SAID IT TWICE...
WHAT ARE YOU HINT-ING?
OH! I'M VERY GRATEFUL TO YOU GUYS.
SHOVE

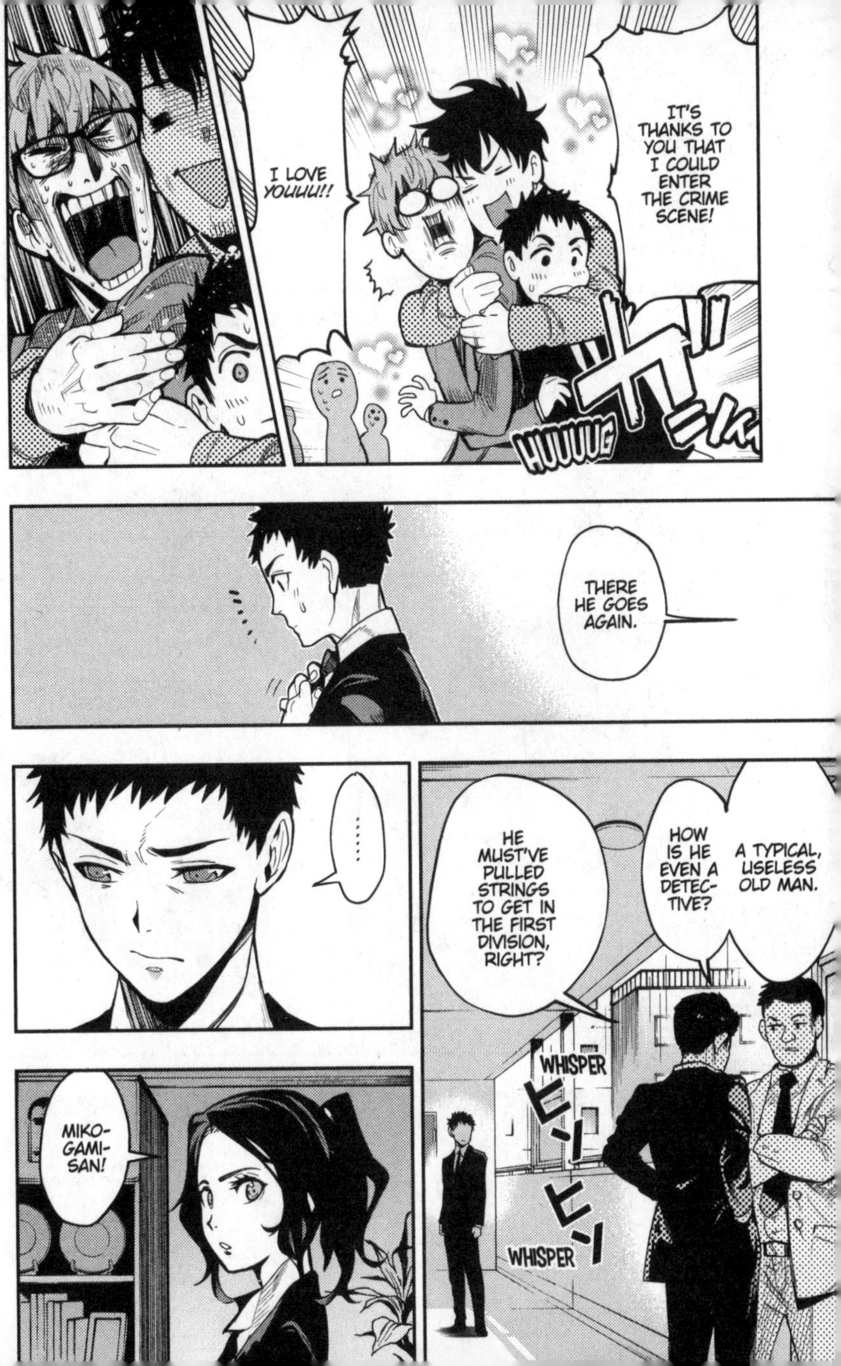
IT'S THANKS TO YOU THAT I COULD ENTER THE CRIME SCENE!
I LOVE YOUUU!!
HUUUUG
THERE HE GOES AGAIN.
A TYPICAL, USELESS OLD MAN.
HOW IS HE EVEN A DETECTIVE?
HE MUST'VE PULLED STRINGS TO GET IN THE FIRST DIVISION, RIGHT?
WHISPER
WHISPER
......
MIKO-GAMI-SAN!

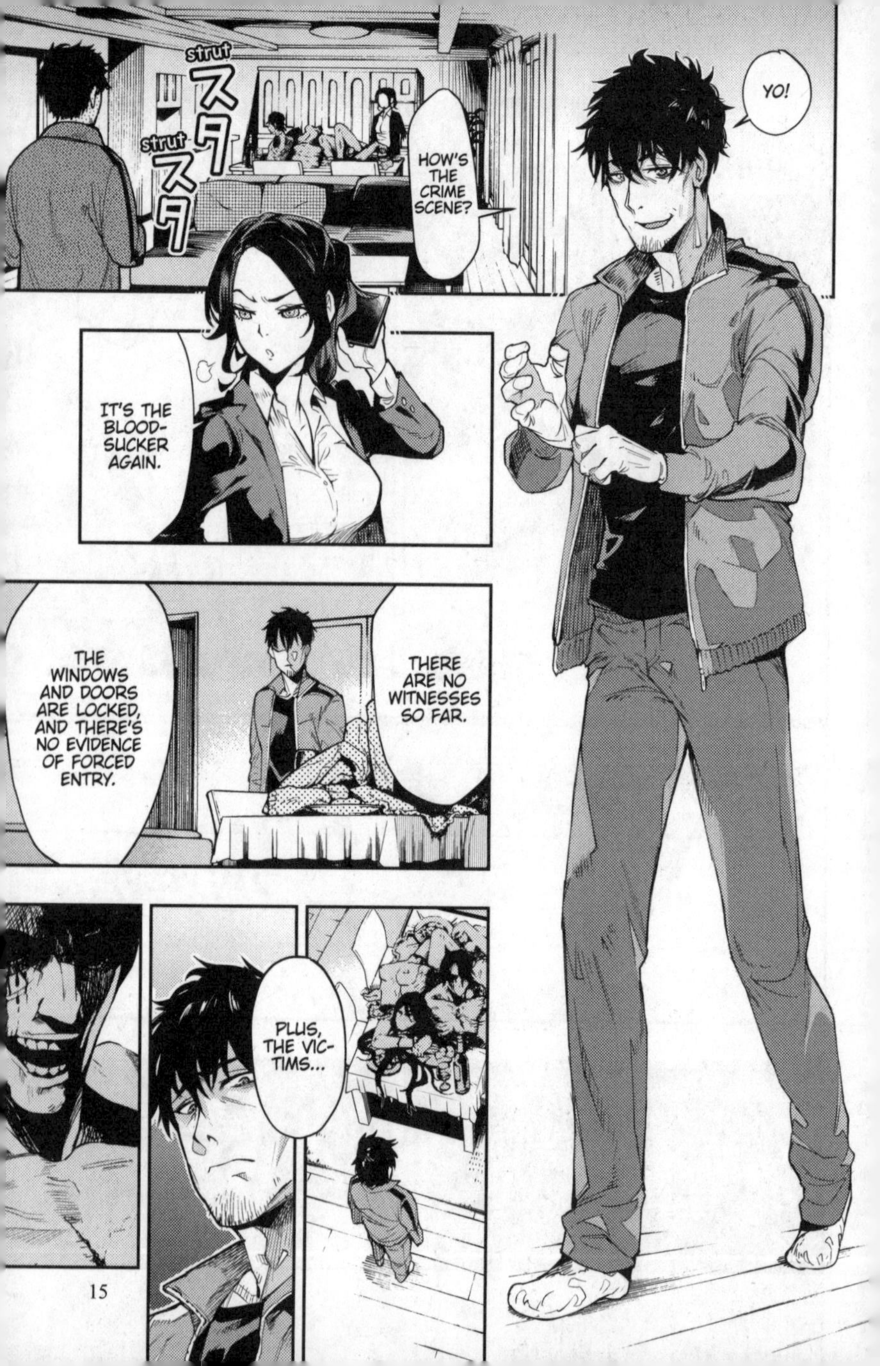
YO!
strut
スタ
strut
スタ
HOW'S THE CRIME SCENE?
IT'S THE BLOOD-SUCKER AGAIN.
THERE ARE NO WITNESSES SO FAR.
THE WINDOWS AND DOORS ARE LOCKED, AND THERE'S NO EVIDENCE OF FORCED ENTRY.
PLUS, THE VIC-TIMS...

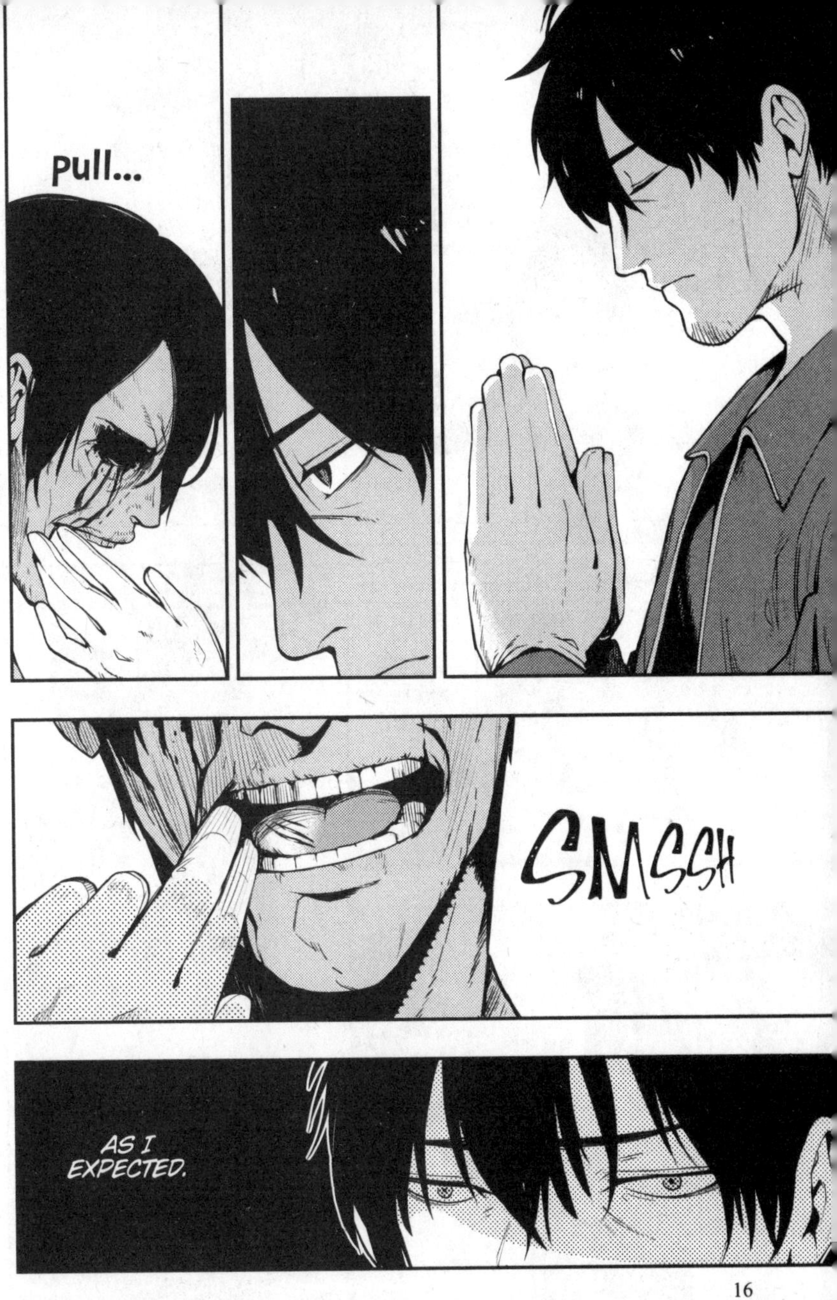
pull...
SMSSH
AS I EXPECTED.

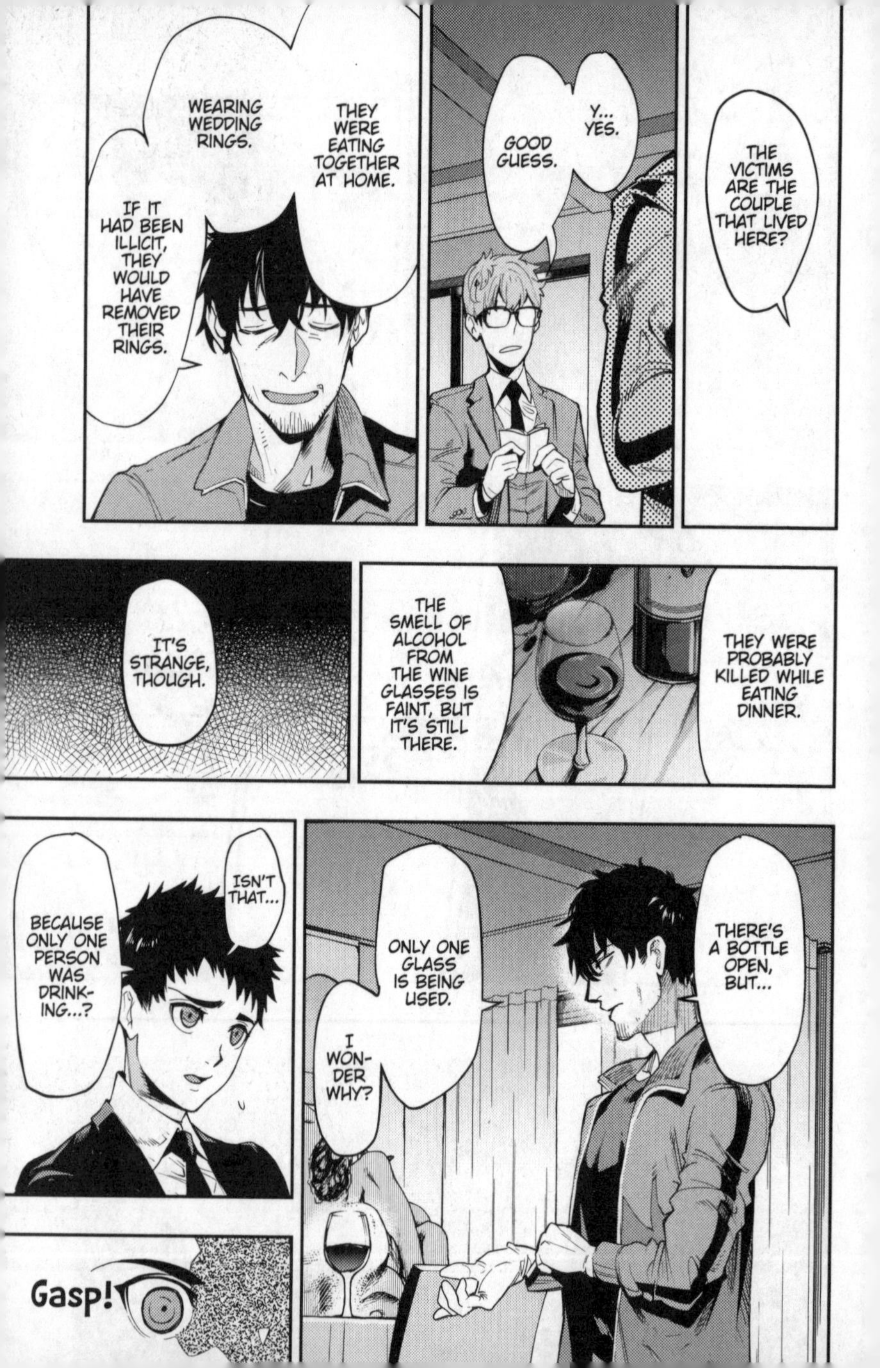
THE VICTIMS ARE THE COUPLE THAT LIVED HERE?
Y... YES.
GOOD GUESS.
THEY WERE EATING TOGETHER AT HOME.
WEARING WEDDING RINGS.
IF IT HAD BEEN ILLICIT, THEY WOULD HAVE REMOVED THEIR RINGS.
THEY WERE PROBABLY KILLED WHILE EATING DINNER.
THE SMELL OF ALCOHOL FROM THE WINE GLASSES IS FAINT, BUT IT'S STILL THERE.
IT'S STRANGE, THOUGH.
THERE'S A BOTTLE OPEN, BUT...
ONLY ONE GLASS IS BEING USED.
I WONDER WHY?
ISN'T THAT...
BECAUSE ONLY ONE PERSON WAS DRINKING...?
Gasp!

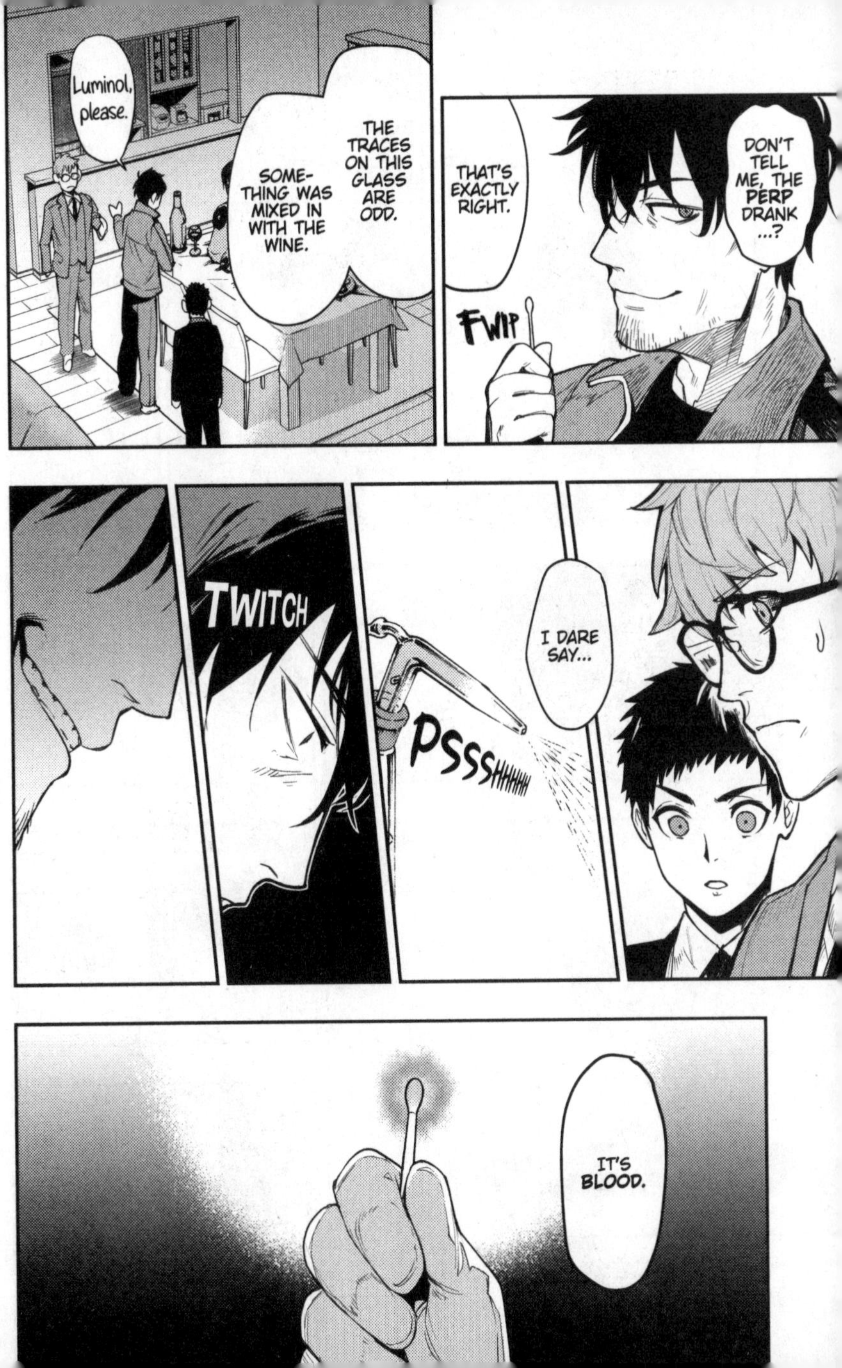
DON'T TELL ME, THE PERP DRANK ...?
THAT'S EXACTLY RIGHT.
FWIP
THE TRACES ON THIS GLASS ARE ODD.
SOME-THING WAS MIXED IN WITH THE WINE.
Luminol, please.
I DARE SAY...
PSSSHHHHH
TWITCH
IT'S BLOOD.

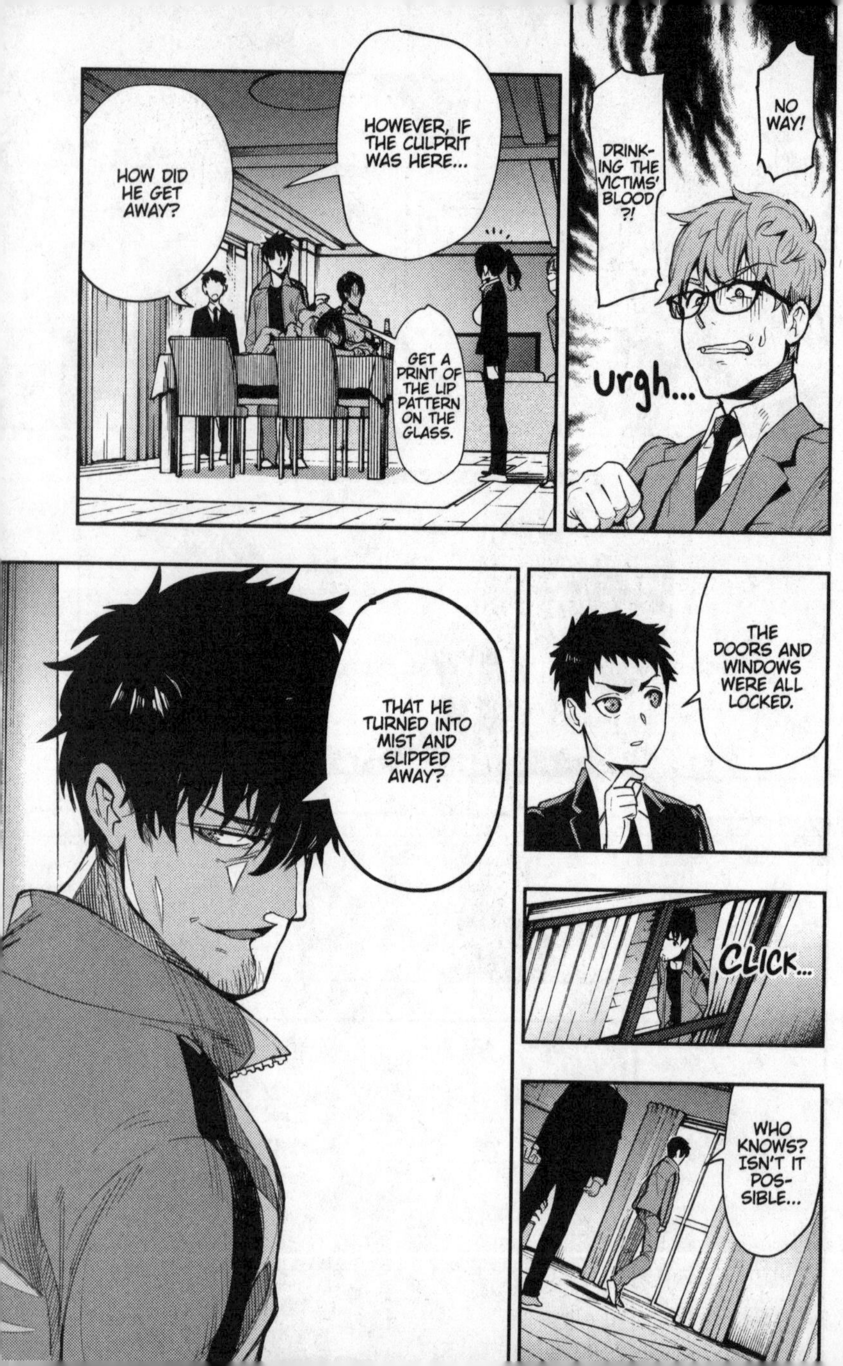
NO WAY!
DRINKING THE VICTIMS' BLOOD?!
Urgh...
HOWEVER, IF THE CULPRIT WAS HERE...
HOW DID HE GET AWAY?
GET A PRINT OF THE LIP PATTERN ON THE GLASS.
THE DOORS AND WINDOWS WERE ALL LOCKED.
CLICK...
WHO KNOWS? ISN'T IT POSSIBLE...
THAT HE TURNED INTO MIST AND SLIPPED AWAY?

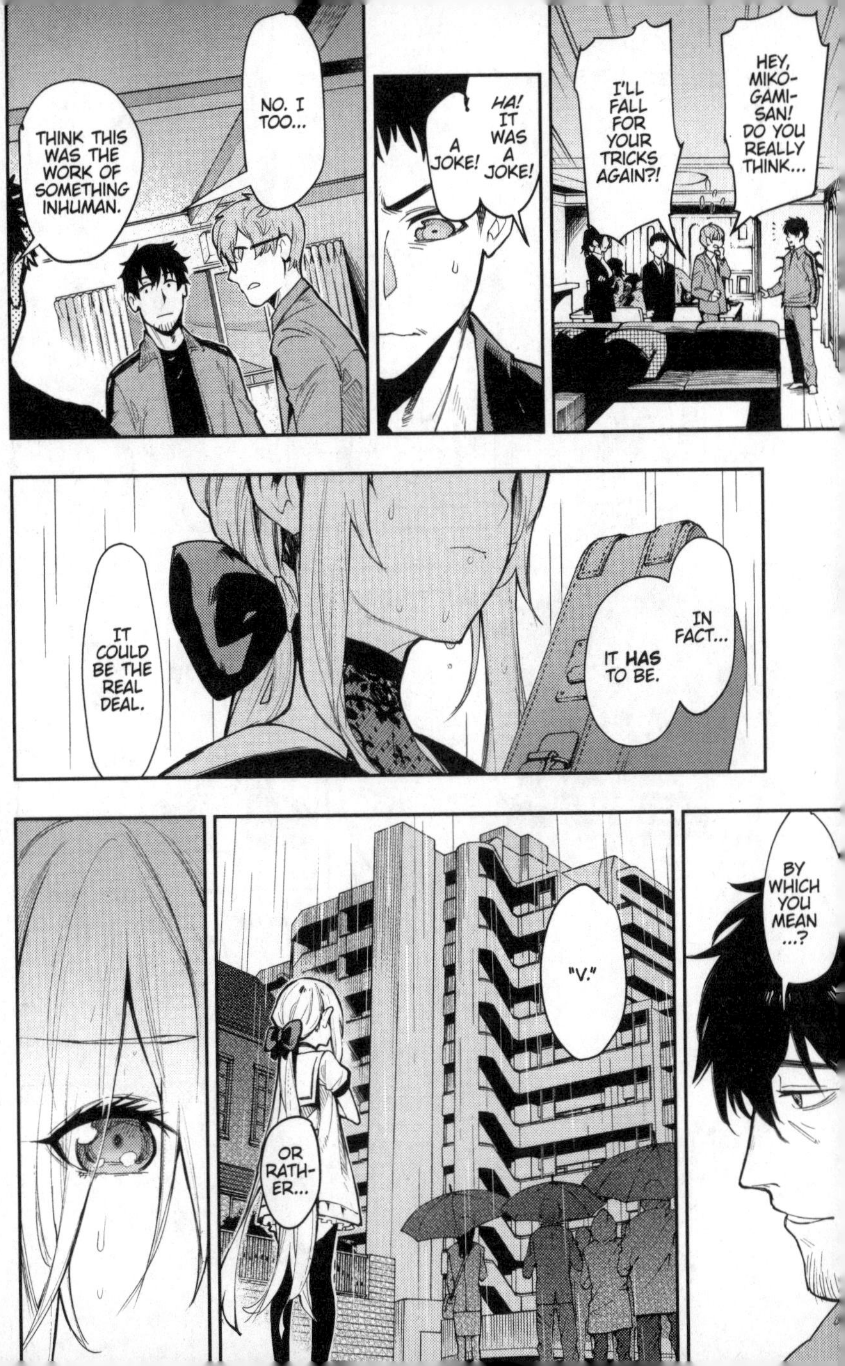
HEY, MIKO-GAMI-SAN! DO YOU REALLY THINK...
I'LL FALL FOR YOUR TRICKS AGAIN?!
HA! IT WAS A JOKE!
A JOKE!
NO. I TOO...
THINK THIS WAS THE WORK OF SOMETHING INHUMAN.
IN FACT...
IT HAS TO BE.
IT COULD BE THE REAL DEAL.
BY WHICH YOU MEAN ...?
"V."
OR RATH-ER...

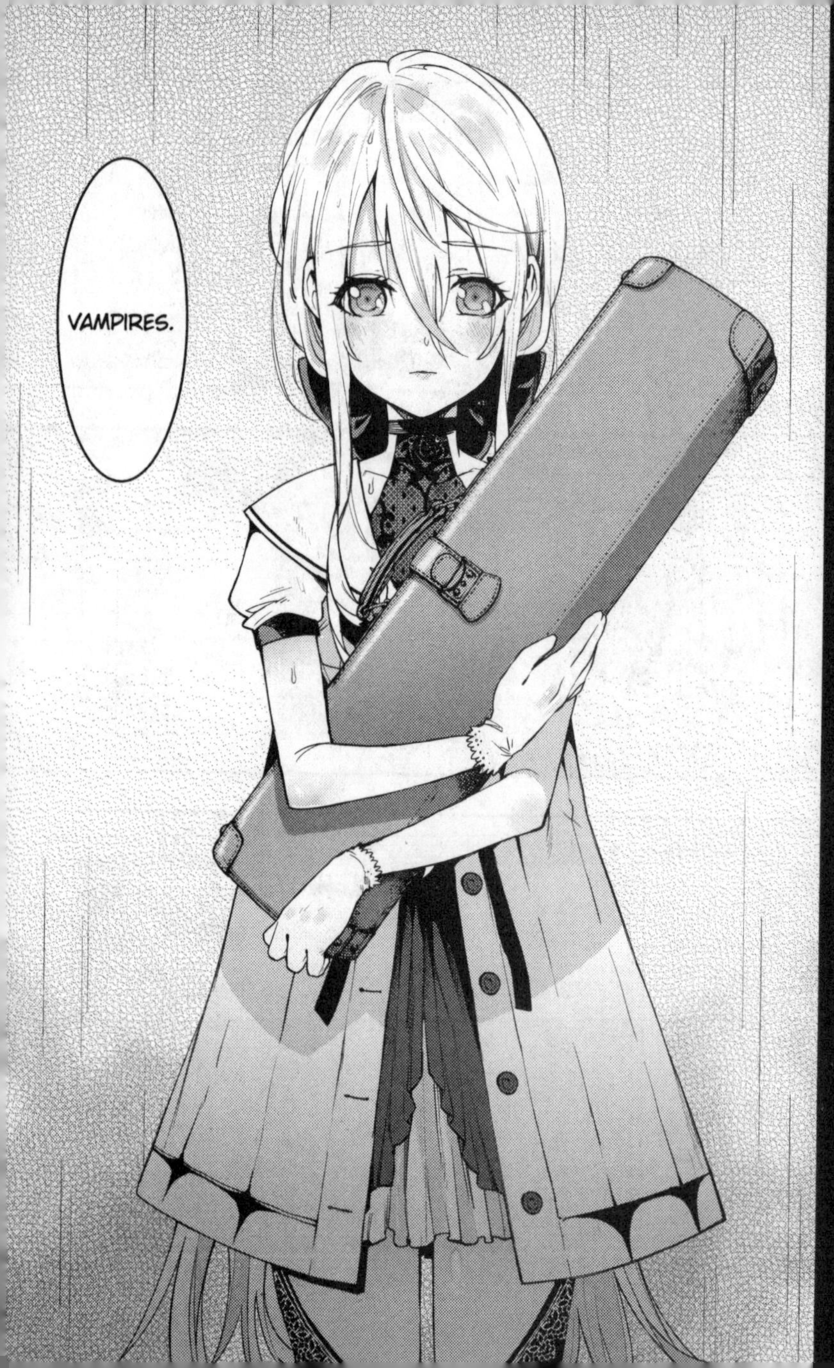
VAMPIRES.

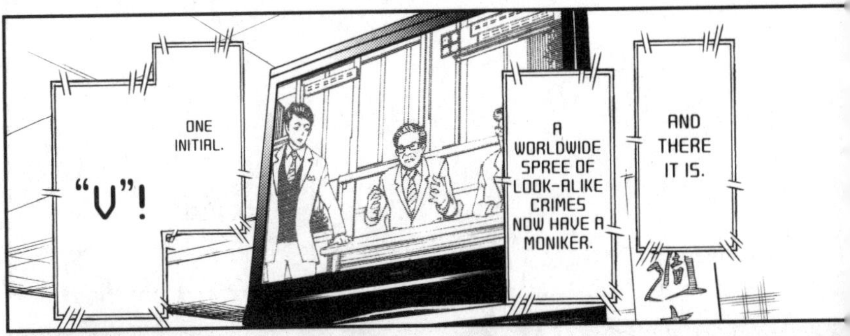
AND THERE IT IS.
A WORLDWIDE SPREE OF LOOK-ALIKE CRIMES NOW HAVE A MONIKER.
ONE INITIAL.
"V"!

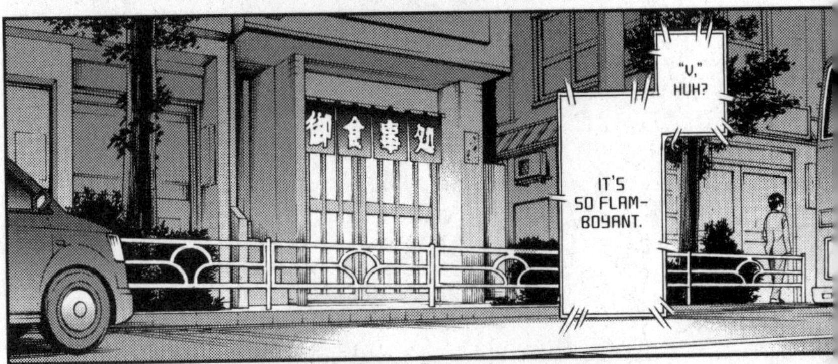
"V," HUH?
IT'S SO FLAM-BOYANT.

Flags: Japanese Restaurant.

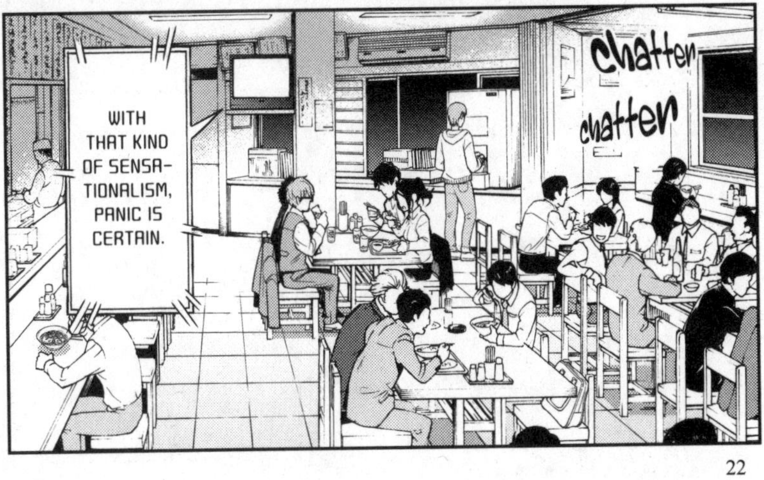
chatter
chatter
WITH THAT KIND OF SENSA-TIONALISM, PANIC IS CERTAIN.

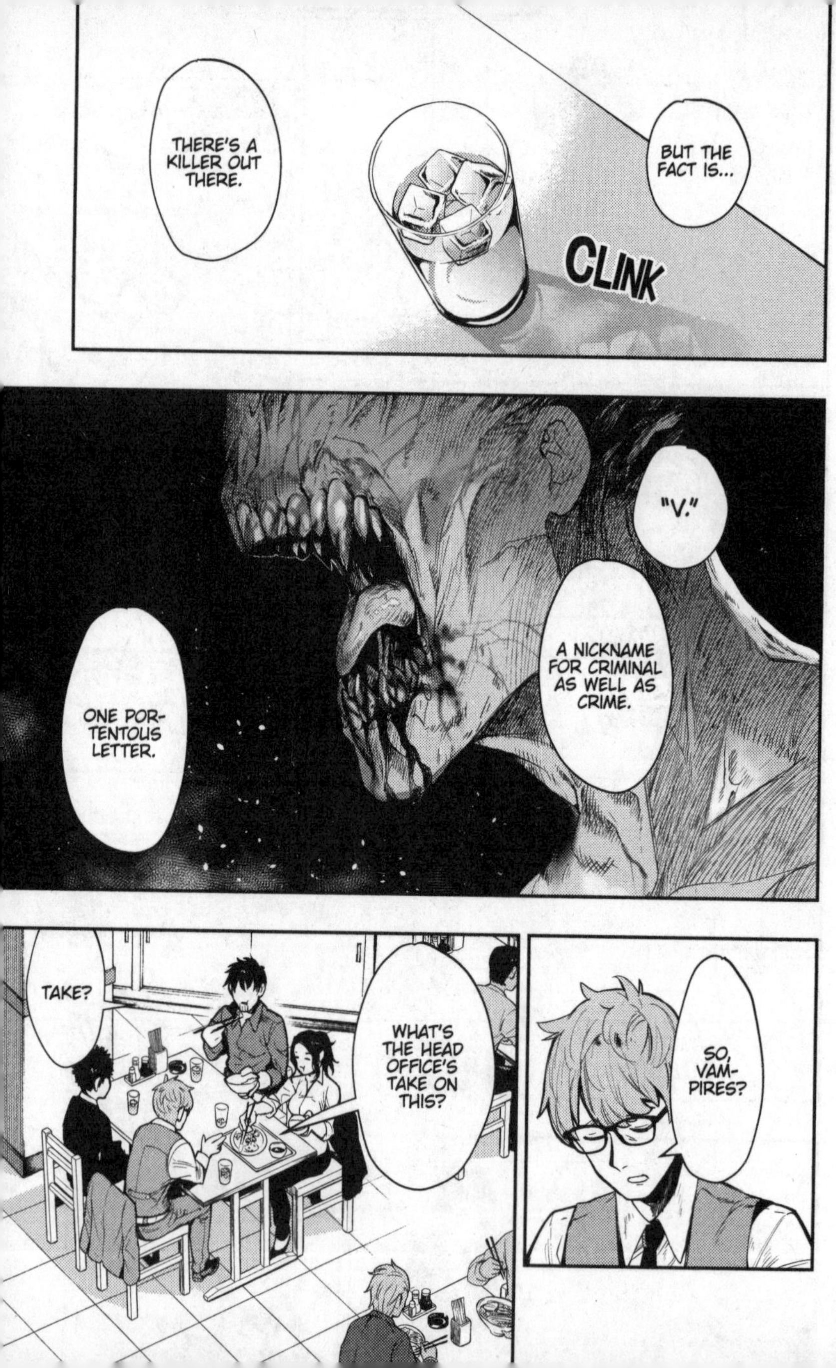
BUT THE FACT IS...
CLINK
THERE'S A KILLER OUT THERE.
"V."
A NICKNAME FOR CRIMINAL AS WELL AS CRIME.
ONE POR-TENTOUS LETTER.
SO, VAM-PIRES?
WHAT'S THE HEAD OFFICE'S TAKE ON THIS?
TAKE?

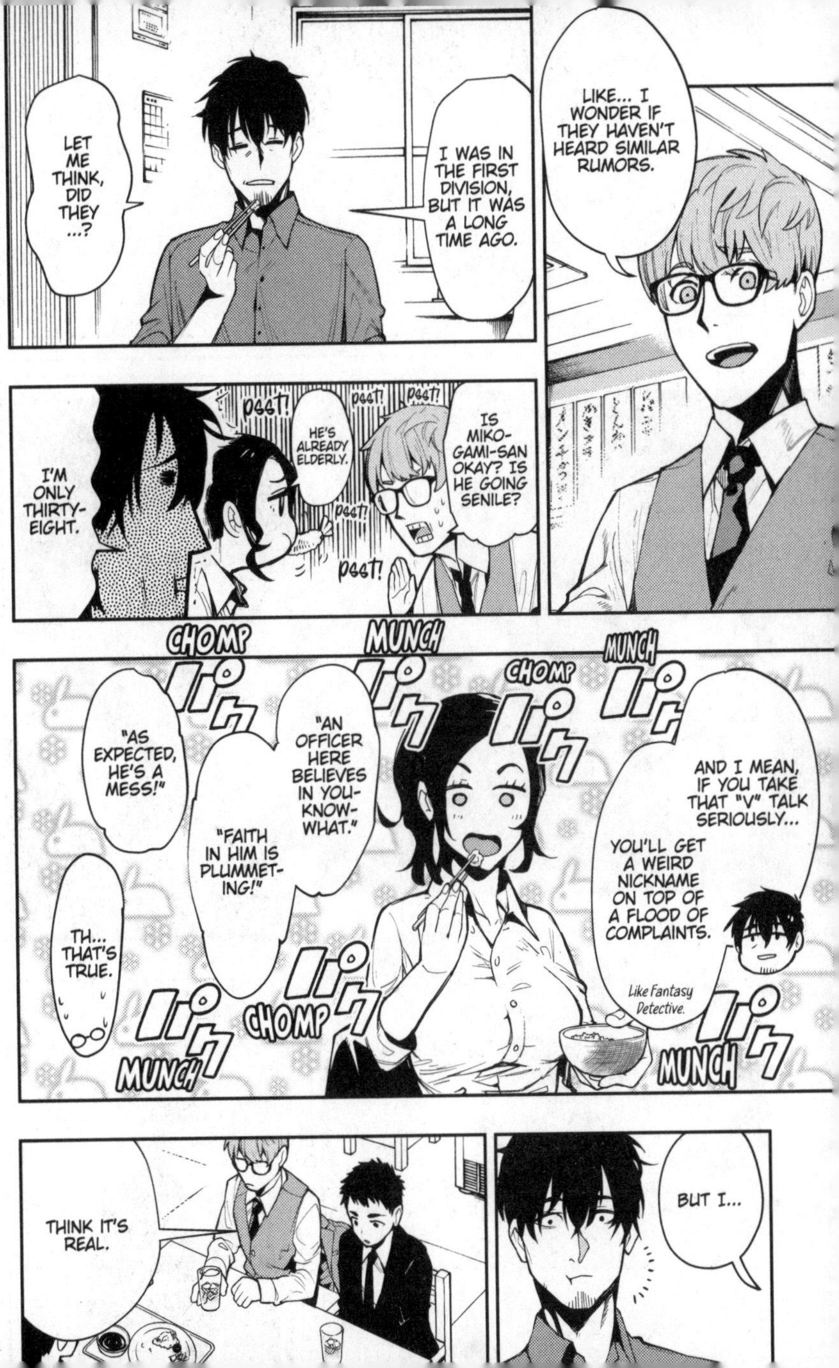
LIKE... I WONDER IF THEY HAVEN'T HEARD SIMILAR RUMORS.
I WAS IN THE FIRST DIVISION, BUT IT WAS A LONG TIME AGO.
LET ME THINK, DID THEY ...?
psst!
psst!
psst!
IS MIKO-GAMI-SAN OKAY? IS HE GOING SENILE?
HE'S ALREADY ELDERLY.
psst!
psst!
I'M ONLY THIRTY-EIGHT.
MUNCH
AND I MEAN, IF YOU TAKE THAT "V" TALK SERIOUSLY...
YOU'LL GET A WEIRD NICKNAME ON TOP OF A FLOOD OF COMPLAINTS.
Like Fantasy Detective.
MUNCH
CHOMP
MUNCH
"AN OFFICER HERE BELIEVES IN YOU-KNOW-WHAT."
"FAITH IN HIM IS PLUMMET-ING!"
CHOMP
CHOMP
"AS EXPECTED, HE'S A MESS!"
TH... THAT'S TRUE.
MUNCH
BUT I...
THINK IT'S REAL.

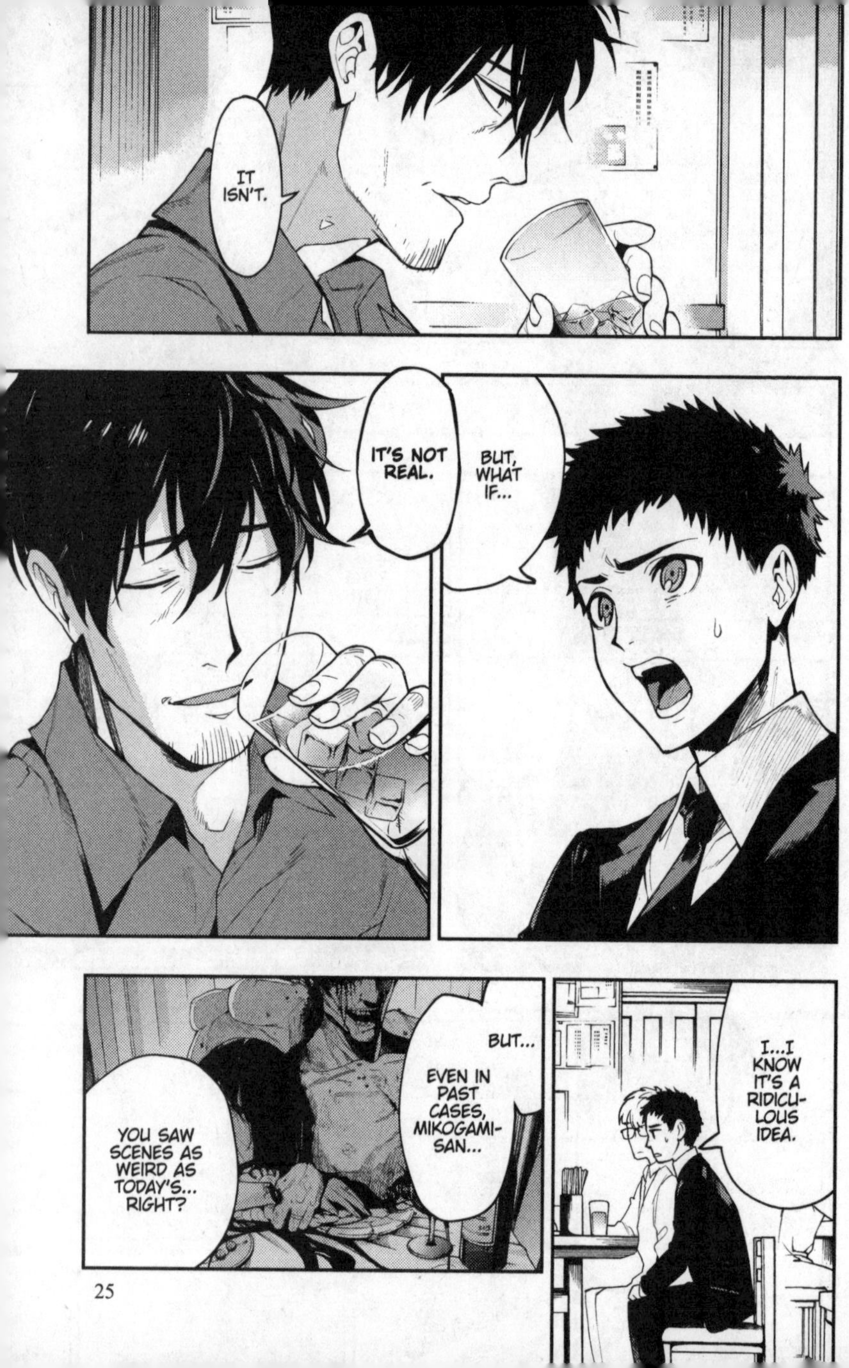
IT ISN'T.
BUT, WHAT IF...
IT'S NOT REAL.
I...I KNOW IT'S A RIDICULOUS IDEA.
BUT...
EVEN IN PAST CASES, MIKOGAMI-SAN...
YOU SAW SCENES AS WEIRD AS TODAY'S... RIGHT?

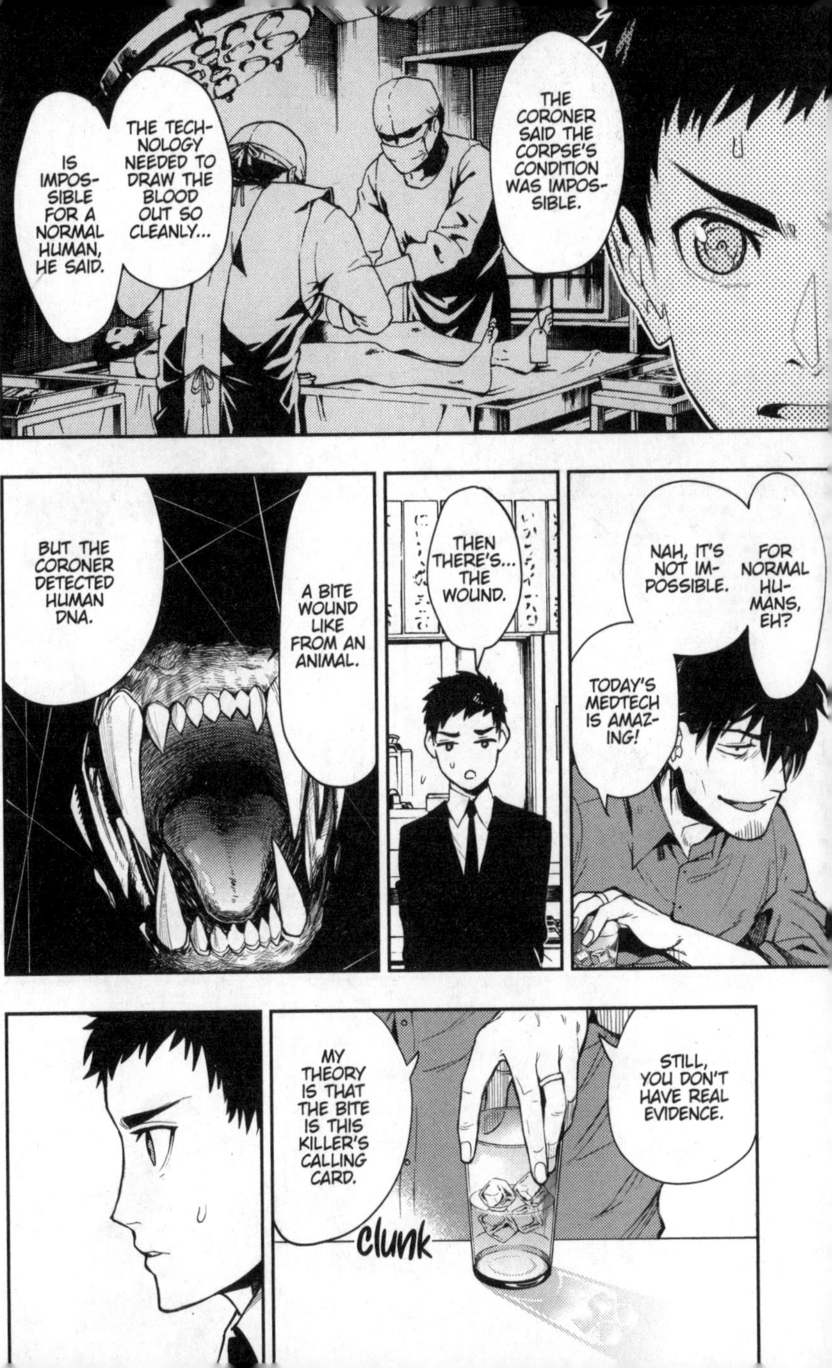
THE CORONER SAID THE CORPSE'S CONDITION WAS IMPOSSIBLE.
THE TECHNOLOGY NEEDED TO DRAW THE BLOOD OUT SO CLEANLY...
IS IMPOSSIBLE FOR A NORMAL HUMAN, HE SAID.
FOR NORMAL HUMANS, EH?
NAH, IT'S NOT IMPOSSIBLE.
TODAY'S MEDTECH IS AMAZING!
THEN THERE'S... THE WOUND.
A BITE WOUND LIKE FROM AN ANIMAL.
BUT THE CORONER DETECTED HUMAN DNA.
STILL, YOU DON'T HAVE REAL EVIDENCE.
MY THEORY IS THAT THE BITE IS THIS KILLER'S CALLING CARD.
Clunk

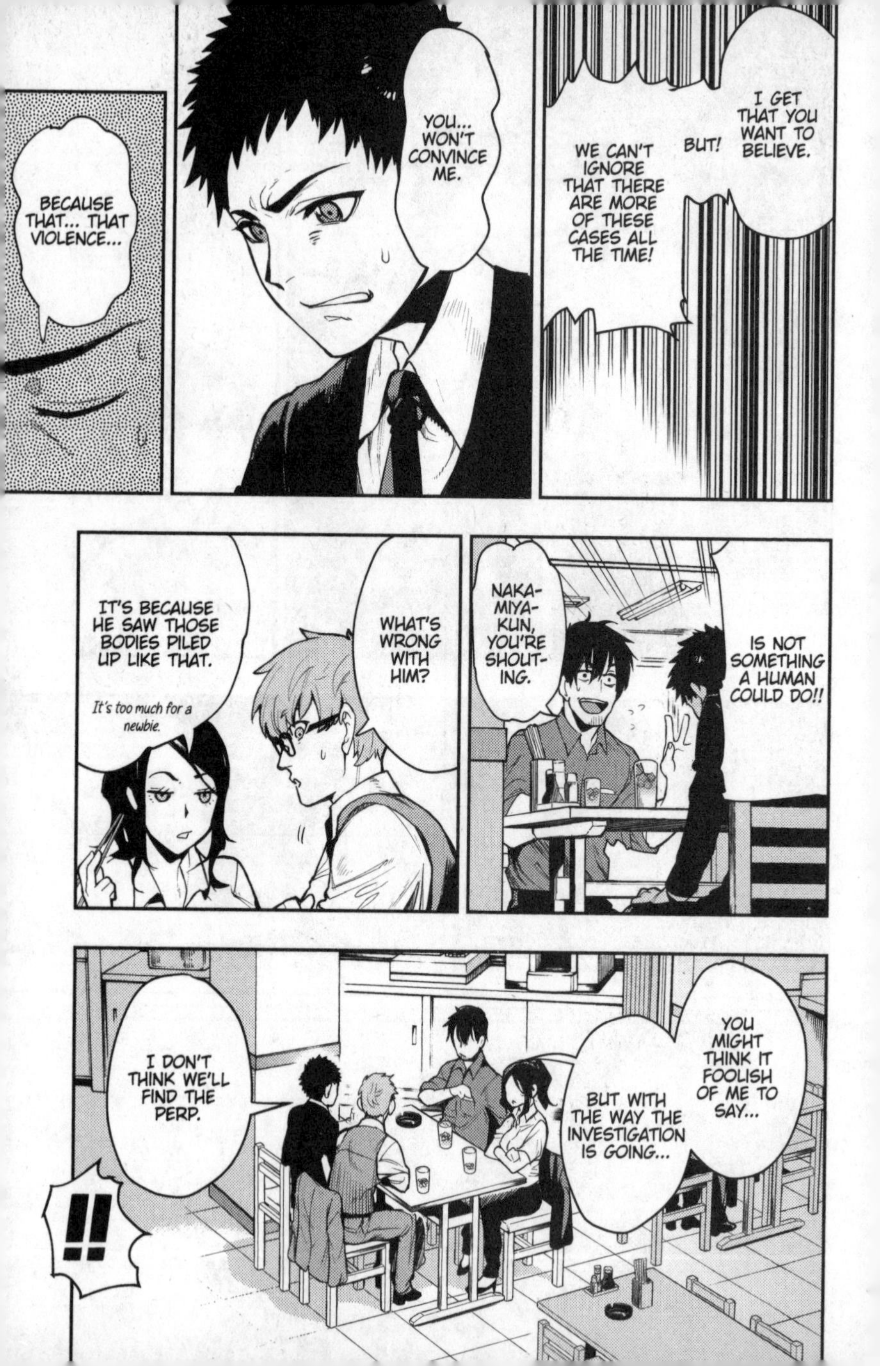
I GET THAT YOU WANT TO BELIEVE.
BUT!
WE CAN'T IGNORE THAT THERE ARE MORE OF THESE CASES ALL THE TIME!
YOU... WON'T CONVINCE ME.
BECAUSE THAT... THAT VIOLENCE...
IS NOT SOMETHING A HUMAN COULD DO!!
NAKA-MIYA-KUN, YOU'RE SHOUT-ING.
WHAT'S WRONG WITH HIM?
IT'S BECAUSE HE SAW THOSE BODIES PILED UP LIKE THAT.
It's too much for a newbie.
YOU MIGHT THINK IT FOOLISH OF ME TO SAY...
BUT WITH THE WAY THE INVESTIGATION IS GOING...
I DON'T THINK WE'LL FIND THE PERP.
!!

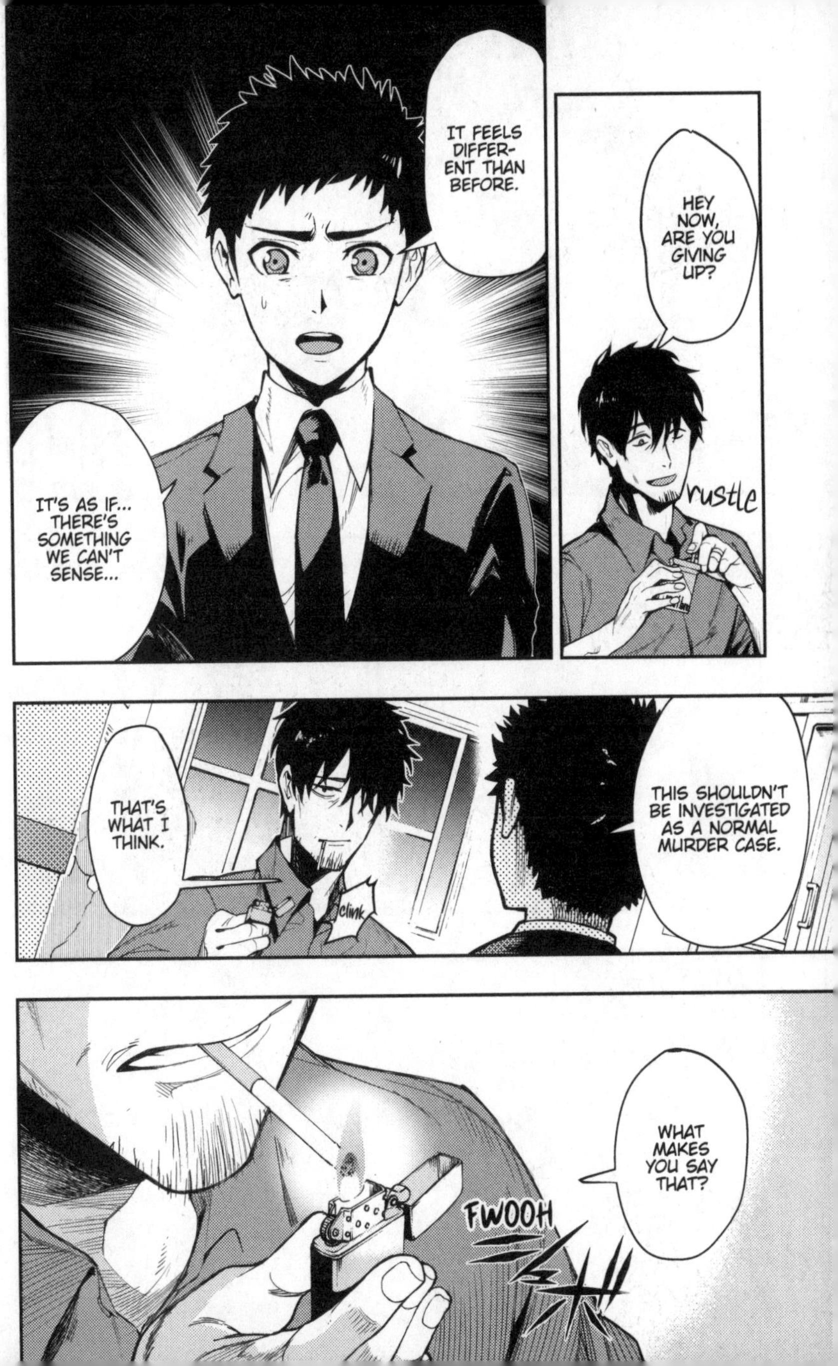
HEY NOW, ARE YOU GIVING UP?
rustle
IT FEELS DIFFER-ENT THAN BEFORE.
IT'S AS IF... THERE'S SOMETHING WE CAN'T SENSE...
THIS SHOULDN'T BE INVESTIGATED AS A NORMAL MURDER CASE.
clink
THAT'S WHAT I THINK.
WHAT MAKES YOU SAY THAT?
FWOOH

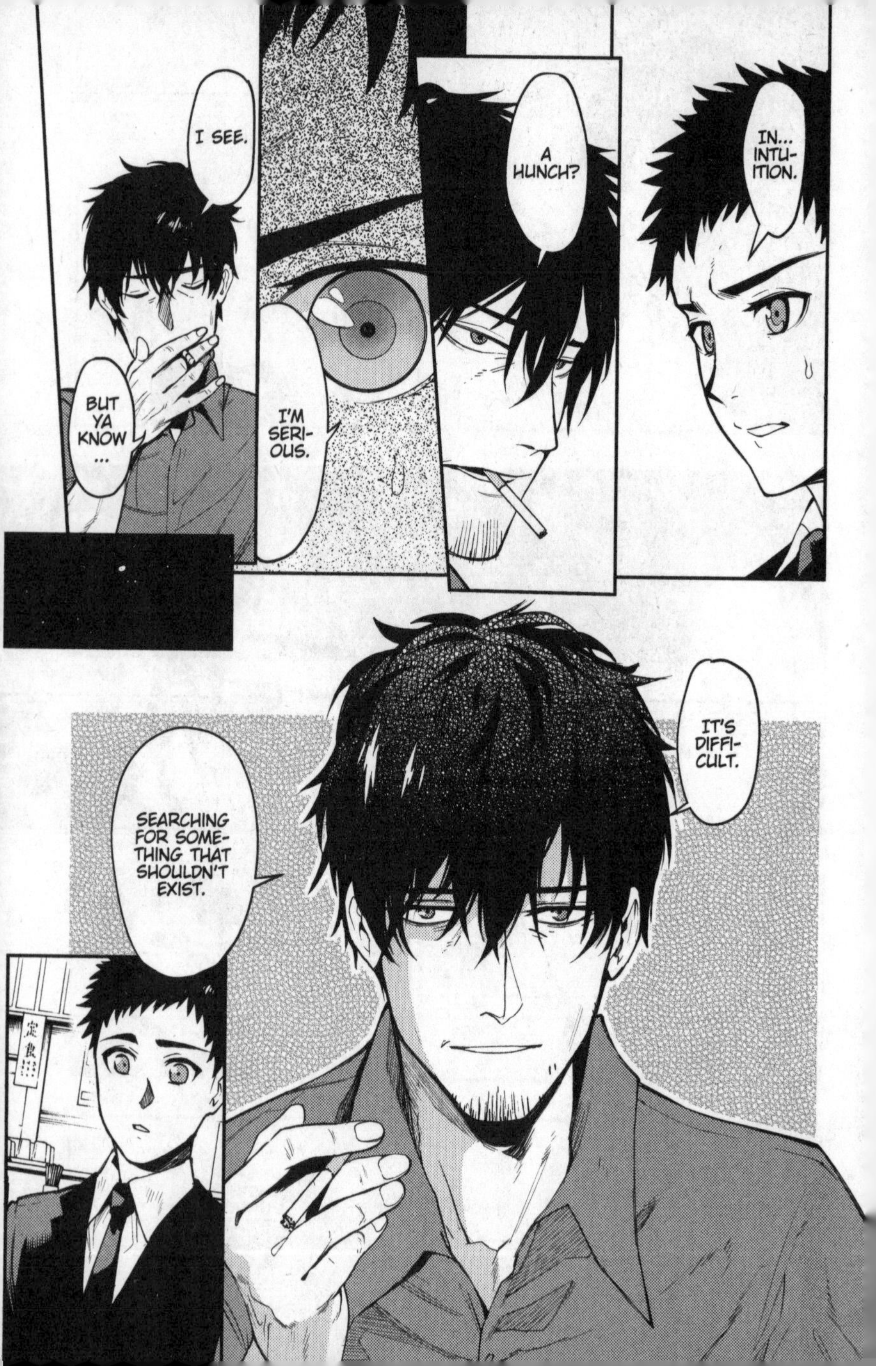
IN... INTUITION.
A HUNCH?
I'M SERIOUS.
I SEE.
BUT YA KNOW ...
IT'S DIFFICULT.
SEARCHING FOR SOMETHING THAT SHOULDN'T EXIST.

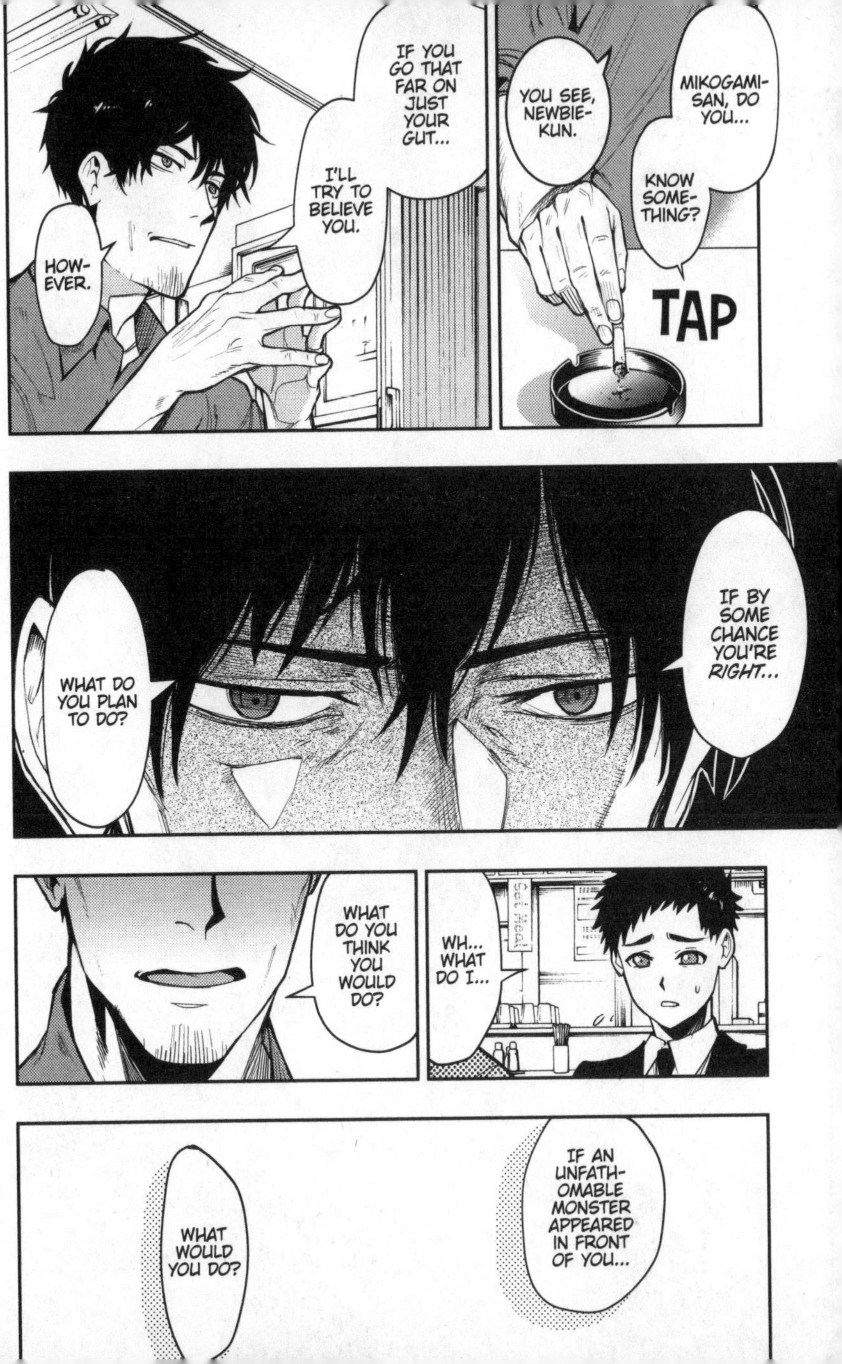
MIKOGAMI-SAN, DO YOU...
KNOW SOMETHING?
YOU SEE, NEWBIE-KUN.
TAP
IF YOU GO THAT FAR ON JUST YOUR GUT...
I'LL TRY TO BELIEVE YOU.
HOW-EVER.
IF BY SOME CHANCE YOU'RE *RIGHT*...
WHAT DO YOU PLAN TO DO?
WH... WHAT DO I...
WHAT DO YOU THINK YOU WOULD DO?
IF AN UNFATH-OMABLE MONSTER APPEARED IN FRONT OF YOU...
WHAT WOULD YOU DO?

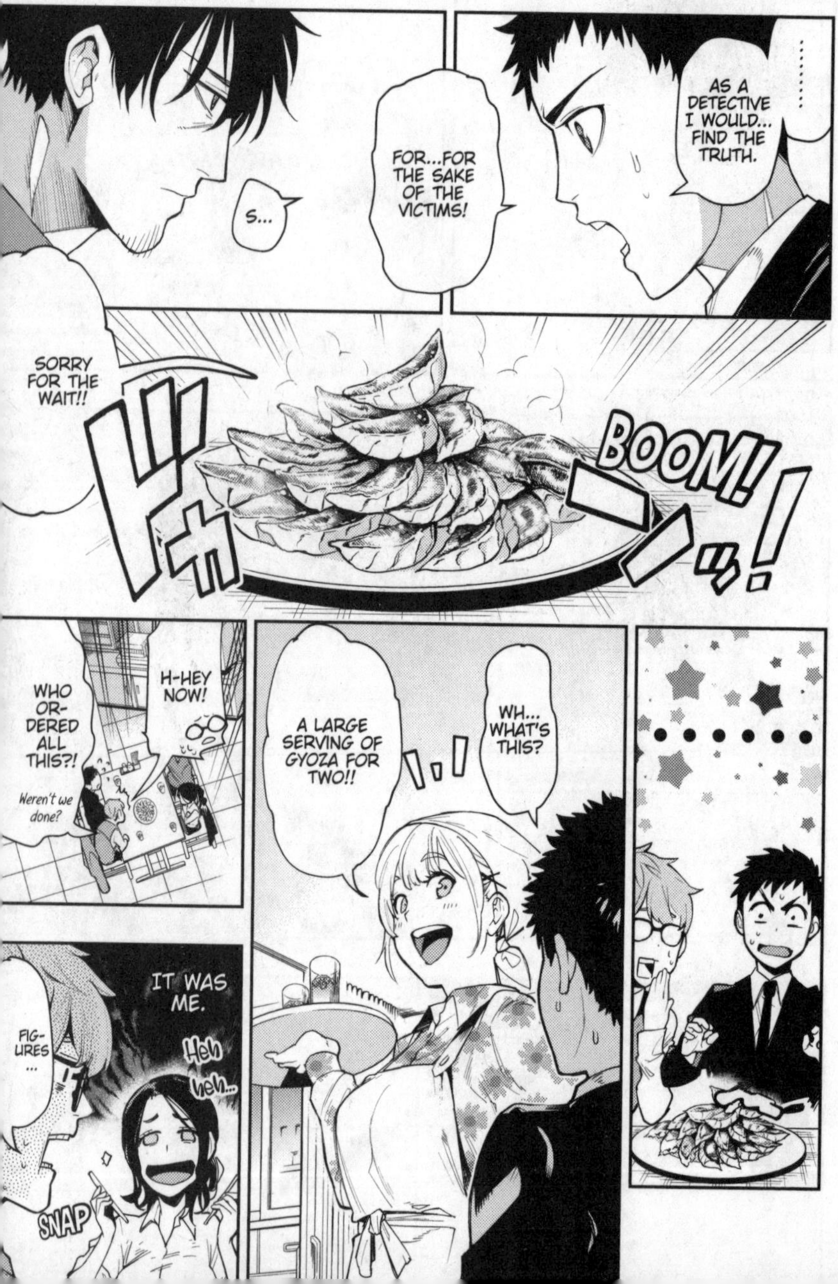
......
AS A DETECTIVE I WOULD... FIND THE TRUTH.
FOR...FOR THE SAKE OF THE VICTIMS!
S...
SORRY FOR THE WAIT!!
BOOM!
....
WH... WHAT'S THIS?
A LARGE SERVING OF GYOZA FOR TWO!!
H-HEY NOW!
WHO ORDERED ALL THIS?!
Weren't we done?
IT WAS ME.
Heh heh...
FIGURES...
SNAP

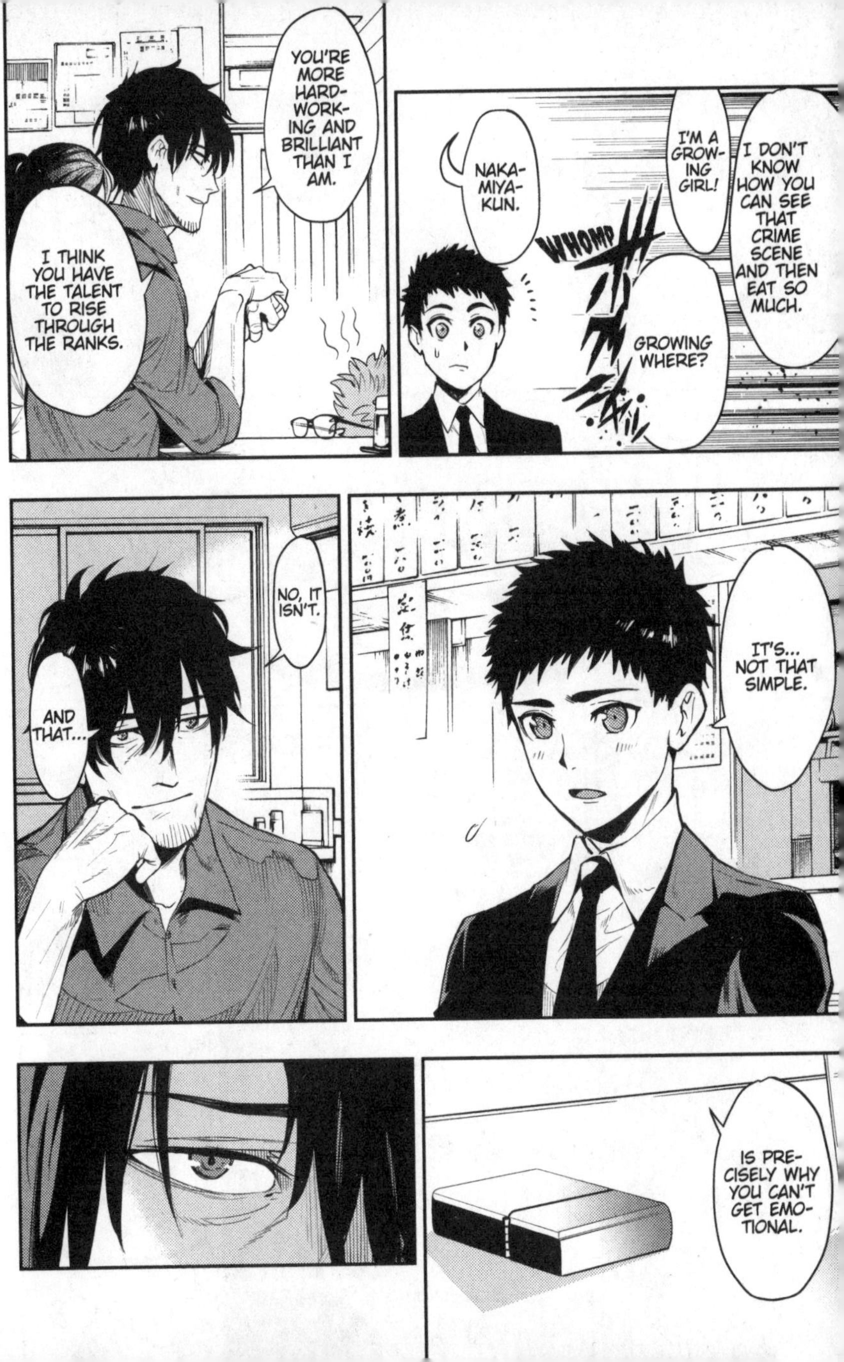
I DON'T KNOW HOW YOU CAN SEE THAT CRIME SCENE AND THEN EAT SO MUCH.
I'M A GROWING GIRL!
GROWING WHERE?
WHOMP
NAKAMIYA-KUN.
YOU'RE MORE HARD-WORKING AND BRILLIANT THAN I AM.
I THINK YOU HAVE THE TALENT TO RISE THROUGH THE RANKS.
IT'S... NOT THAT SIMPLE.
NO, IT ISN'T.
AND THAT...
IS PRECISELY WHY YOU CAN'T GET EMOTIONAL.

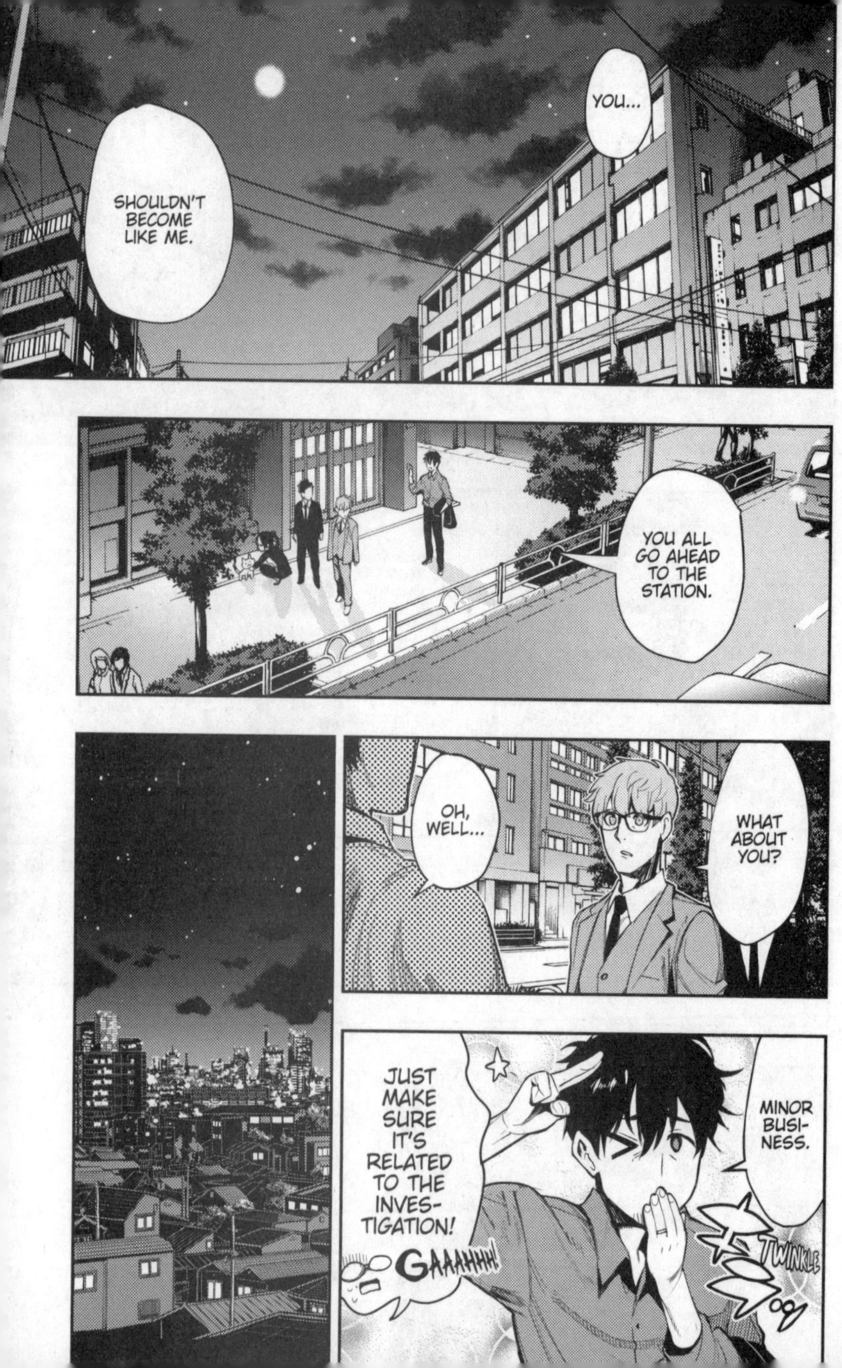
YOU...
SHOULDN'T BECOME LIKE ME.
YOU ALL GO AHEAD TO THE STATION.
WHAT ABOUT YOU?
OH, WELL...
MINOR BUSI-NESS.
TWINKLE
JUST MAKE SURE IT'S RELATED TO THE INVES-TIGATION!
GAAAHHH!

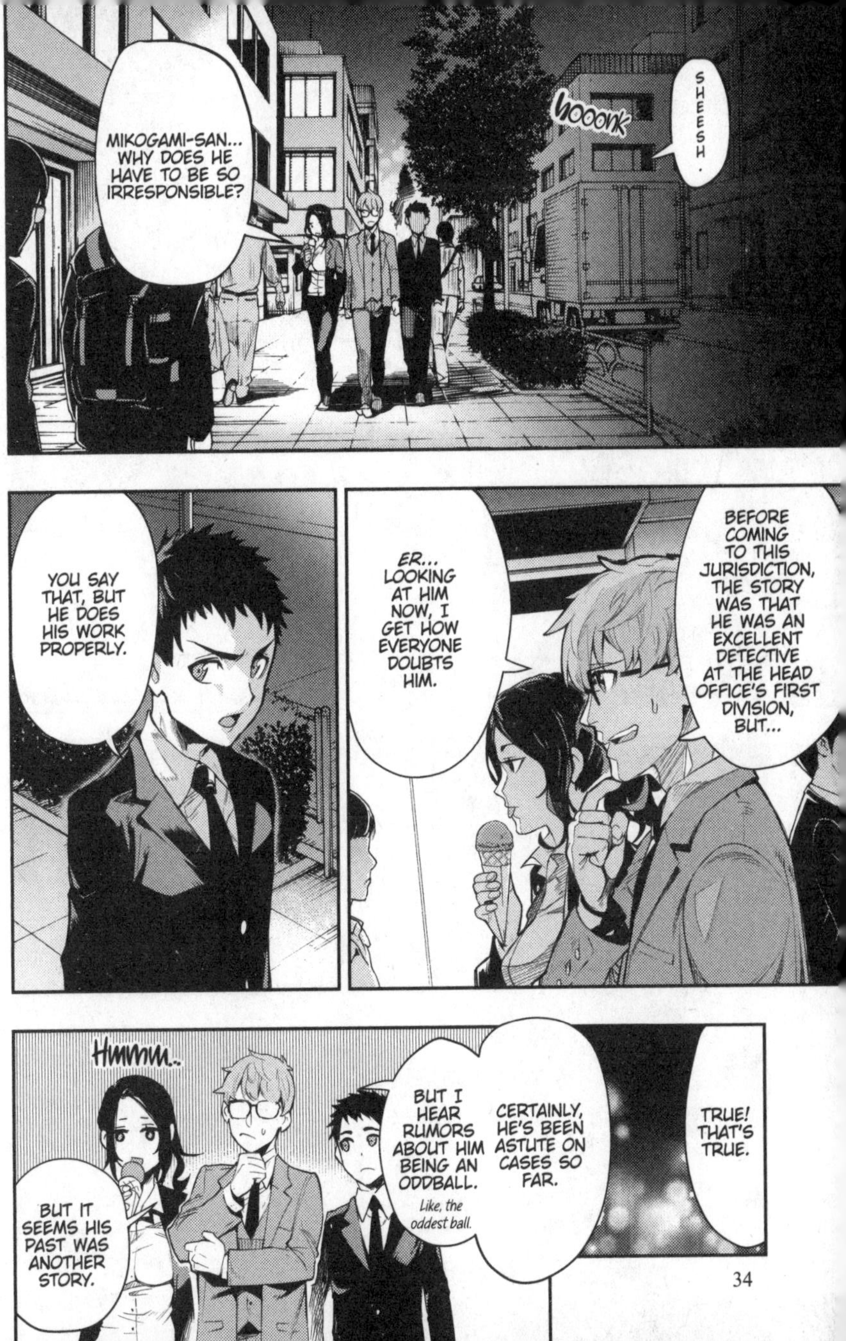
SHEESH.
Hooonk
MIKOGAMI-SAN... WHY DOES HE HAVE TO BE SO IRRESPONSIBLE?
BEFORE COMING TO THIS JURISDICTION, THE STORY WAS THAT HE WAS AN EXCELLENT DETECTIVE AT THE HEAD OFFICE'S FIRST DIVISION, BUT...
ER... LOOKING AT HIM NOW, I GET HOW EVERYONE DOUBTS HIM.
YOU SAY THAT, BUT HE DOES HIS WORK PROPERLY.
TRUE! THAT'S TRUE.
CERTAINLY, HE'S BEEN ASTUTE ON CASES SO FAR.
BUT I HEAR RUMORS ABOUT HIM BEING AN ODDBALL.
Like, the oddest ball.
Hmmm..
BUT IT SEEMS HIS PAST WAS ANOTHER STORY.

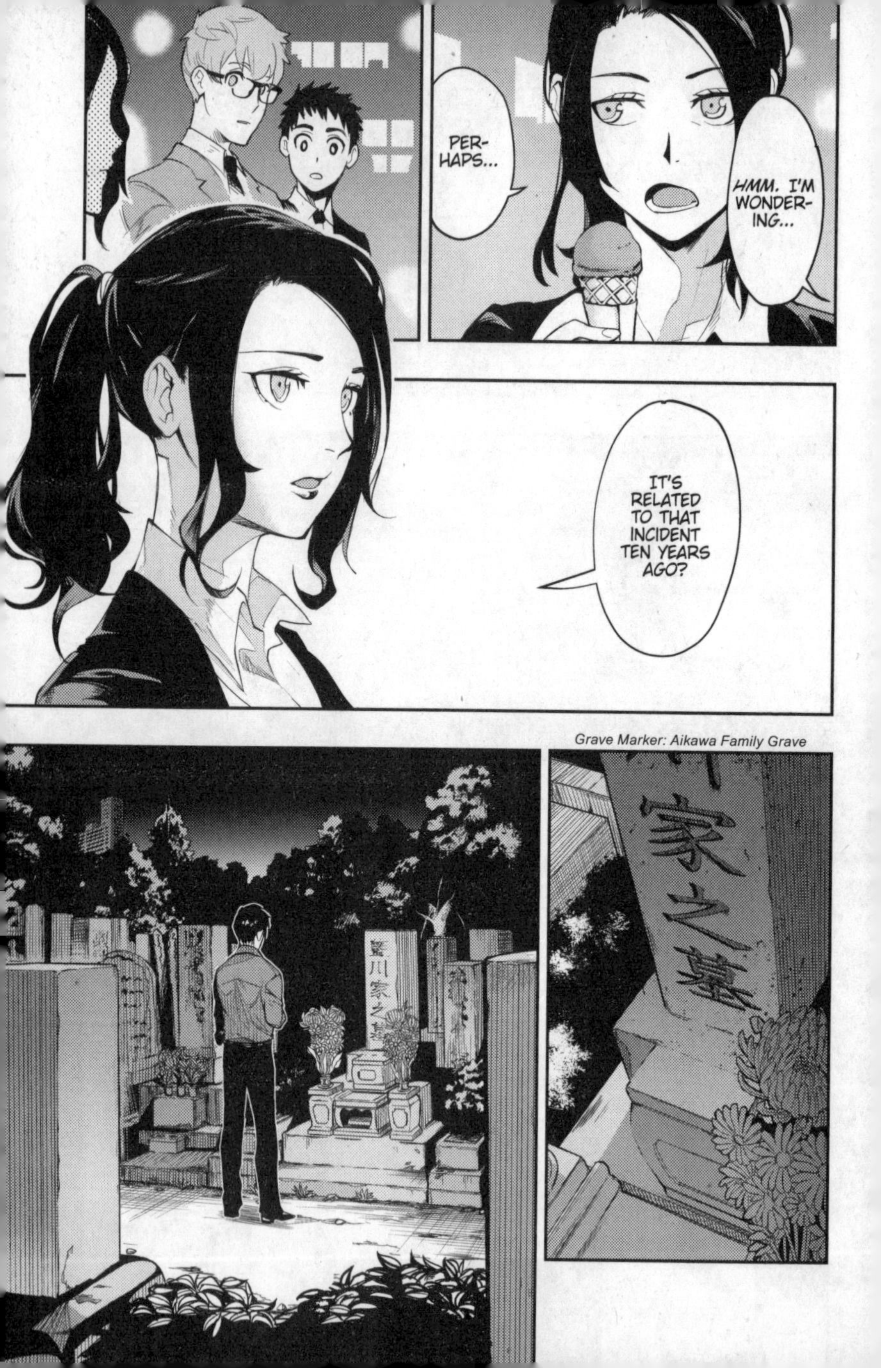
HMM. I'M WONDERING...
PER-HAPS...
IT'S RELATED TO THAT INCIDENT TEN YEARS AGO?
Grave Marker: Aikawa Family Grave

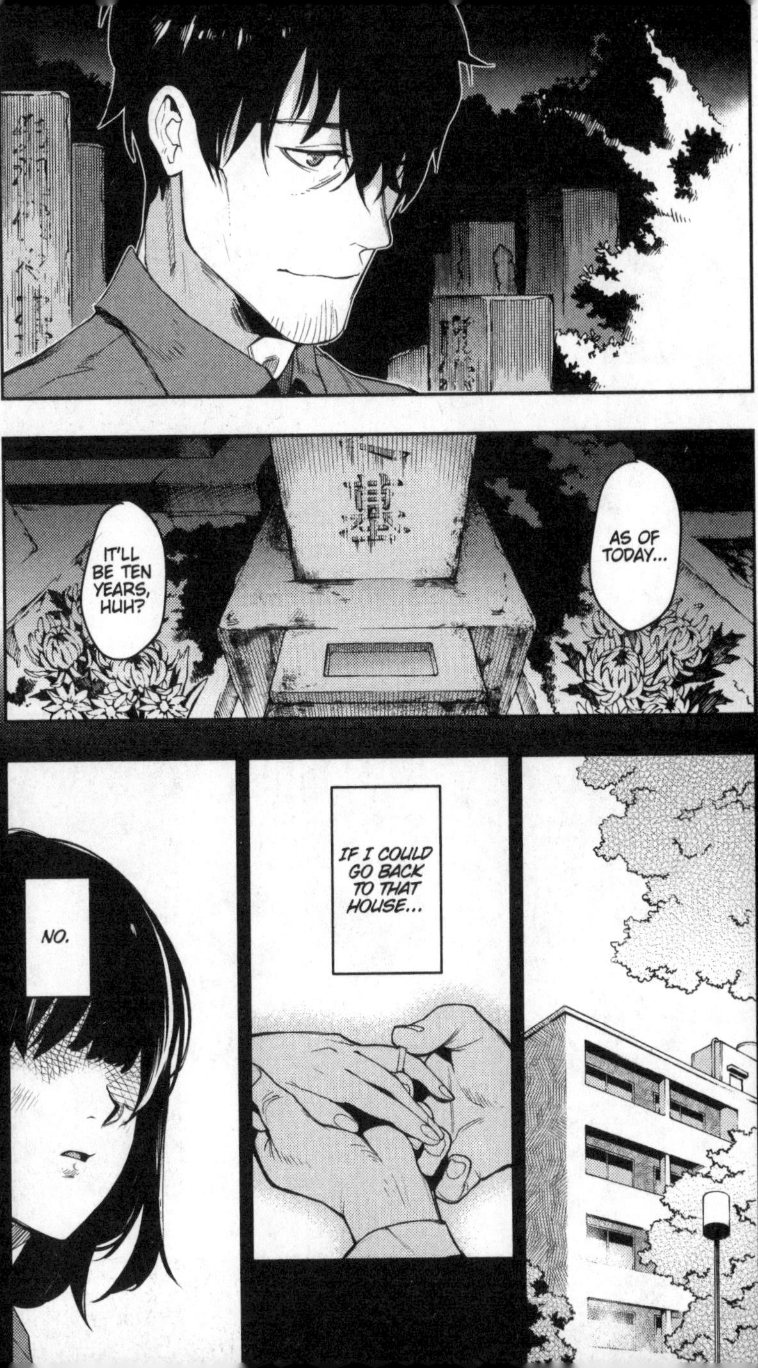
AS OF TODAY...
IT'LL BE TEN YEARS, HUH?
IF I COULD GO BACK TO THAT HOUSE...
NO.

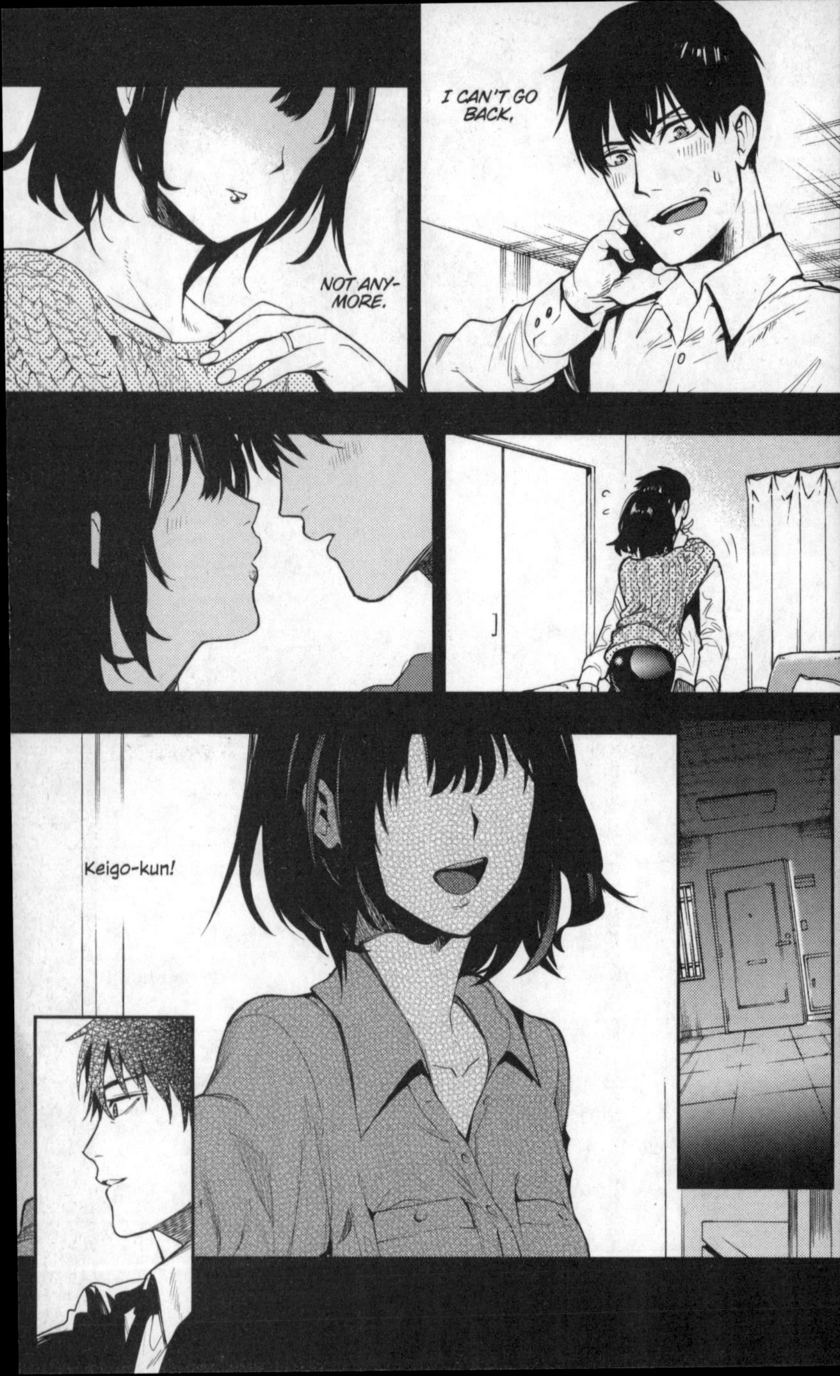
I CAN'T GO BACK.
NOT ANY-MORE.
Keigo-kun!

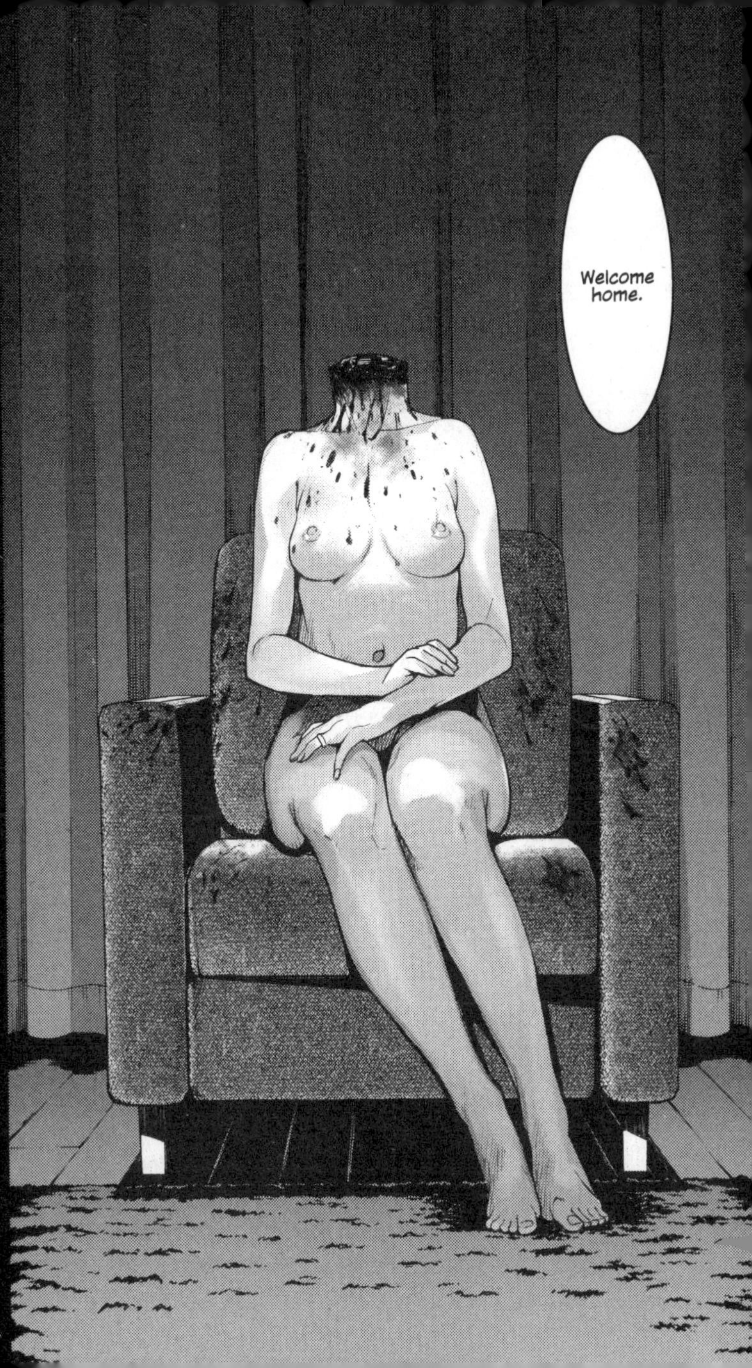
Welcome home.

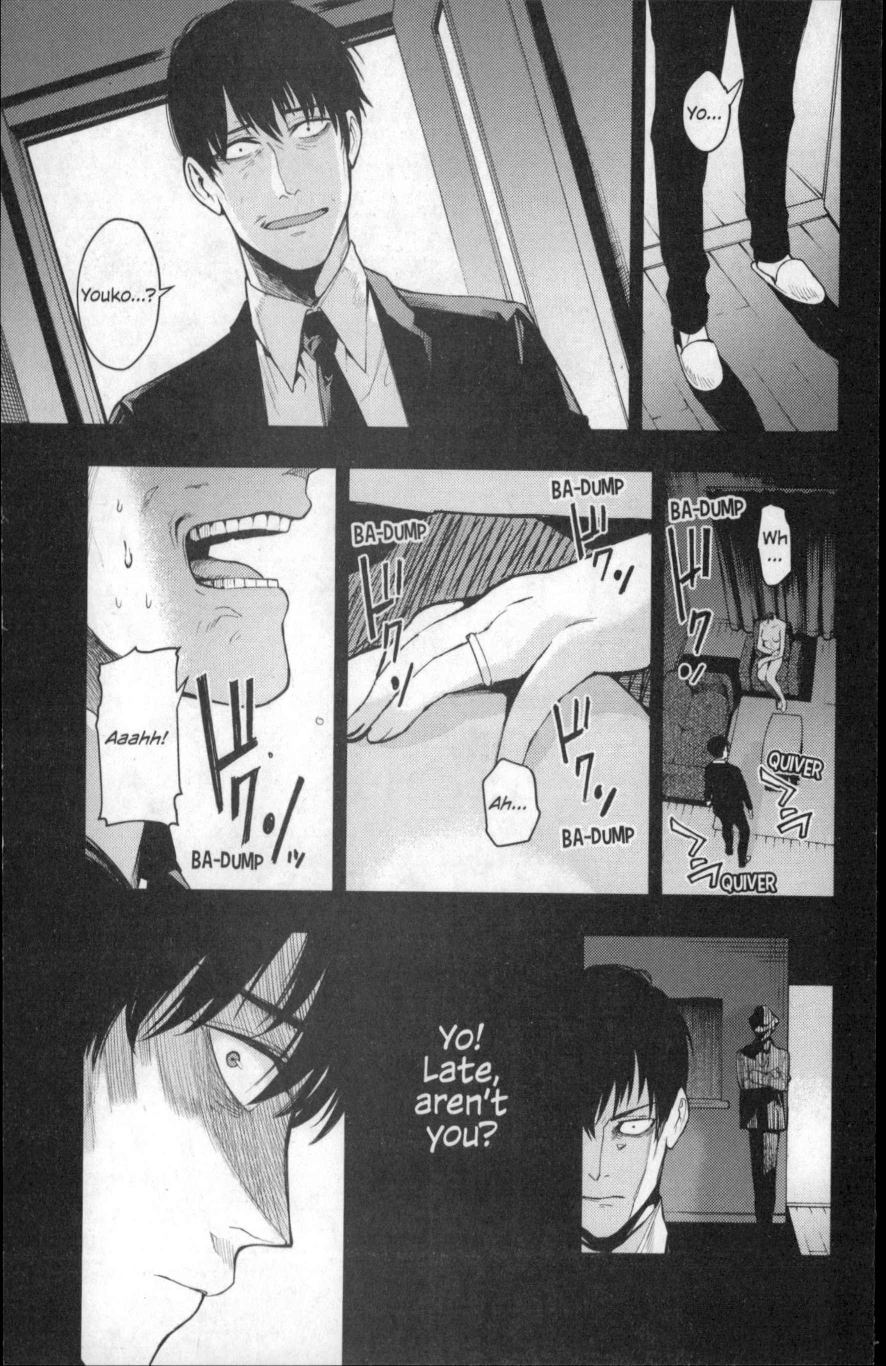

Yo...
Youko...?
BA-DUMP
Wh...
QUIVER
QUIVER
BA-DUMP
BA-DUMP
Ah...
BA-DUMP
Aaahh!
BA-DUMP
Yo! Late, aren't you?

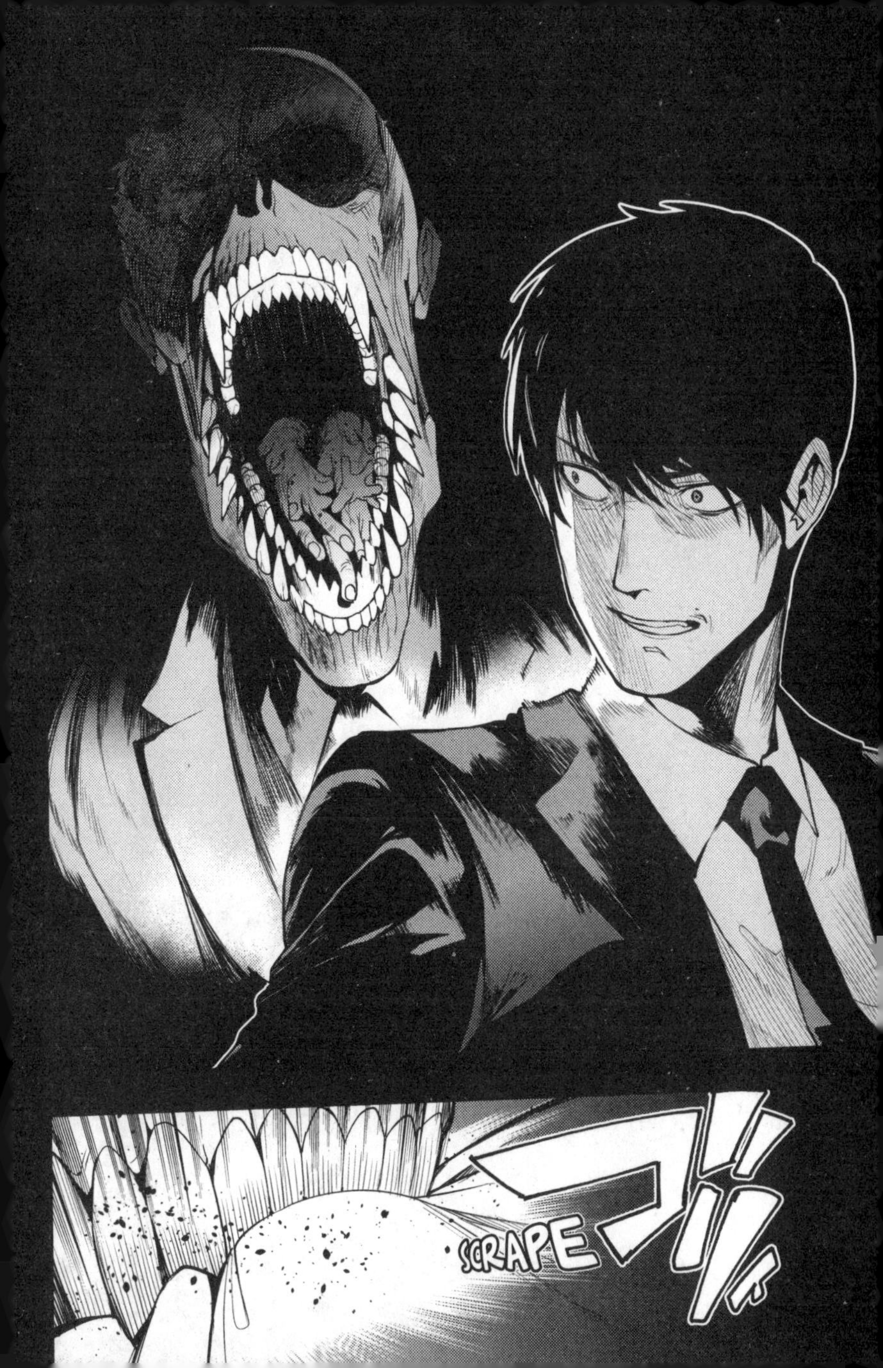
SCRAPE

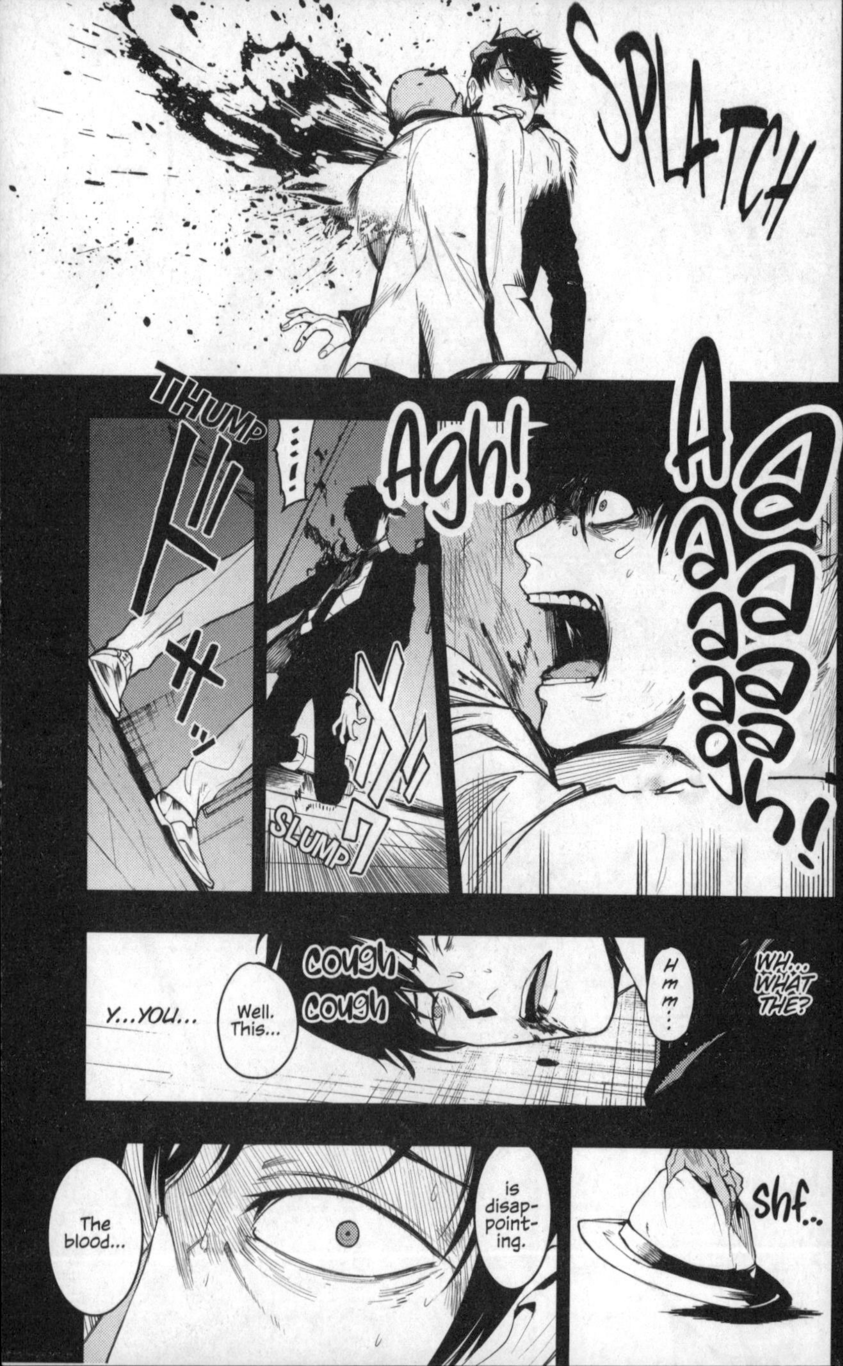

SPLATCH
Aaaaaaaaaaagh!
Agh!
...!
SLUMP
THUMP
WH... WHAT THE?
Hmm...
cough cough
Well. This...
Y...YOU...
shf...
is disap-pointing.
The blood...

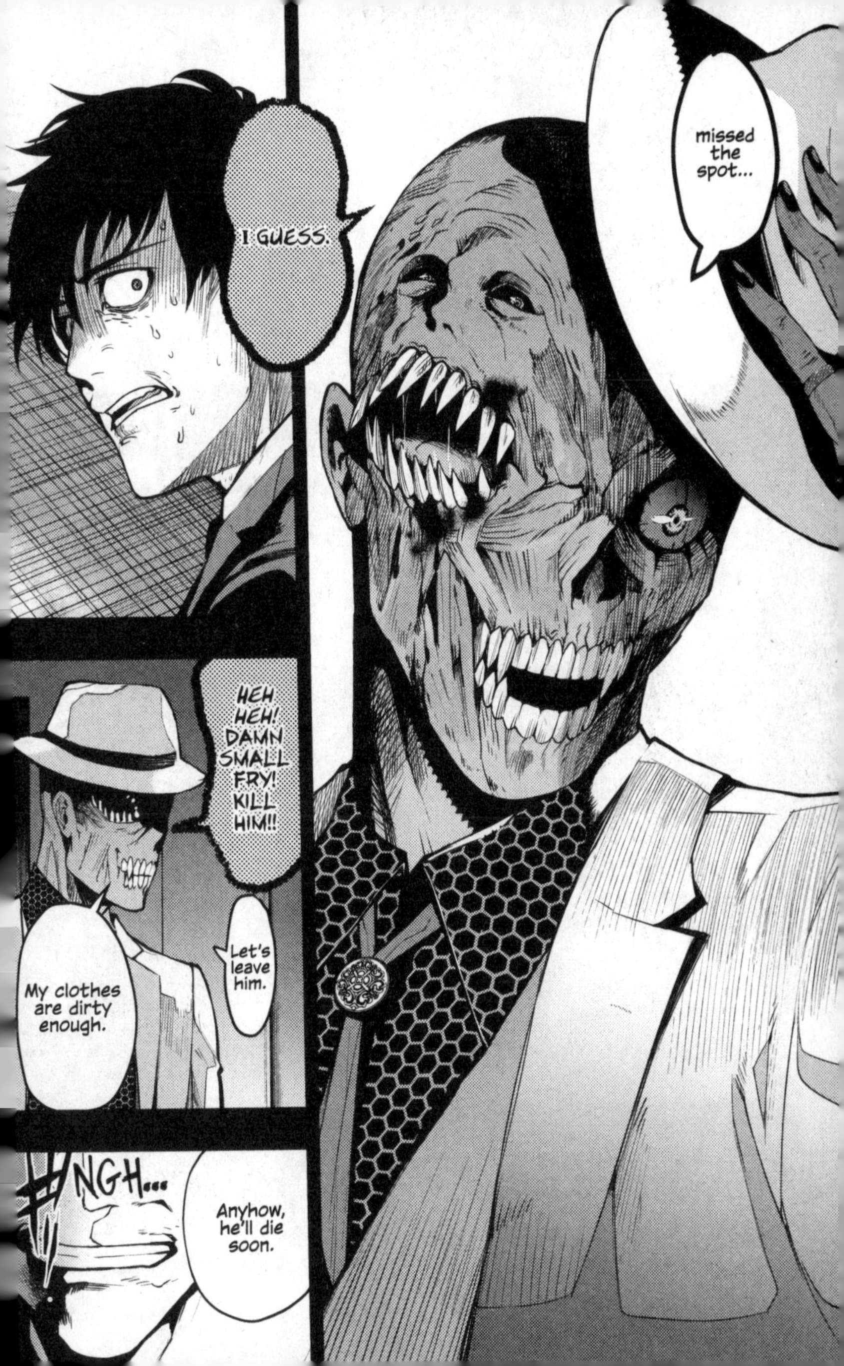

missed the spot...
I GUESS.
HEH HEH! DAMN SMALL FRY! KILL HIM!!
Let's leave him.
My clothes are dirty enough.
Anyhow, he'll die soon.
NGH...

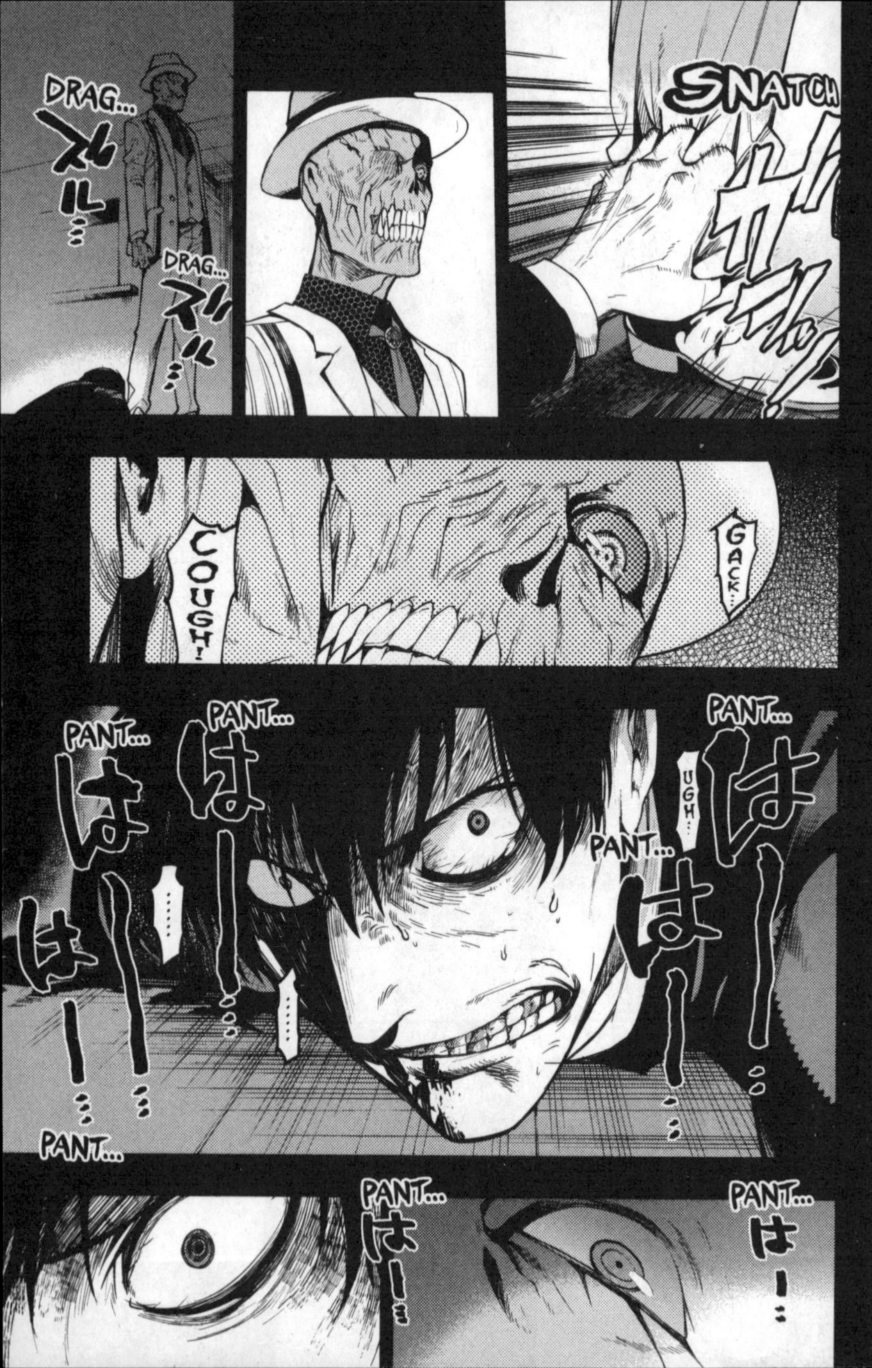
SNATCH
DRAG...
ズル…
DRAG...
ズル…
GACK...
COUGH!
PANT...
はー…
UGH...
PANT...
はー…
PANT...
はー…
......
......
PANT...
はー…
PANT...
PANT...
はー…
PANT...
はー…

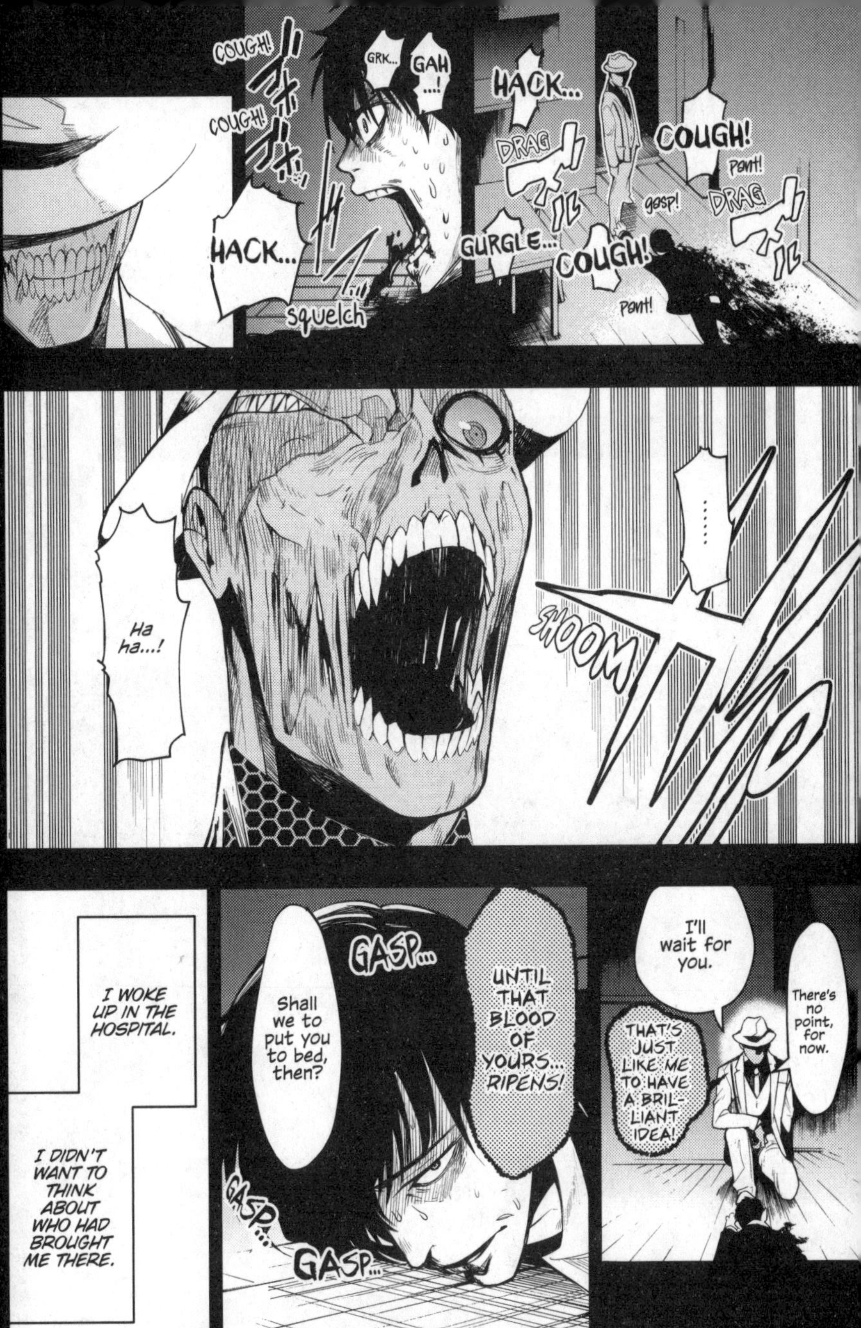
HACK...
COUGH!
Pant!
DRAG
gasp!
DRAG
GURGLE...
COUGH!
Pant!
GAH ...!
GRK...
COUGH!
COUGH!
HACK...
squelch
......
SHOOM
Ha ha...!
I'll wait for you.
There's no point, for now.
THAT'S JUST LIKE ME TO HAVE A BRIL-LIANT IDEA!
UNTIL THAT BLOOD OF YOURS... RIPENS!
GASP...
Shall we to put you to bed, then?
GASP...
GASP...
I WOKE UP IN THE HOSPITAL.
I DIDN'T WANT TO THINK ABOUT WHO HAD BROUGHT ME THERE.

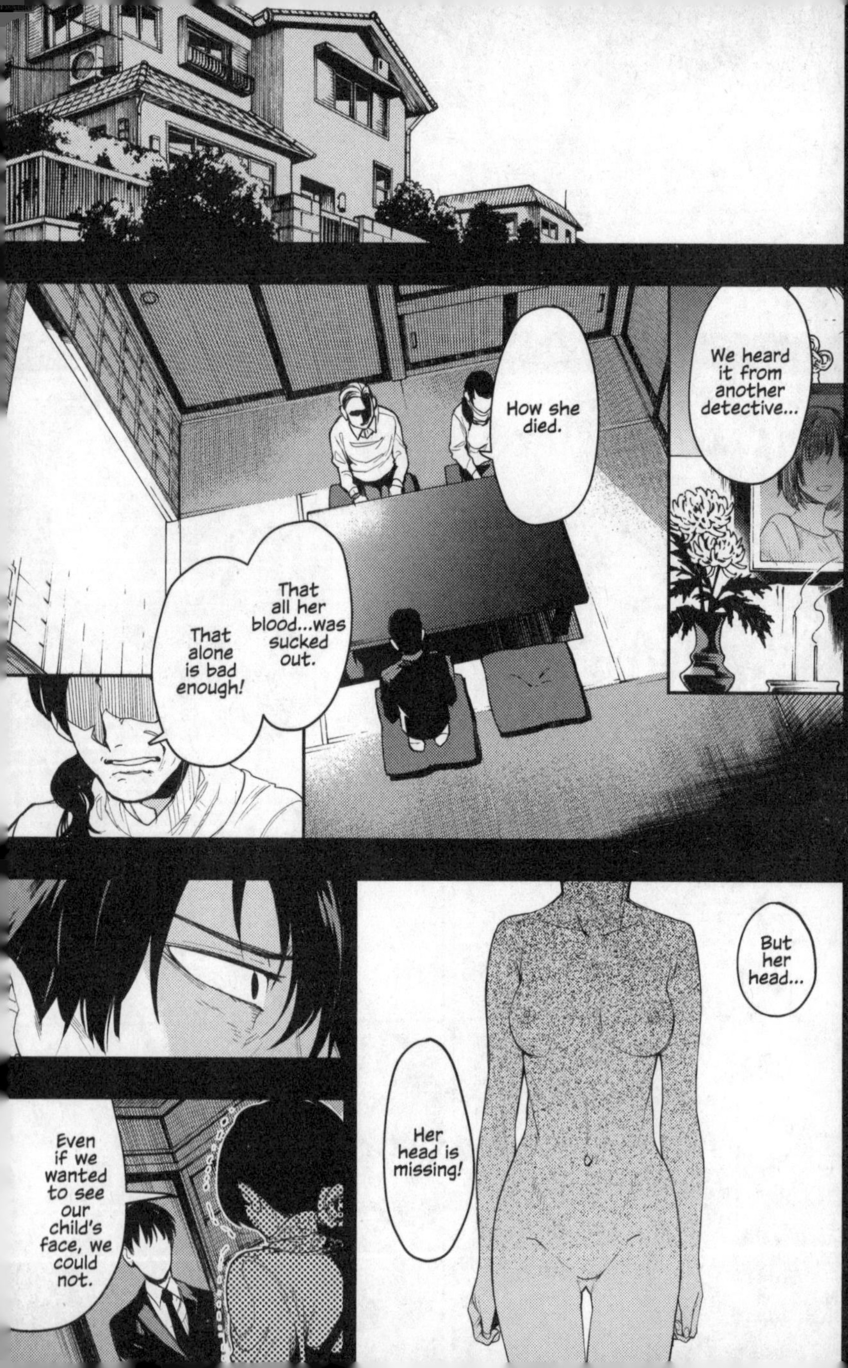
We heard it from another detective...
How she died.
That all her blood...was sucked out.
That alone is bad enough!
But her head...
Her head is missing!
Even if we wanted to see our child's face, we could not.

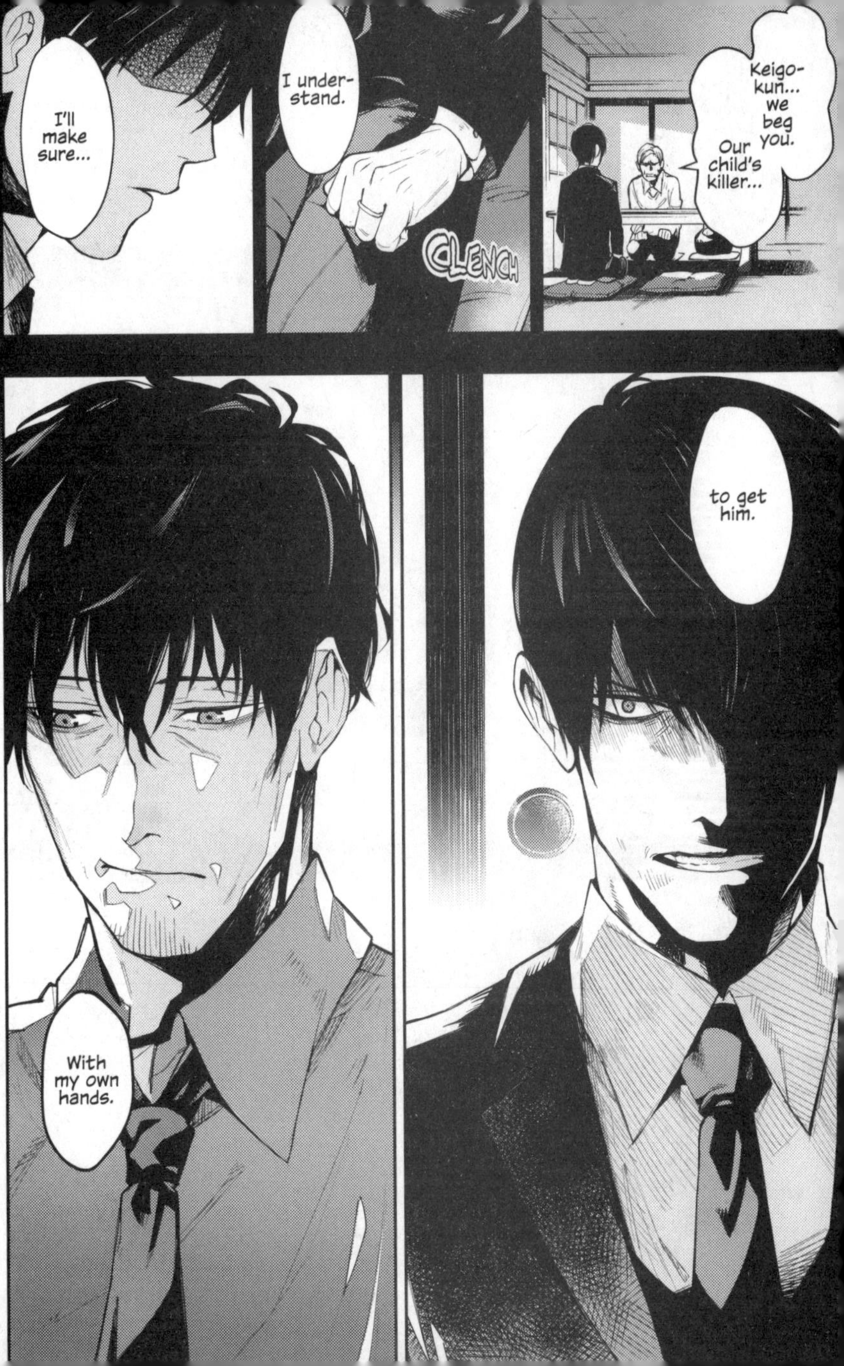
Keigo-kun... we beg you. Our child's killer...
I under-stand.
CLENCH
I'll make sure...
to get him.
With my own hands.

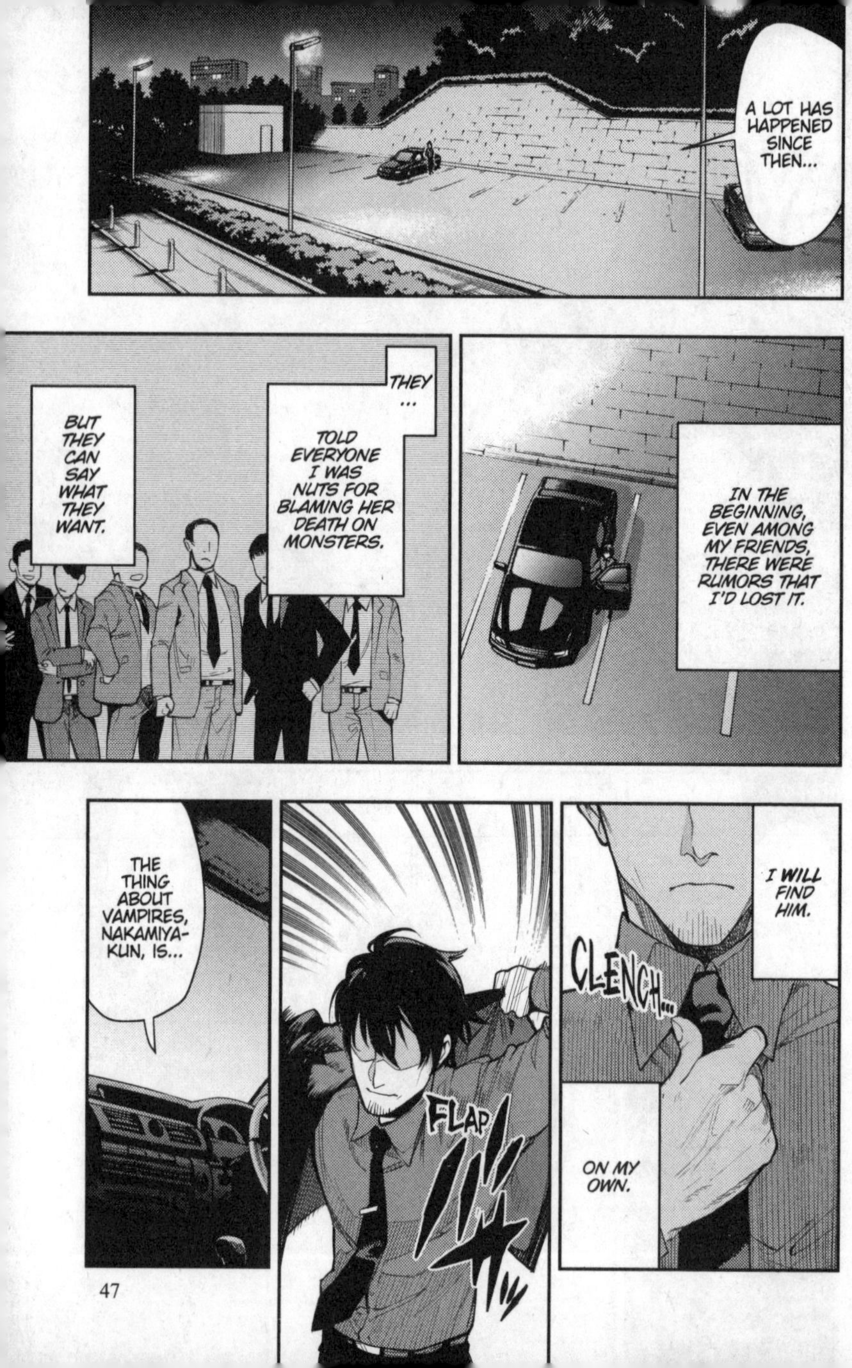
A LOT HAS HAPPENED SINCE THEN...
IN THE BEGINNING, EVEN AMONG MY FRIENDS, THERE WERE RUMORS THAT I'D LOST IT.
THEY ...
TOLD EVERYONE I WAS NUTS FOR BLAMING HER DEATH ON MONSTERS.
BUT THEY CAN SAY WHAT THEY WANT.
I WILL FIND HIM.
CLENCH...
ON MY OWN.
FLAP
THE THING ABOUT VAMPIRES, NAKAMIYA-KUN, IS...

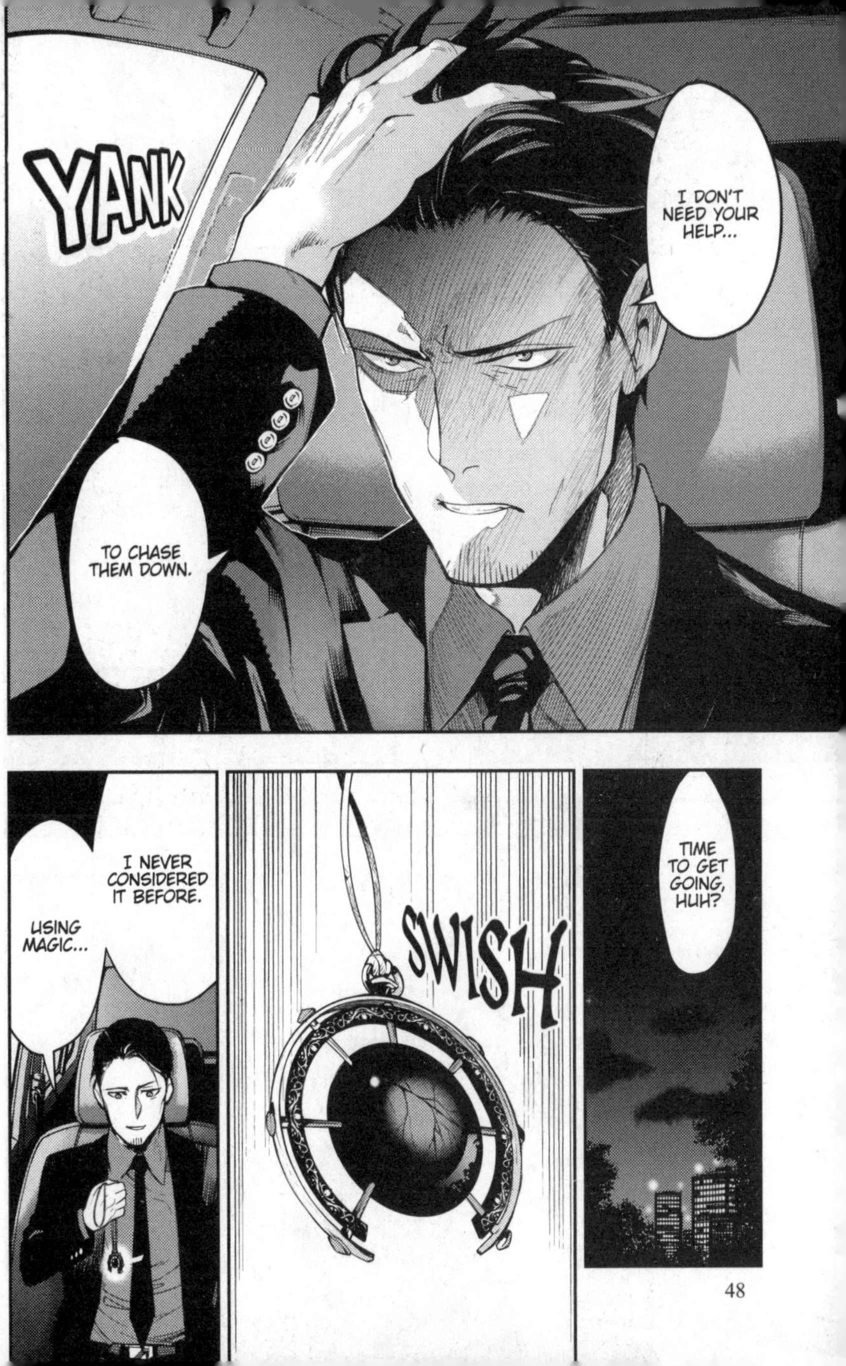
I DON'T NEED YOUR HELP...
YANK
TO CHASE THEM DOWN.
TIME TO GET GOING, HUH?
SWISH
I NEVER CONSIDERED IT BEFORE.
USING MAGIC...

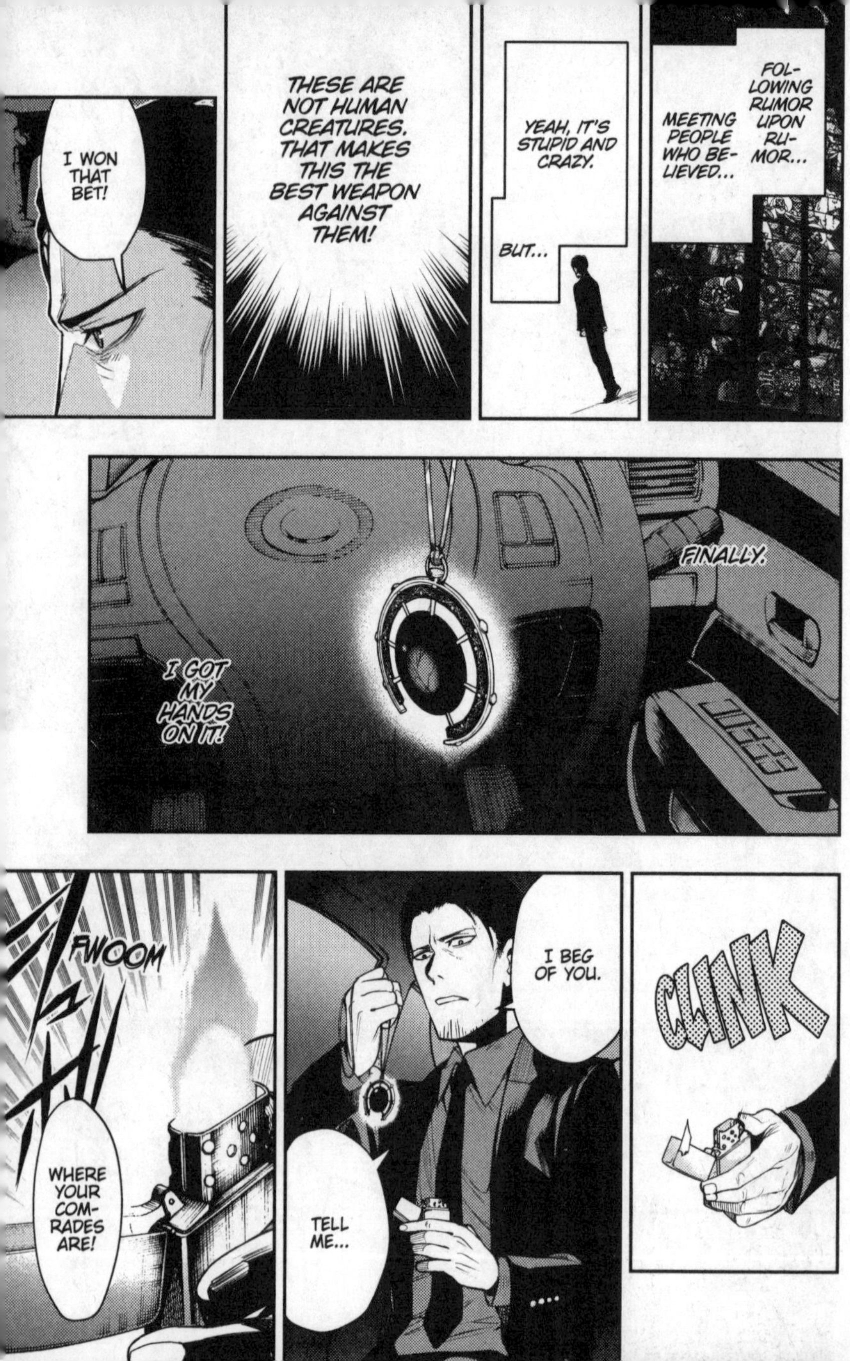

FOL-LOWING RUMOR UPON RU-MOR...
MEETING PEOPLE WHO BE-LIEVED...
YEAH, IT'S STUPID AND CRAZY.
BUT...
THESE ARE NOT HUMAN CREATURES. THAT MAKES THIS THE BEST WEAPON AGAINST THEM!
I WON THAT BET!
FINALLY.
I GOT MY HANDS ON IT!
CLINK
I BEG OF YOU.
TELL ME...
FWOOM
WHERE YOUR COM-RADES ARE!

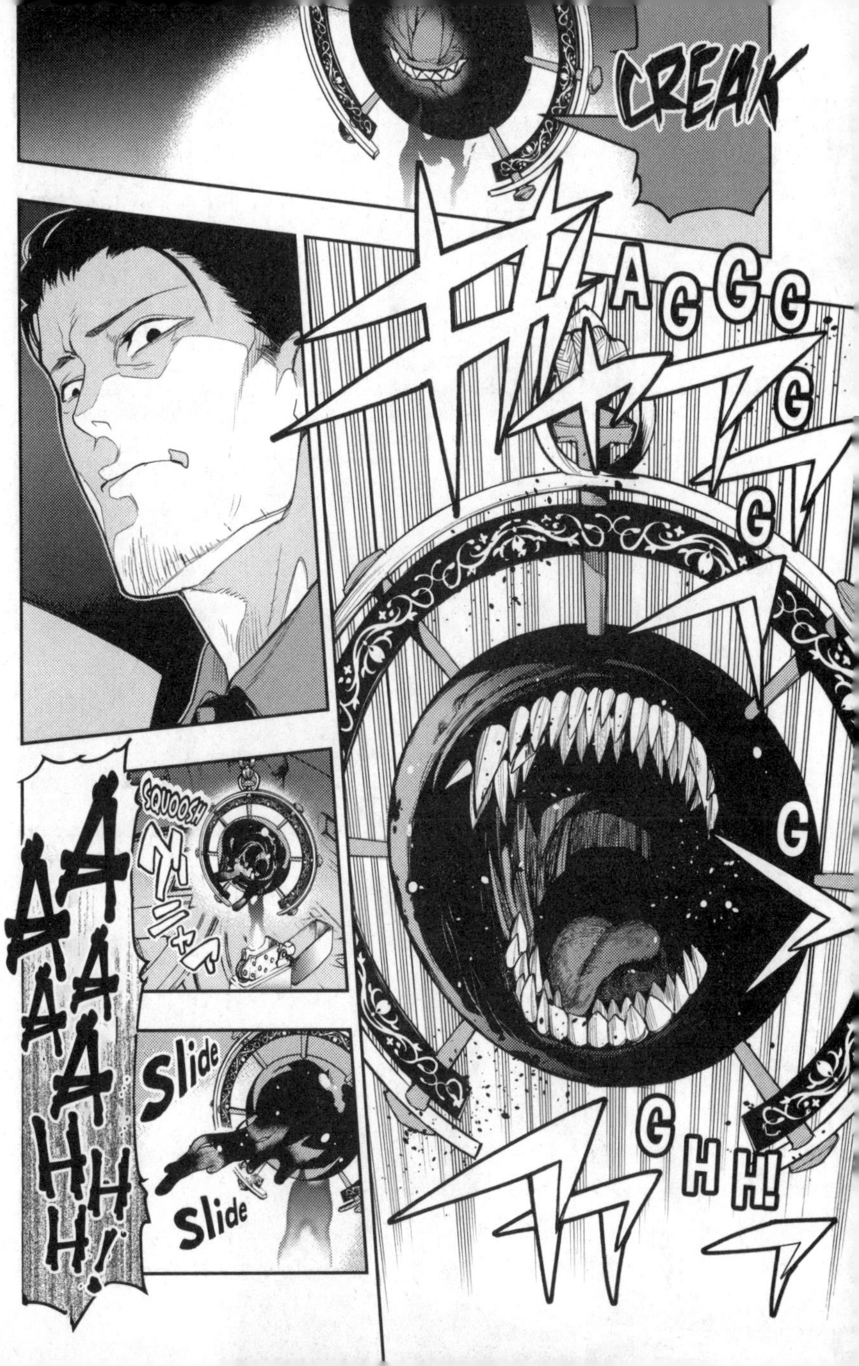
CREAK
AGGGGGGGHH!
AAAAAHHH!
SQUOOSH
Slide
Slide

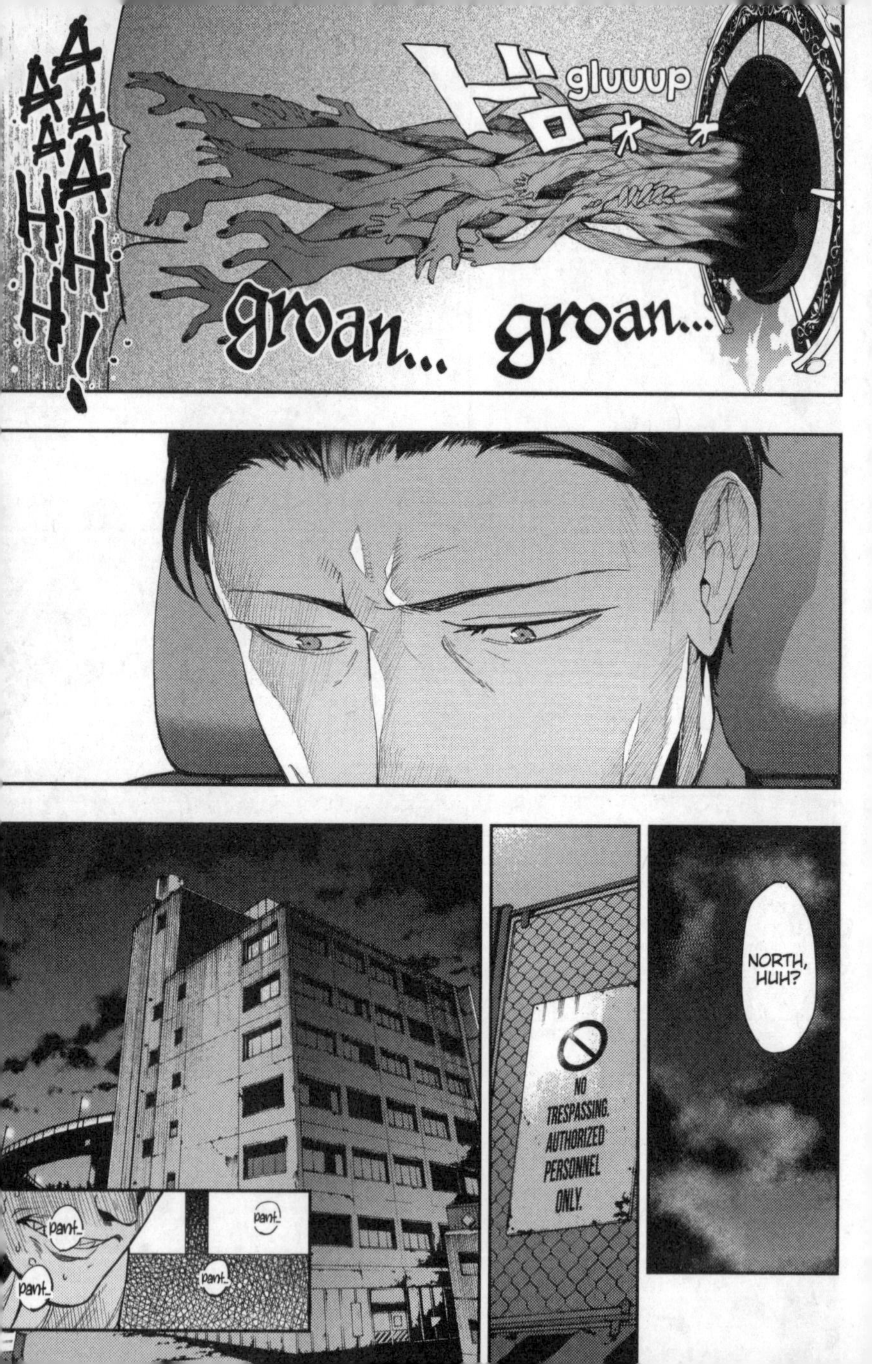

gluuup
ドロォォ
groan... groan...
AAAAAHHH!
NORTH, HUH?
NO TRESPASSING. AUTHORIZED PERSONNEL ONLY.
pant_
pant_
pant_
pant_

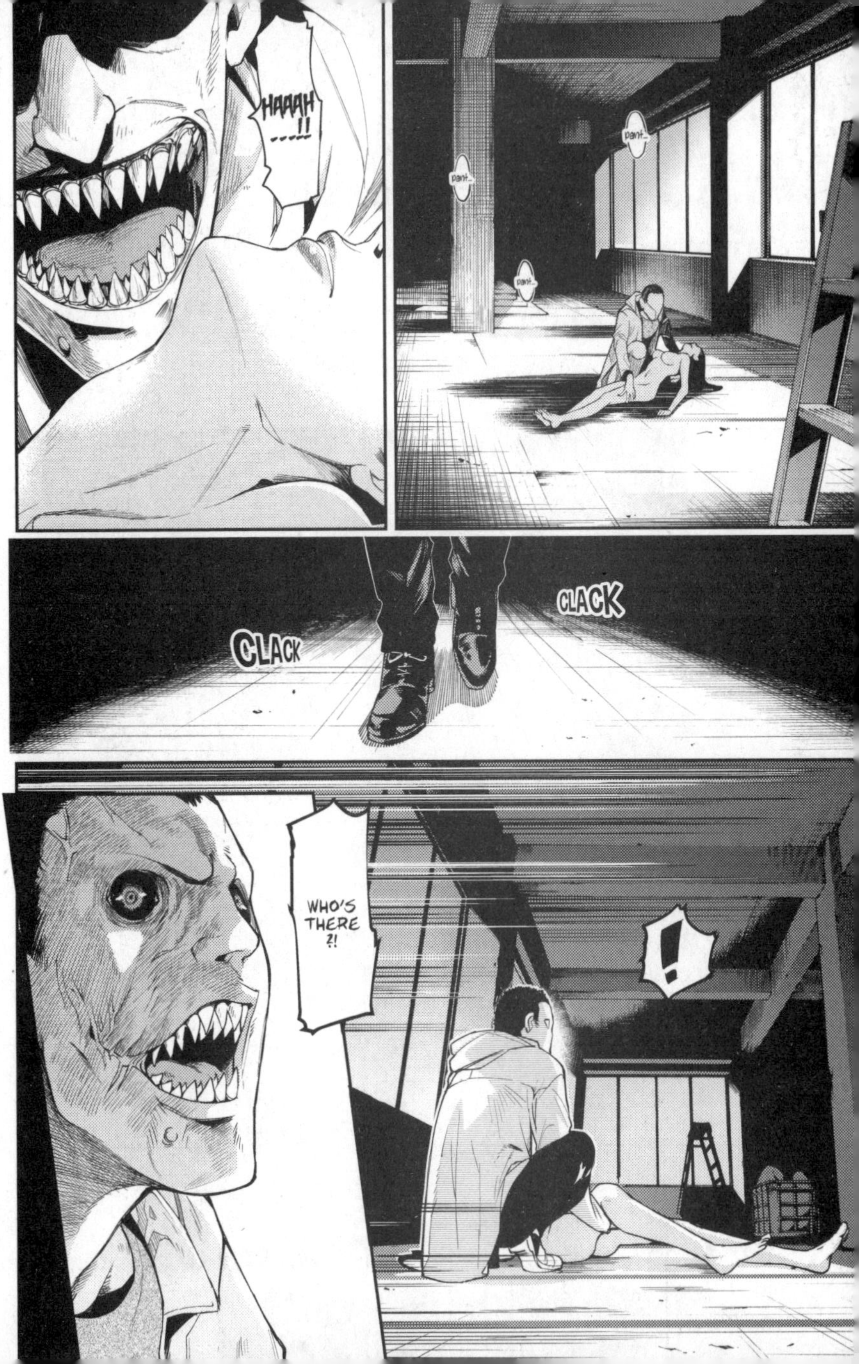
pant...
pant...
pant...
HAAAH.....!!
CLACK
CLACK
!
WHO'S THERE?!

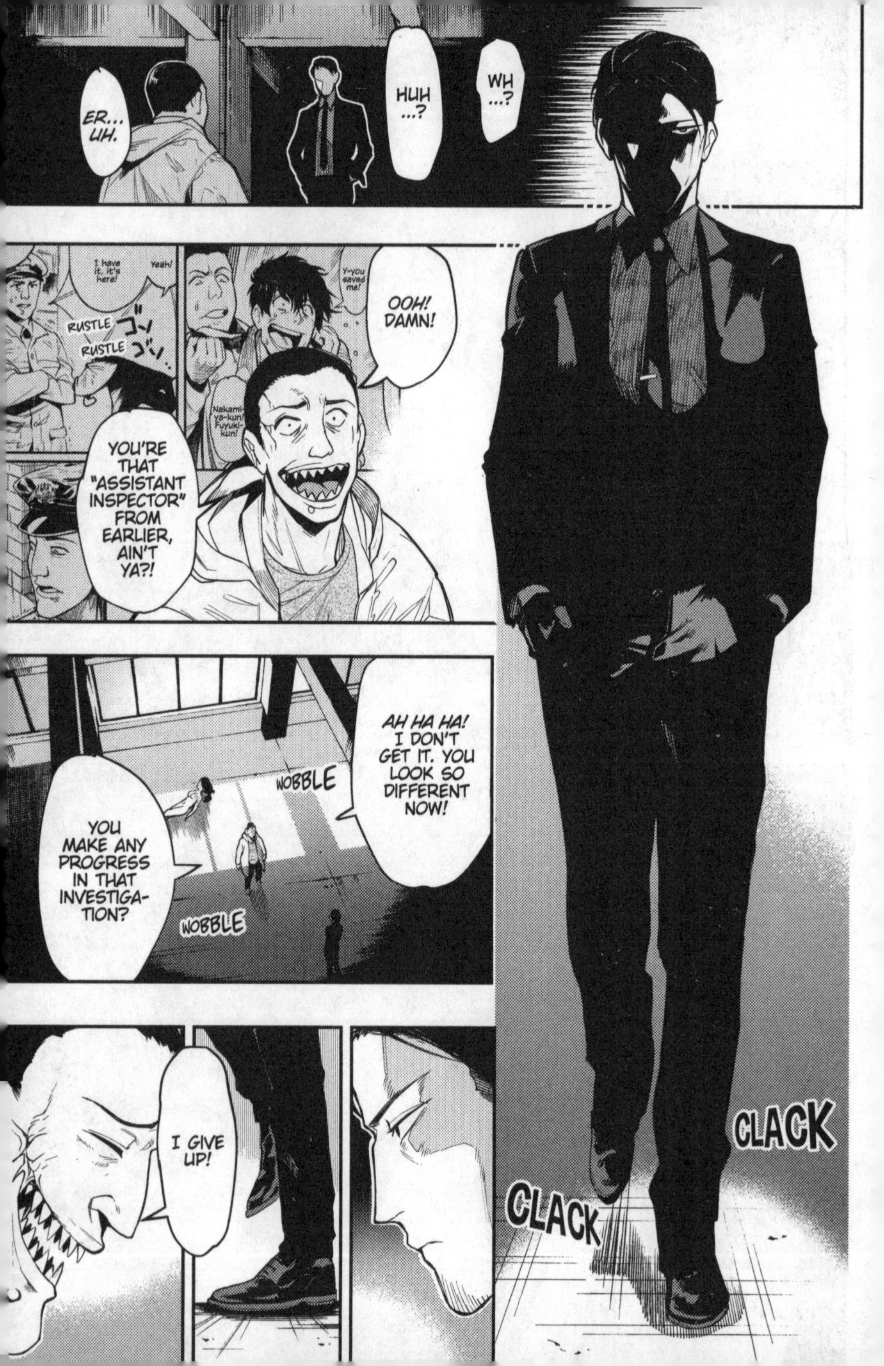
CLACK
CLACK
WH ...?
HUH ...?
ER... UH.
Y-you saved me!
OOH! DAMN!
YOU'RE THAT "ASSISTANT INSPECTOR" FROM EARLIER, AIN'T YA?!
Nakamiya-kun! Fuyuki-kun!
Yeah!
I have it, it's here!
RUSTLE
RUSTLE
AH HA HA! I DON'T GET IT. YOU LOOK SO DIFFERENT NOW!
WOBBLE
YOU MAKE ANY PROGRESS IN THAT INVESTIGATION?
WOBBLE
I GIVE UP!

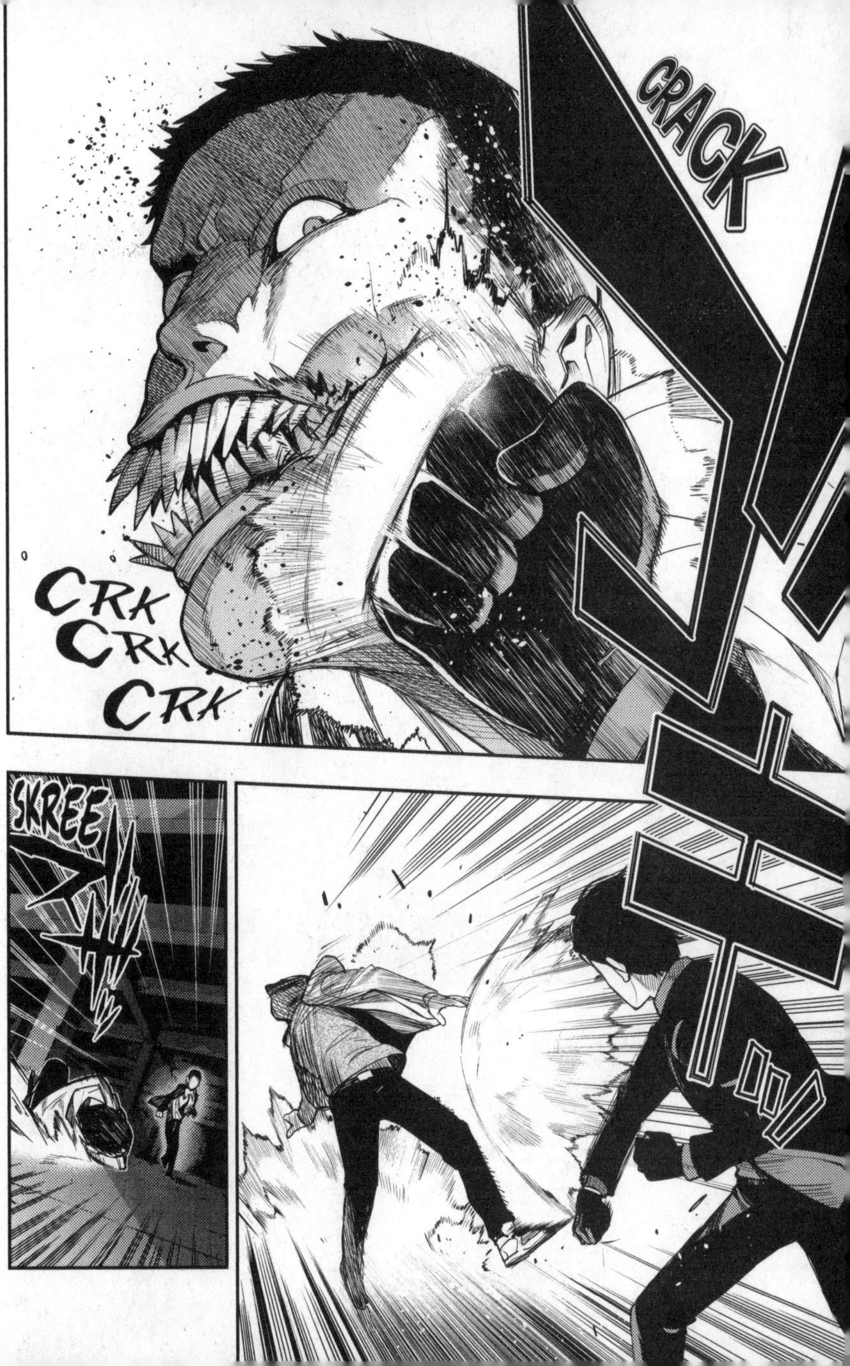
CRACK
CRK CRK CRK
SKREE

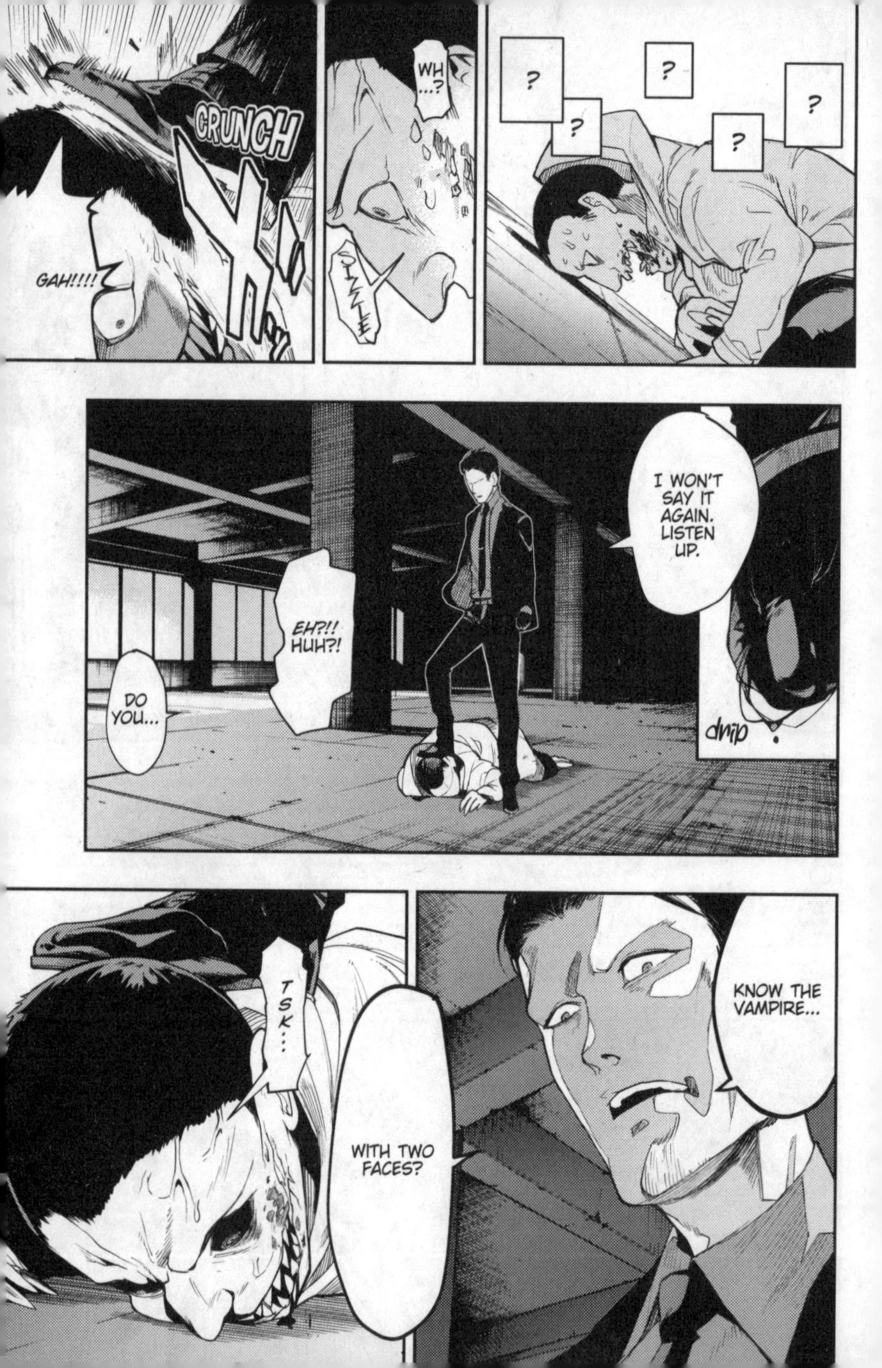
?
?
?
?
?
WH ...?
SIZZLE
CRUNCH
GAH!!!!
I WON'T SAY IT AGAIN. LISTEN UP.
drip
EH?!! HUH?!
DO YOU...
KNOW THE VAMPIRE...
WITH TWO FACES?
TSK...

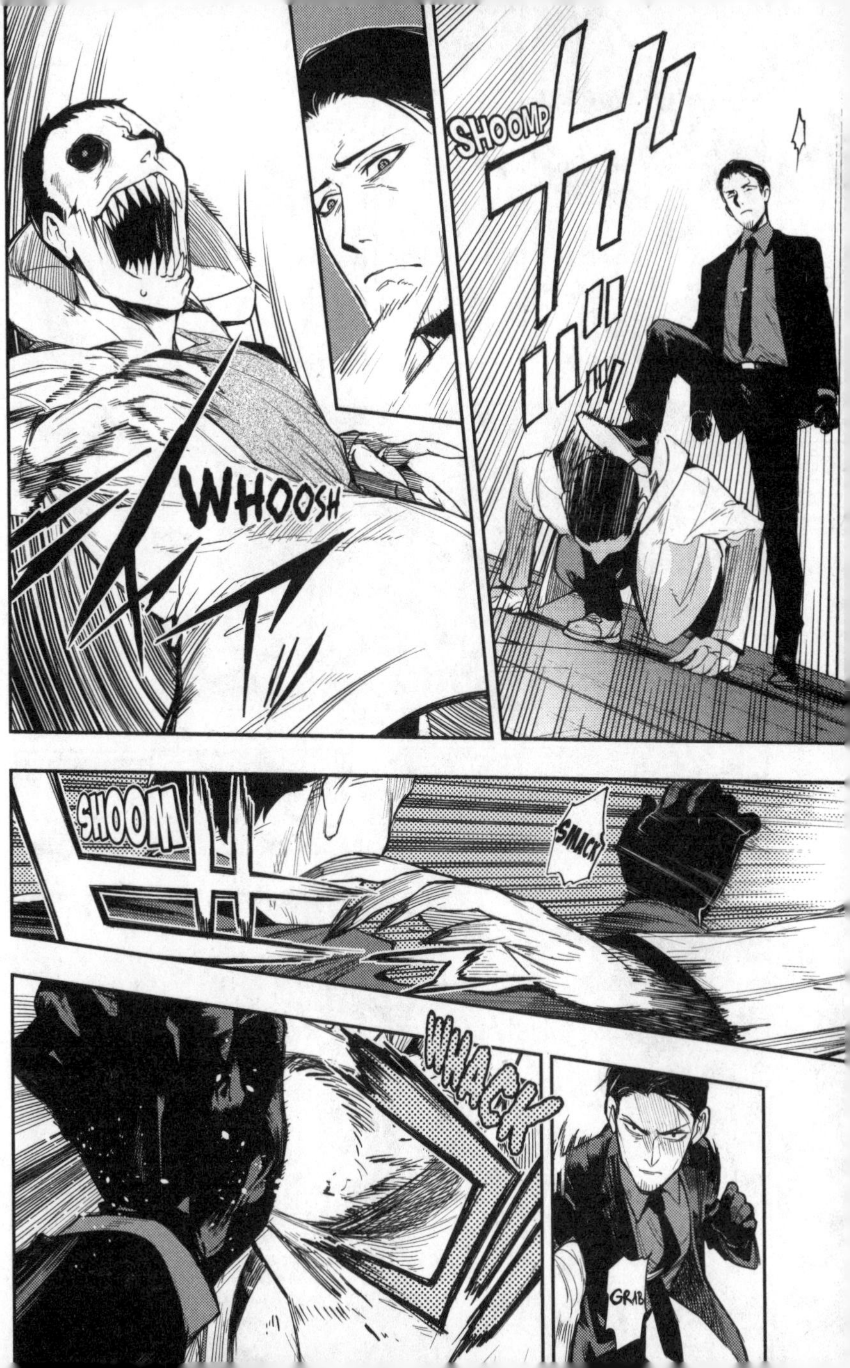
SHOOMP
WHOOSH
SMACK
SHOOM
GRAB
WHACK

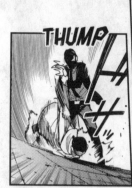

THUMP

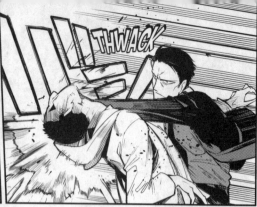

THWACK

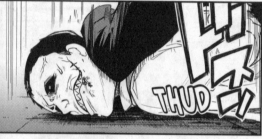

THUD

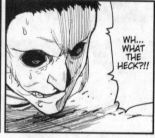

WH... WHAT THE HECK?!!

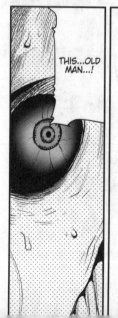

THIS...OLD MAN...!

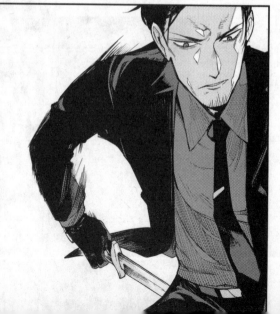

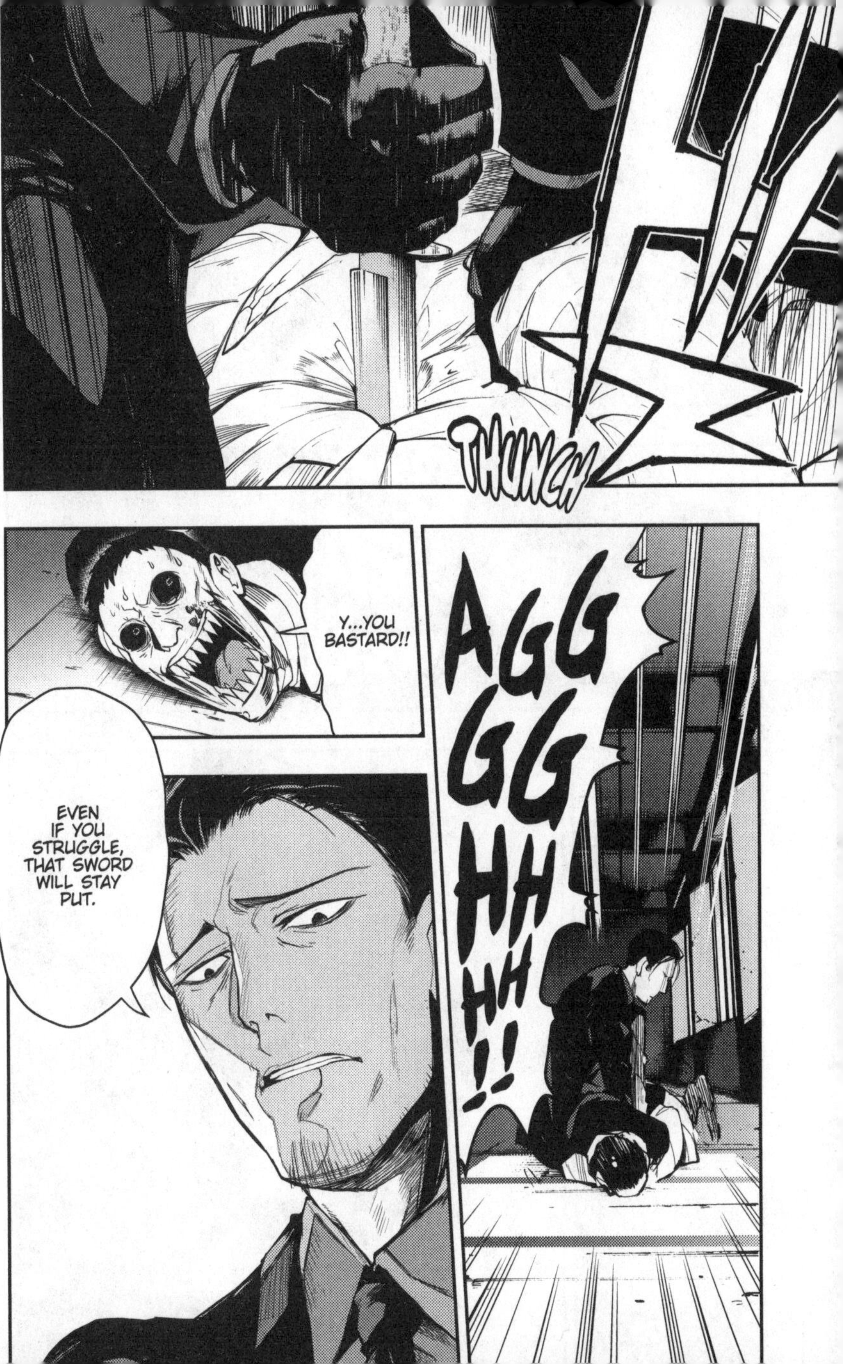
THUNCH
AGGGGHHHHHH!!
Y...YOU BASTARD!!
EVEN IF YOU STRUGGLE, THAT SWORD WILL STAY PUT.

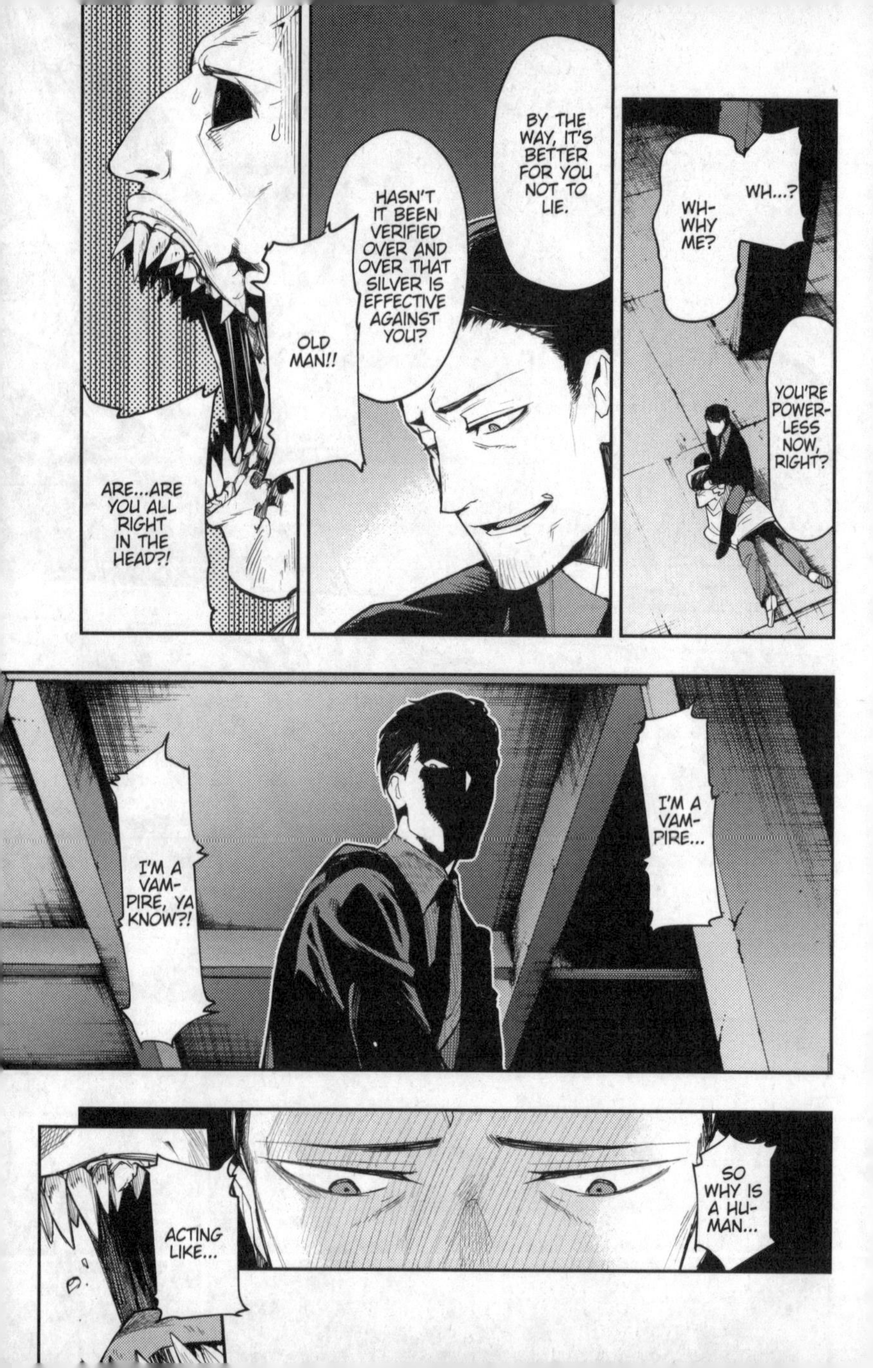
WH...?
WH-WHY ME?
YOU'RE POWERLESS NOW, RIGHT?
BY THE WAY, IT'S BETTER FOR YOU NOT TO LIE.
HASN'T IT BEEN VERIFIED OVER AND OVER THAT SILVER IS EFFECTIVE AGAINST YOU?
OLD MAN!!
ARE...ARE YOU ALL RIGHT IN THE HEAD?!
I'M A VAMPIRE...
I'M A VAMPIRE, YA KNOW?!
SO WHY IS A HUMAN...
ACTING LIKE...

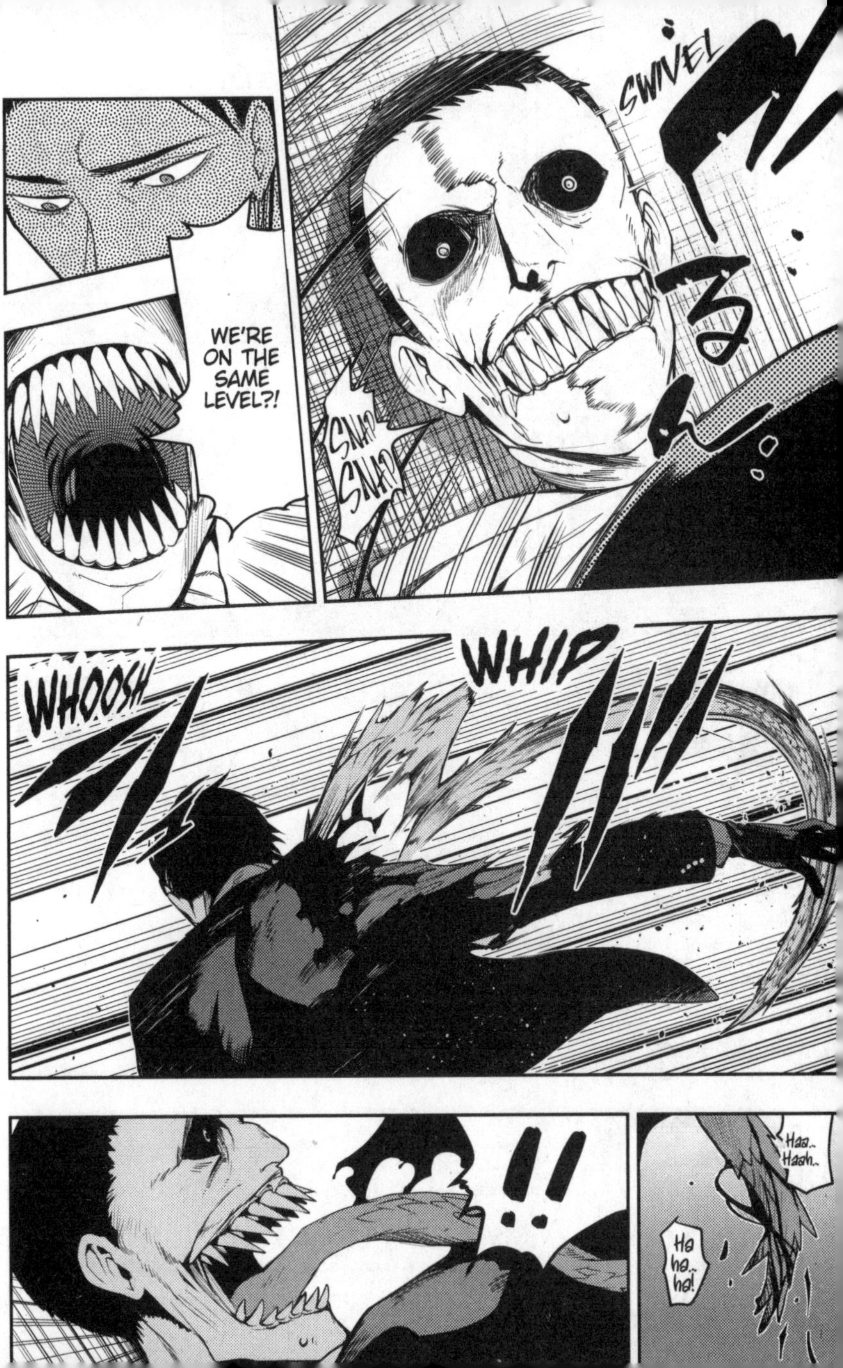
SWIVEL
SNAP SNAP
WE'RE ON THE SAME LEVEL?!
WHIP
WHOOSH
Haa.. Haah..
Ha ha.. ha!
!!

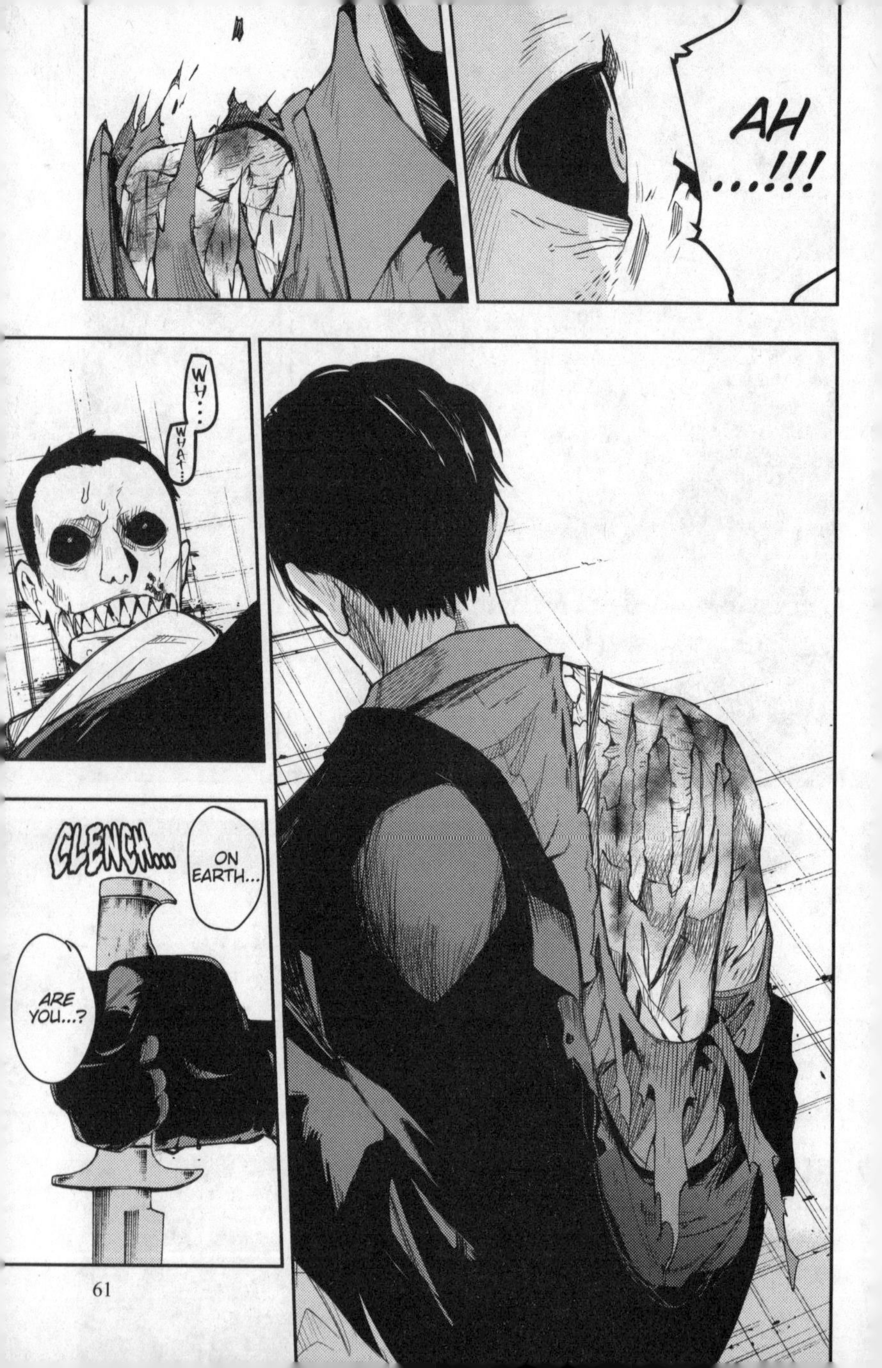
AH ...!!!
WH... WHAT...
ON EARTH...
CLENCH...
ARE YOU...?

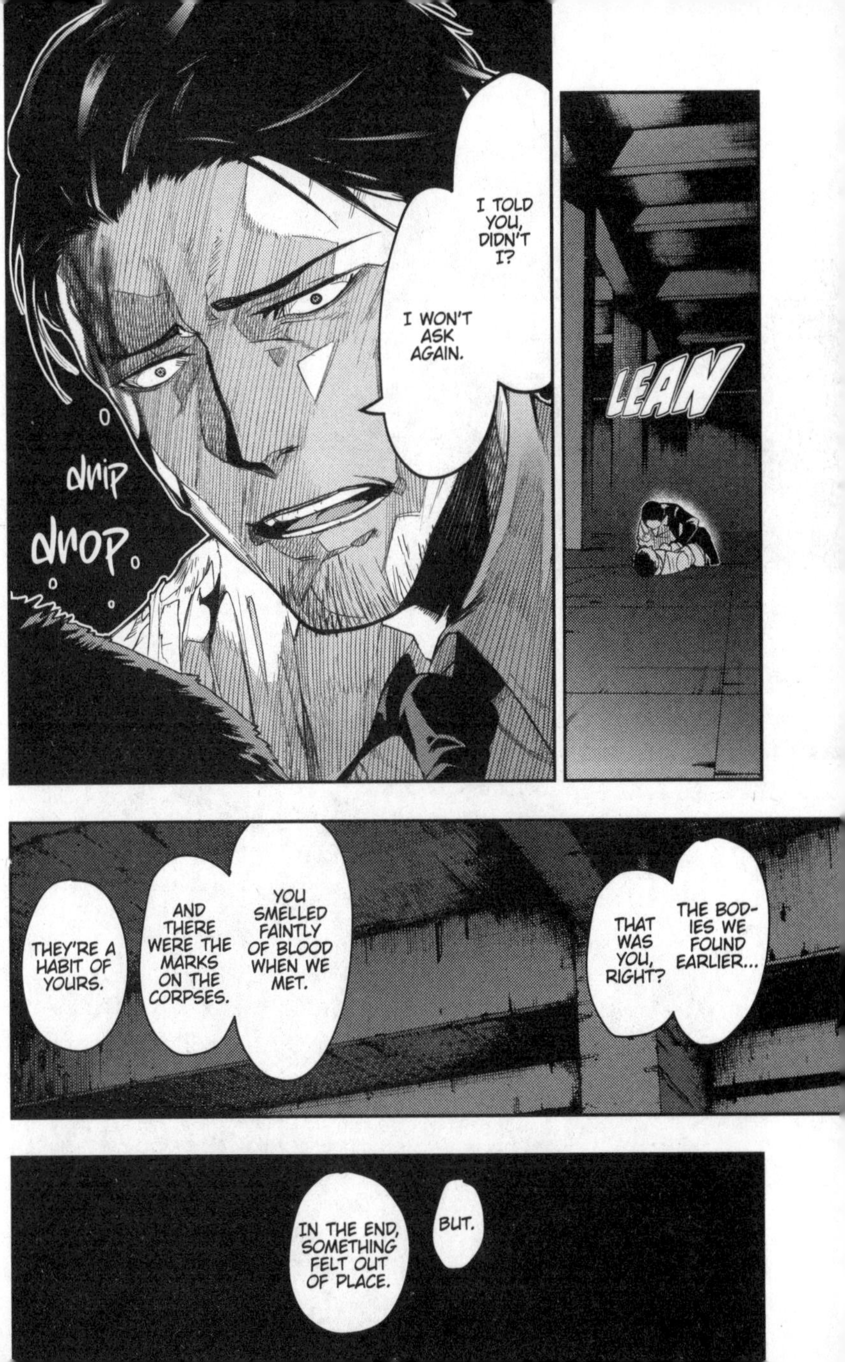
LEAN
I TOLD YOU, DIDN'T I?
I WON'T ASK AGAIN.
drip
drop
THE BOD-IES WE FOUND EARLIER...
THAT WAS YOU, RIGHT?
YOU SMELLED FAINTLY OF BLOOD WHEN WE MET.
AND THERE WERE THE MARKS ON THE CORPSES.
THEY'RE A HABIT OF YOURS.
BUT.
IN THE END, SOMETHING FELT OUT OF PLACE.

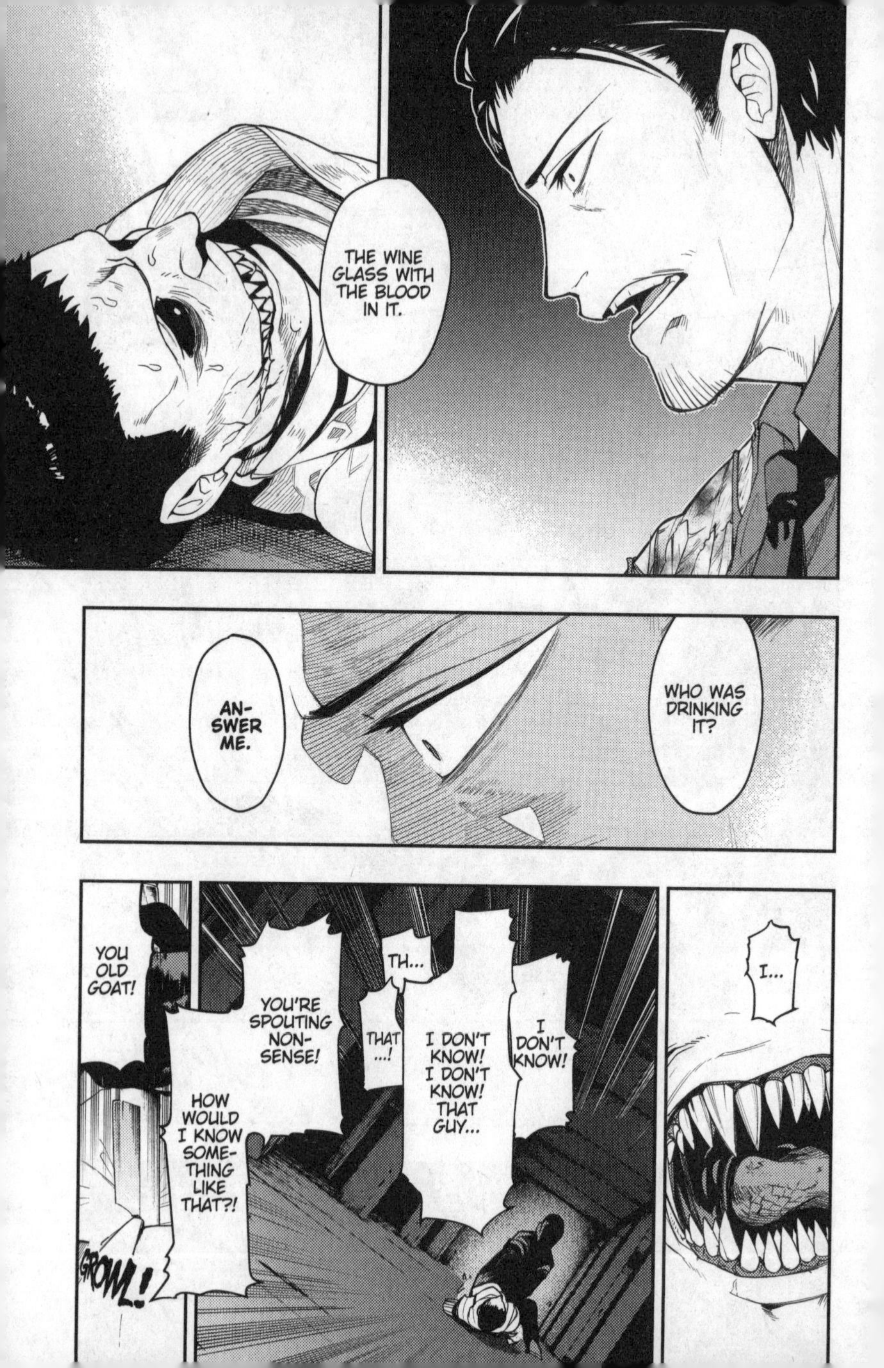
THE WINE GLASS WITH THE BLOOD IN IT.
WHO WAS DRINKING IT?
AN-SWER ME.
I...
I DON'T KNOW!
TH...
I DON'T KNOW! I DON'T KNOW! THAT GUY...
THAT ...!
YOU'RE SPOUTING NON-SENSE!
HOW WOULD I KNOW SOME-THING LIKE THAT?!
YOU OLD GOAT!
GROWL!

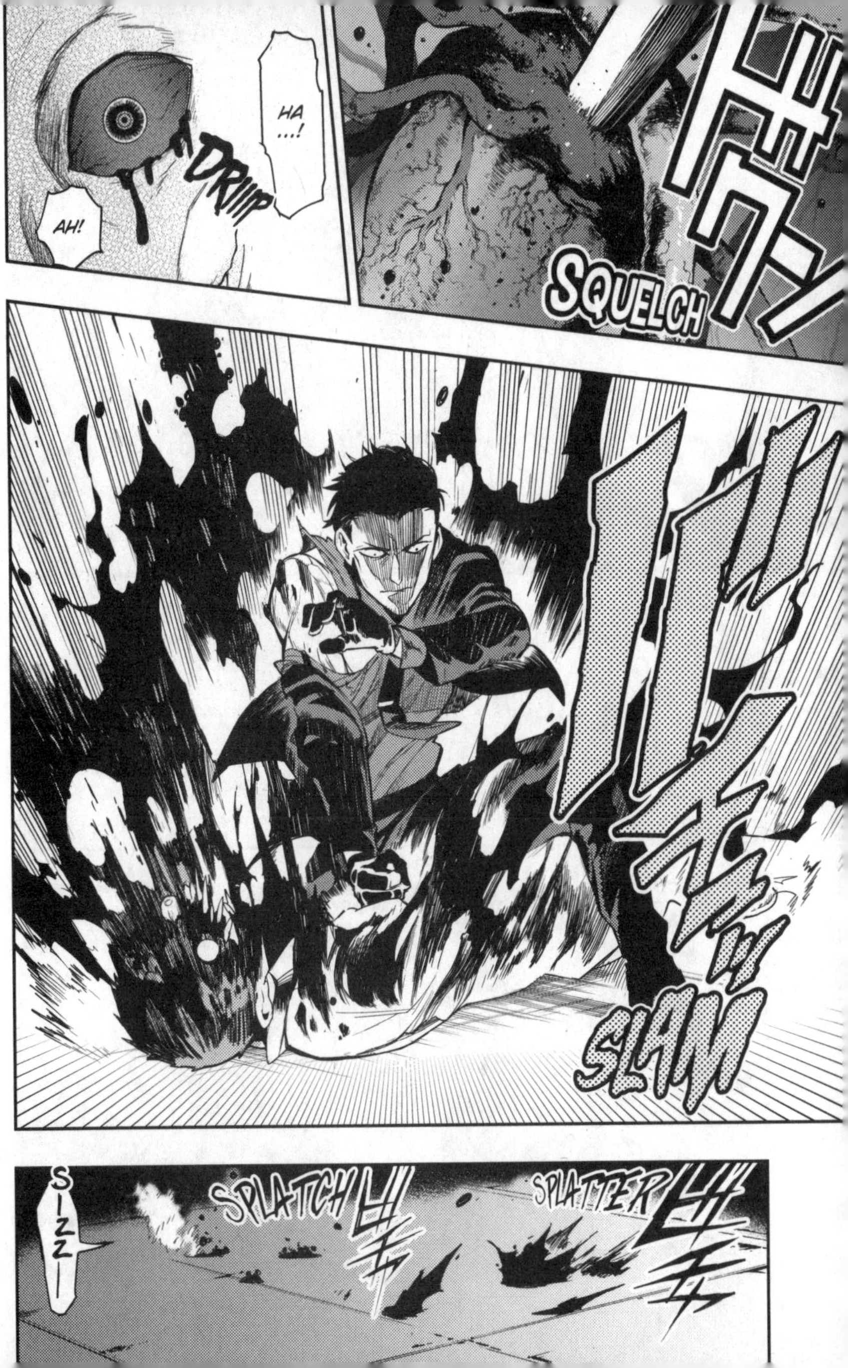
SQUELCH
HA ...!
DRIIP
AH!
SLAM
SPLATTER
SPLATCH
SIZZ

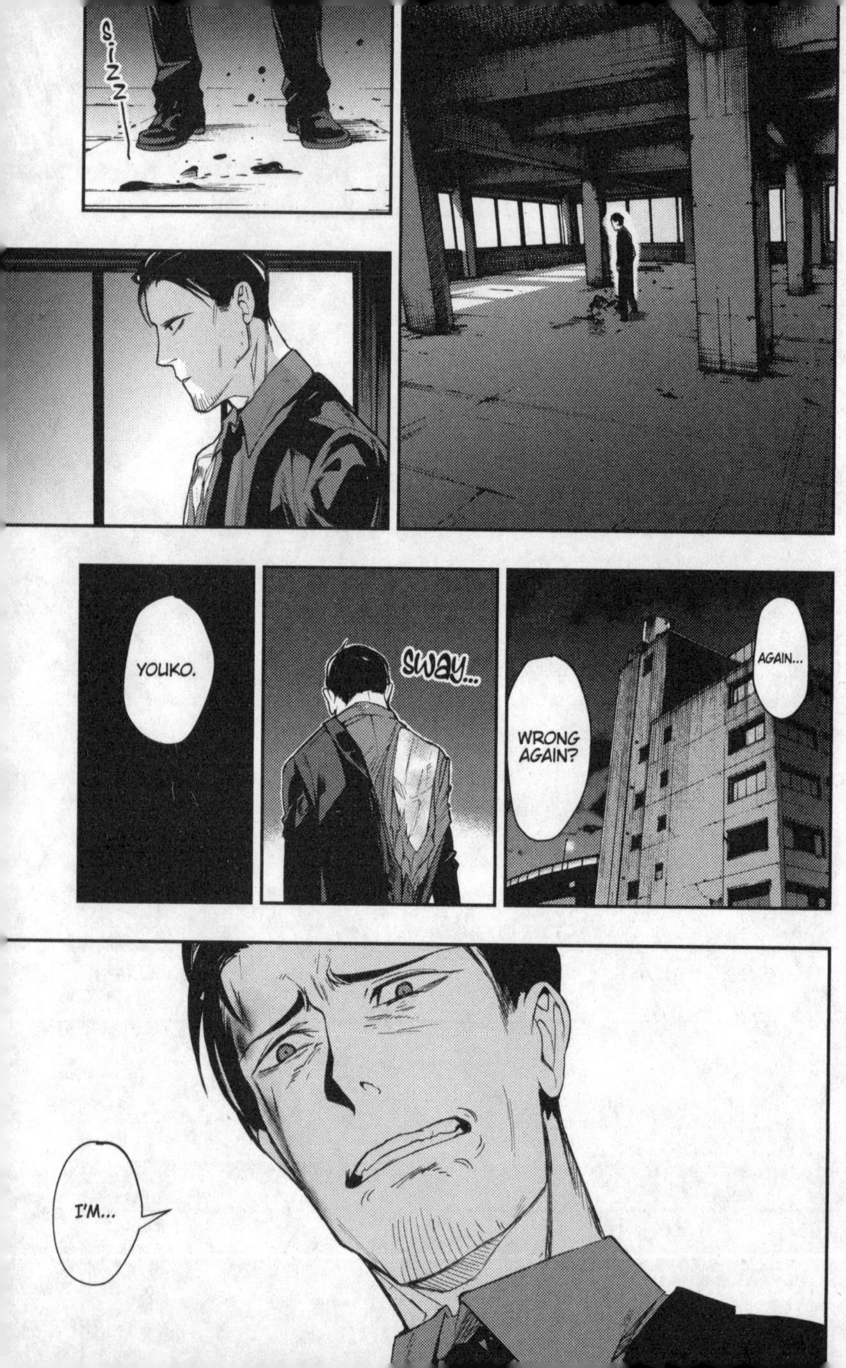
SIZZ
AGAIN...
WRONG AGAIN?
SWAY...
YOUKO.
I'M...

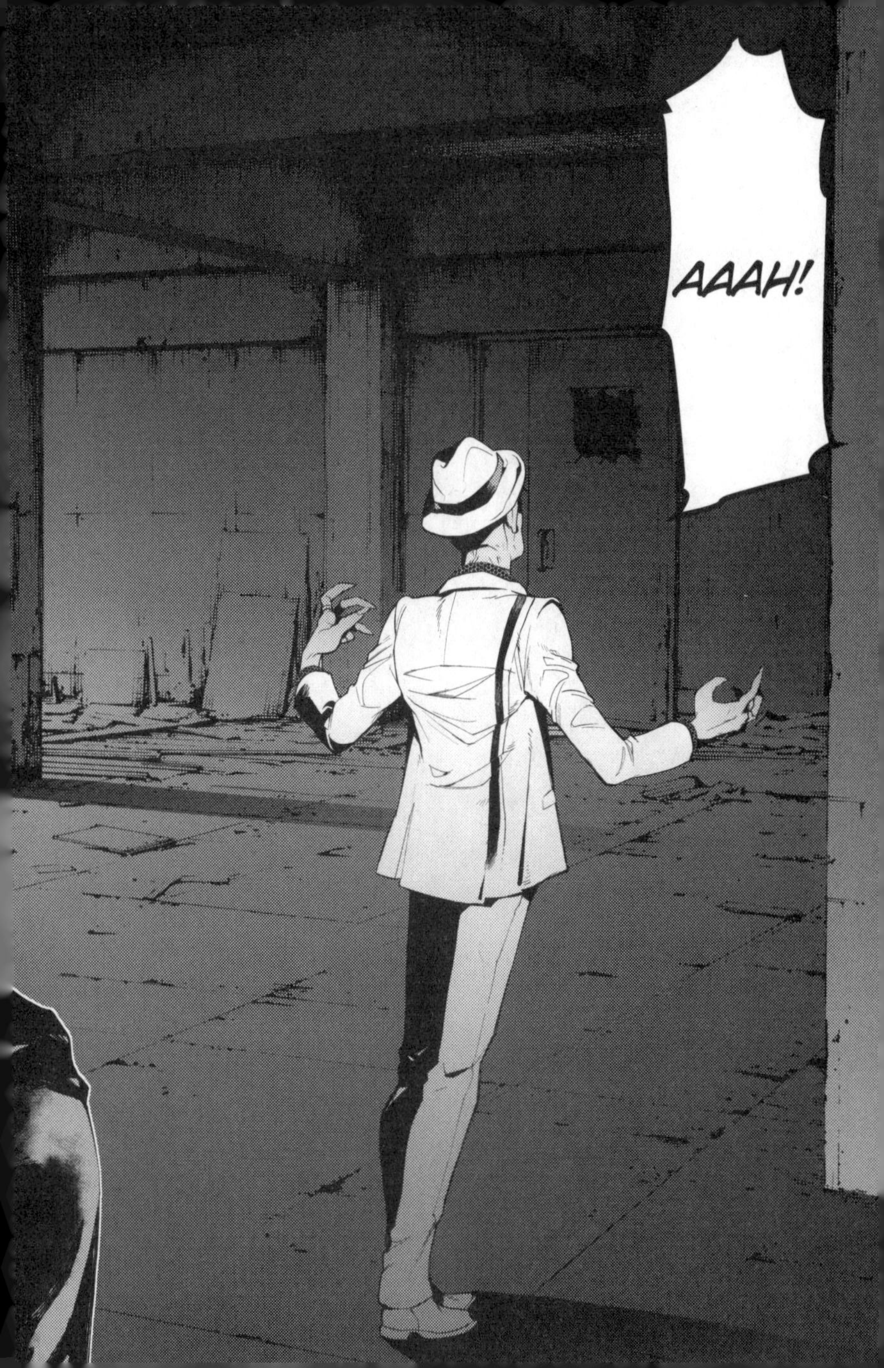
AAAH!

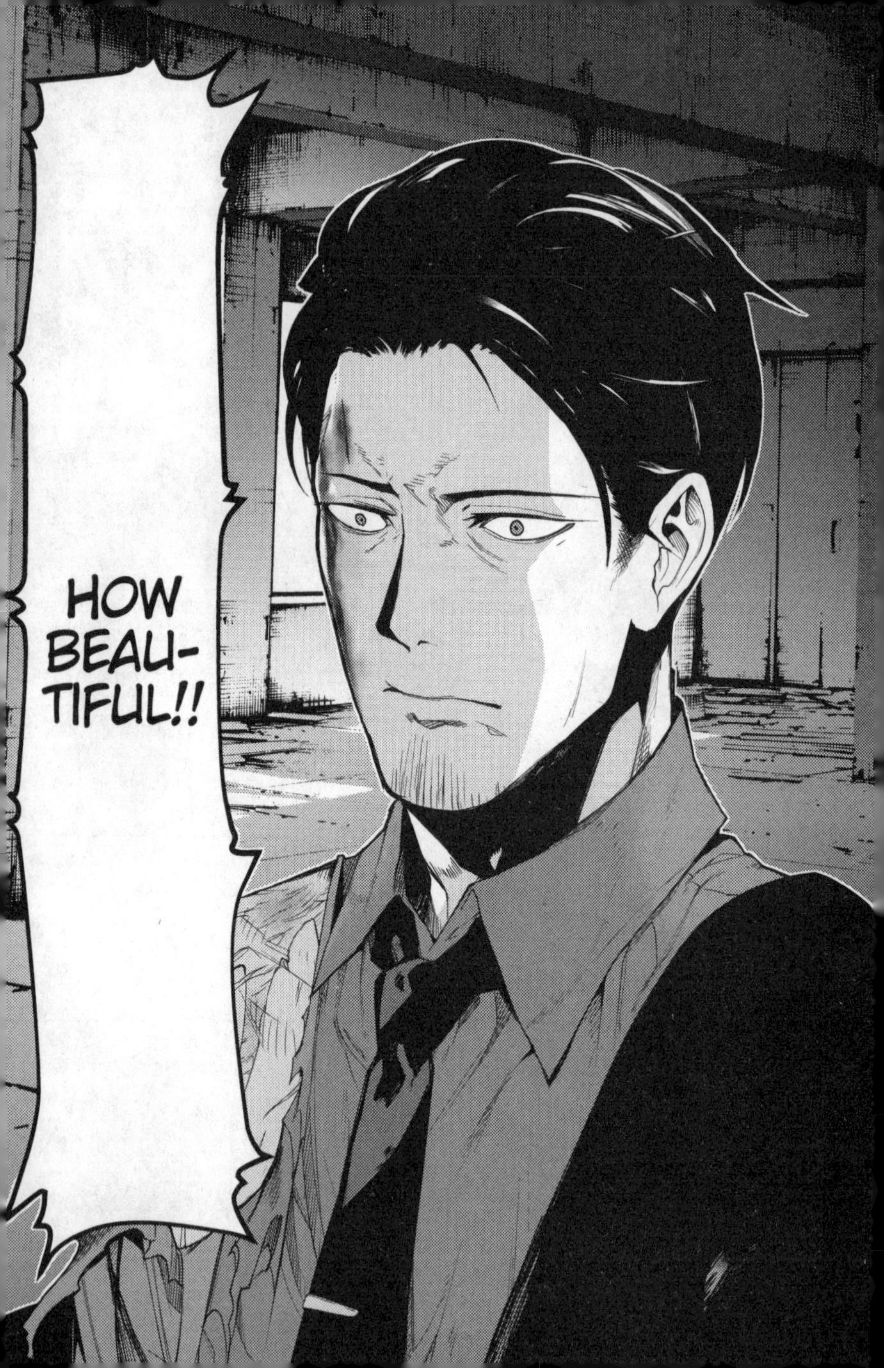
HOW BEAU-TIFUL!!

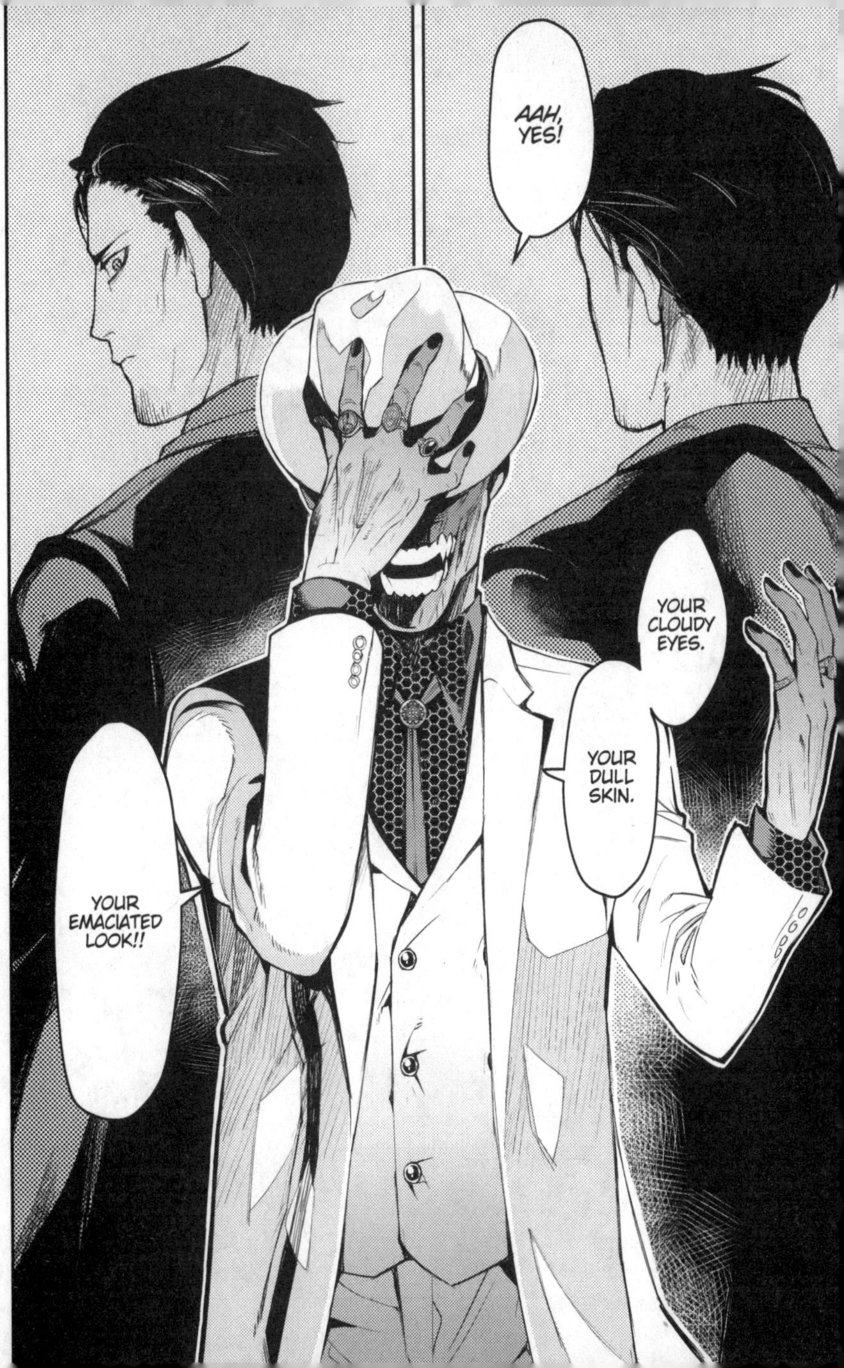
AAH, YES!
YOUR CLOUDY EYES.
YOUR DULL SKIN.
YOUR EMACIATED LOOK!!

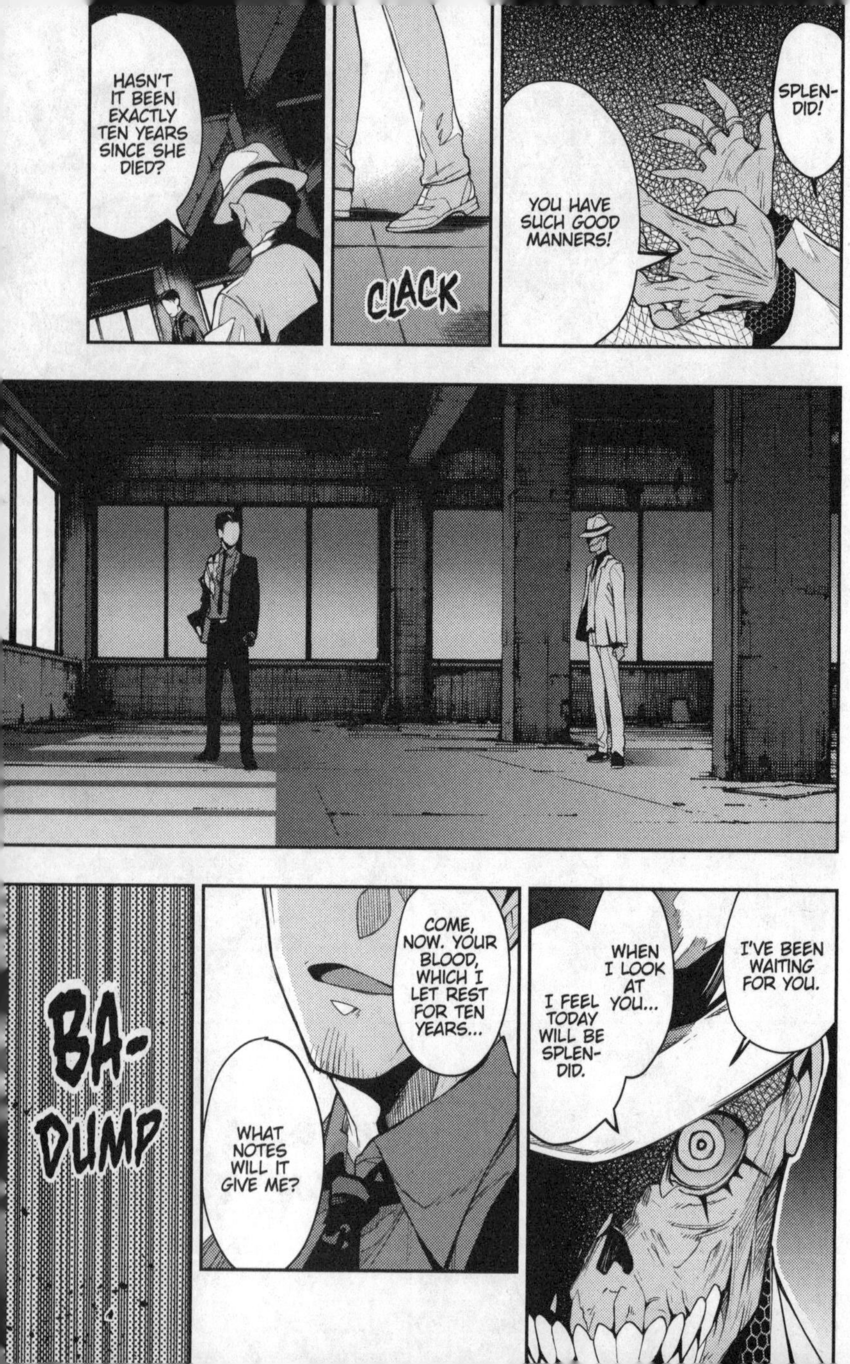
SPLEN-DID!
YOU HAVE SUCH GOOD MANNERS!
CLACK
HASN'T IT BEEN EXACTLY TEN YEARS SINCE SHE DIED?
I'VE BEEN WAITING FOR YOU.
WHEN I LOOK AT YOU...
I FEEL TODAY WILL BE SPLEN-DID.
COME, NOW. YOUR BLOOD, WHICH I LET REST FOR TEN YEARS...
WHAT NOTES WILL IT GIVE ME?
BA-DUMP

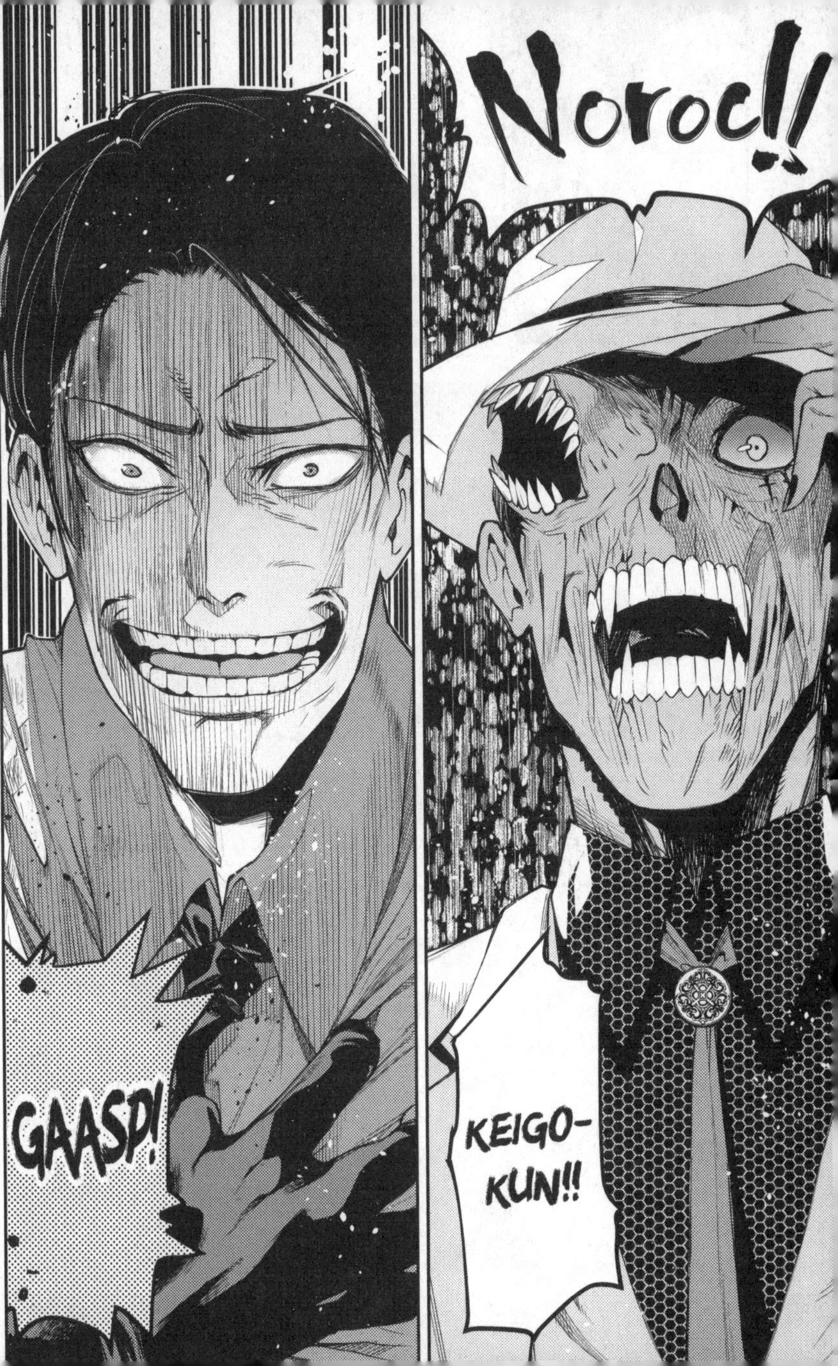

Noroc!!
KEIGO-KUN!!
GAASP!

*Noroc is a Romanian word used as a greeting, to say "bless you" or "good luck," or as a toast.

MoMo
the blood taker

MOMO
the blood taker

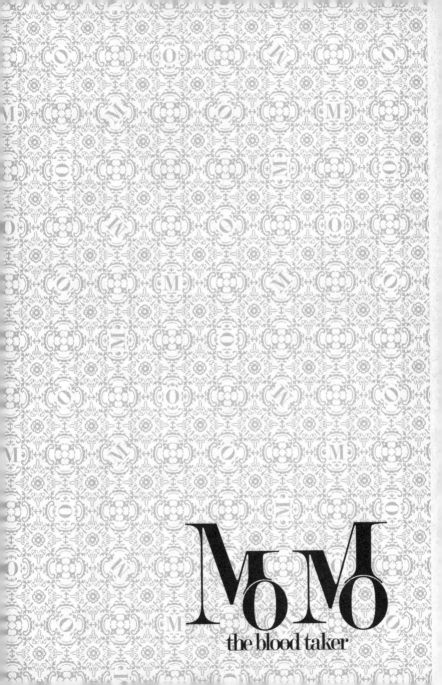

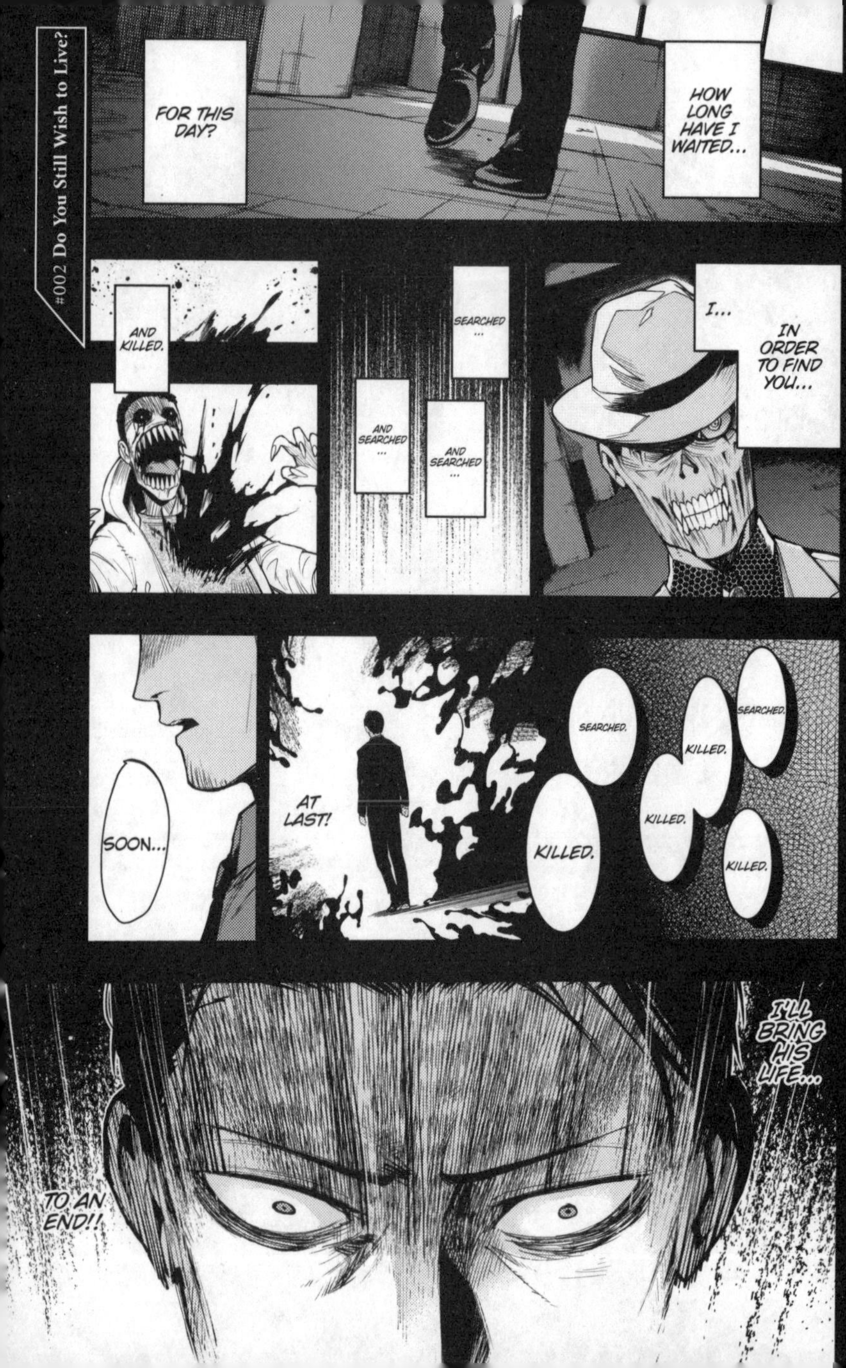
#002 Do You Still Wish to Live?
HOW LONG HAVE I WAITED...
FOR THIS DAY?
I...
IN ORDER TO FIND YOU...
SEARCHED...
AND SEARCHED...
AND SEARCHED...
AND KILLED.
SEARCHED.
KILLED.
SEARCHED.
KILLED.
KILLED.
KILLED.
AT LAST!
SOON...
I'LL BRING HIS LIFE...
TO AN END!!

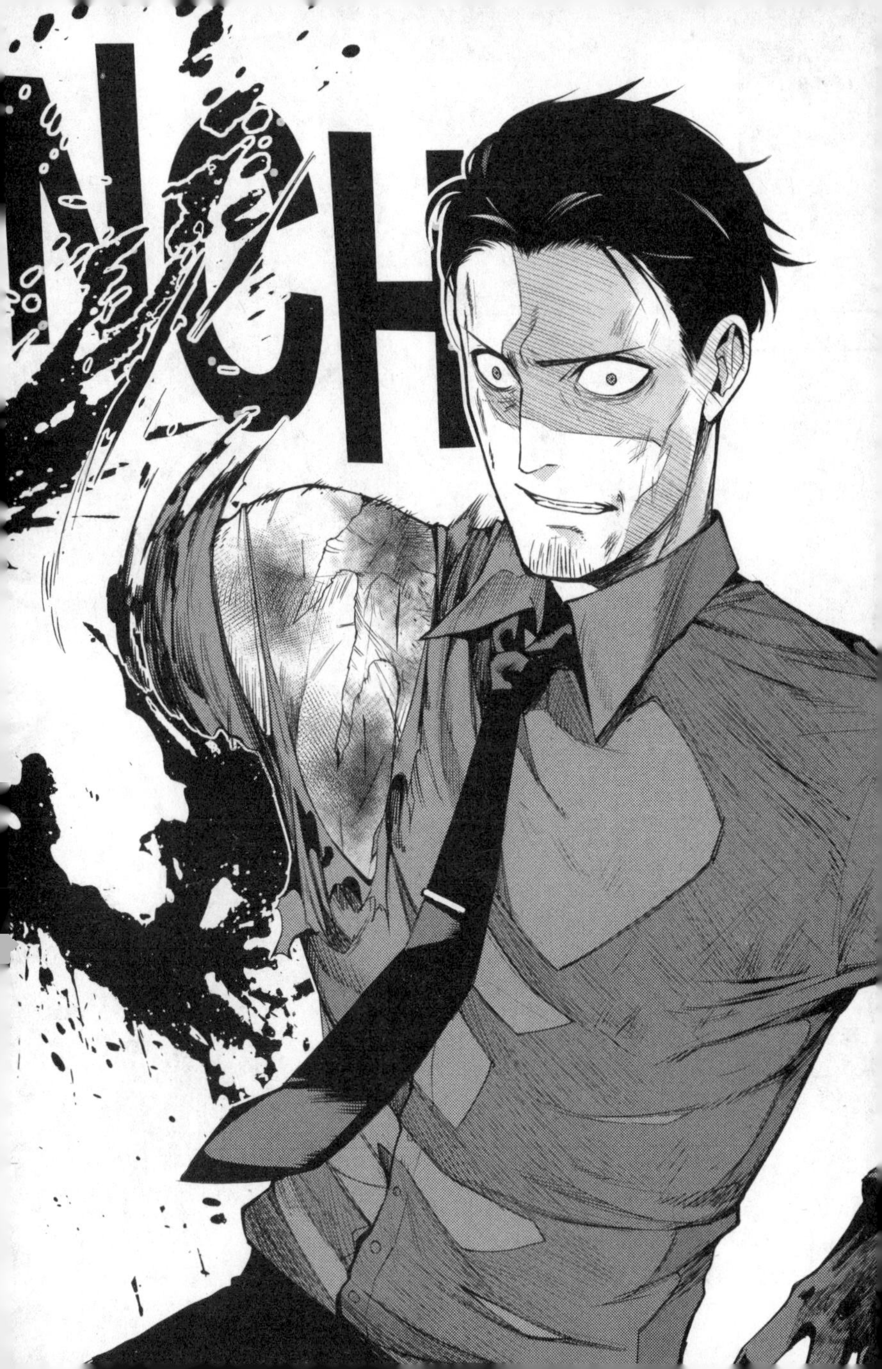
NCH

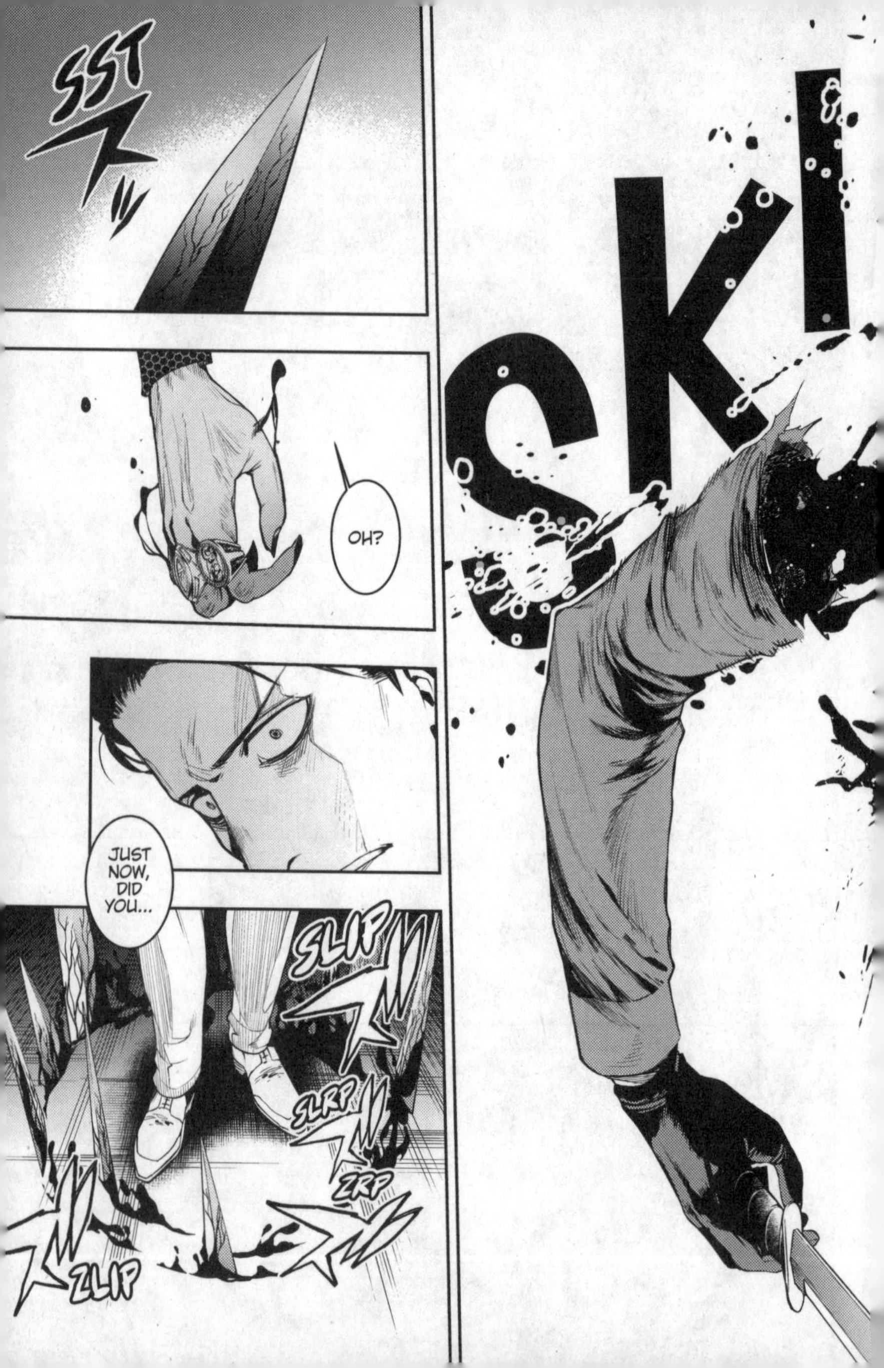

SKI
SST
OH?
JUST NOW, DID YOU...
SLIP
SLRP
ZRP
ZLIP

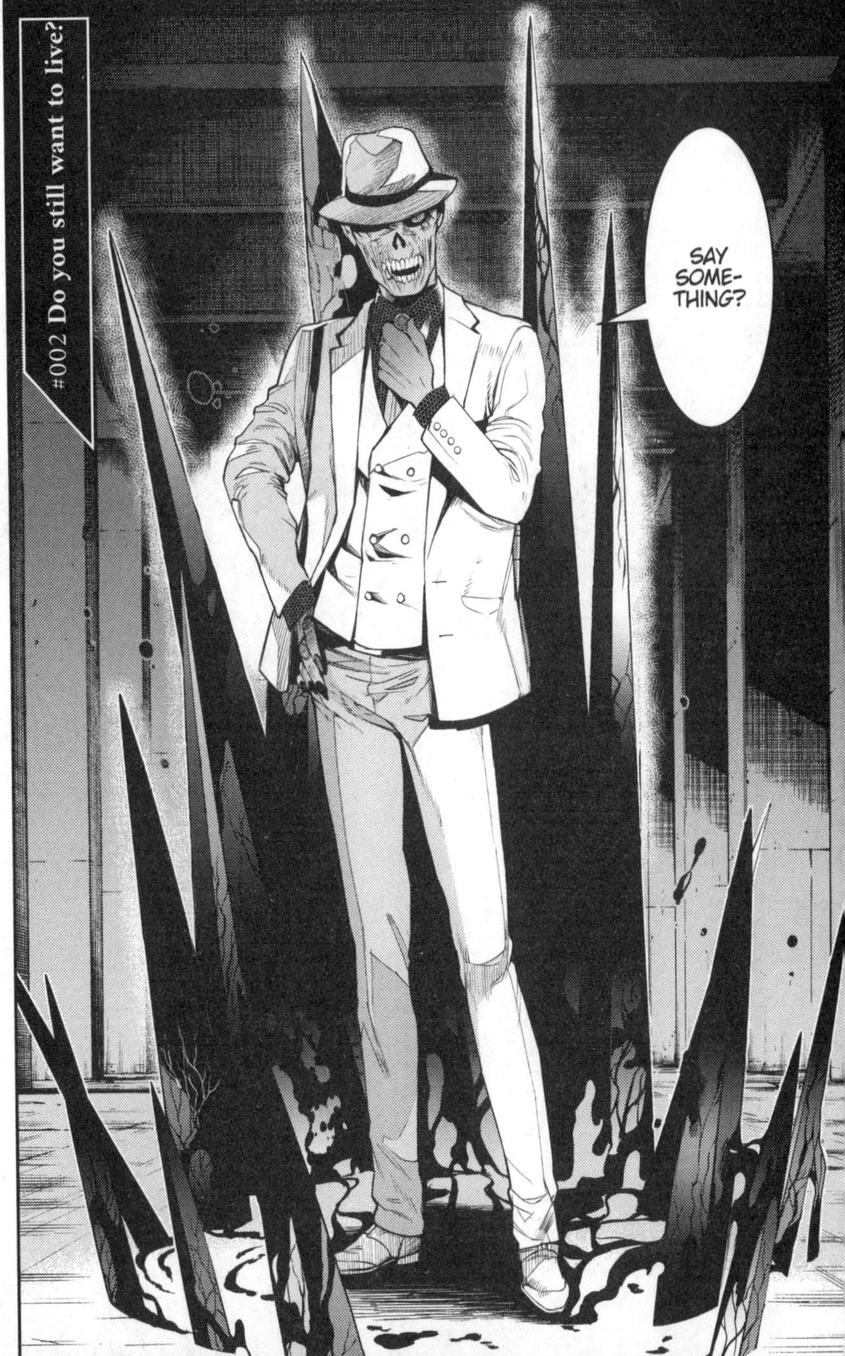
#002 Do you still want to live?
SAY SOME-THING?

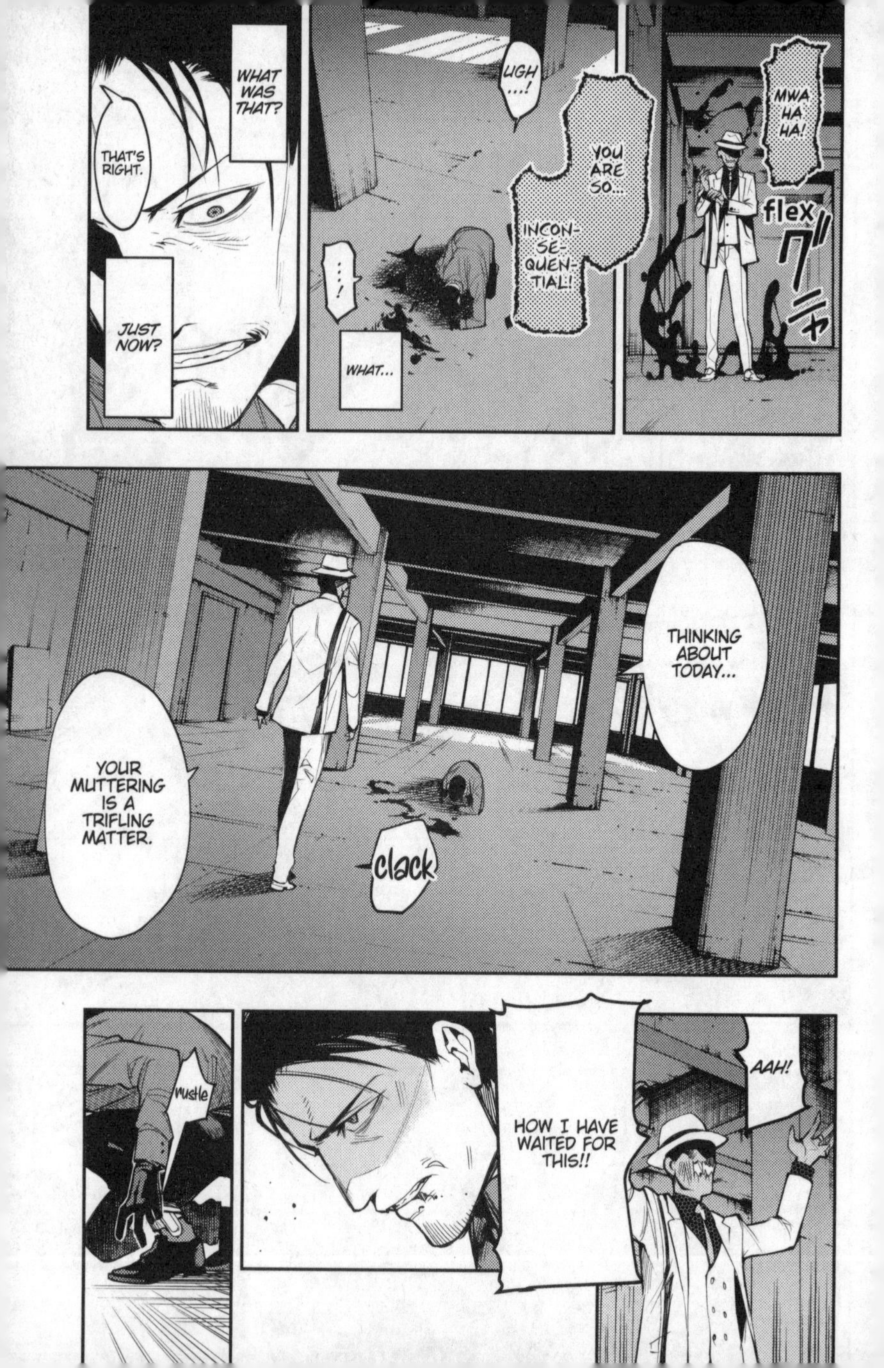
MWA HA HA!
flex
YOU ARE SO... INCON-SE-QUEN-TIAL!
UGH ...!
...!
WHAT...
WHAT WAS THAT?
THAT'S RIGHT.
JUST NOW?
THINKING ABOUT TODAY...
YOUR MUTTERING IS A TRIFLING MATTER.
clack
AAH!
HOW I HAVE WAITED FOR THIS!!
rustle

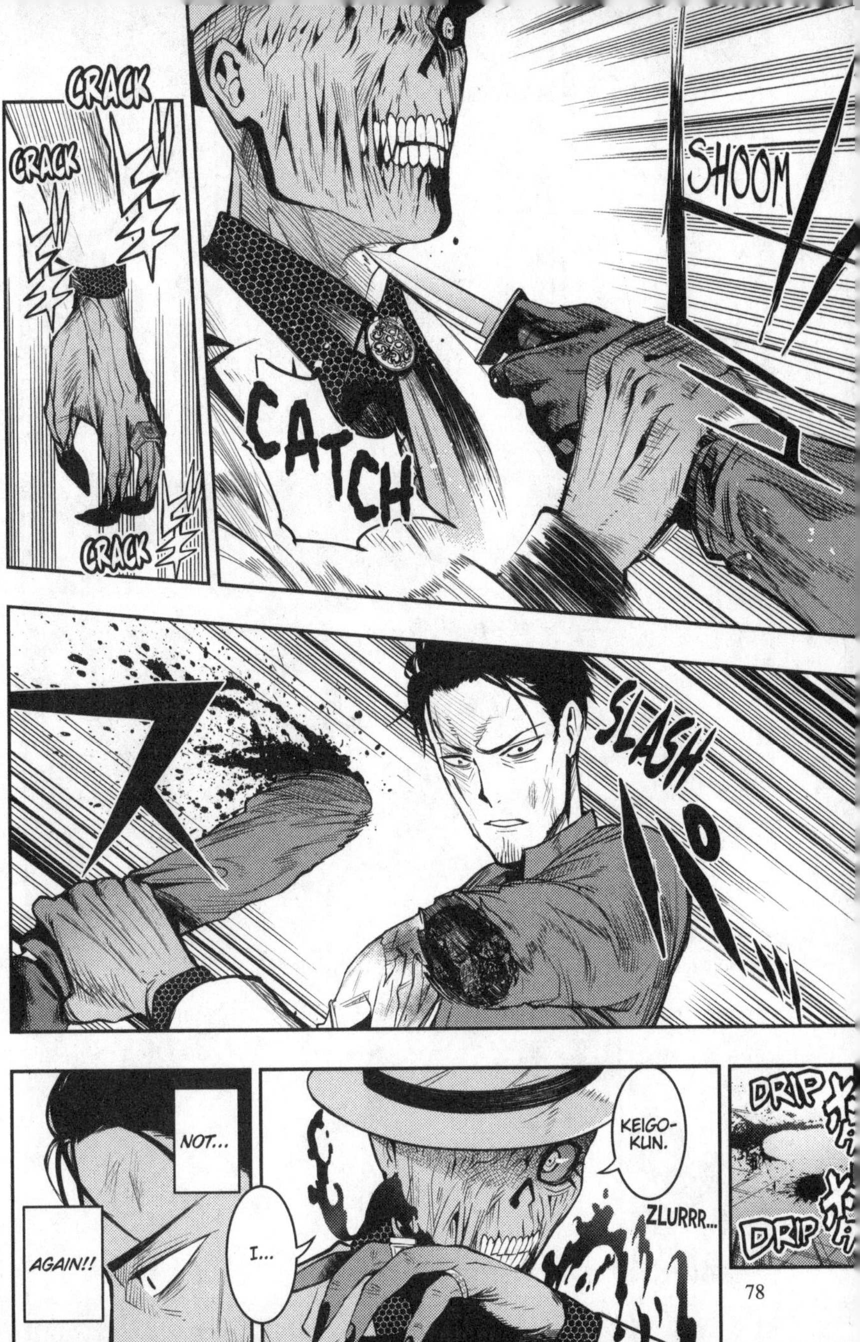
SHOOM
CATCH
CRACK
CRACK
CRACK
SLASH
DRIP
DRIP
KEIGO-KUN.
ZLURRR...
I...
NOT...
AGAIN!!

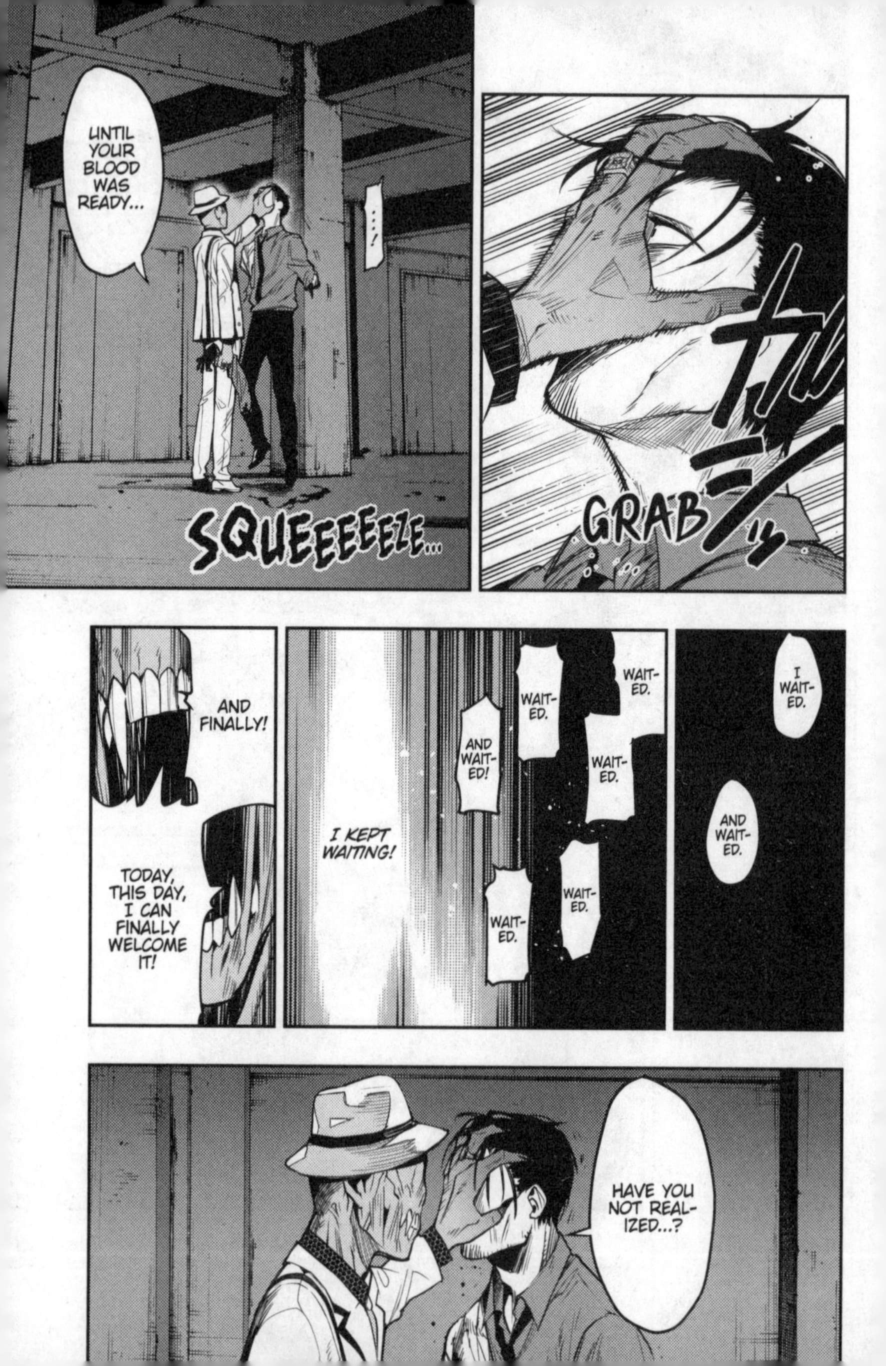
GRAB
UNTIL YOUR BLOOD WAS READY...
...!
SQUEEEEEEZE...
I WAIT-ED.
AND WAIT-ED.
WAIT-ED.
WAIT-ED.
AND WAIT-ED!
WAIT-ED.
WAIT-ED.
WAIT-ED.
I KEPT WAITING!
AND FINALLY!
TODAY, THIS DAY, I CAN FINALLY WELCOME IT!
HAVE YOU NOT REAL-IZED...?

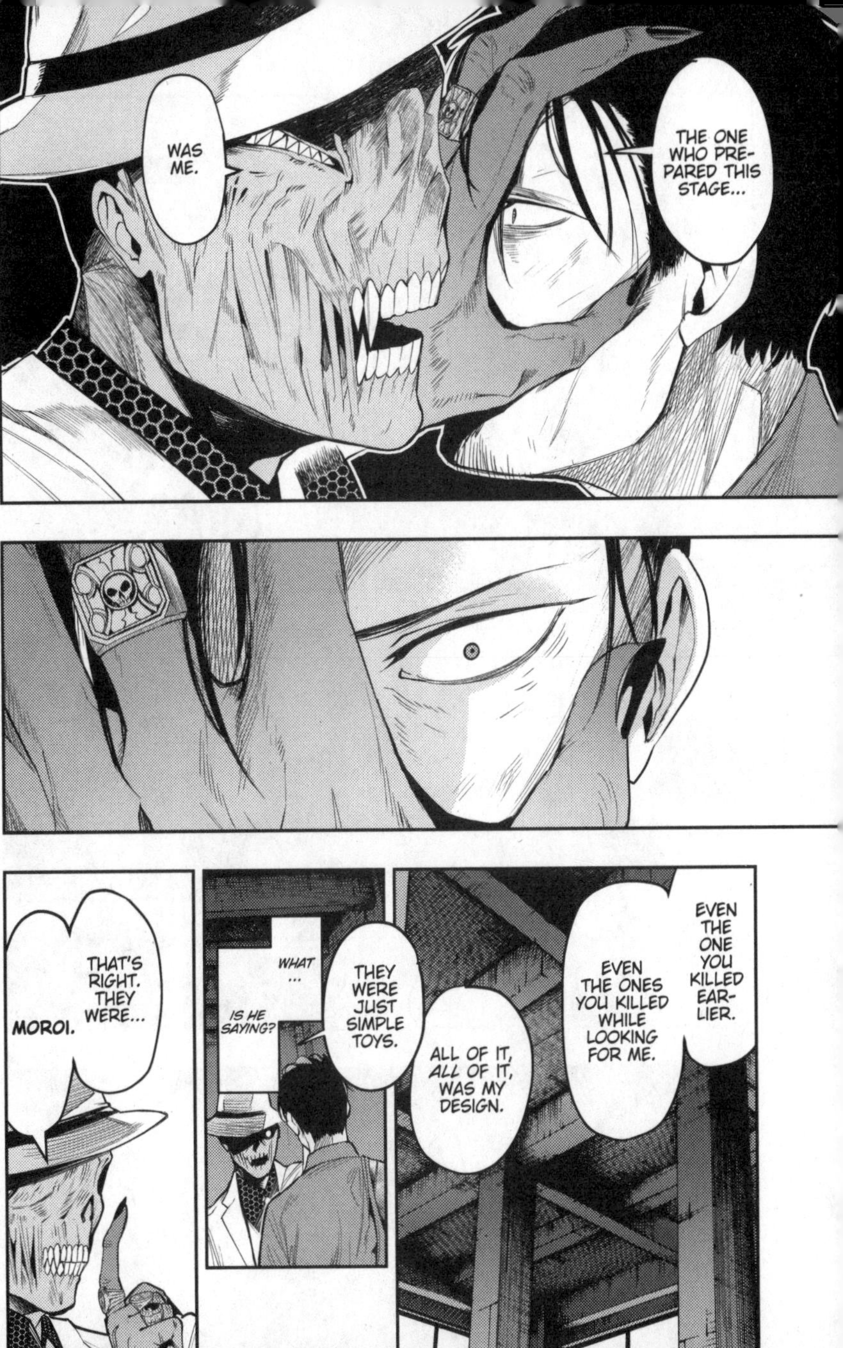
THE ONE WHO PREPARED THIS STAGE...
WAS ME.
EVEN THE ONE YOU KILLED EARLIER.
EVEN THE ONES YOU KILLED WHILE LOOKING FOR ME.
ALL OF IT, *ALL OF IT*, WAS MY DESIGN.
THEY WERE JUST SIMPLE TOYS.
WHAT ... IS HE SAYING?
THAT'S RIGHT. THEY WERE...
MOROI.

*Moroi: Romanian for a kind of vampire or phantom.

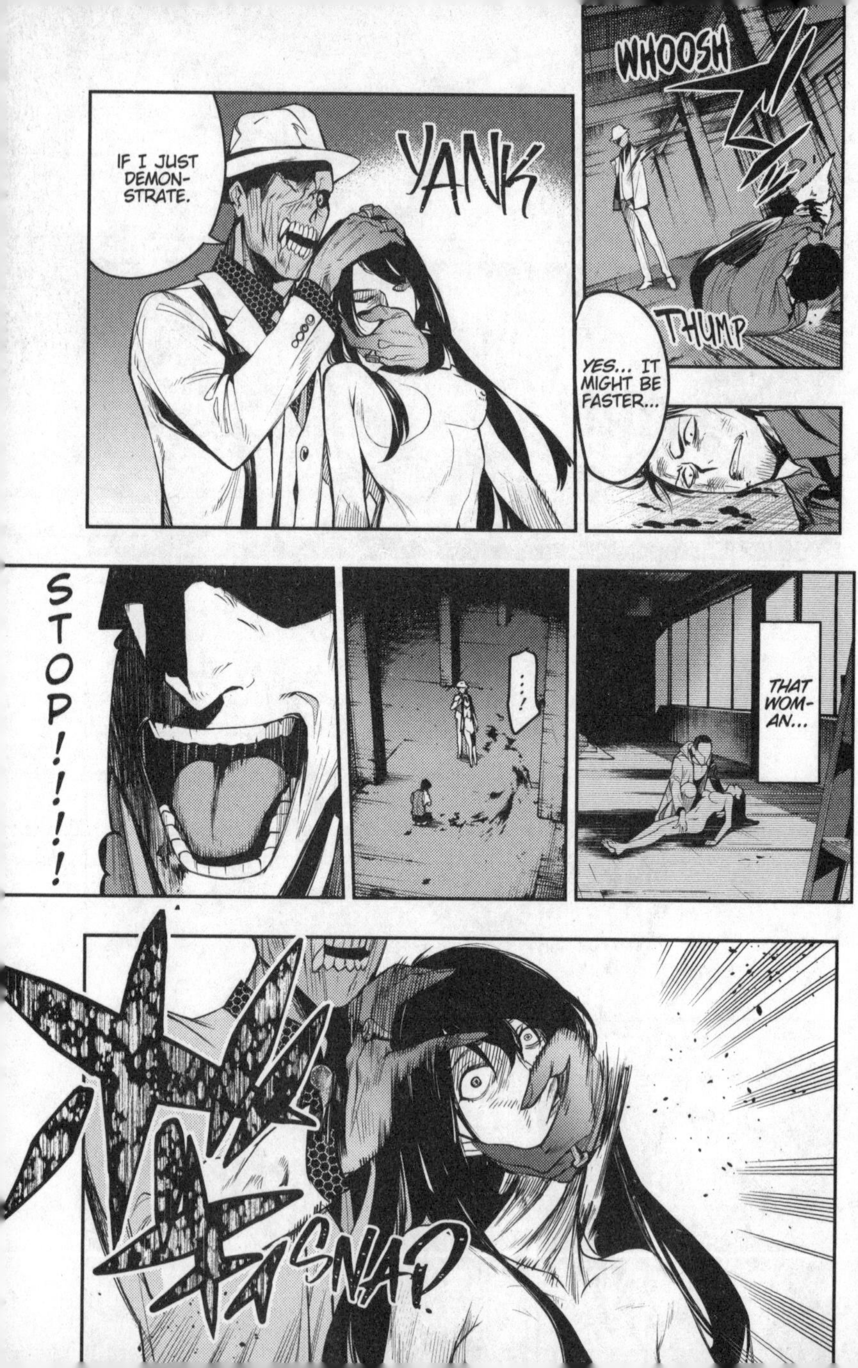
WHOOSH
THUMP
YES... IT MIGHT BE FASTER...
IF I JUST DEMON-STRATE.
YANK
THAT WOM-AN...
...!
STOP!!!!!
SNAP

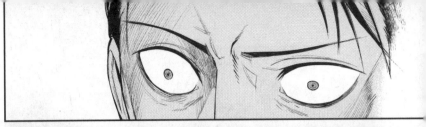

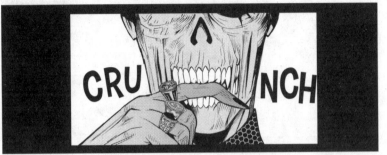

CRU NCH

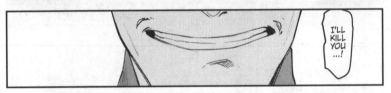

I'LL
KILL
YOU
...!

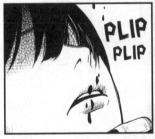

PLIP
PLIP

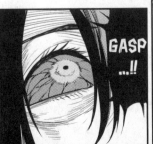

GASP
...!!

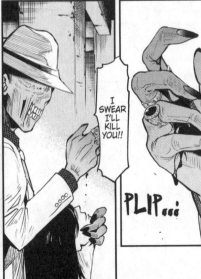

I
SWEAR
I'LL
KILL
YOU!!

PLIP...

82

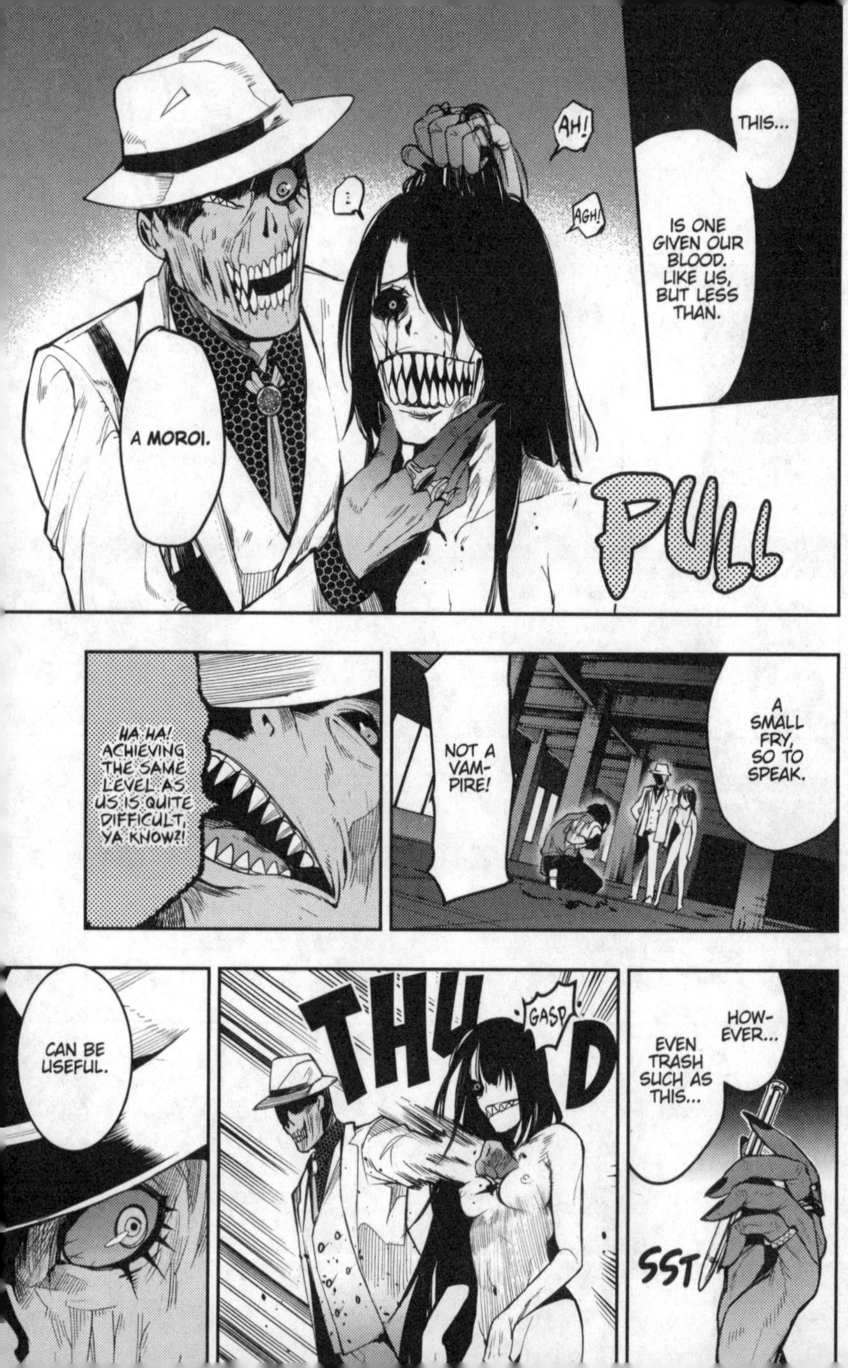
THIS...
IS ONE GIVEN OUR BLOOD. LIKE US, BUT LESS THAN.
AH!
AGH!
!
PULL
A MOROI.
A SMALL FRY, SO TO SPEAK.
NOT A VAMPIRE!
HA HA! ACHIEVING THE SAME LEVEL AS US IS QUITE DIFFICULT, YA KNOW?!
HOW-EVER...
EVEN TRASH SUCH AS THIS...
SST
GASP
THUD
CAN BE USEFUL.

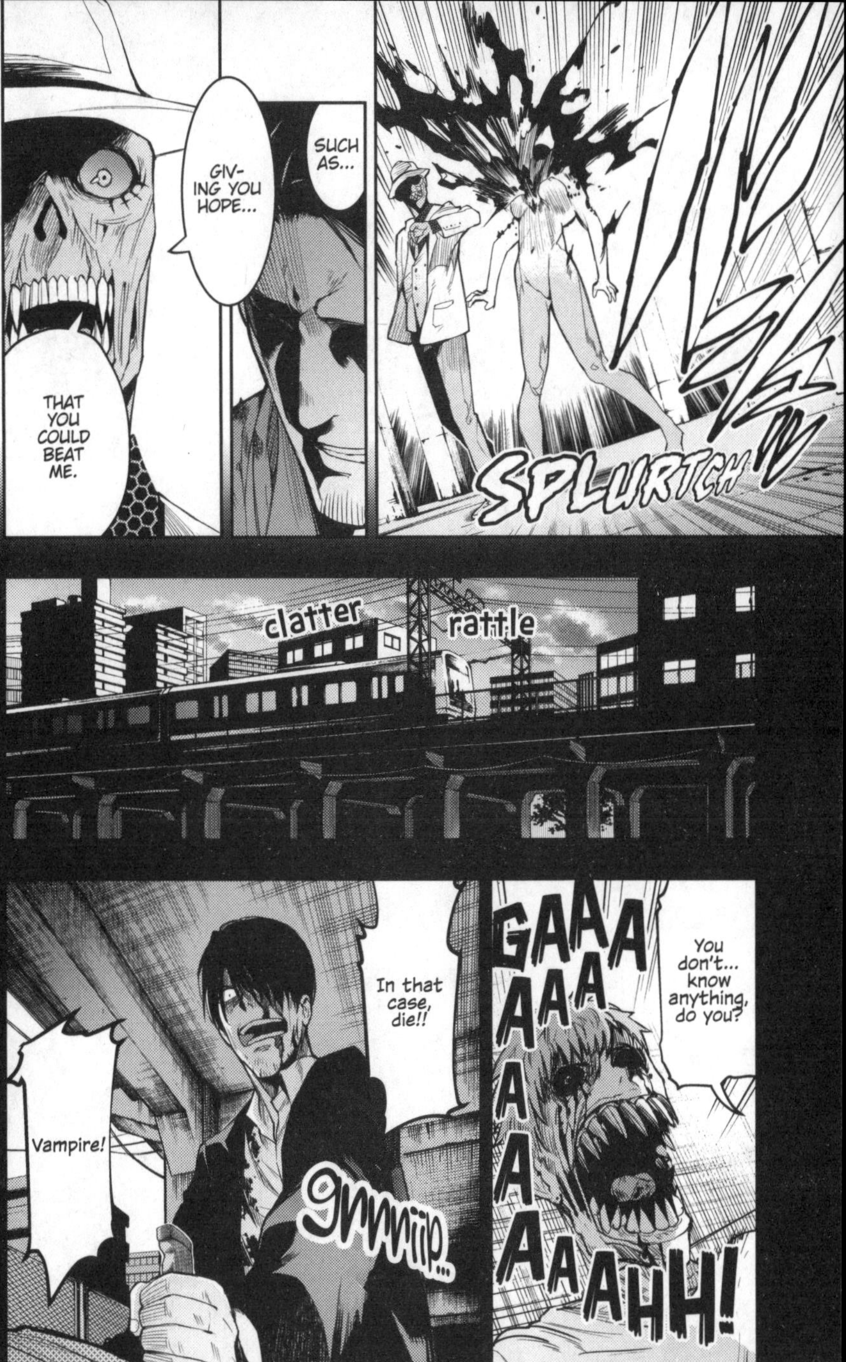
SPLURTCH
SUCH AS...
GIV-ING YOU HOPE...
THAT YOU COULD BEAT ME.
rattle
clatter
You don't... know anything, do you?
GAAAAAAAAAAAAAAAHH!
In that case, die!!
grrrriip...
Vampire!

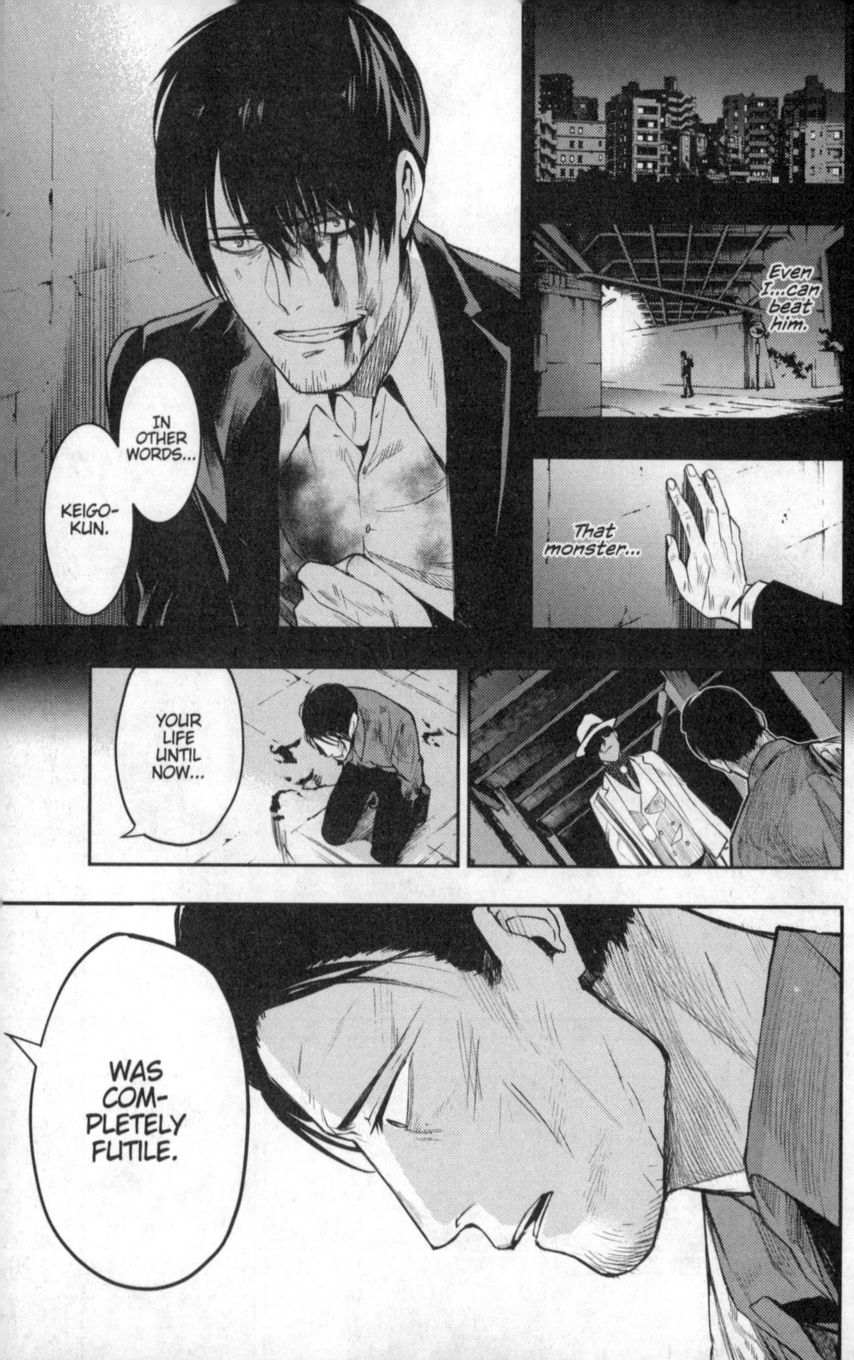
Even I...can beat him.
That monster...
IN OTHER WORDS...
KEIGO-KUN.
YOUR LIFE UNTIL NOW...
WAS COM-PLETELY FUTILE.

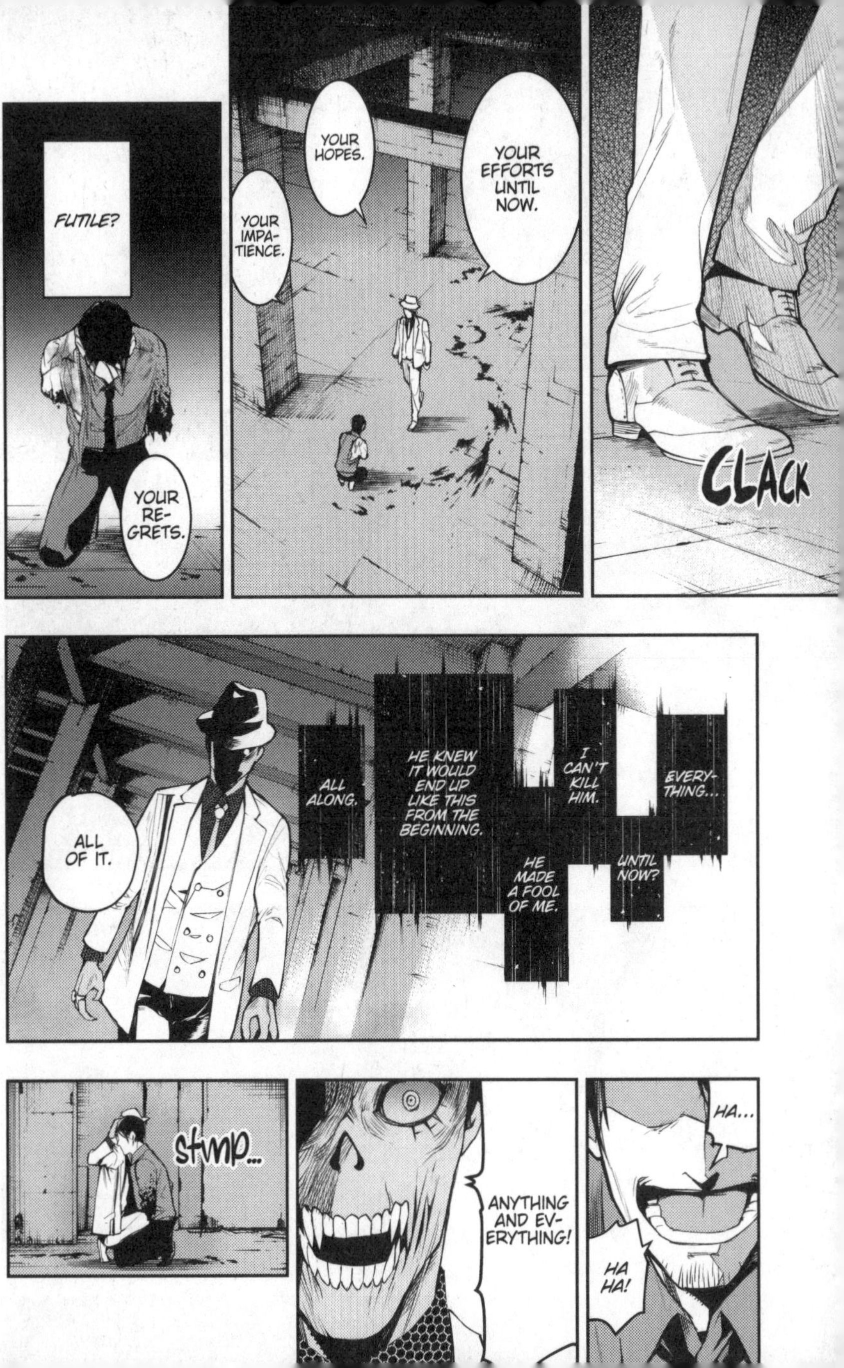
CLACK
YOUR EFFORTS UNTIL NOW.
YOUR HOPES.
YOUR IMPATIENCE.
FUTILE?
YOUR REGRETS.
EVERYTHING...
I CAN'T KILL HIM.
UNTIL NOW?
HE KNEW IT WOULD END UP LIKE THIS FROM THE BEGINNING.
HE MADE A FOOL OF ME.
ALL ALONG.
ALL OF IT.
HA...
HA HA!
ANYTHING AND EVERYTHING!
stmp...

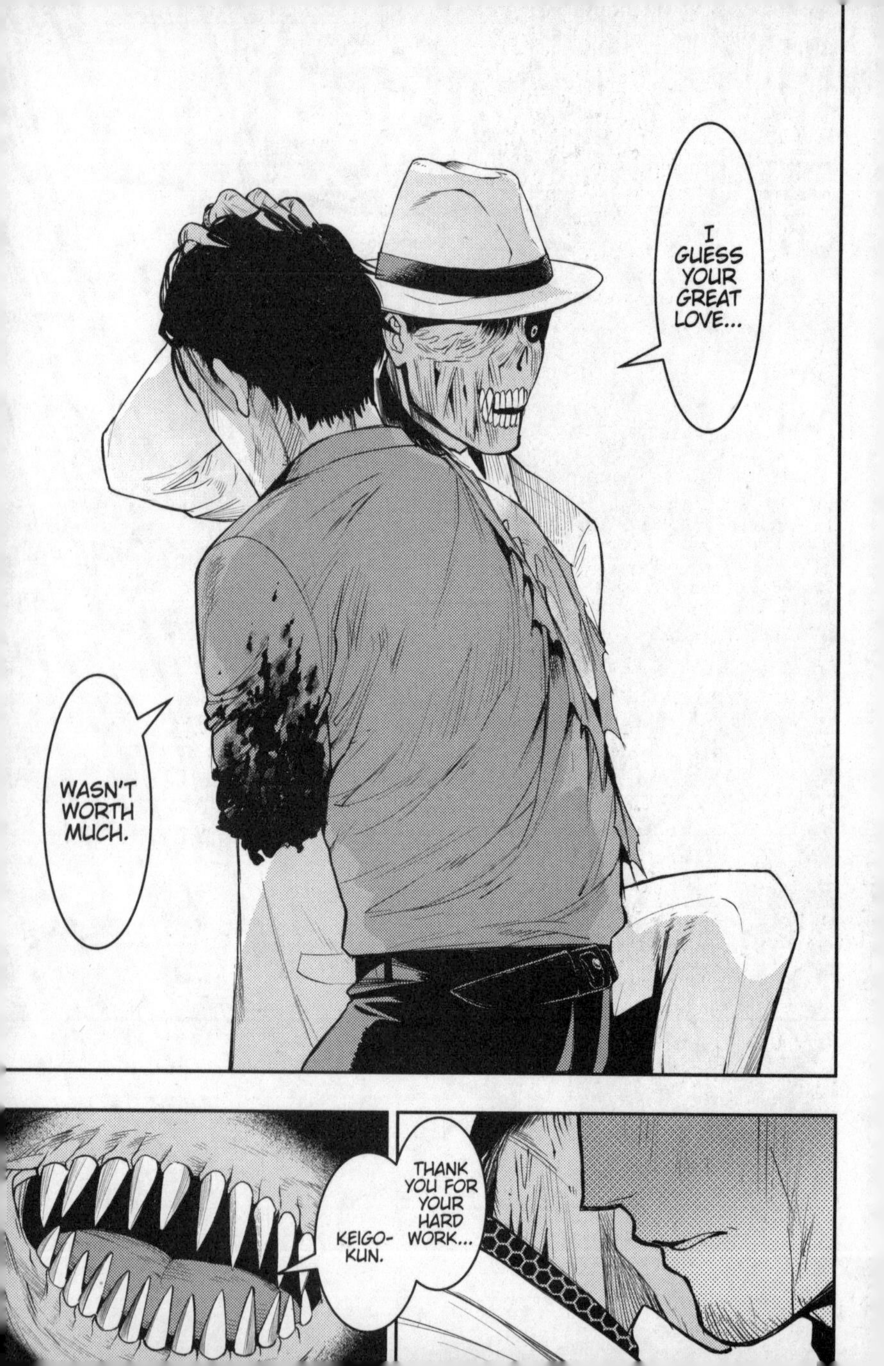
I GUESS YOUR GREAT LOVE...
WASN'T WORTH MUCH.
THANK YOU FOR YOUR HARD WORK...
KEIGO-KUN.

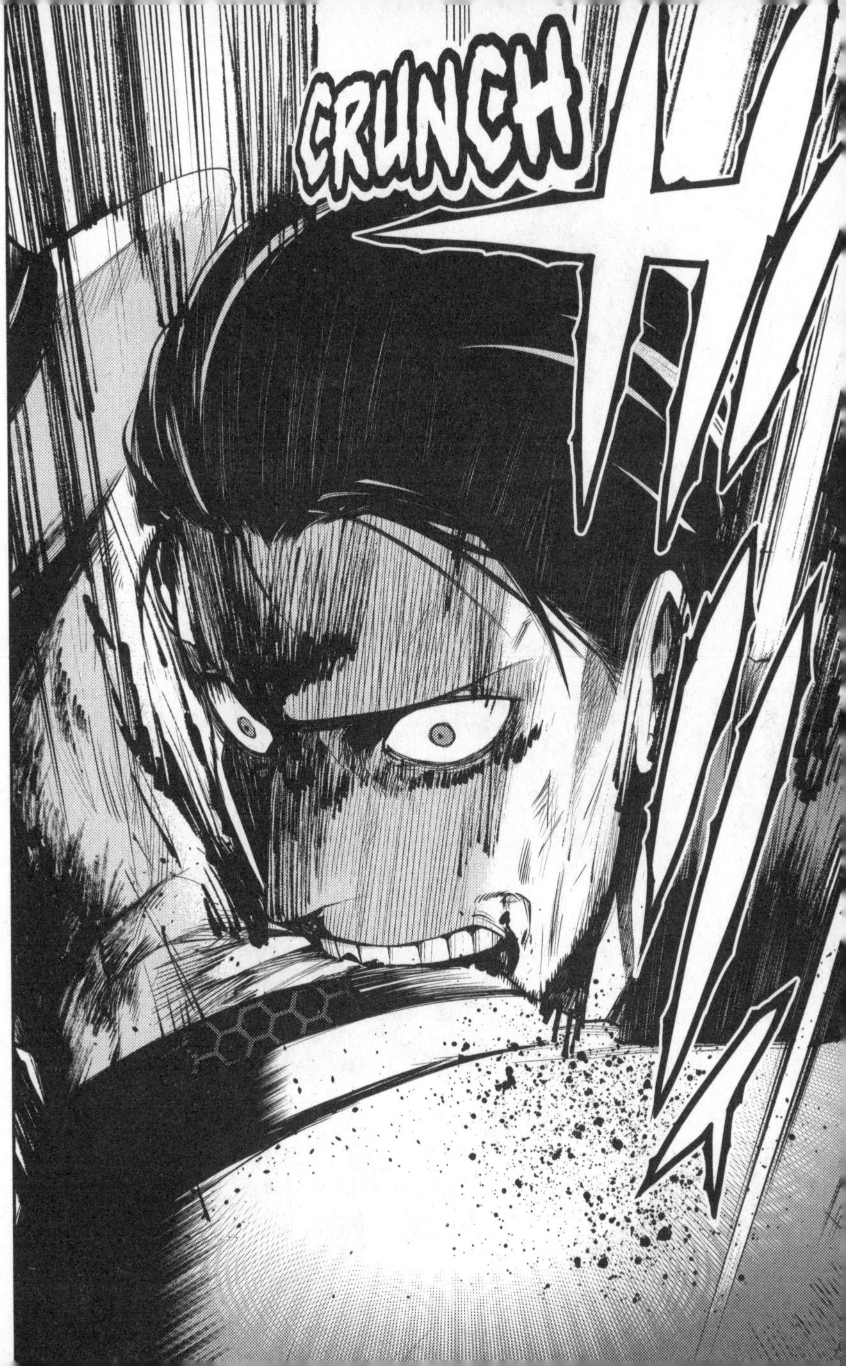
CRUNCH

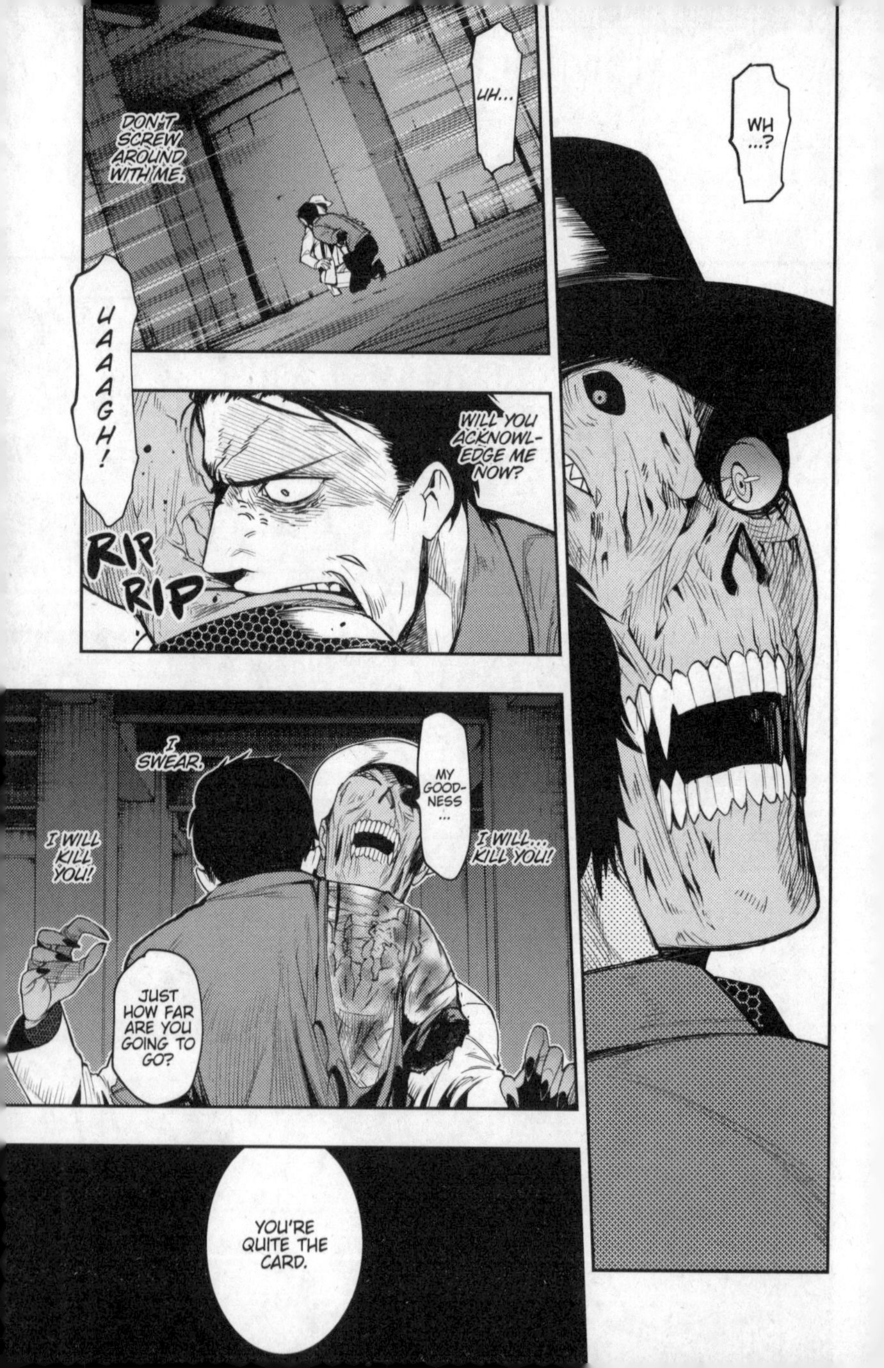
WH ...?
UH...
DON'T SCREW AROUND WITH ME.
UAAAAGH!
WILL YOU ACKNOWL-EDGE ME NOW?
RIP RIP
MY GOOD-NESS ...
I WILL... KILL YOU!
I SWEAR.
I WILL KILL YOU!
JUST HOW FAR ARE YOU GOING TO GO?
YOU'RE QUITE THE CARD.

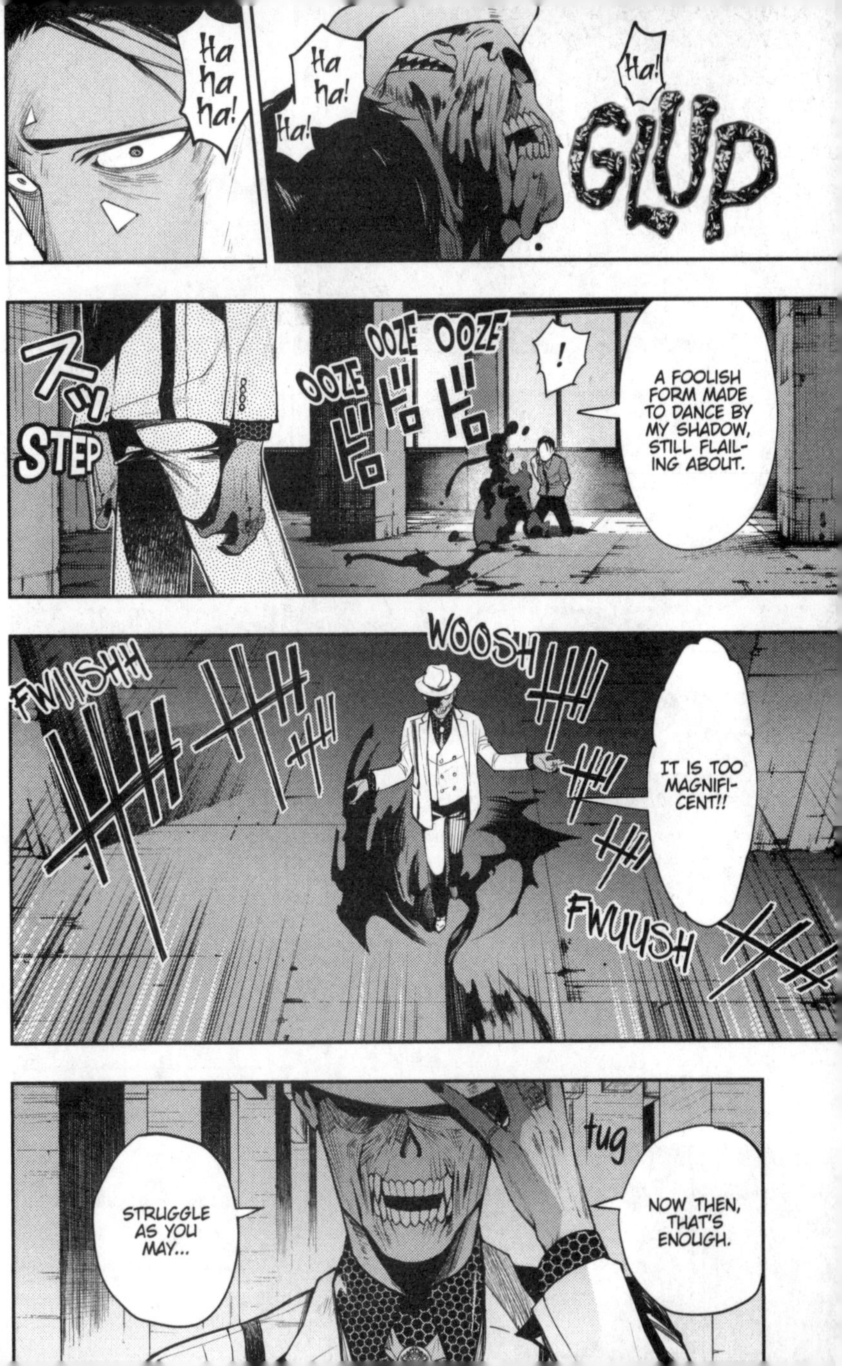

Ha!
GLUP
Ha ha!
Ha!
Ha ha ha!
A FOOLISH FORM MADE TO DANCE BY MY SHADOW, STILL FLAILING ABOUT.
!
OOZE OOZE
ドドド
OOZE
スッ
STEP
WOOSH
IT IS TOO MAGNIFICENT!!
FWUUSH
FWUSHH
NOW THEN, THAT'S ENOUGH.
tug
STRUGGLE AS YOU MAY...

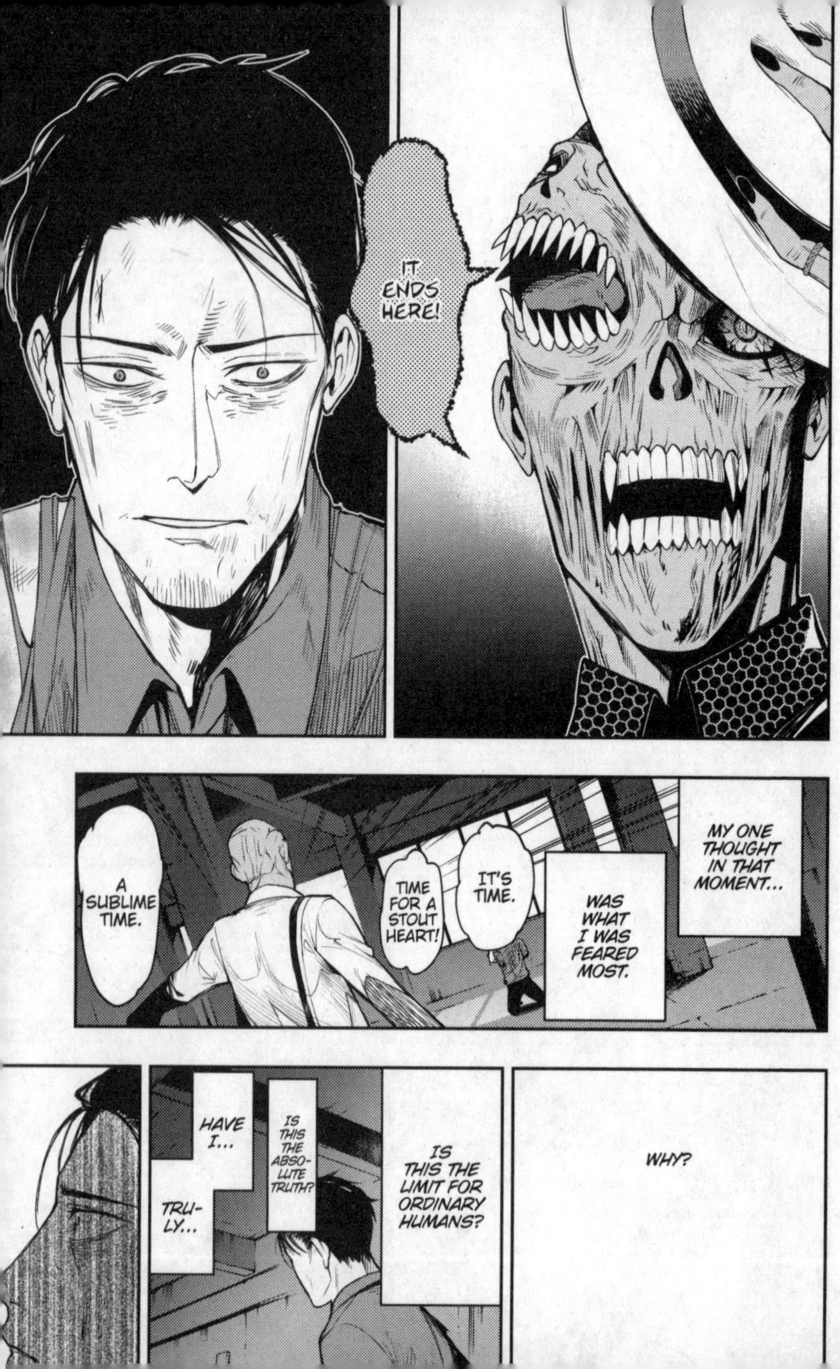
IT ENDS HERE!
MY ONE THOUGHT IN THAT MOMENT...
WAS WHAT I WAS FEARED MOST.
IT'S TIME.
TIME FOR A STOUT HEART!
A SUBLIME TIME.
WHY?
IS THIS THE LIMIT FOR ORDINARY HUMANS?
IS THIS THE ABSO-LUTE TRUTH?
HAVE I...
TRU-LY...

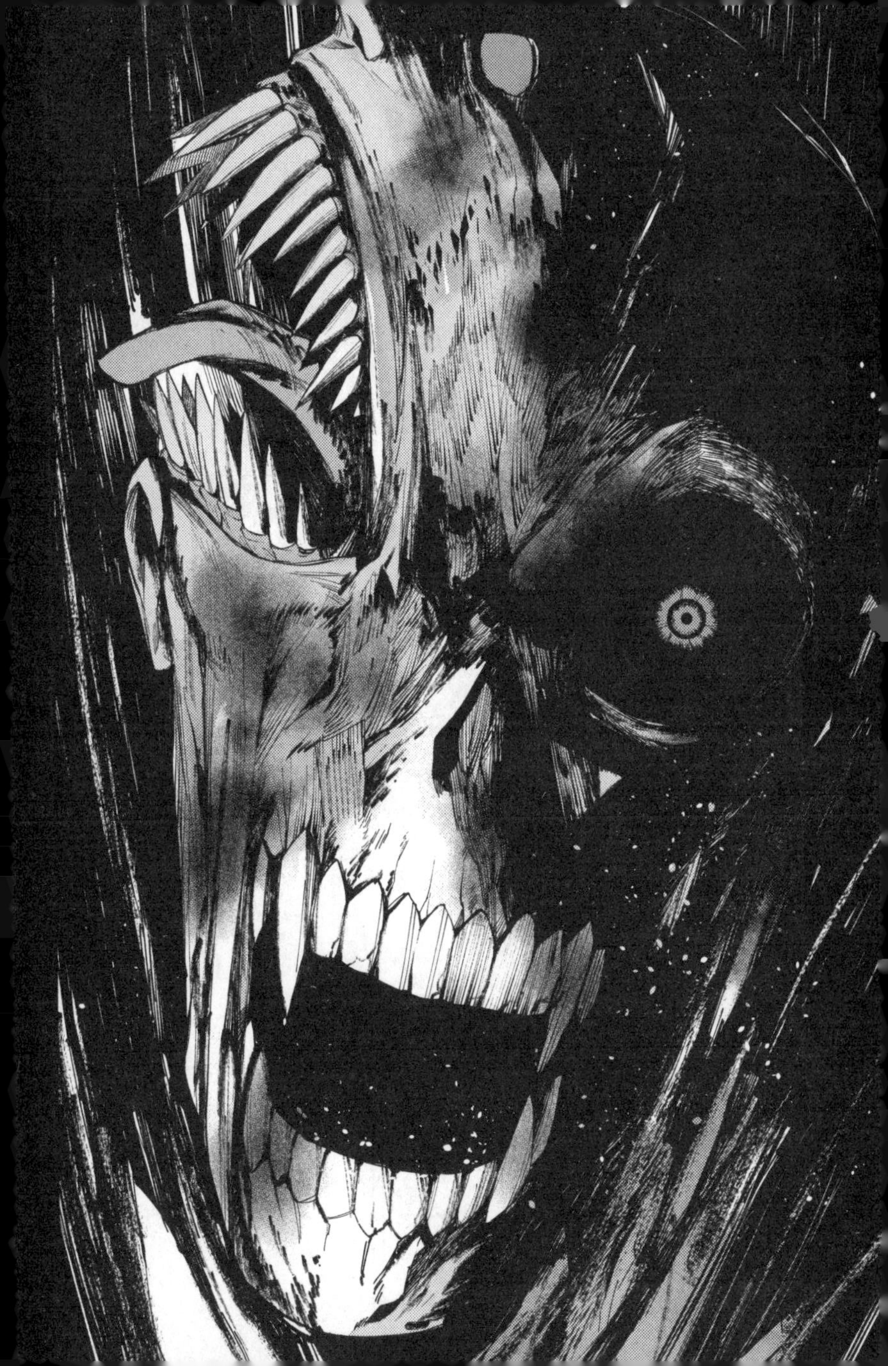

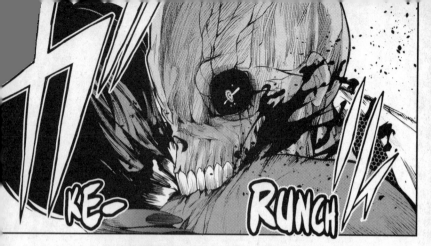

KE-

RUNCH

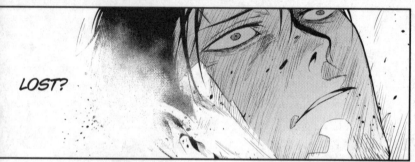

LOST?

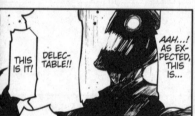

THIS IS IT! DELEC-TABLE!!

AAH...! AS EX-PECTED, THIS IS...

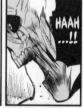

HAAH.....!!

smack

AAH...

YOUKO.

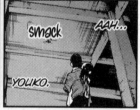

THE IDEAL I WAS LOOKING FOR!

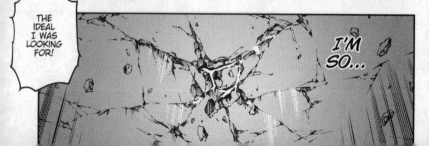

I'M SO...

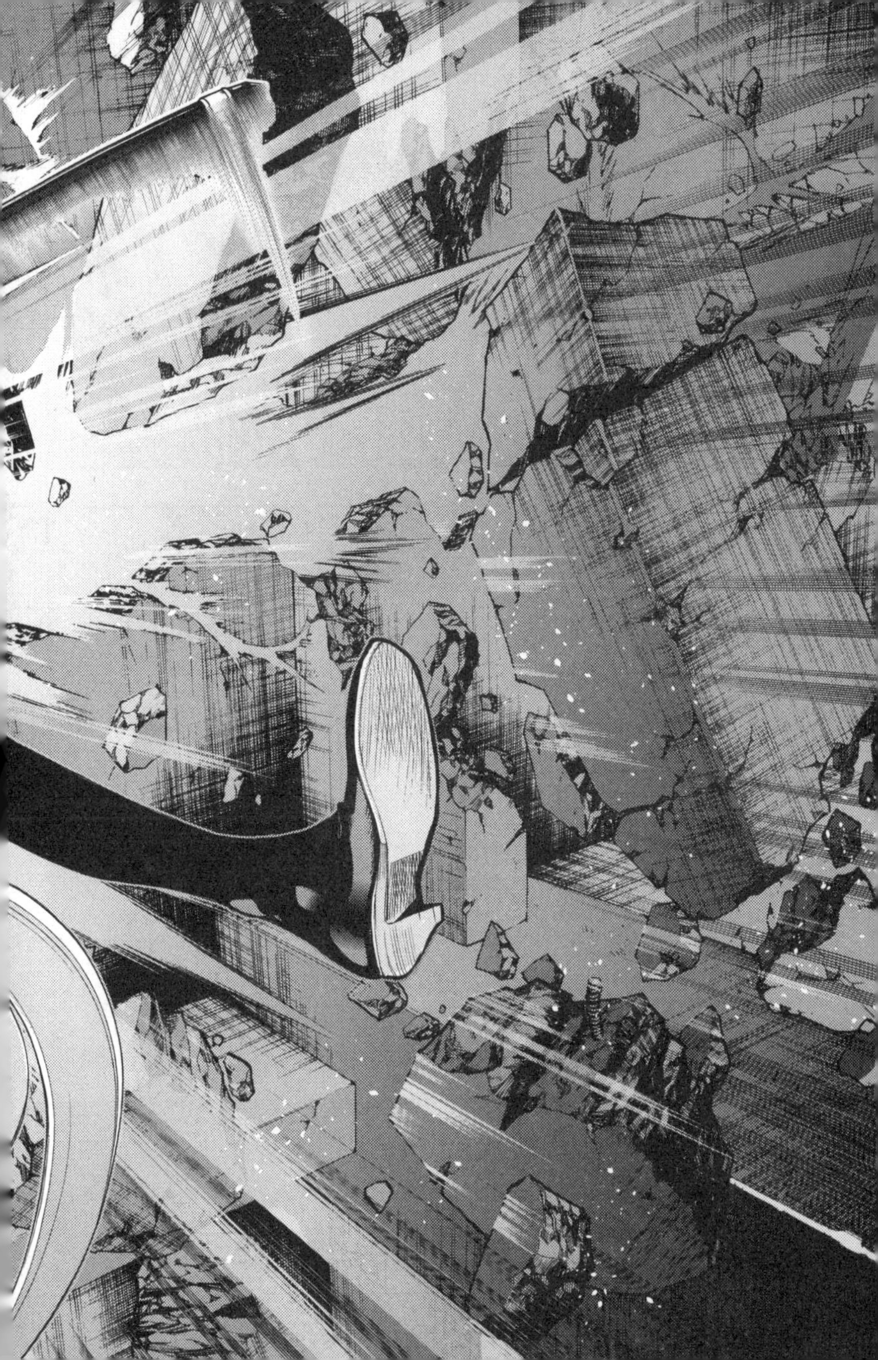

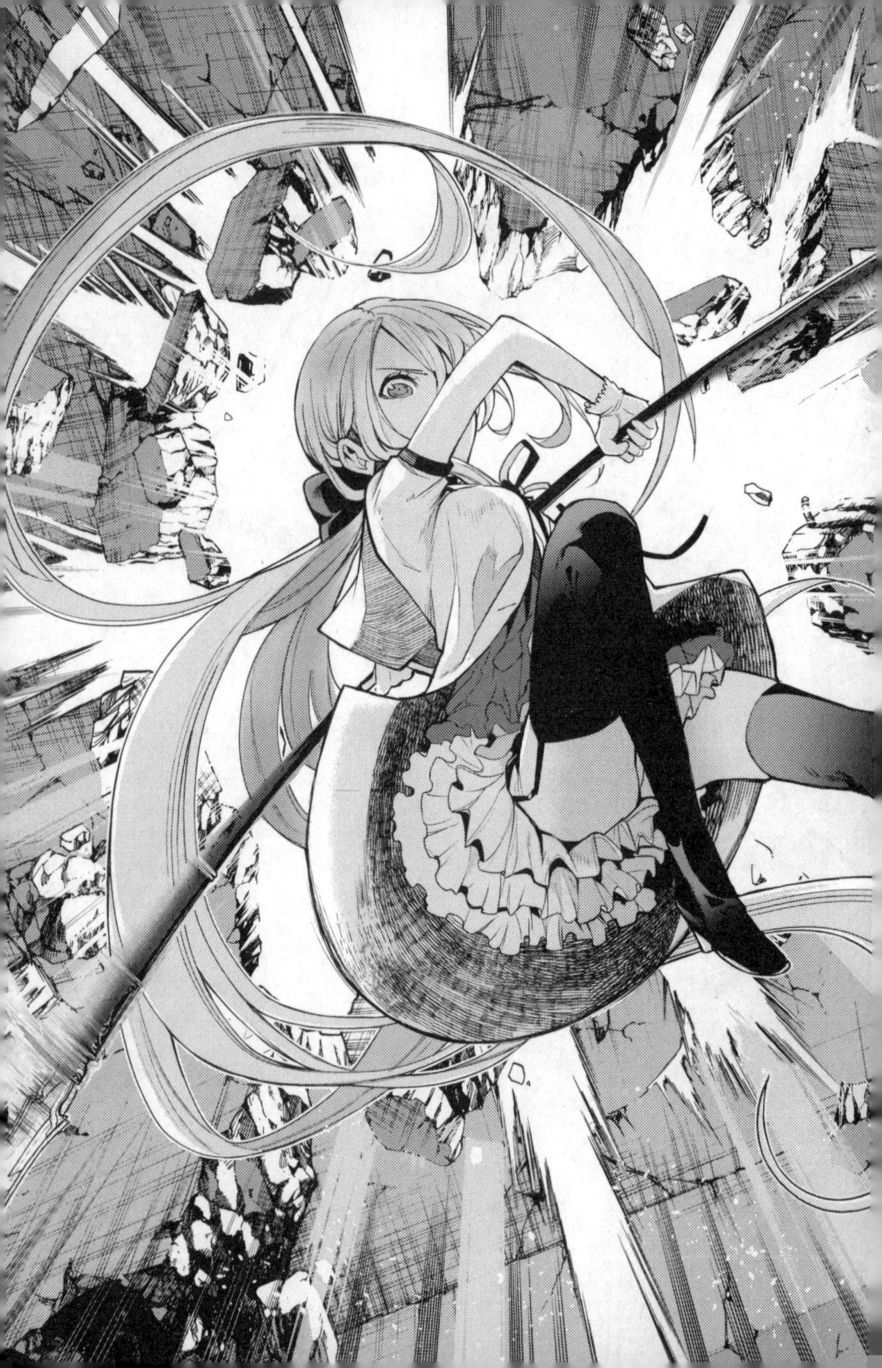

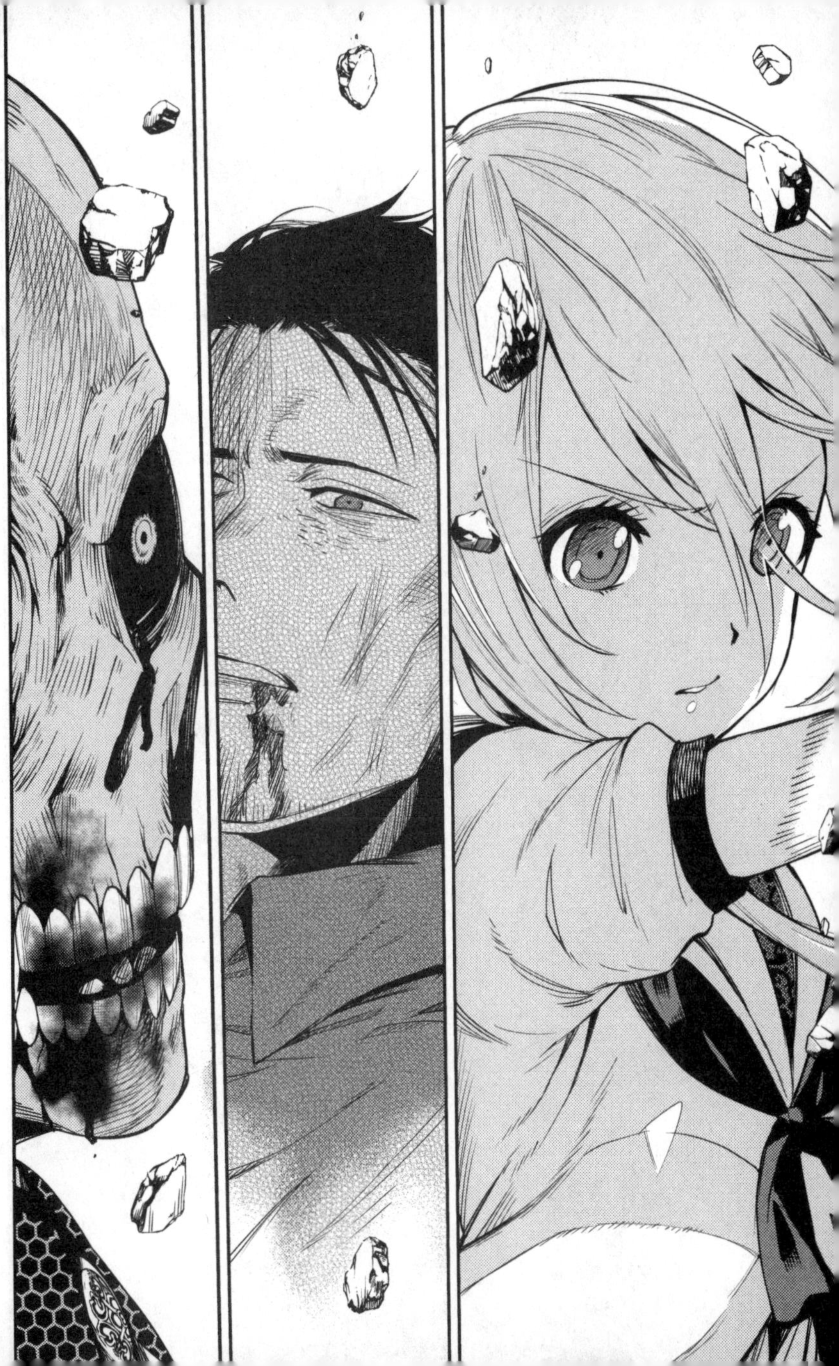

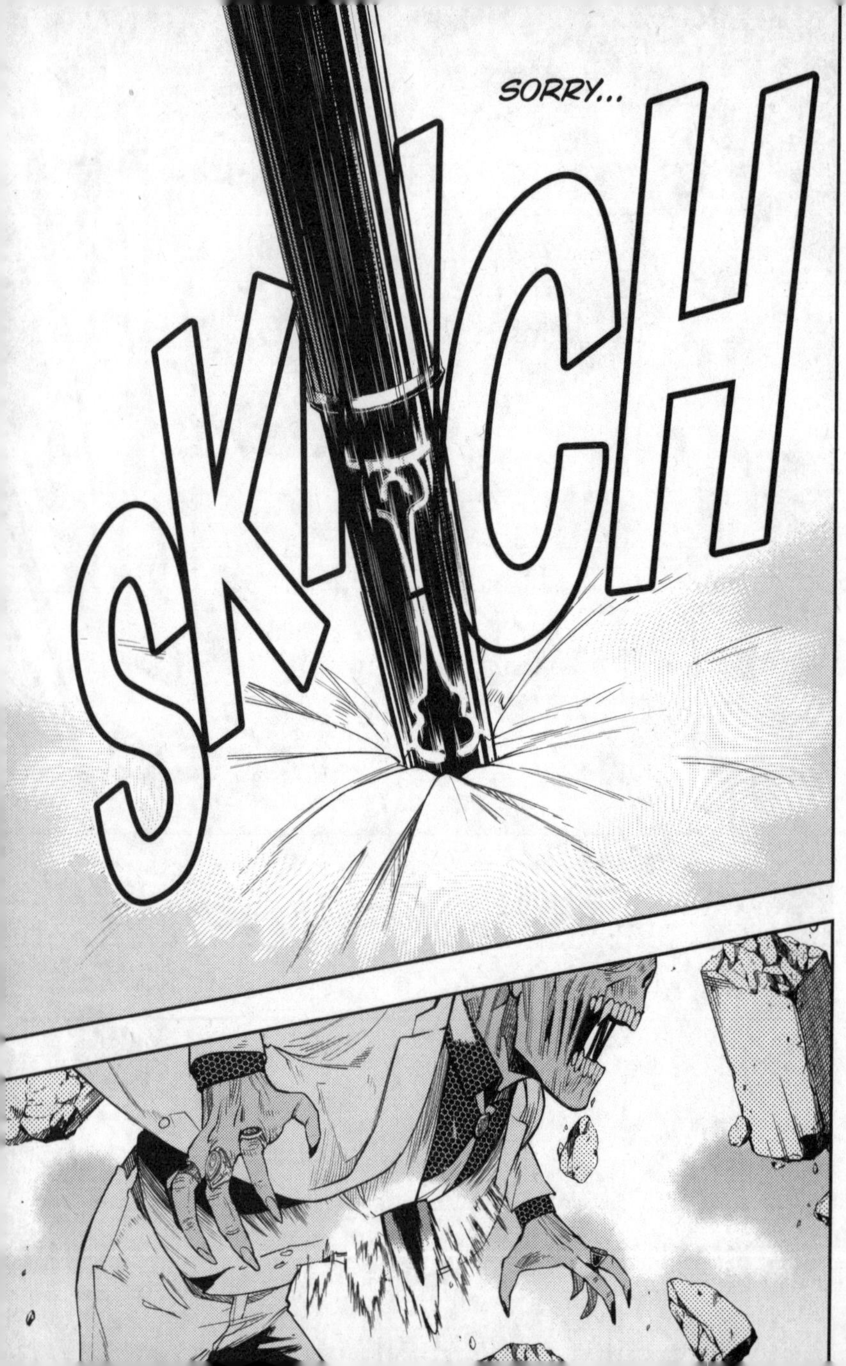
SORRY...
SKNCH

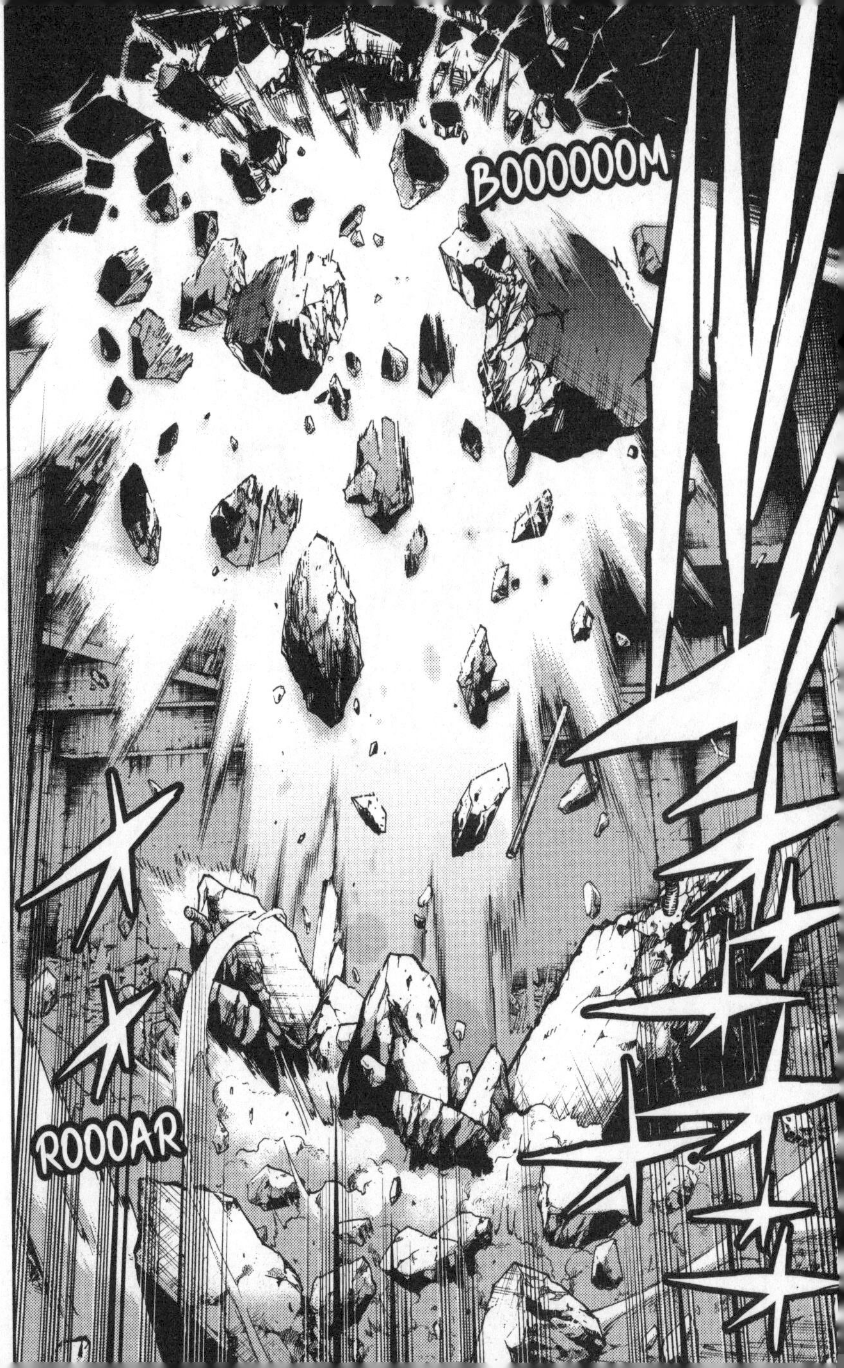
BOOOOOOM
ROOOAR

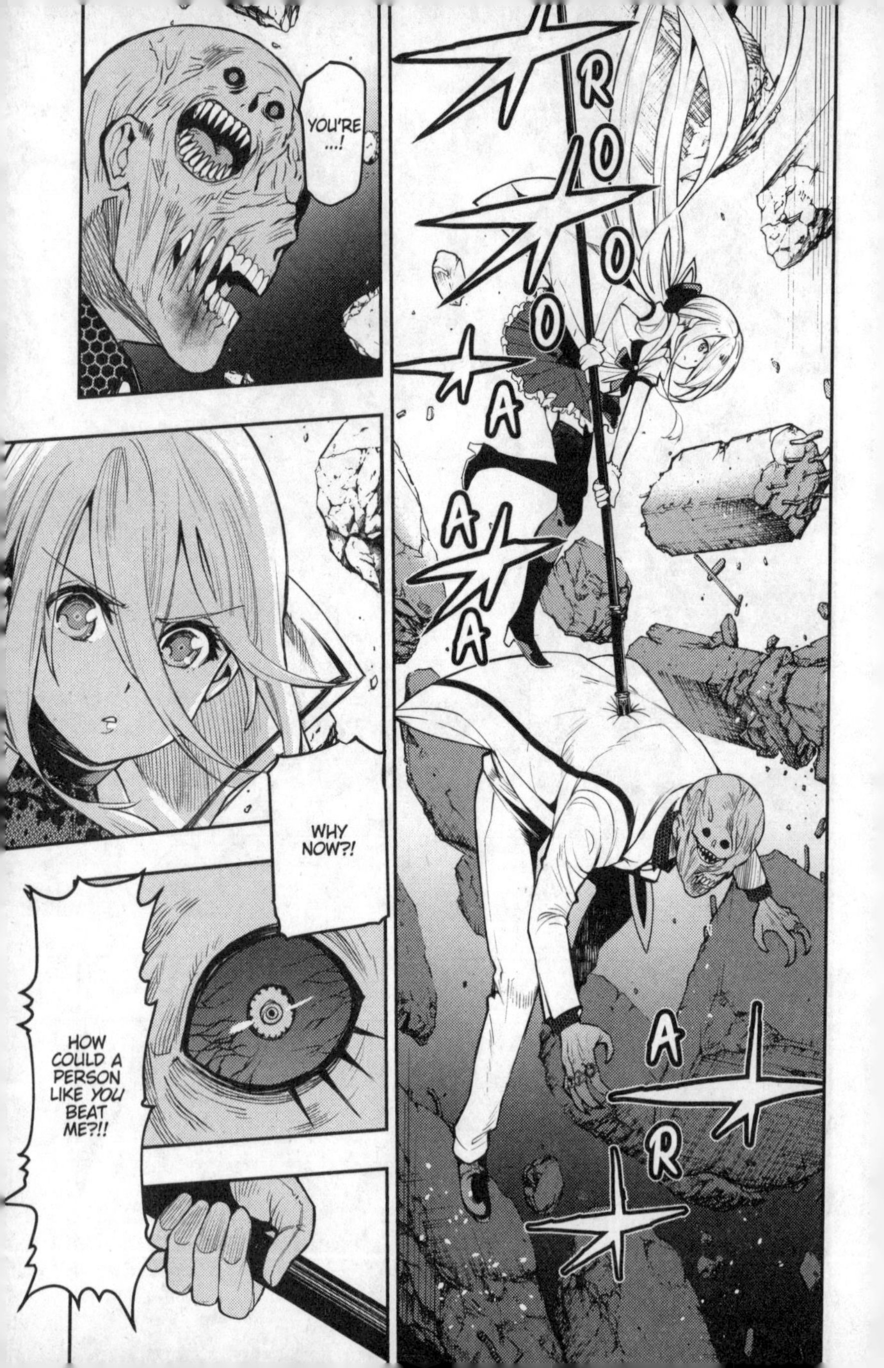
ROOOAAA
AR
YOU'RE ...!
WHY NOW?!
HOW COULD A PERSON LIKE YOU BEAT ME?!!

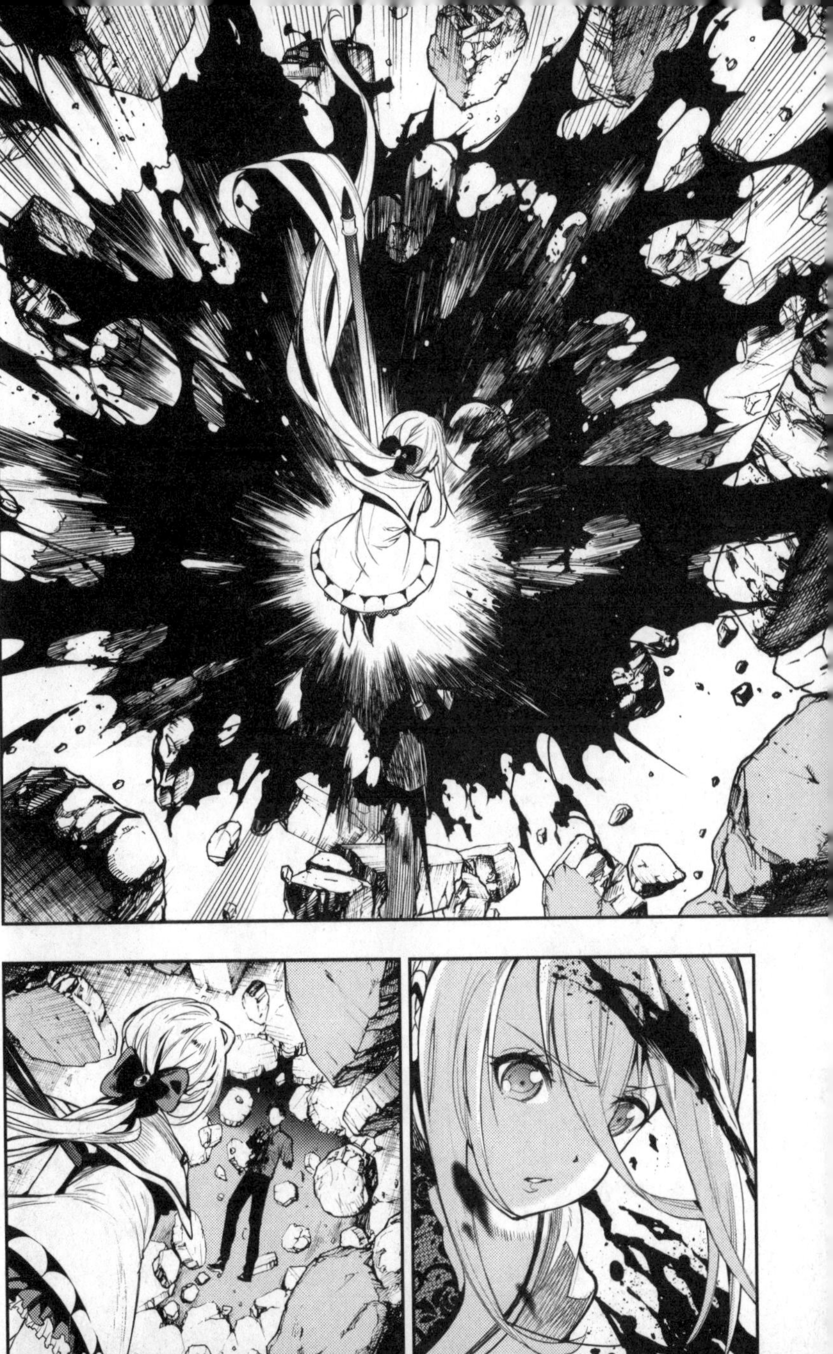

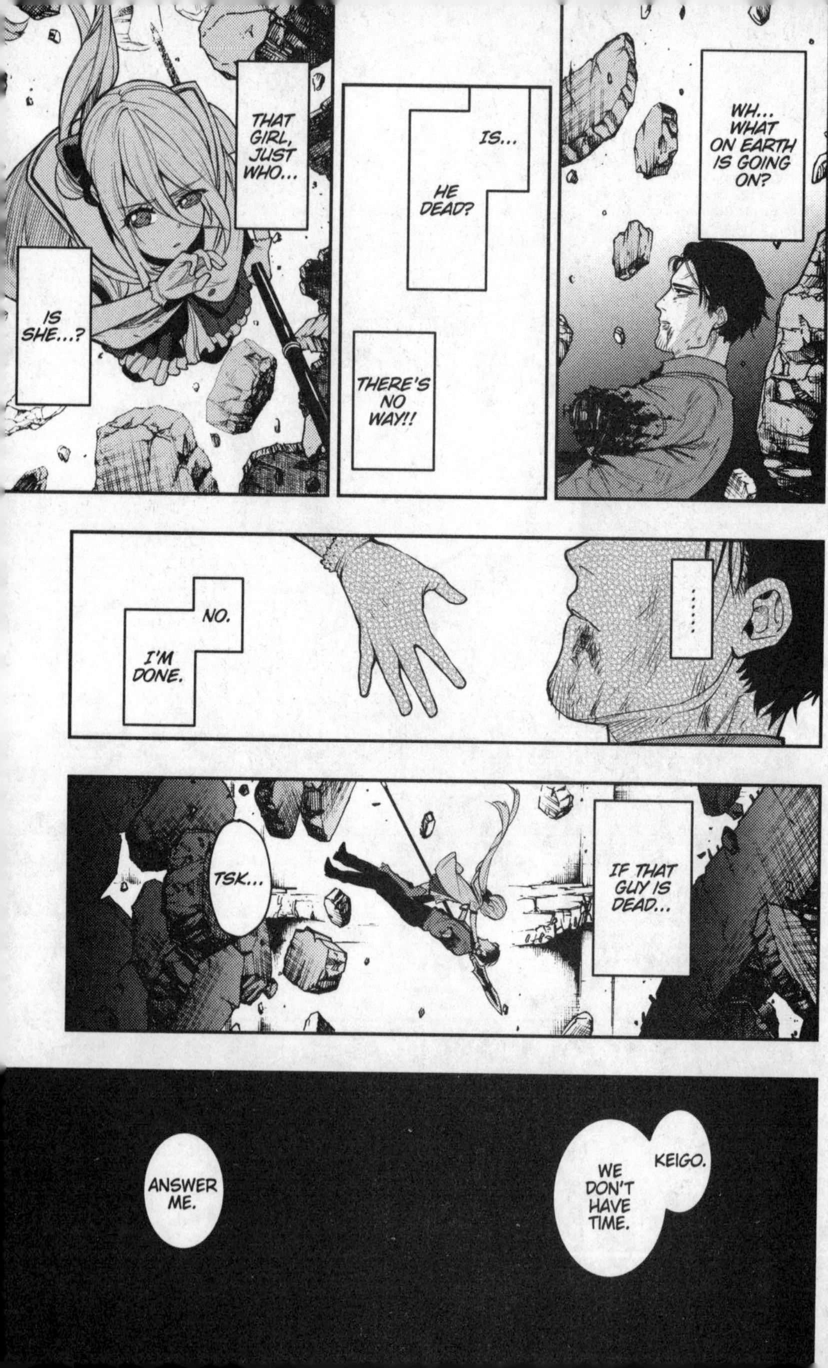
WH... WHAT ON EARTH IS GOING ON?
IS... HE DEAD?
THERE'S NO WAY!!
THAT GIRL, JUST WHO...
IS SHE...?
......
NO. I'M DONE.
IF THAT GUY IS DEAD...
TSK...
KEIGO.
WE DON'T HAVE TIME.
ANSWER ME.

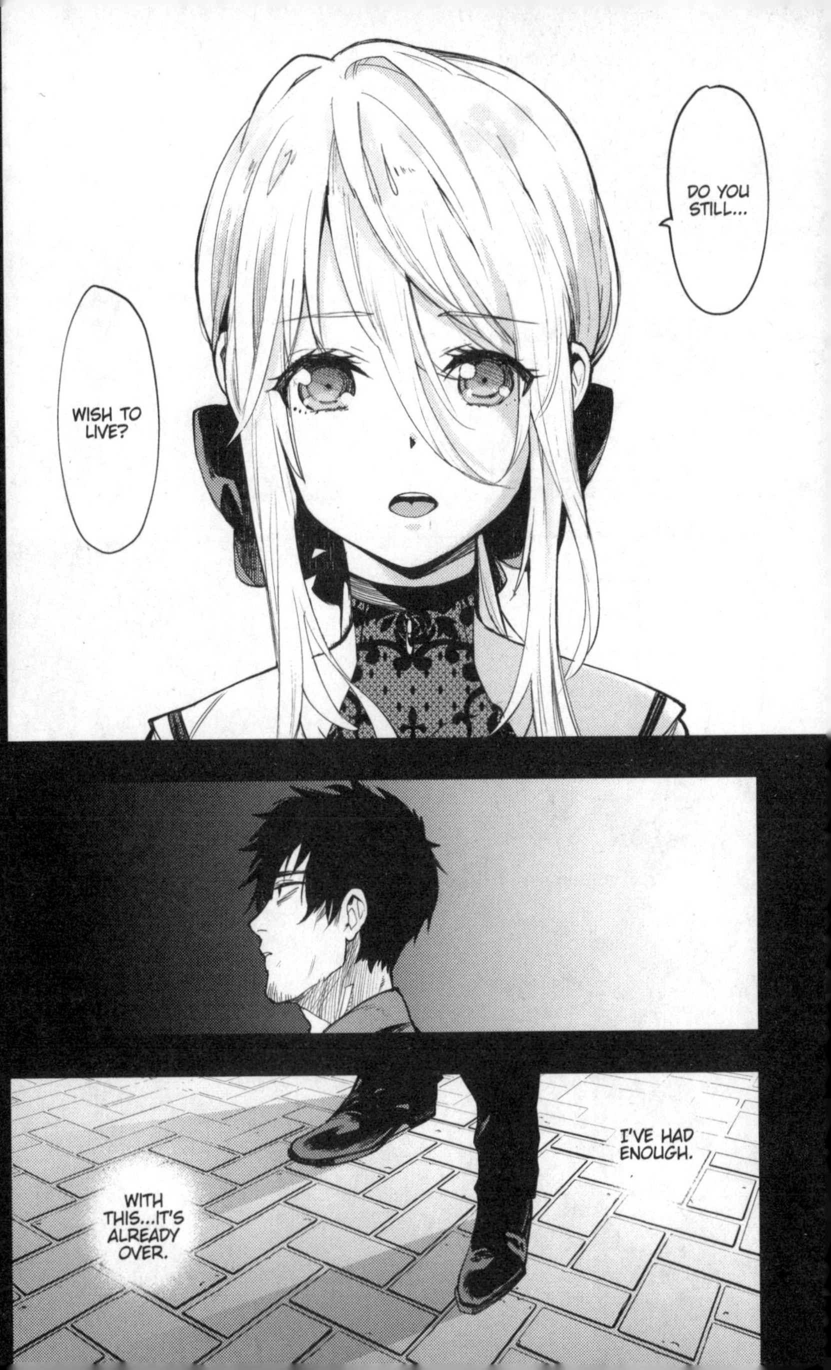
DO YOU STILL...
WISH TO LIVE?
I'VE HAD ENOUGH.
WITH THIS...IT'S ALREADY OVER.

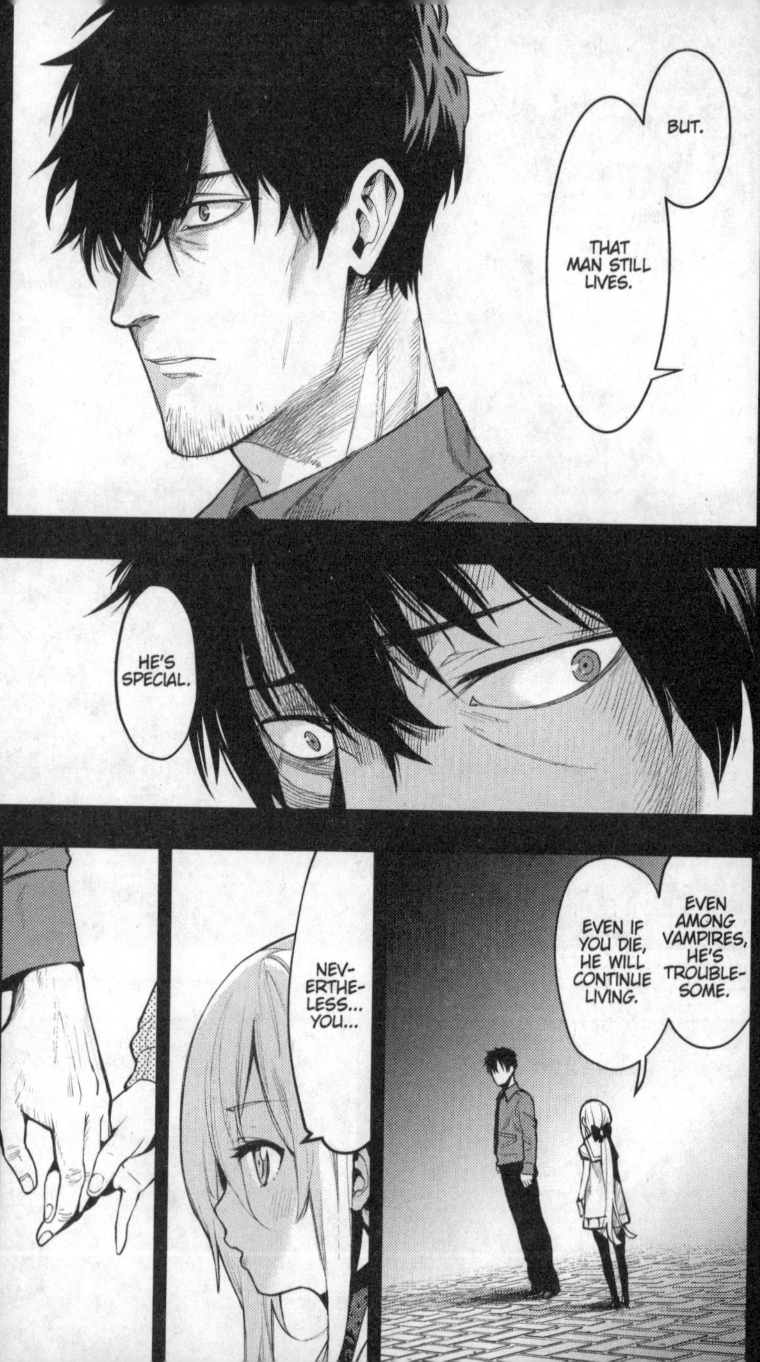
BUT.
THAT MAN STILL LIVES.
HE'S SPECIAL.
EVEN AMONG VAMPIRES, HE'S TROUBLE-SOME.
EVEN IF YOU DIE, HE WILL CONTINUE LIVING.
NEV-ERTHE-LESS... YOU...

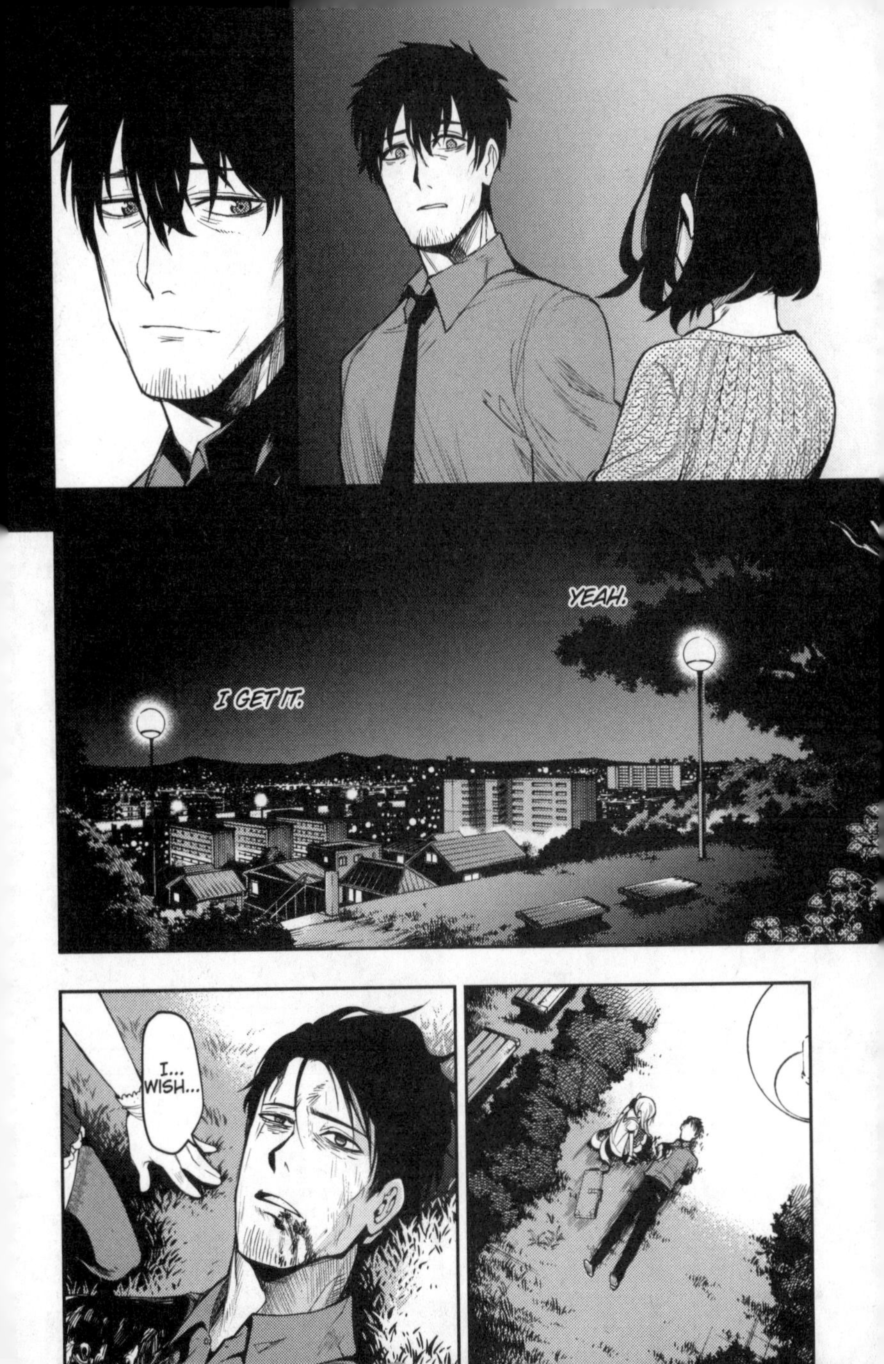
YEAH.
I GET IT.
I... WISH...

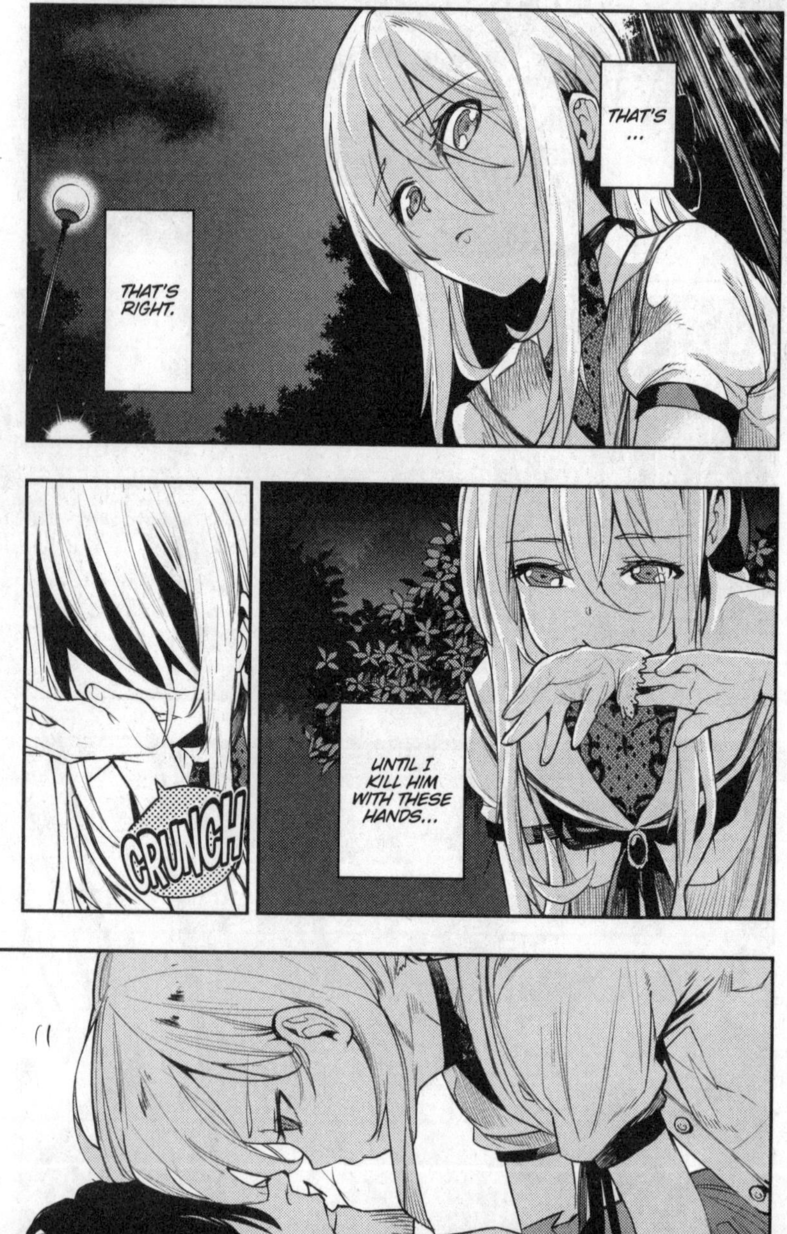
THAT'S ...
THAT'S RIGHT.
UNTIL I KILL HIM WITH THESE HANDS...
CRUNCH

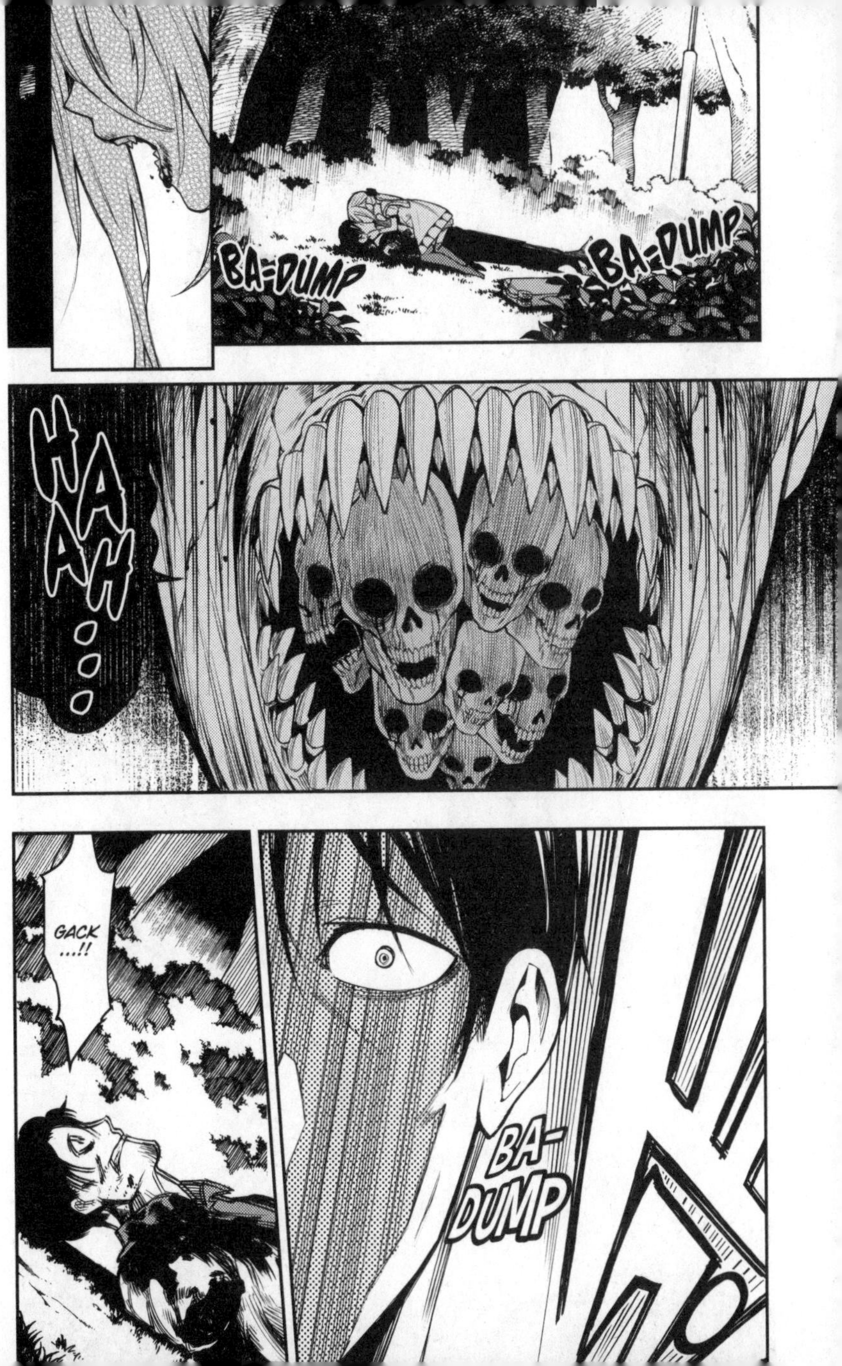
BA-DUMP
BA-DUMP
HAAH...
BA-DUMP
GACK ...!!

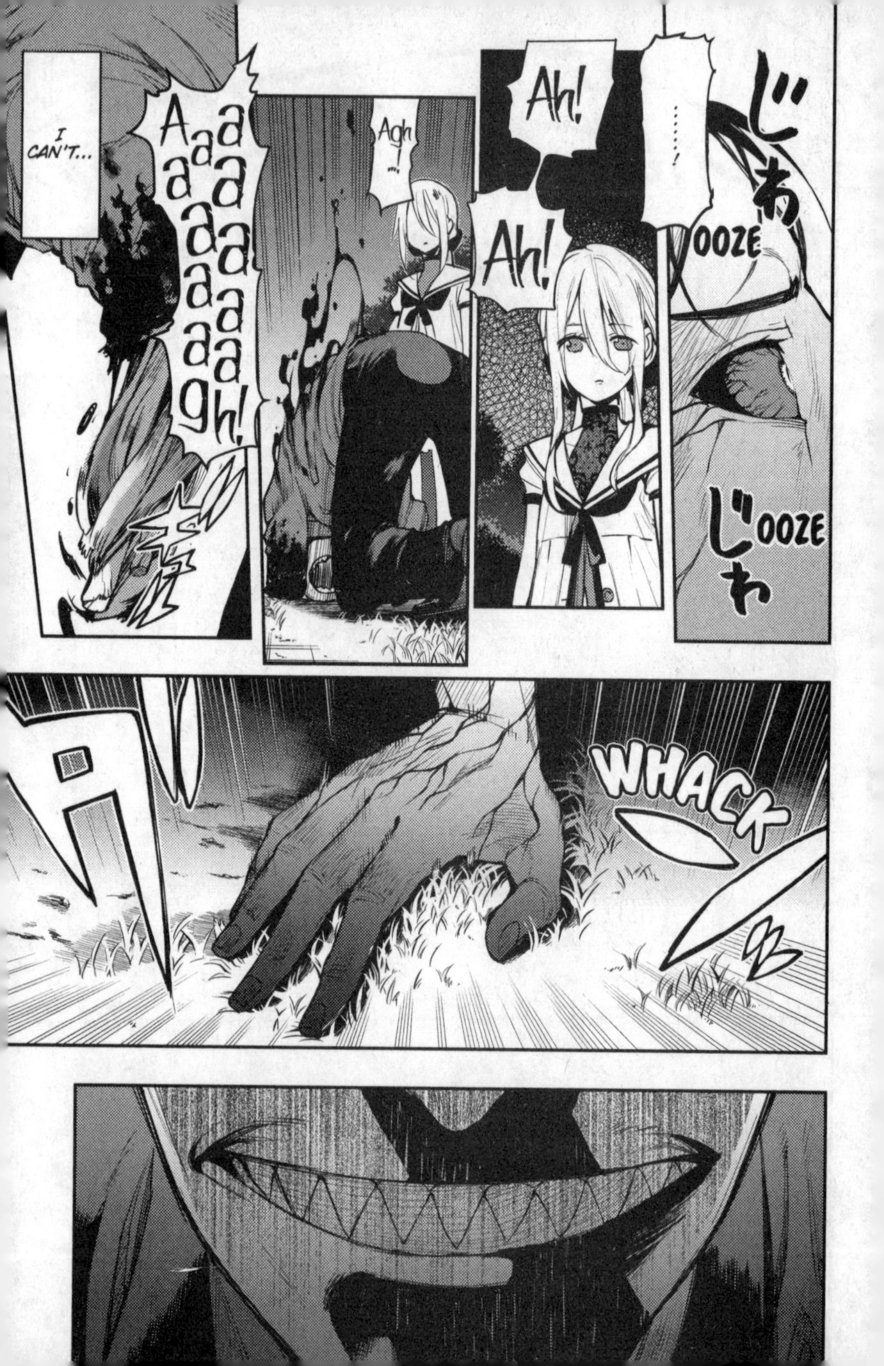
じあ
OOZE
じや
OOZE
……!
Ah!
Ah!
Agh …!
Aaaaaaaaaaaagh!
I CAN'T…
WHACK

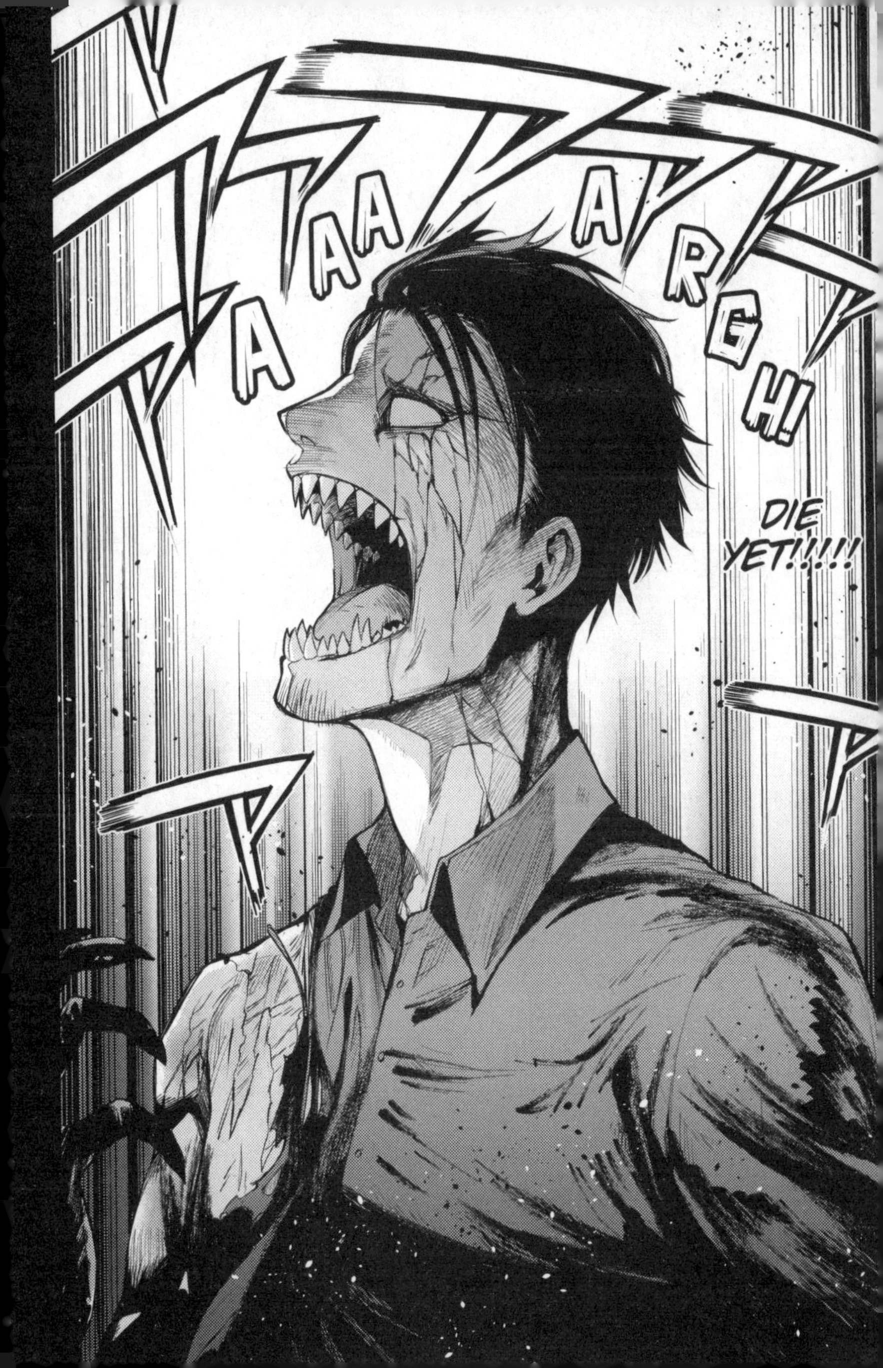
AAAAAARGH!
DIE YET!!!!!

MOMO
the blood taker

MOMO
the blood taker

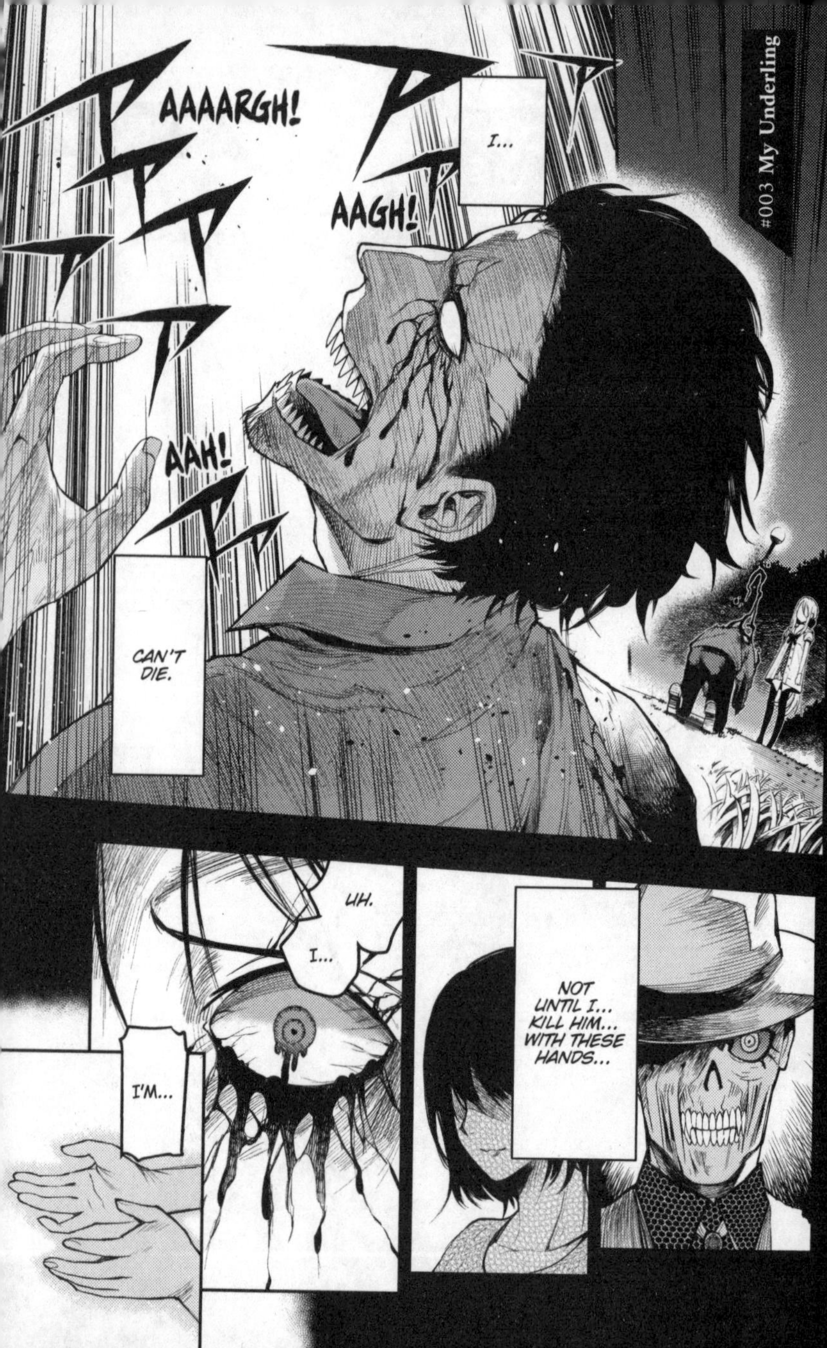
#003 My Underling
I...
AAAARGH!
AAGH!
AAH!
CAN'T DIE.
NOT UNTIL I... KILL HIM... WITH THESE HANDS...
UH.
I...
I'M...

#003 My Underling

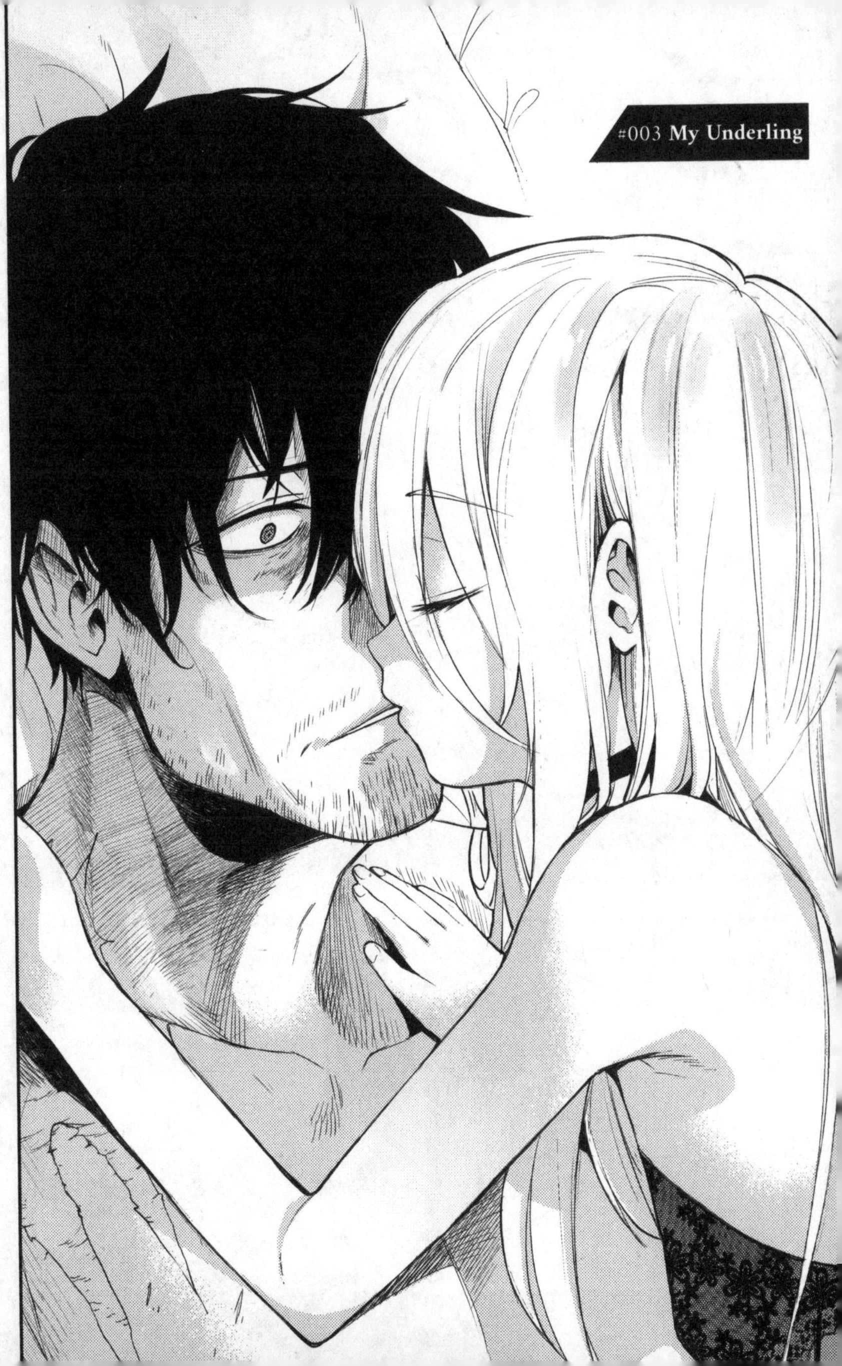

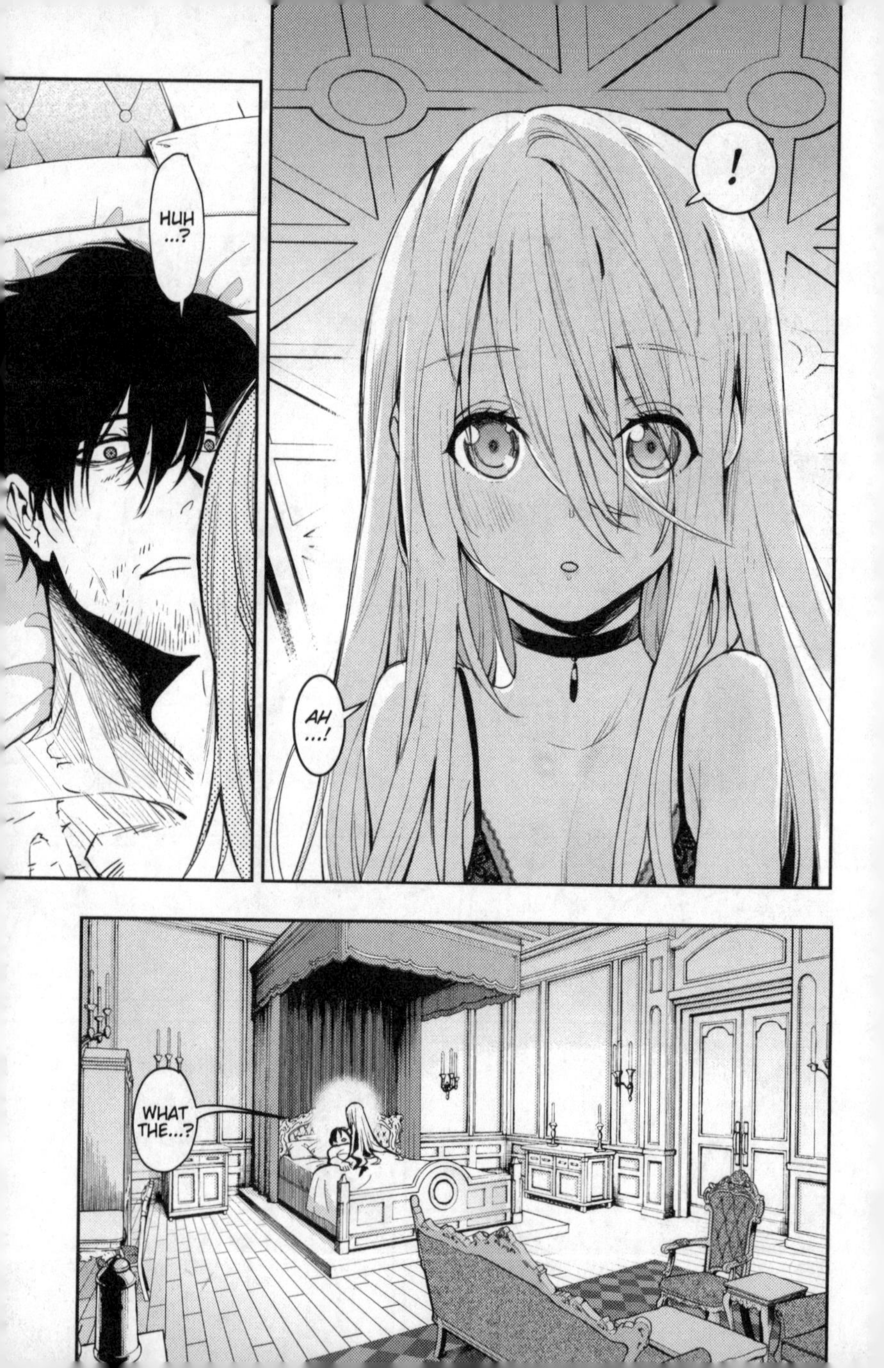
!
AH ...!
HUH ...?
WHAT THE...?

gaze...

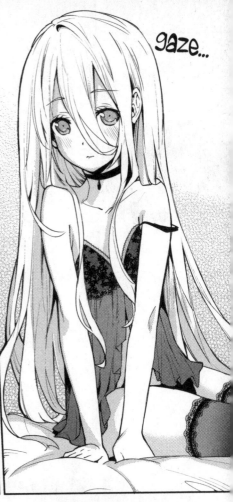

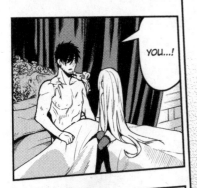

YOU...!

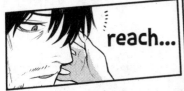

reach...

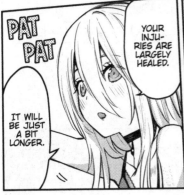

PAT PAT

YOUR INJURIES ARE LARGELY HEALED.

IT WILL BE JUST A BIT LONGER.

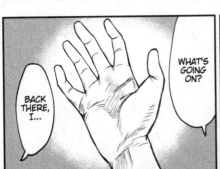

WHAT'S GOING ON?

BACK THERE, I...

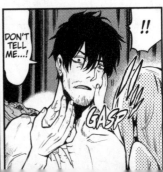

!!

DON'T TELL ME...!

GASP

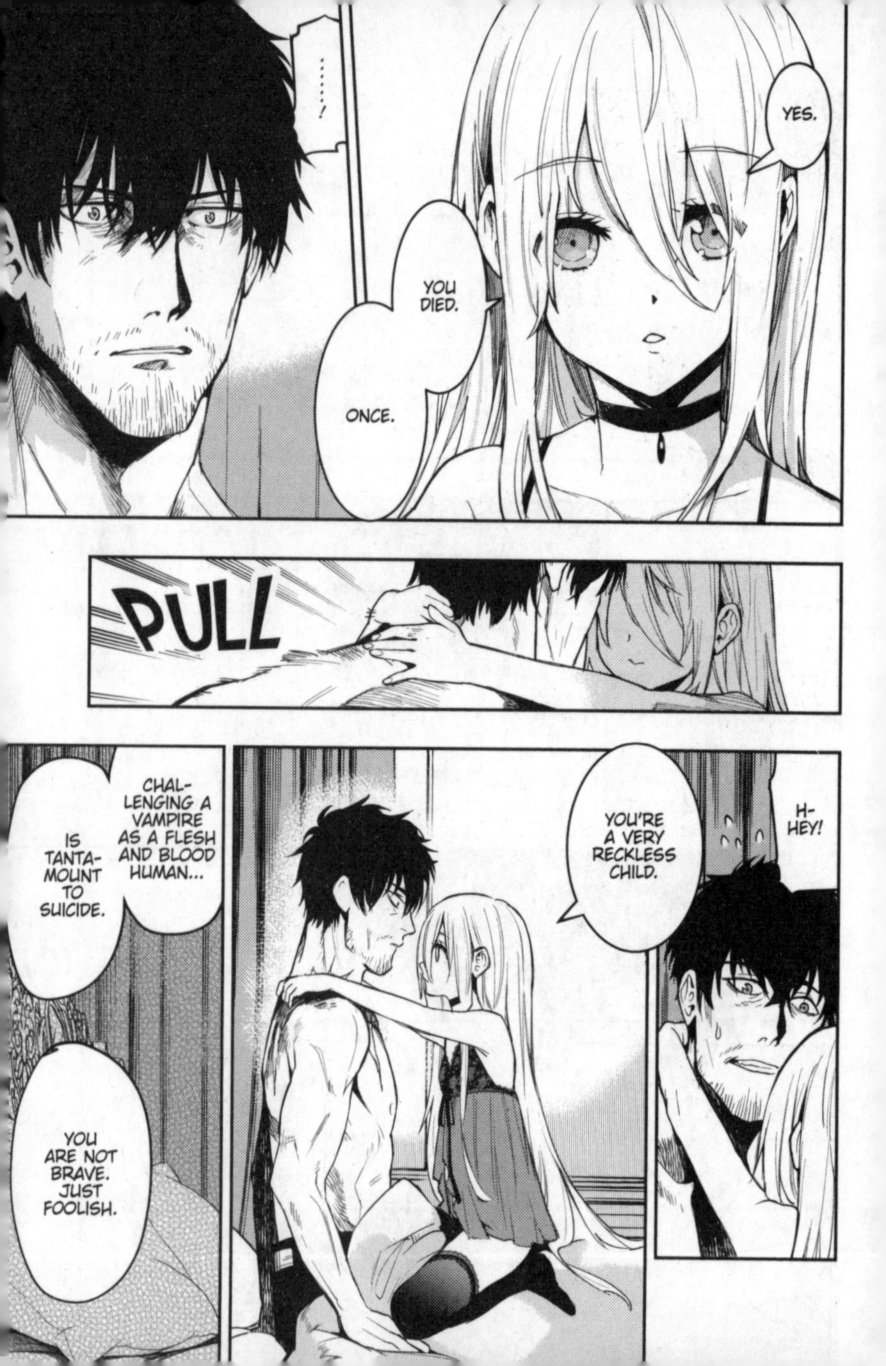
YES.
YOU DIED.
ONCE.
......!
PULL
H-HEY!
YOU'RE A VERY RECKLESS CHILD.
CHALLENGING A VAMPIRE AS A FLESH AND BLOOD HUMAN...
IS TANTAMOUNT TO SUICIDE.
YOU ARE NOT BRAVE. JUST FOOLISH.

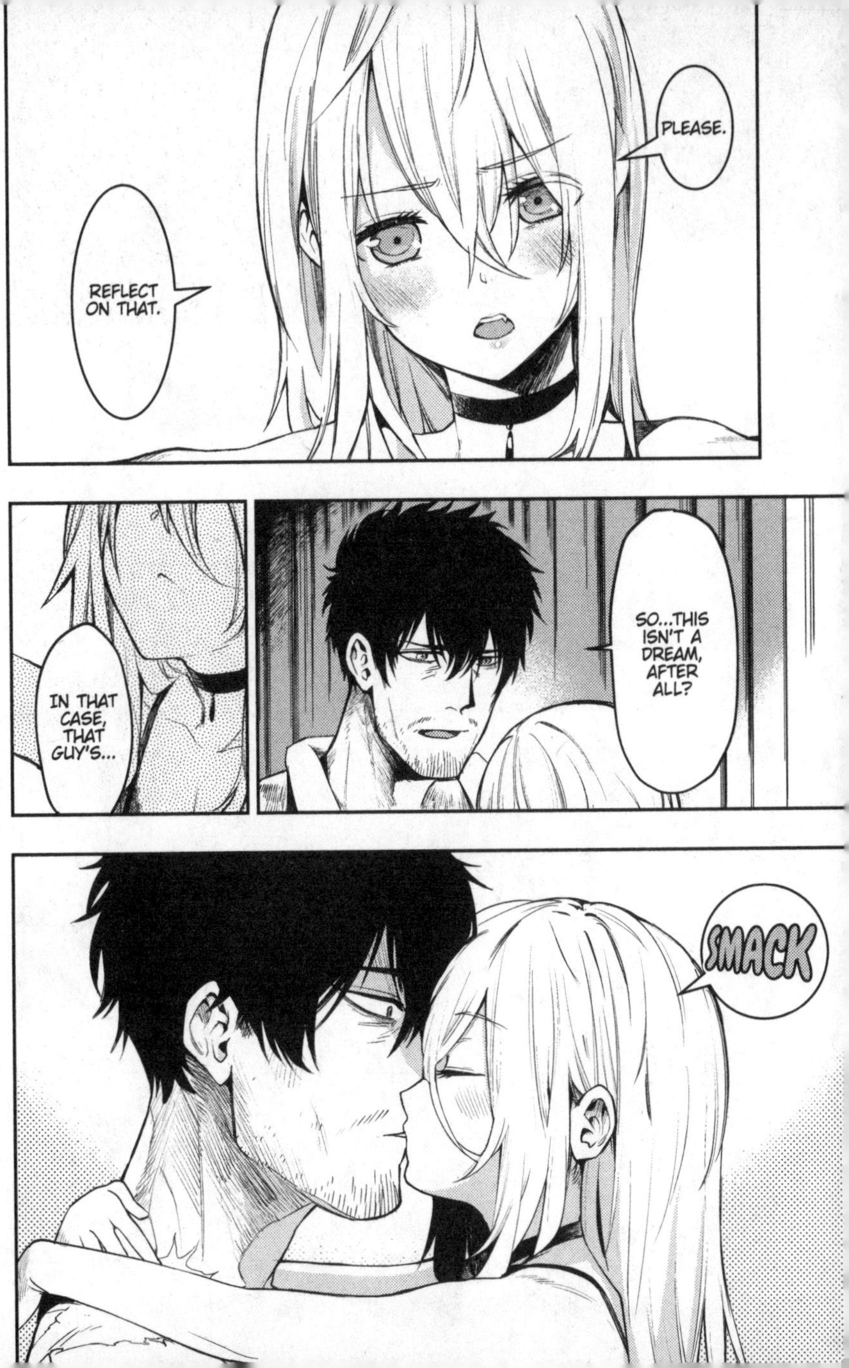
PLEASE.
REFLECT ON THAT.
SO...THIS ISN'T A DREAM, AFTER ALL?
IN THAT CASE, THAT GUY'S...
SMACK

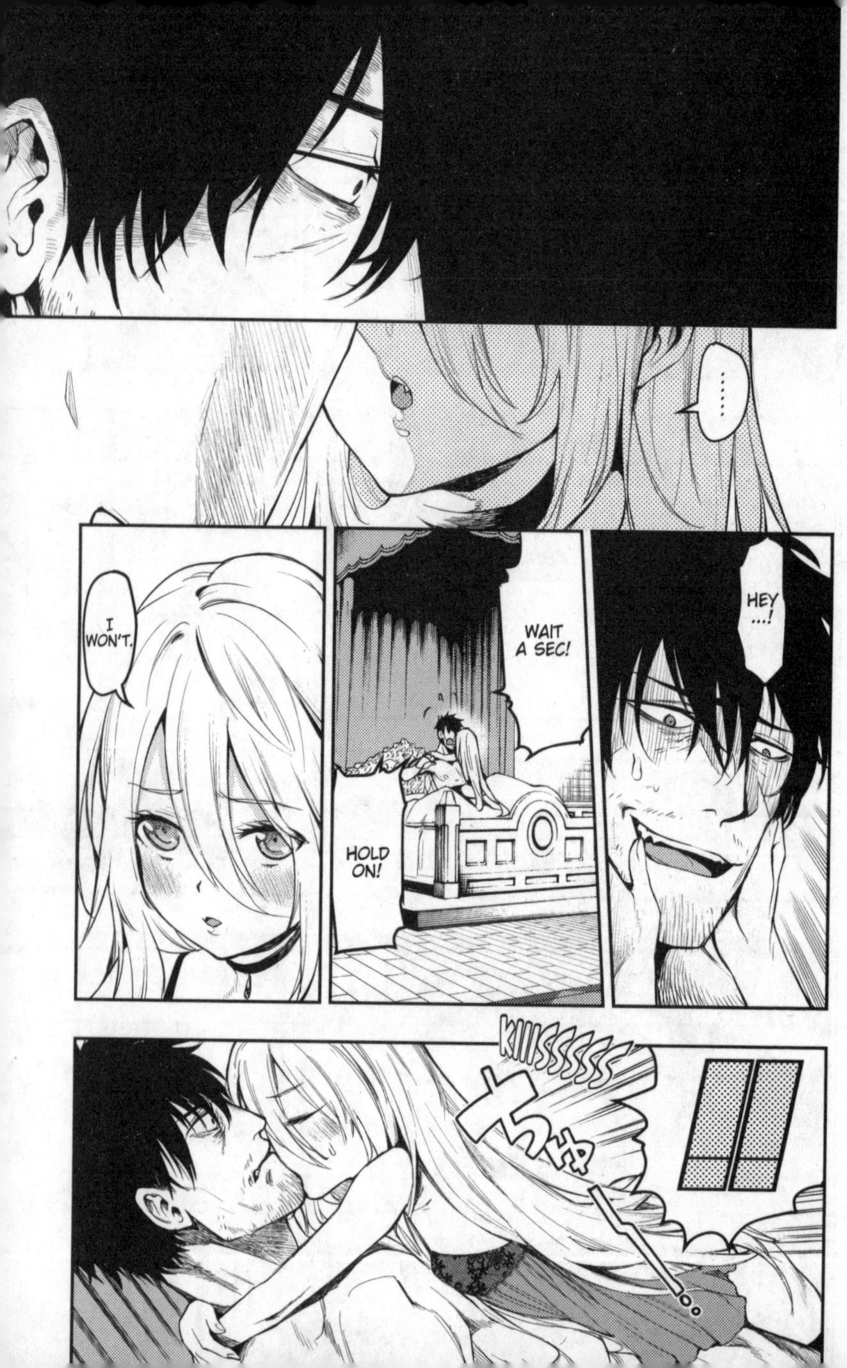
......
HEY ...!
WAIT A SEC!
HOLD ON!
I WON'T.
KIIISSSSSS
ちゅ

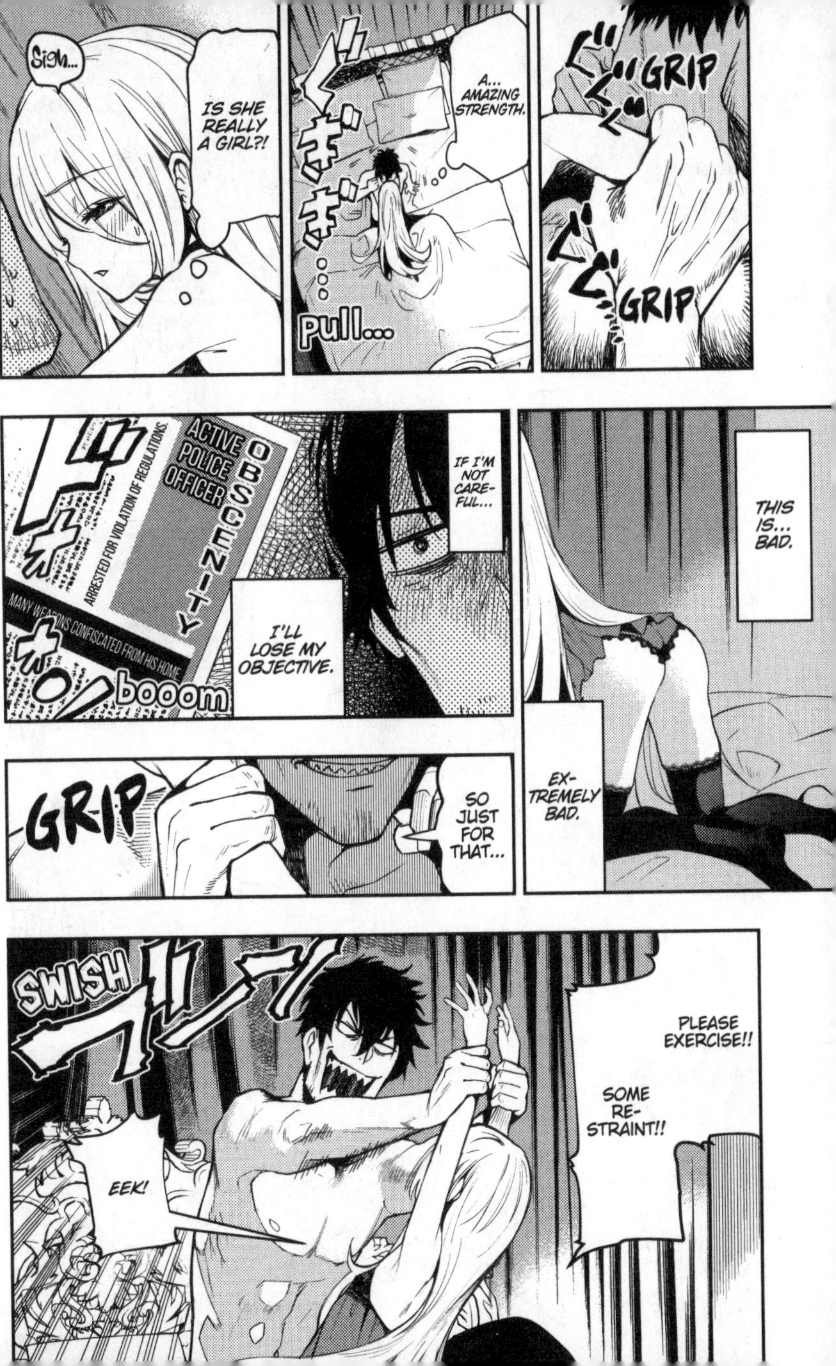
GRIP
GRIP
A... AMAZING STRENGTH.
pull...
Sigh...
IS SHE REALLY A GIRL?!
THIS IS... BAD.
EX-TREMELY BAD.
IF I'M NOT CARE-FUL...
I'LL LOSE MY OBJECTIVE.
OBSCENITY
ACTIVE POLICE OFFICER
ARRESTED FOR VIOLATION OF REGULATIONS.
MANY WEAPONS CONFISCATED FROM HIS HOME
booom
SO JUST FOR THAT...
GRIP
PLEASE EXERCISE!!
SOME RE-STRAINT!!
SWISH
EEK!

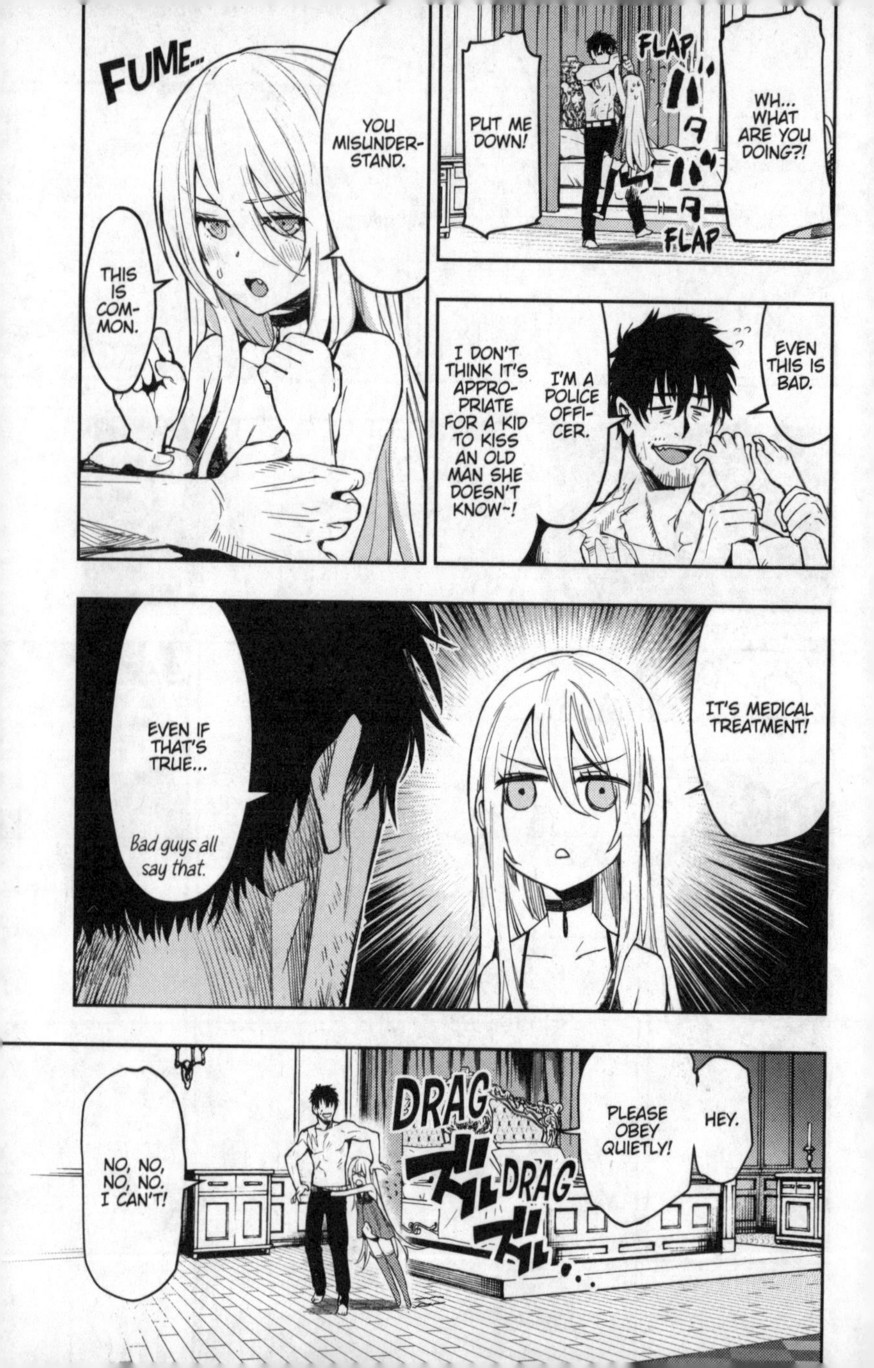
WH... WHAT ARE YOU DOING?!
FLAP
PUT ME DOWN!
FLAP
EVEN THIS IS BAD.
I'M A POLICE OFFICER.
I DON'T THINK IT'S APPROPRIATE FOR A KID TO KISS AN OLD MAN SHE DOESN'T KNOW~!
YOU MISUNDERSTAND.
FUME...
THIS IS COMMON.
IT'S MEDICAL TREATMENT!
EVEN IF THAT'S TRUE...
Bad guys all say that.
HEY.
PLEASE OBEY QUIETLY!
DRAG
DRAG
NO, NO, NO, NO. I CAN'T!

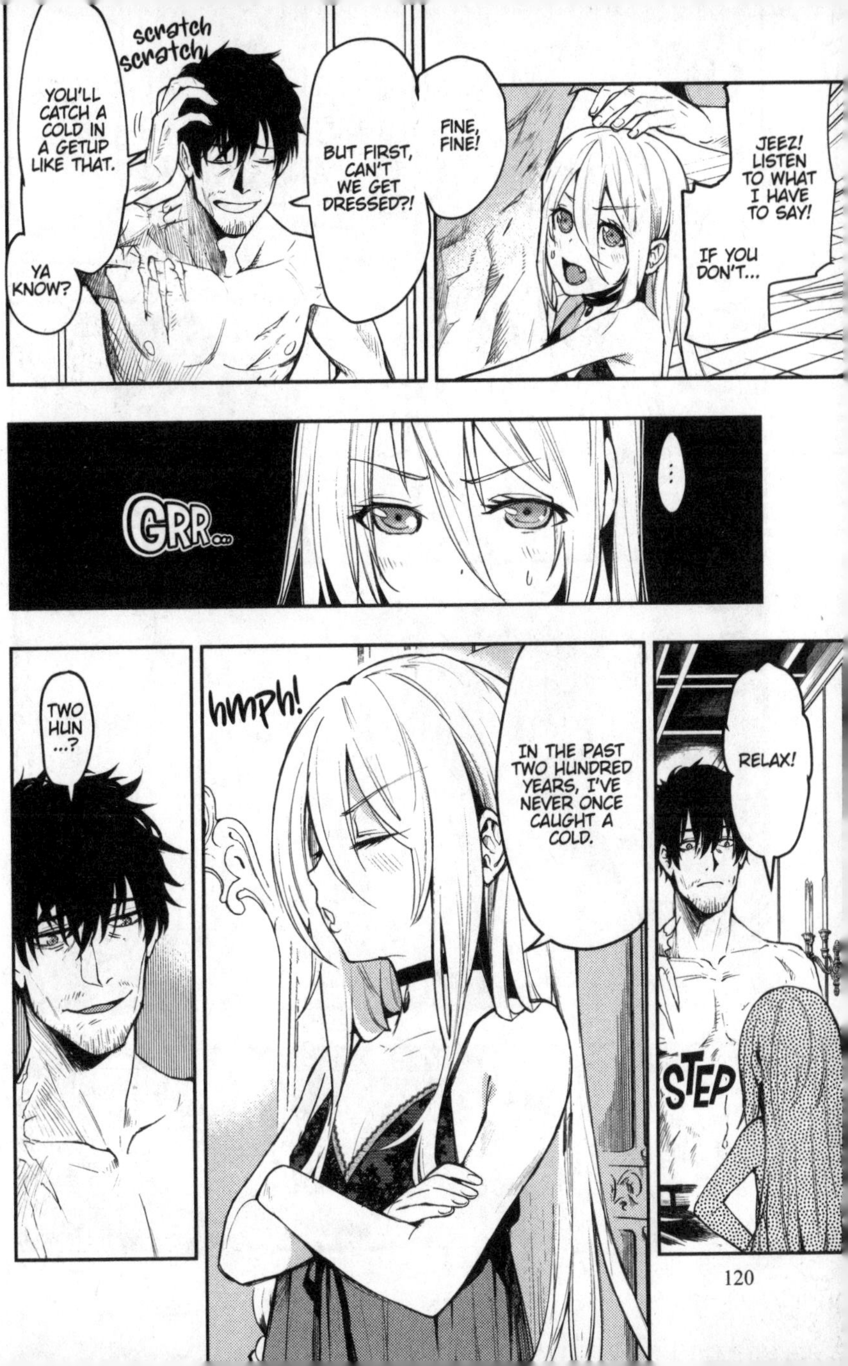
JEEZ! LISTEN TO WHAT I HAVE TO SAY!
IF YOU DON'T...
FINE, FINE!
BUT FIRST, CAN'T WE GET DRESSED?!
scratch scratch
YOU'LL CATCH A COLD IN A GETUP LIKE THAT.
YA KNOW?
...
GRR...
RELAX!
STEP
IN THE PAST TWO HUNDRED YEARS, I'VE NEVER ONCE CAUGHT A COLD.
hmph!
TWO HUN ...?

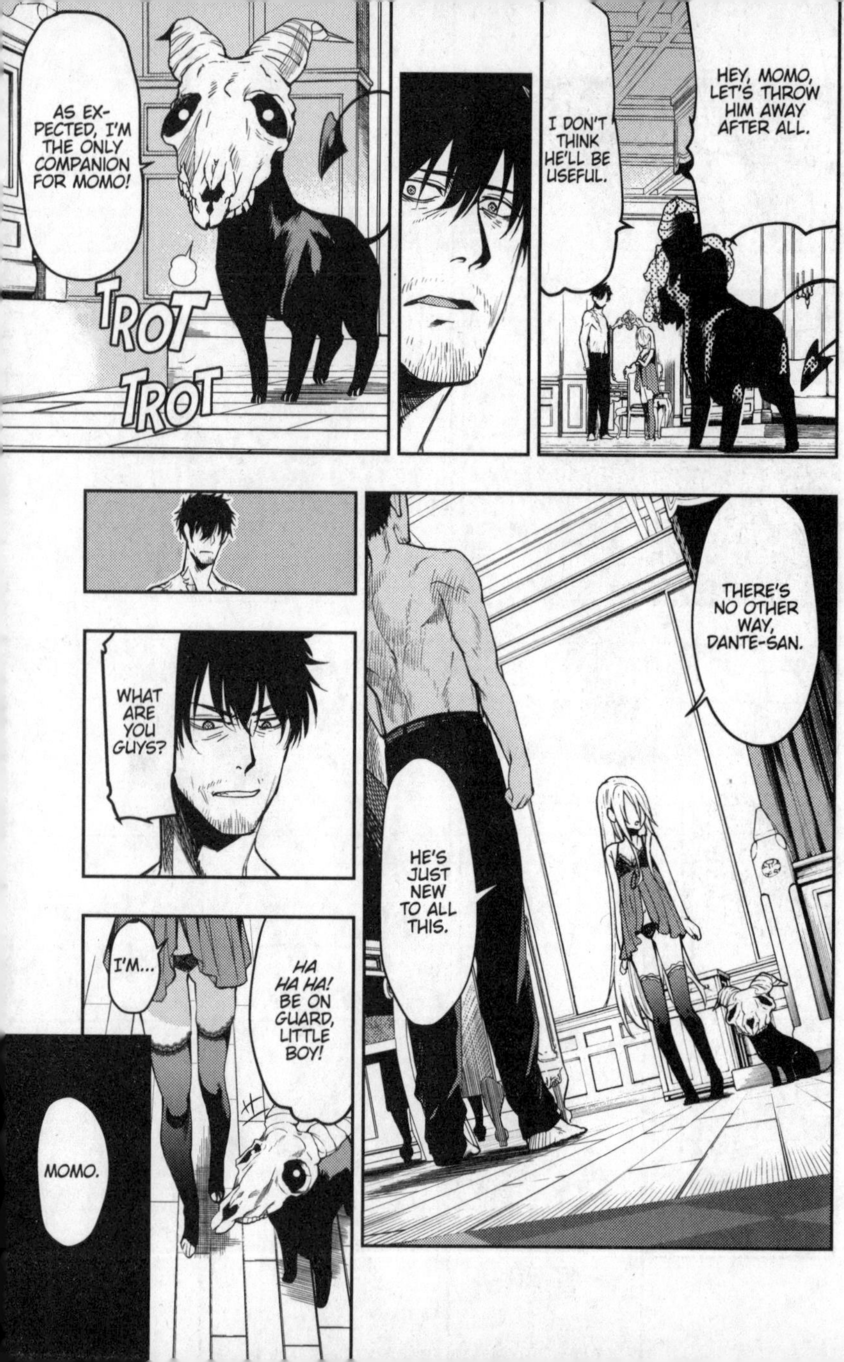
HEY, MOMO, LET'S THROW HIM AWAY AFTER ALL.
I DON'T THINK HE'LL BE USEFUL.
AS EX-PECTED, I'M THE ONLY COMPANION FOR MOMO!
TROT
TROT
THERE'S NO OTHER WAY, DANTE-SAN.
HE'S JUST NEW TO ALL THIS.
WHAT ARE YOU GUYS?
I'M...
HA HA HA! BE ON GUARD, LITTLE BOY!
MOMO.

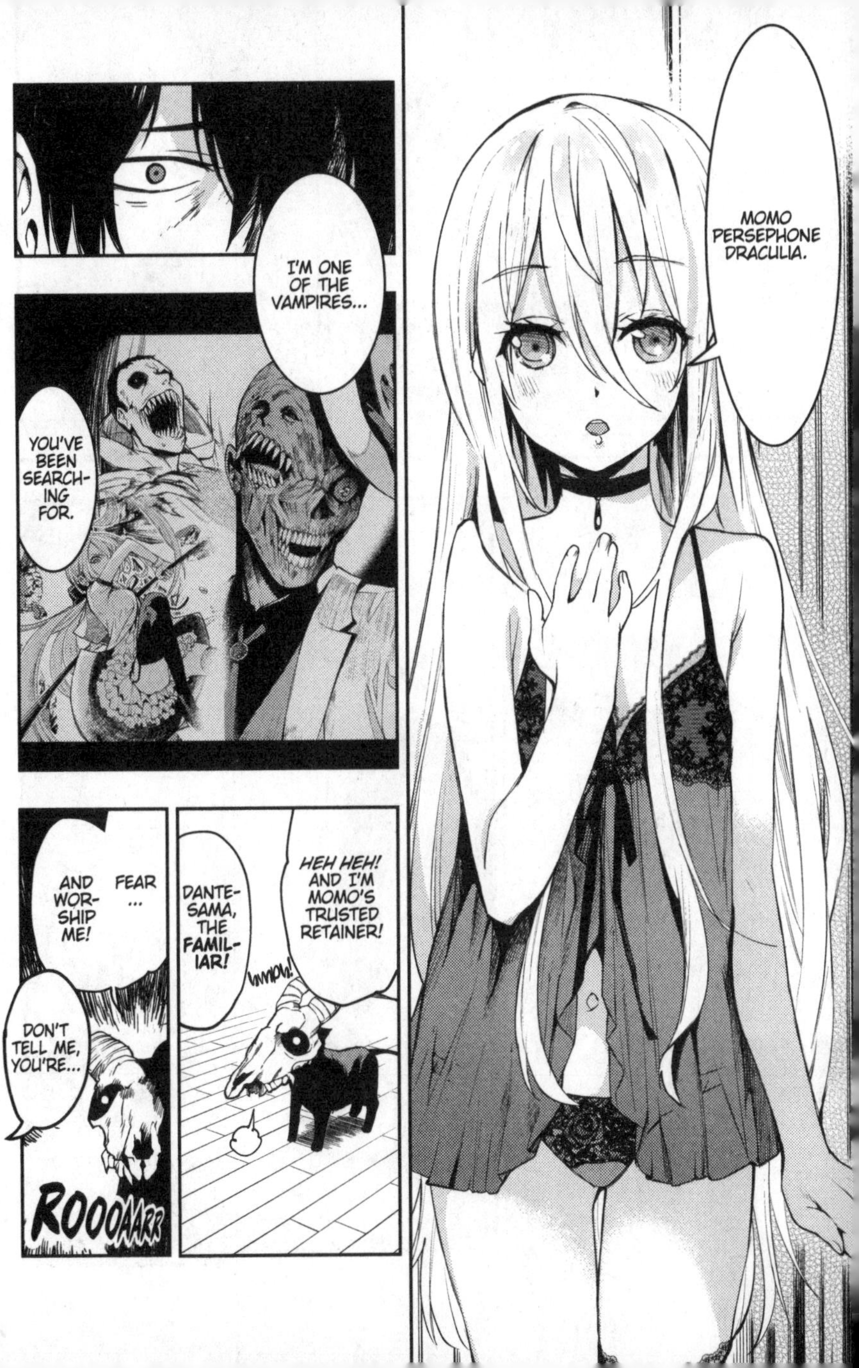
MOMO PERSEPHONE DRACULIA.
I'M ONE OF THE VAMPIRES...
YOU'VE BEEN SEARCHING FOR.
HEH HEH! AND I'M MOMO'S TRUSTED RETAINER!
DANTE-SAMA, THE FAMILIAR!
FEAR ...
AND WORSHIP ME!
DON'T TELL ME, YOU'RE...
ROOOAARR

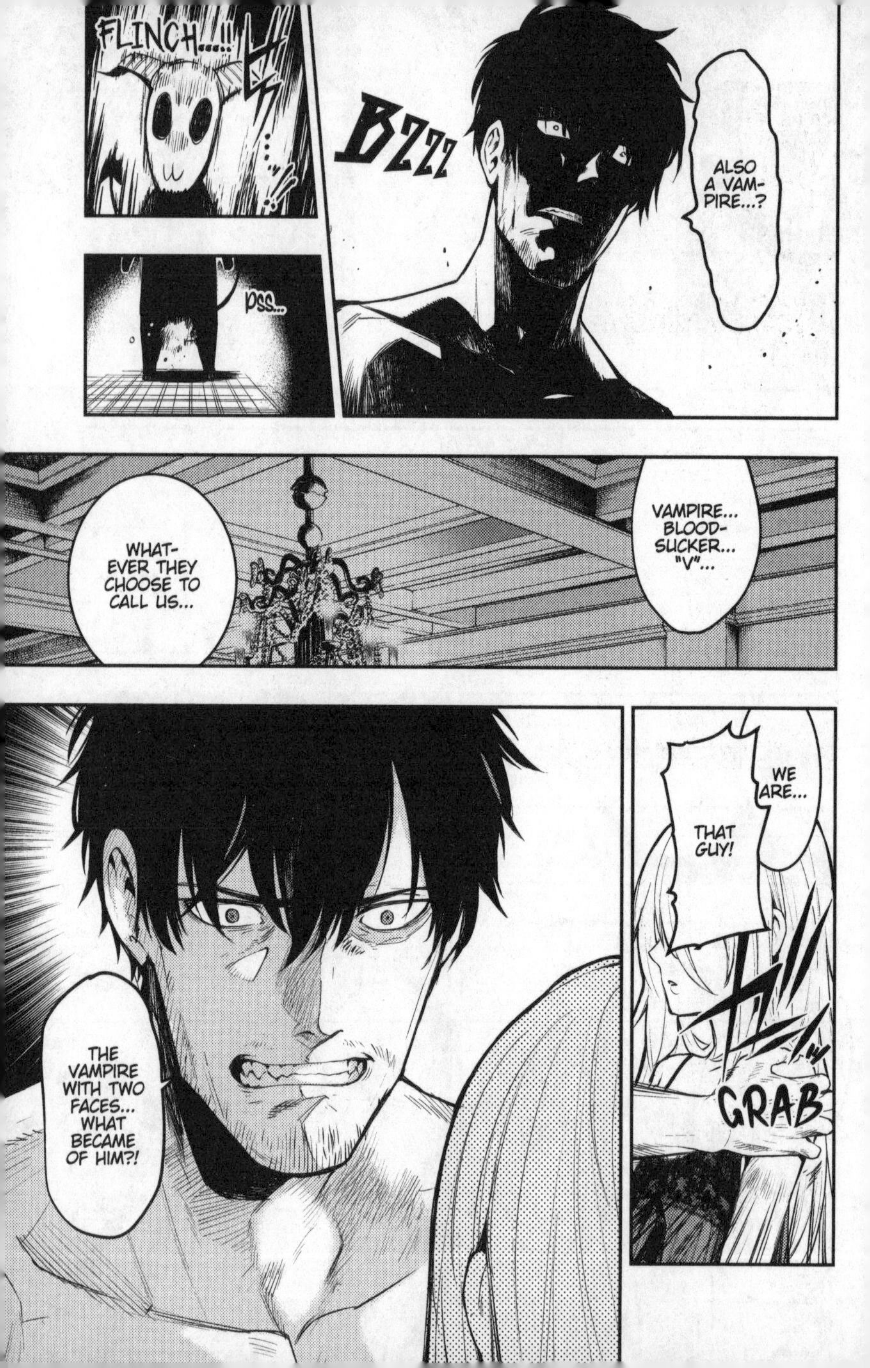
ALSO A VAMPIRE...?
BZZZ
FLINCH...!!
pss...
VAMPIRE... BLOODSUCKER... "V"...
WHATEVER THEY CHOOSE TO CALL US...
WE ARE...
THAT GUY!
GRAB
THE VAMPIRE WITH TWO FACES... WHAT BECAME OF HIM?!

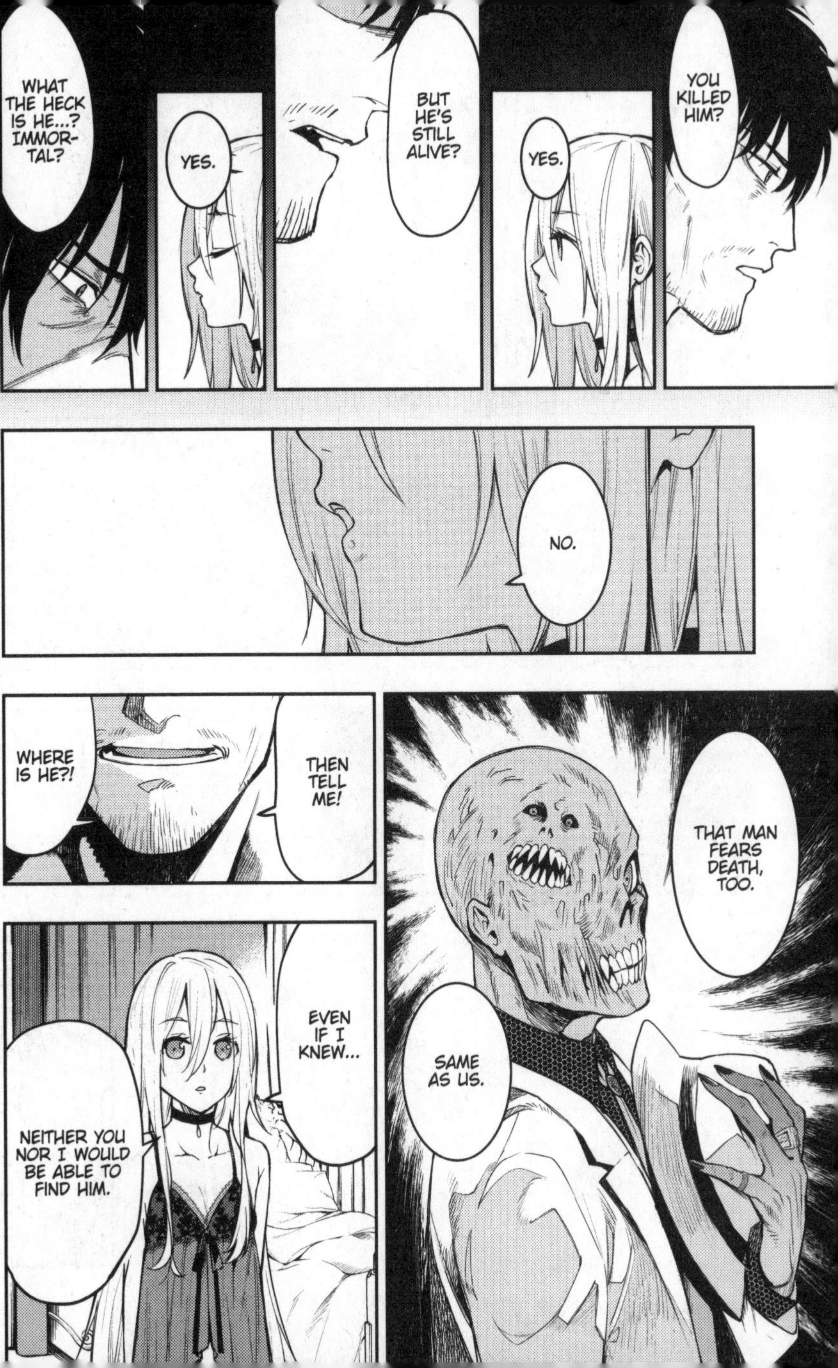
YOU KILLED HIM?
YES.
BUT HE'S STILL ALIVE?
YES.
WHAT THE HECK IS HE...? IMMORTAL?
NO.
THAT MAN FEARS DEATH, TOO.
SAME AS US.
THEN TELL ME!
WHERE IS HE?!
EVEN IF I KNEW...
NEITHER YOU NOR I WOULD BE ABLE TO FIND HIM.

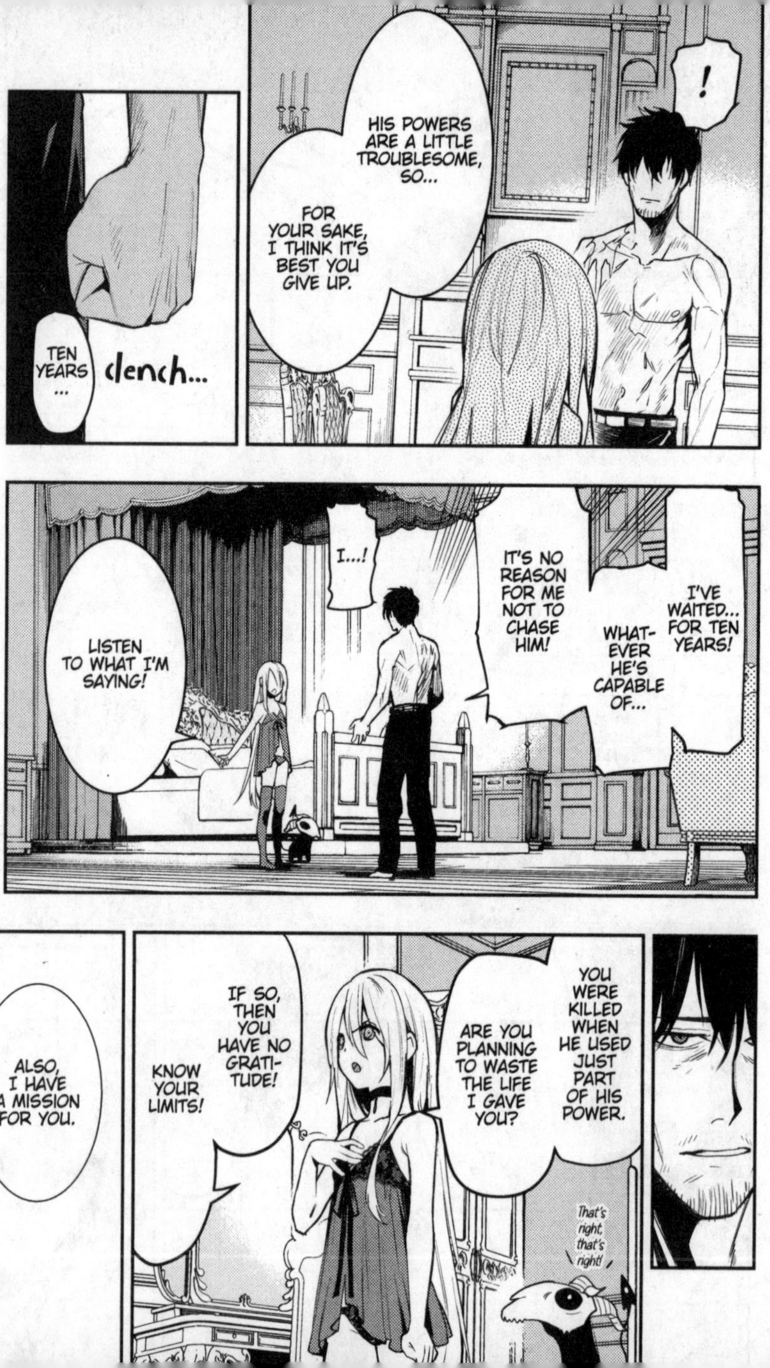
!
HIS POWERS ARE A LITTLE TROUBLESOME, SO...
FOR YOUR SAKE, I THINK IT'S BEST YOU GIVE UP.
TEN YEARS...
clench...
I'VE WAITED... FOR TEN YEARS!
WHATEVER HE'S CAPABLE OF...
IT'S NO REASON FOR ME NOT TO CHASE HIM!
I...!
LISTEN TO WHAT I'M SAYING!
YOU WERE KILLED WHEN HE USED JUST PART OF HIS POWER.
ARE YOU PLANNING TO WASTE THE LIFE I GAVE YOU?
That's right, that's right!
IF SO, THEN YOU HAVE NO GRATITUDE!
KNOW YOUR LIMITS!
ALSO, I HAVE A MISSION FOR YOU.

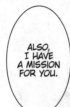

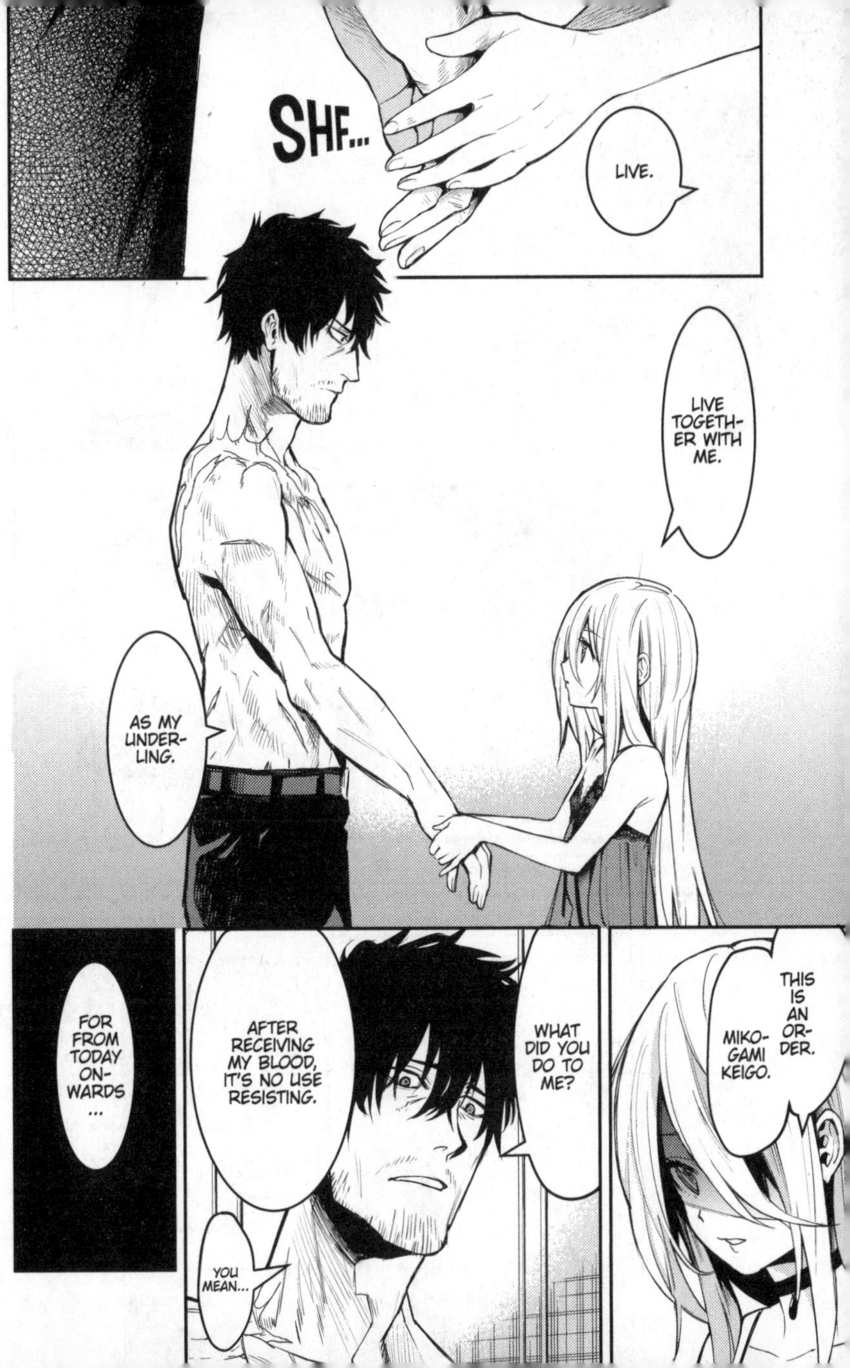
SHF...
LIVE.
LIVE TOGETHER WITH ME.
AS MY UNDERLING.
THIS IS AN ORDER.
MIKOGAMI KEIGO.
WHAT DID YOU DO TO ME?
AFTER RECEIVING MY BLOOD, IT'S NO USE RESISTING.
YOU MEAN...
FOR FROM TODAY ONWARDS...

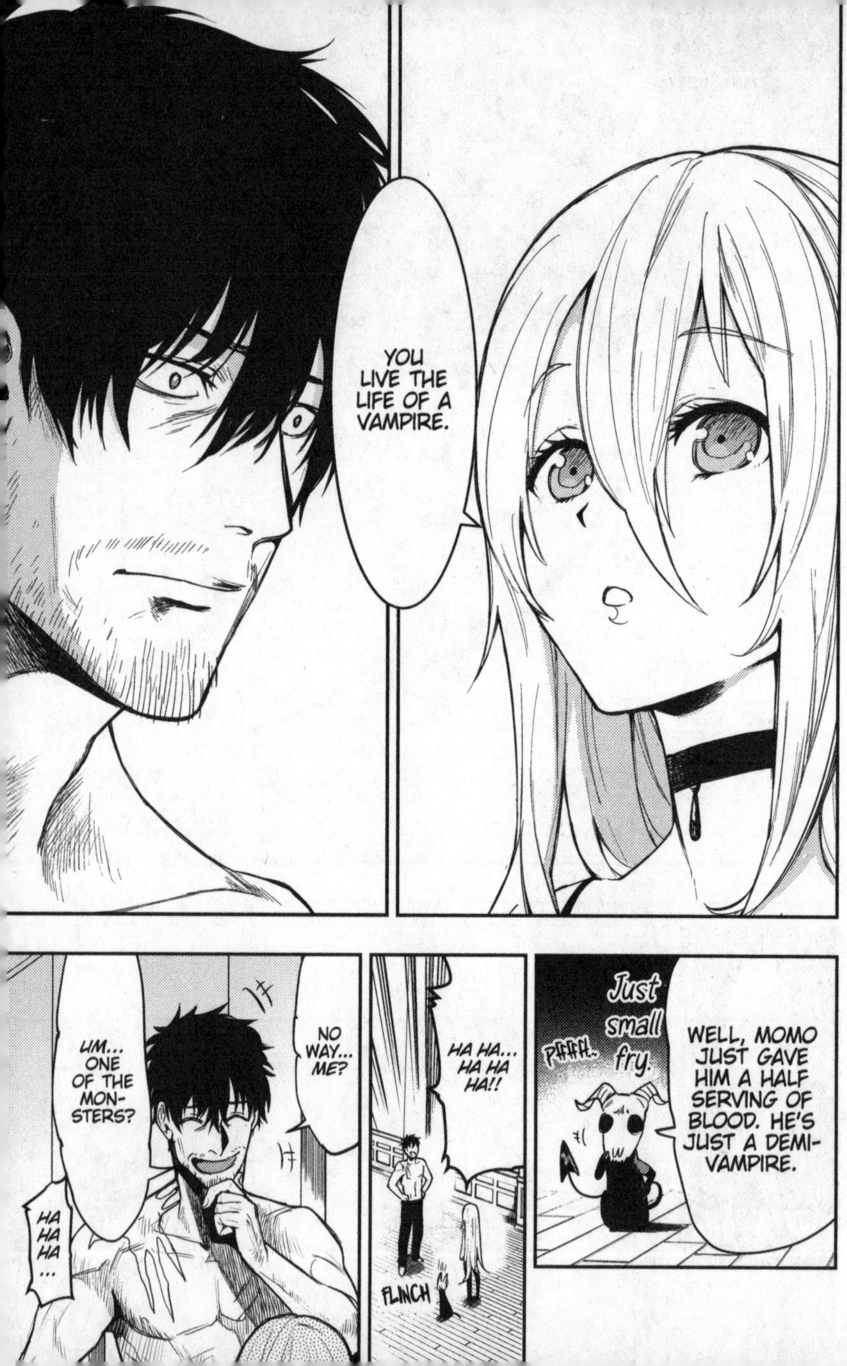
YOU LIVE THE LIFE OF A VAMPIRE.
WELL, MOMO JUST GAVE HIM A HALF SERVING OF BLOOD. HE'S JUST A DEMI-VAMPIRE.
Just small fry.
PFFFH...
HA HA... HA HA HA!!
FLINCH
NO WAY... ME?
UM... ONE OF THE MON-STERS?
HA HA HA HA ...

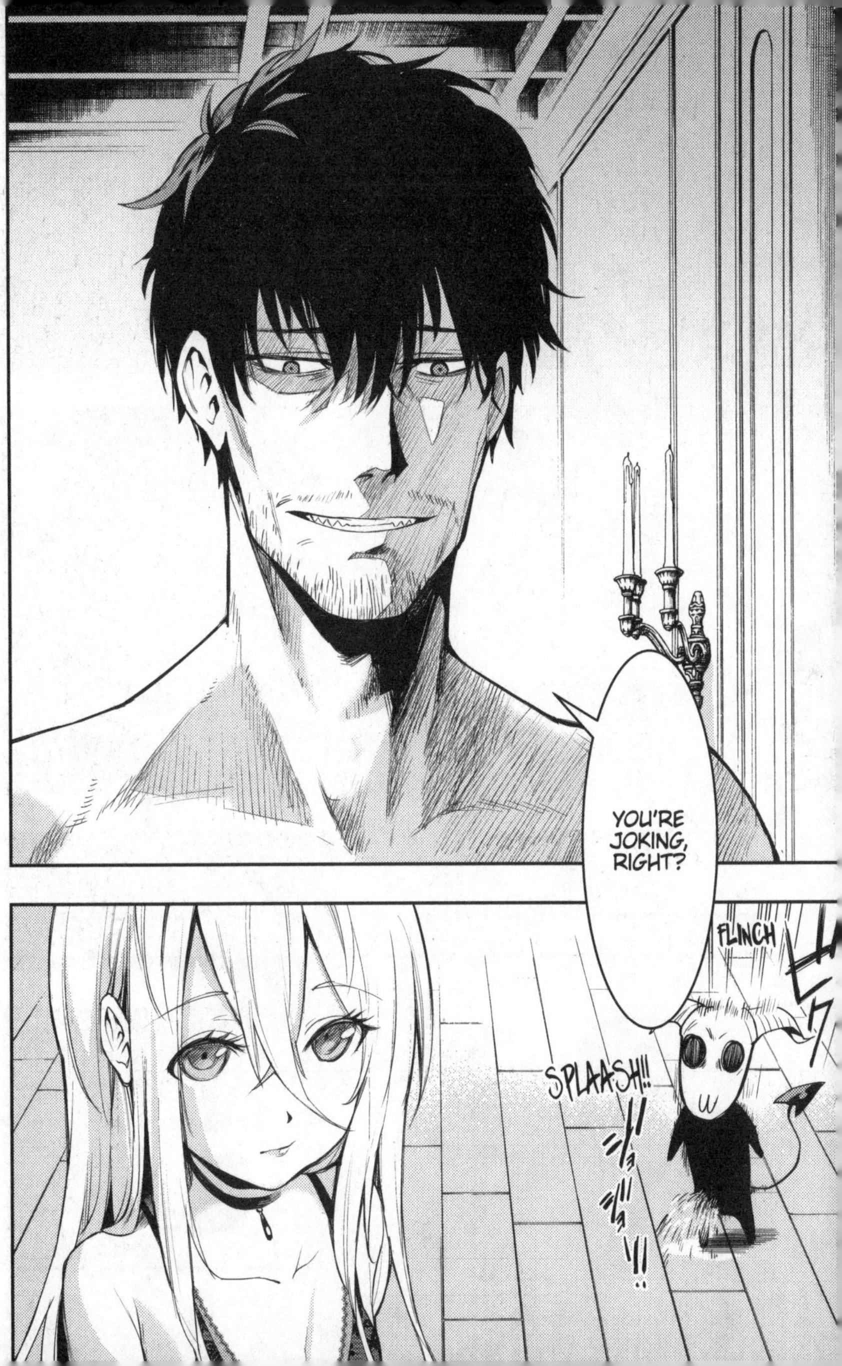
YOU'RE JOKING, RIGHT?
FLINCH
SPLAASH!!

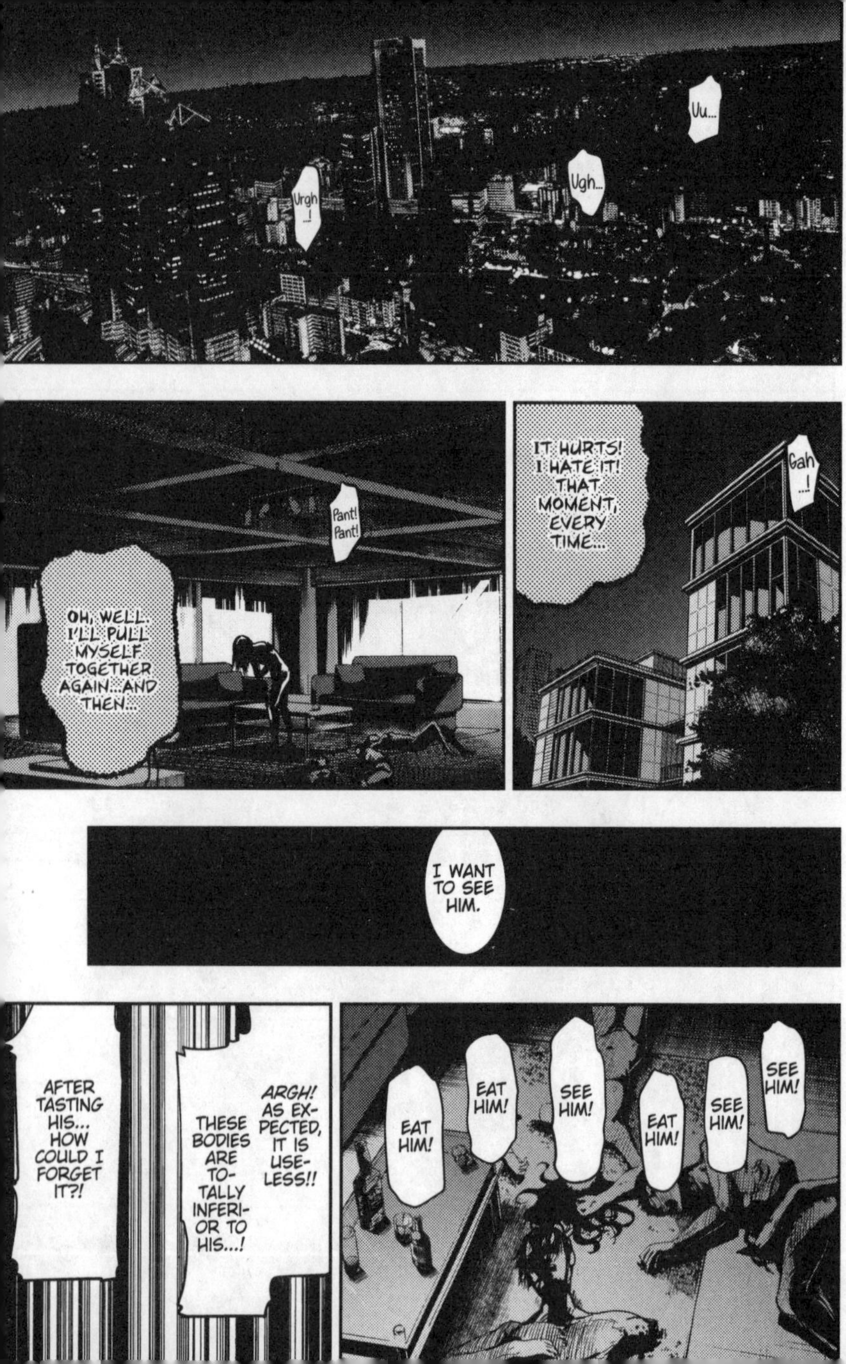

Uu...
Ugh...
Urgh ...!
Gah ...!
IT HURTS! I HATE IT! THAT MOMENT, EVERY TIME...
Pant! Pant!
OH, WELL. I'LL PULL MYSELF TOGETHER AGAIN...AND THEN...
I WANT TO SEE HIM.
SEE HIM!
SEE HIM!
EAT HIM!
SEE HIM!
EAT HIM!
EAT HIM!
ARGH! AS EXPECTED, IT IS USELESS!!
THESE BODIES ARE TOTALLY INFERIOR TO HIS...!
AFTER TASTING HIS... HOW COULD I FORGET IT?!

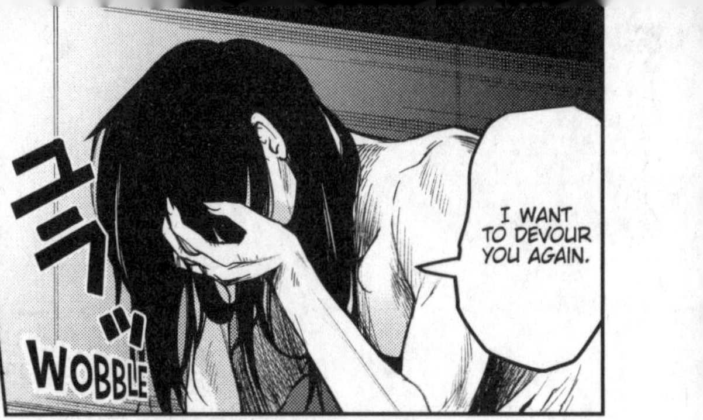
ユラッ
WOBBLE
I WANT TO DEVOUR YOU AGAIN.
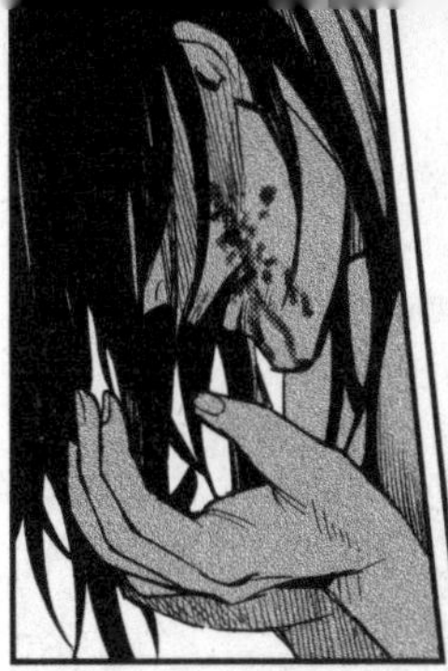
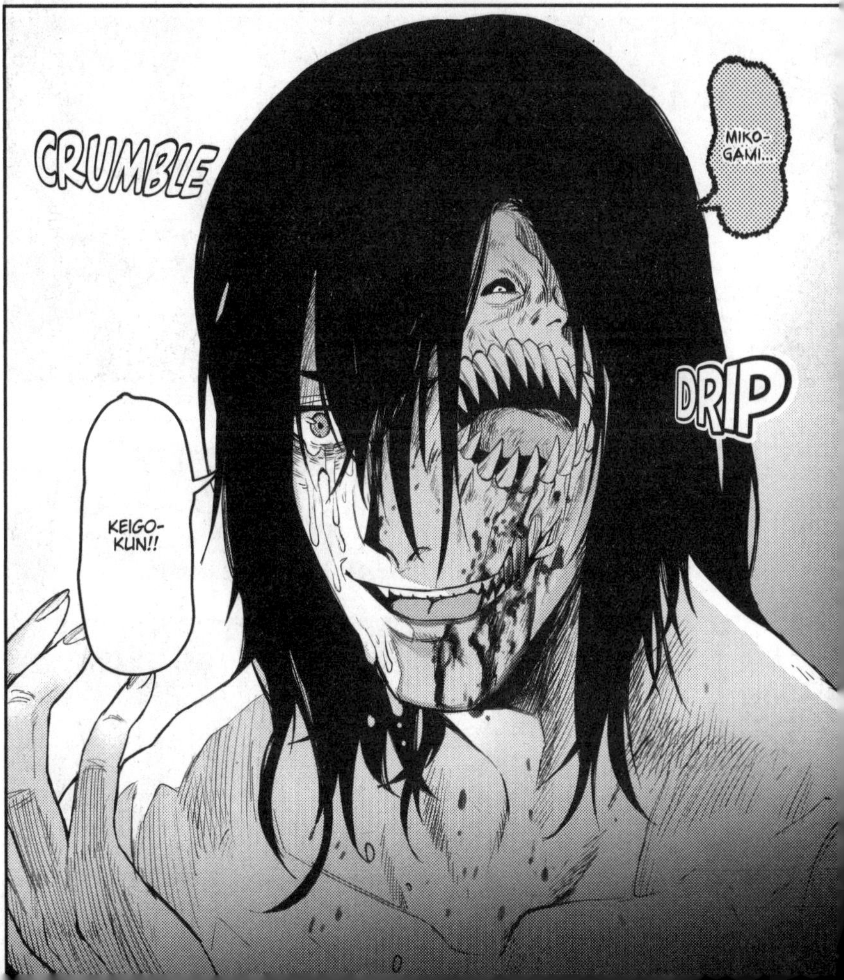
MIKO-GAMI...
CRUMBLE
DRIP
KEIGO-KUN!!

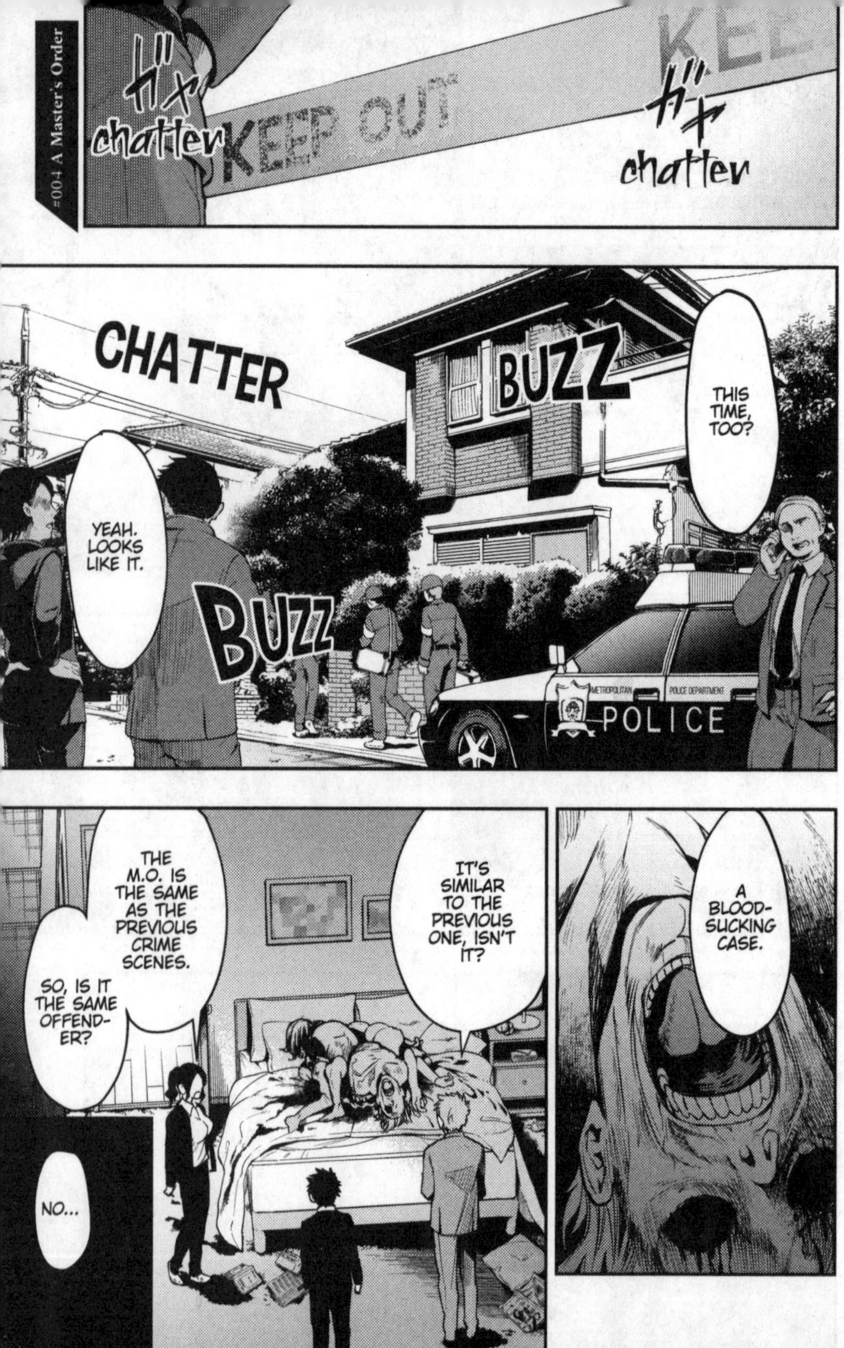
KEEP OUT
ガヤ
chatter
ガヤ
chatter
THIS TIME, TOO?
CHATTER
BUZZ
YEAH. LOOKS LIKE IT.
BUZZ
METROPOLITAN POLICE DEPARTMENT
POLICE
A BLOOD-SUCKING CASE.
IT'S SIMILAR TO THE PREVIOUS ONE, ISN'T IT?
THE M.O. IS THE SAME AS THE PREVIOUS CRIME SCENES.
SO, IS IT THE SAME OFFENDER?
NO...

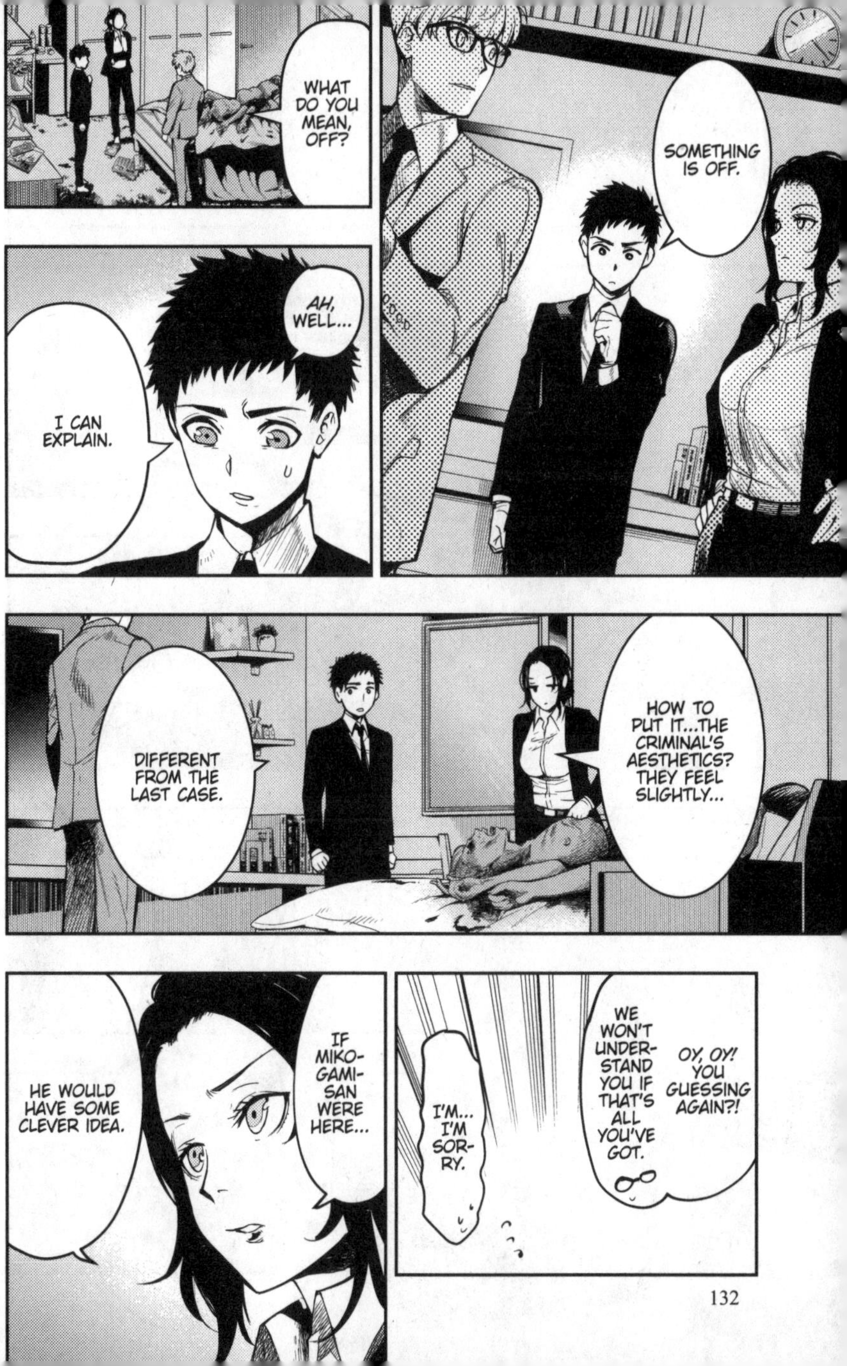
SOMETHING IS OFF.
WHAT DO YOU MEAN, OFF?
AH, WELL...
I CAN EXPLAIN.
HOW TO PUT IT...THE CRIMINAL'S AESTHETICS? THEY FEEL SLIGHTLY...
DIFFERENT FROM THE LAST CASE.
OY, OY! YOU GUESSING AGAIN?!
WE WON'T UNDER-STAND YOU IF THAT'S ALL YOU'VE GOT.
I'M... I'M SOR-RY.
IF MIKO-GAMI-SAN WERE HERE...
HE WOULD HAVE SOME CLEVER IDEA.

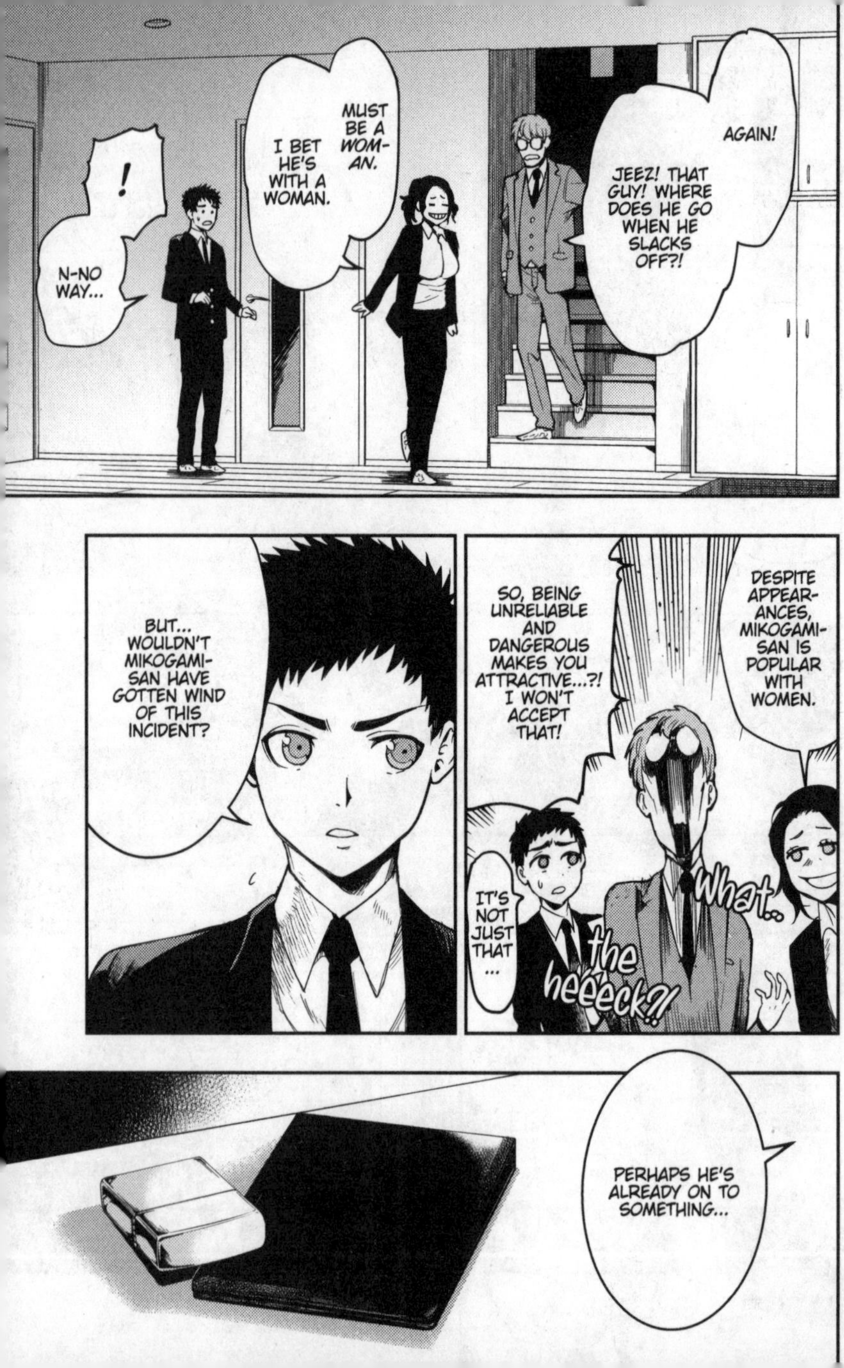
AGAIN!
JEEZ! THAT GUY! WHERE DOES HE GO WHEN HE SLACKS OFF?!
MUST BE A WOMAN.
I BET HE'S WITH A WOMAN.
!
N-NO WAY...
DESPITE APPEARANCES, MIKOGAMI-SAN IS POPULAR WITH WOMEN.
SO, BEING UNRELIABLE AND DANGEROUS MAKES YOU ATTRACTIVE...?! I WON'T ACCEPT THAT!
What... the heeeck?!
IT'S NOT JUST THAT...
BUT... WOULDN'T MIKOGAMI-SAN HAVE GOTTEN WIND OF THIS INCIDENT?
PERHAPS HE'S ALREADY ON TO SOMETHING...

#004 A Master's Order

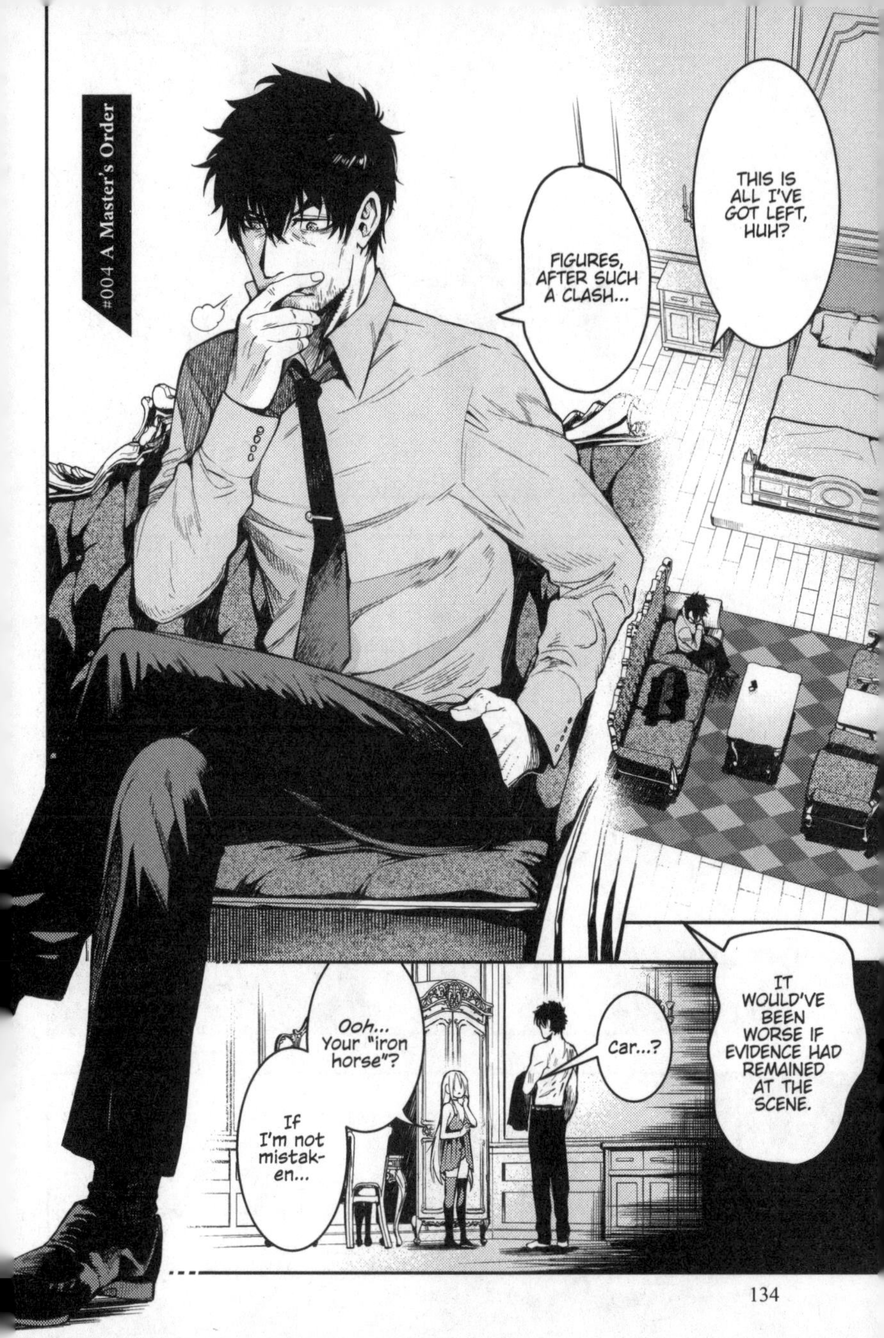
THIS IS ALL I'VE GOT LEFT, HUH?
FIGURES, AFTER SUCH A CLASH...
IT WOULD'VE BEEN WORSE IF EVIDENCE HAD REMAINED AT THE SCENE.
Car...?
Ooh... Your "iron horse"?
If I'm not mistak-en...

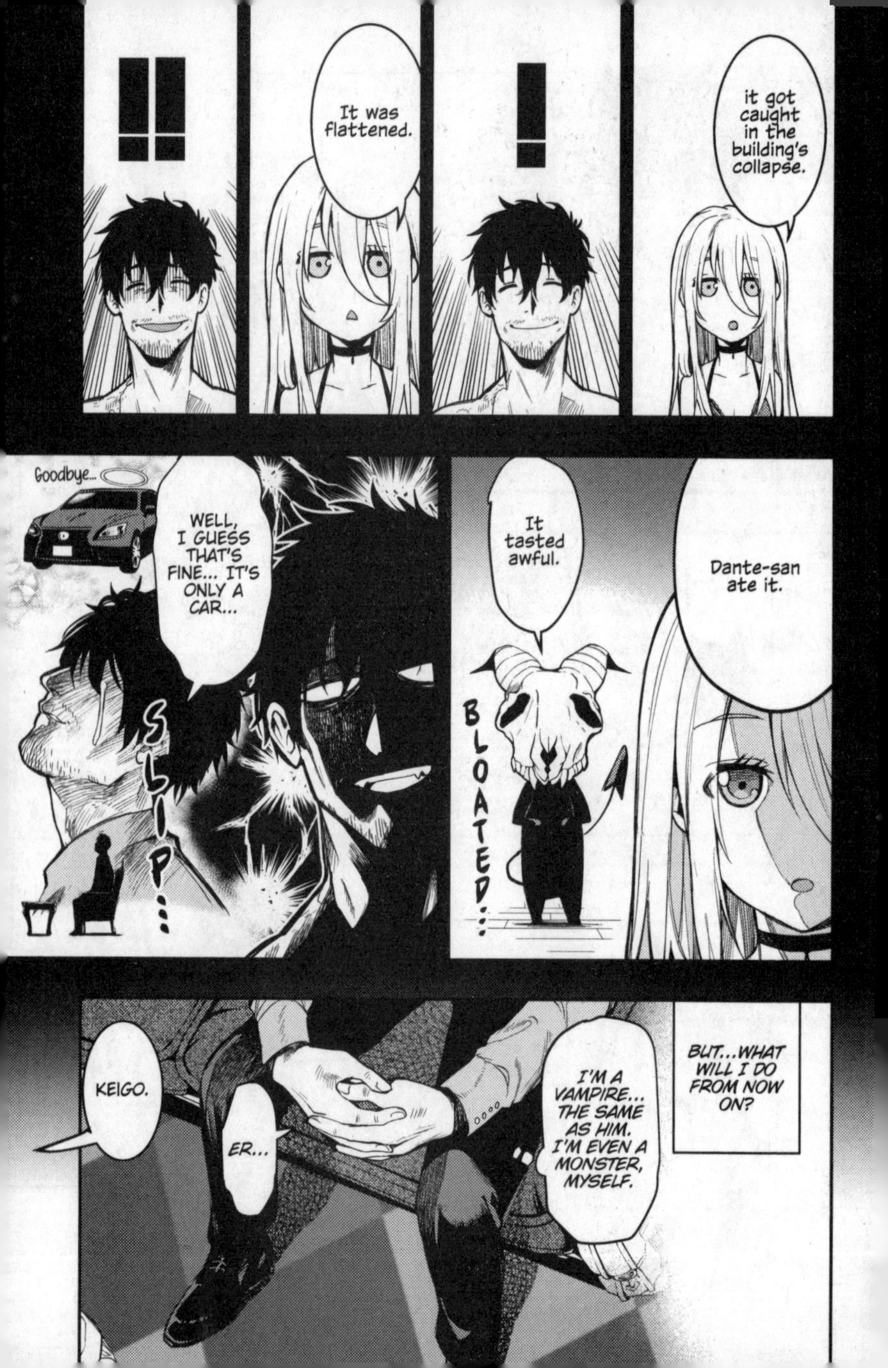
it got caught in the building's collapse.
!
It was flattened.
!!
Dante-san ate it.
It tasted awful.
BLOATED...
WELL, I GUESS THAT'S FINE... IT'S ONLY A CAR...
Goodbye...
SLIP...
BUT...WHAT WILL I DO FROM NOW ON?
I'M A VAMPIRE... THE SAME AS HIM. I'M EVEN A MONSTER, MYSELF.
ER...
KEIGO.

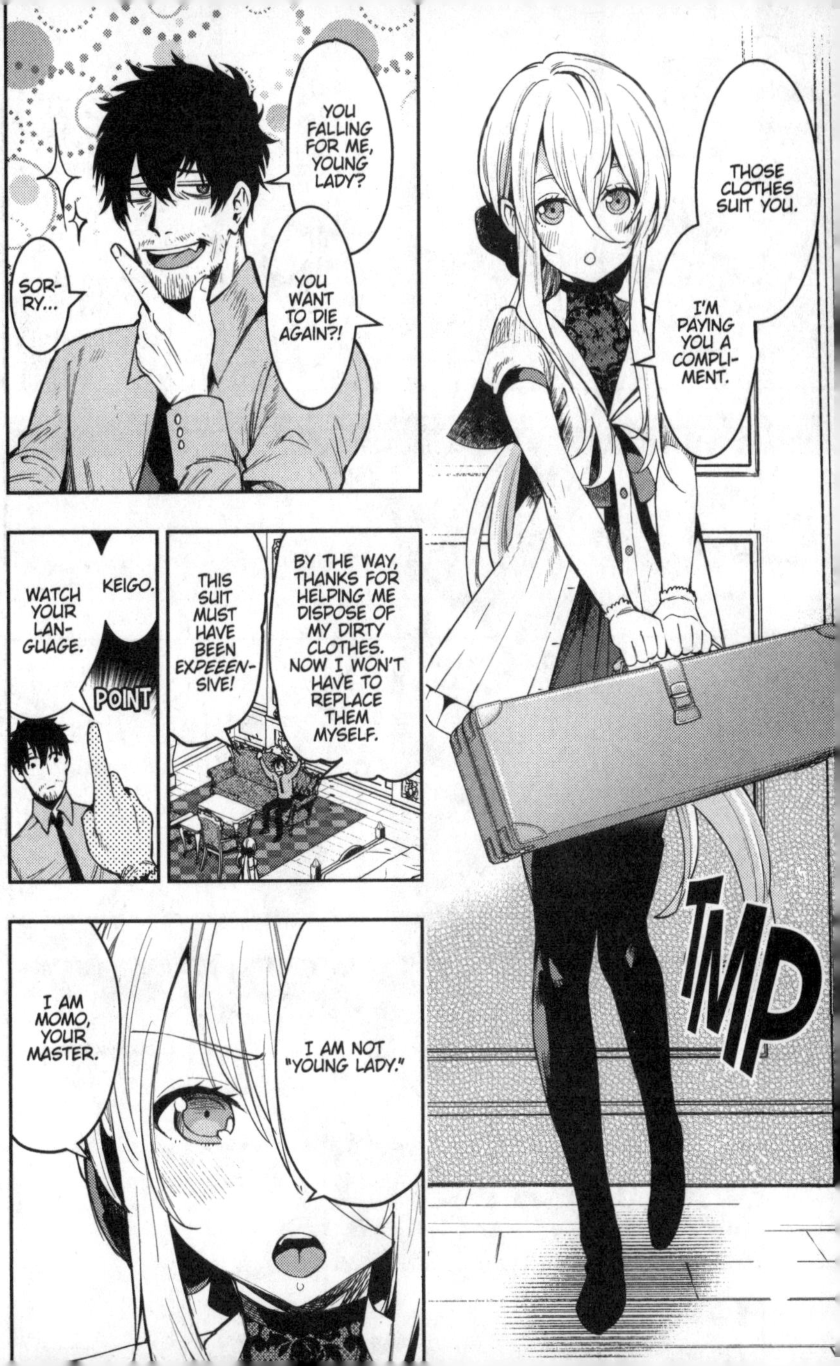
THOSE CLOTHES SUIT YOU.
I'M PAYING YOU A COMPLI-MENT.
TMP
YOU FALLING FOR ME, YOUNG LADY?
YOU WANT TO DIE AGAIN?!
SOR-RY...
BY THE WAY, THANKS FOR HELPING ME DISPOSE OF MY DIRTY CLOTHES. NOW I WON'T HAVE TO REPLACE THEM MYSELF.
THIS SUIT MUST HAVE BEEN EXPEEEN-SIVE!
KEIGO.
WATCH YOUR LAN-GUAGE.
POINT
I AM NOT "YOUNG LADY."
I AM MOMO, YOUR MASTER.

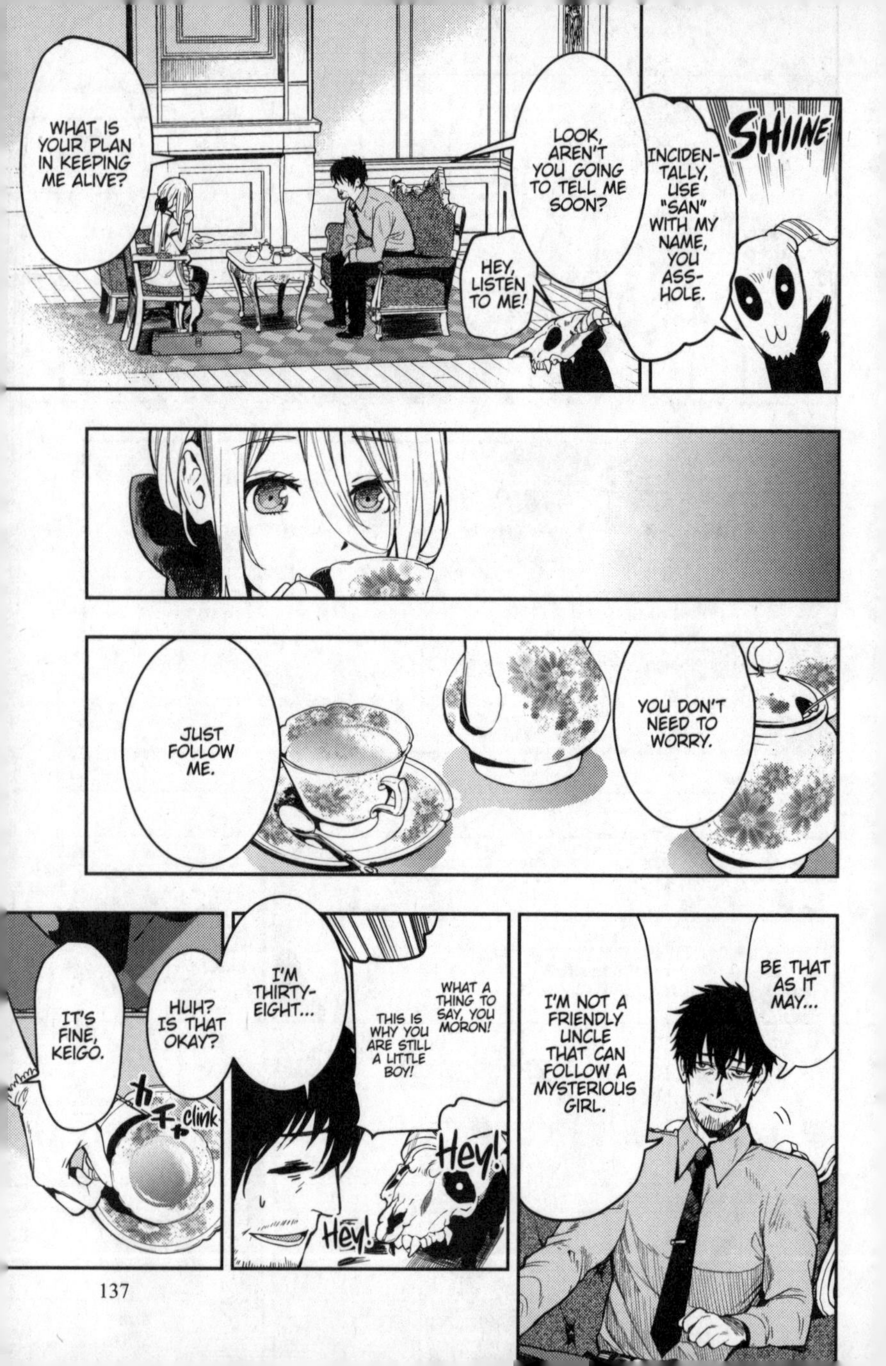
SHIINE
INCIDENTALLY, USE "SAN" WITH MY NAME, YOU ASSHOLE.
LOOK, AREN'T YOU GOING TO TELL ME SOON?
HEY, LISTEN TO ME!
WHAT IS YOUR PLAN IN KEEPING ME ALIVE?
YOU DON'T NEED TO WORRY.
JUST FOLLOW ME.
BE THAT AS IT MAY...
I'M NOT A FRIENDLY UNCLE THAT CAN FOLLOW A MYSTERIOUS GIRL.
I'M THIRTY-EIGHT...
WHAT A THING TO SAY, YOU MORON!
THIS IS WHY YOU ARE STILL A LITTLE BOY!
Hey!
Hey!
HUH? IS THAT OKAY?
IT'S FINE, KEIGO.
clink

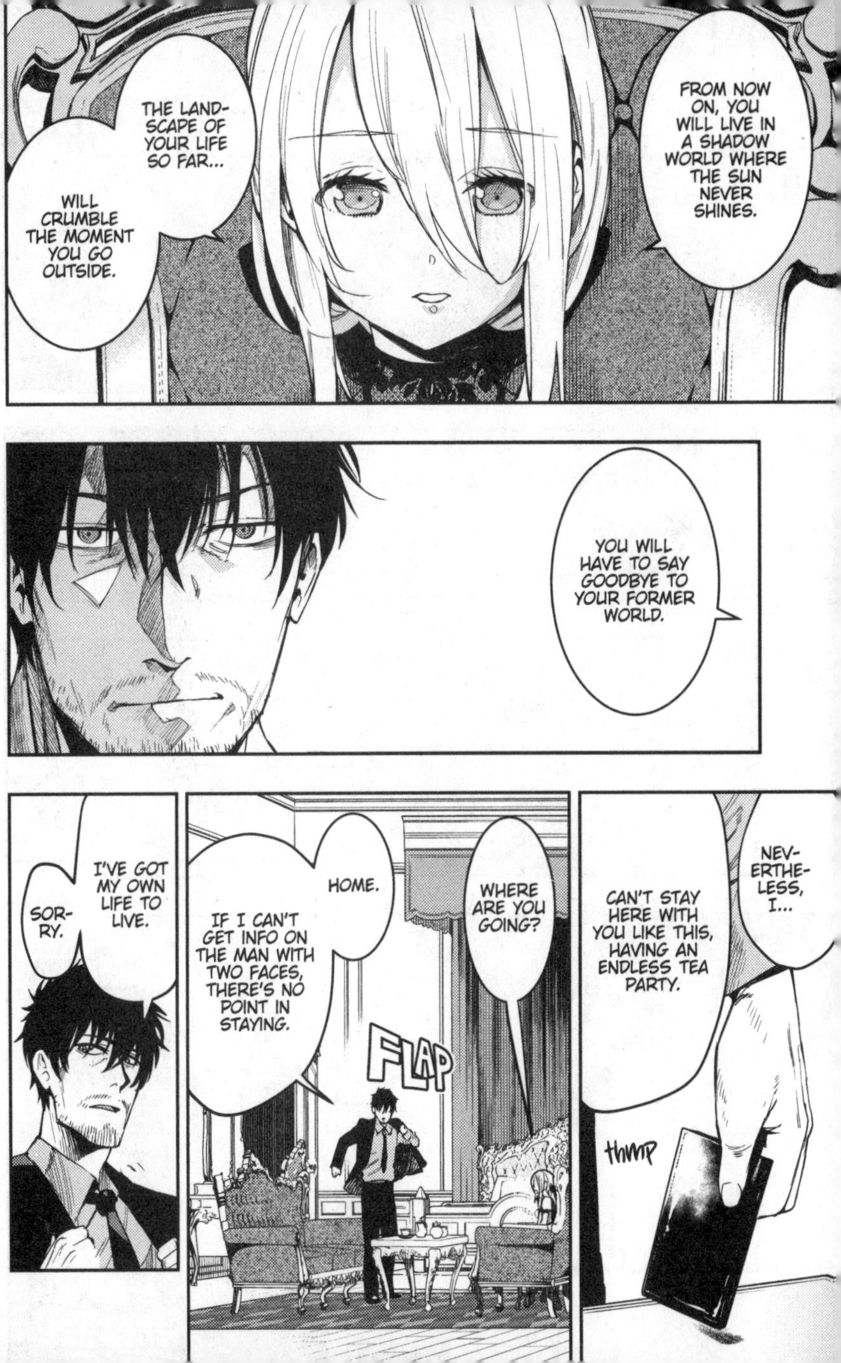
FROM NOW ON, YOU WILL LIVE IN A SHADOW WORLD WHERE THE SUN NEVER SHINES.
THE LANDSCAPE OF YOUR LIFE SO FAR...
WILL CRUMBLE THE MOMENT YOU GO OUTSIDE.
YOU WILL HAVE TO SAY GOODBYE TO YOUR FORMER WORLD.
NEVERTHELESS, I...
CAN'T STAY HERE WITH YOU LIKE THIS, HAVING AN ENDLESS TEA PARTY.
thmp
WHERE ARE YOU GOING?
HOME.
IF I CAN'T GET INFO ON THE MAN WITH TWO FACES, THERE'S NO POINT IN STAYING.
FLAP
I'VE GOT MY OWN LIFE TO LIVE.
SORRY.

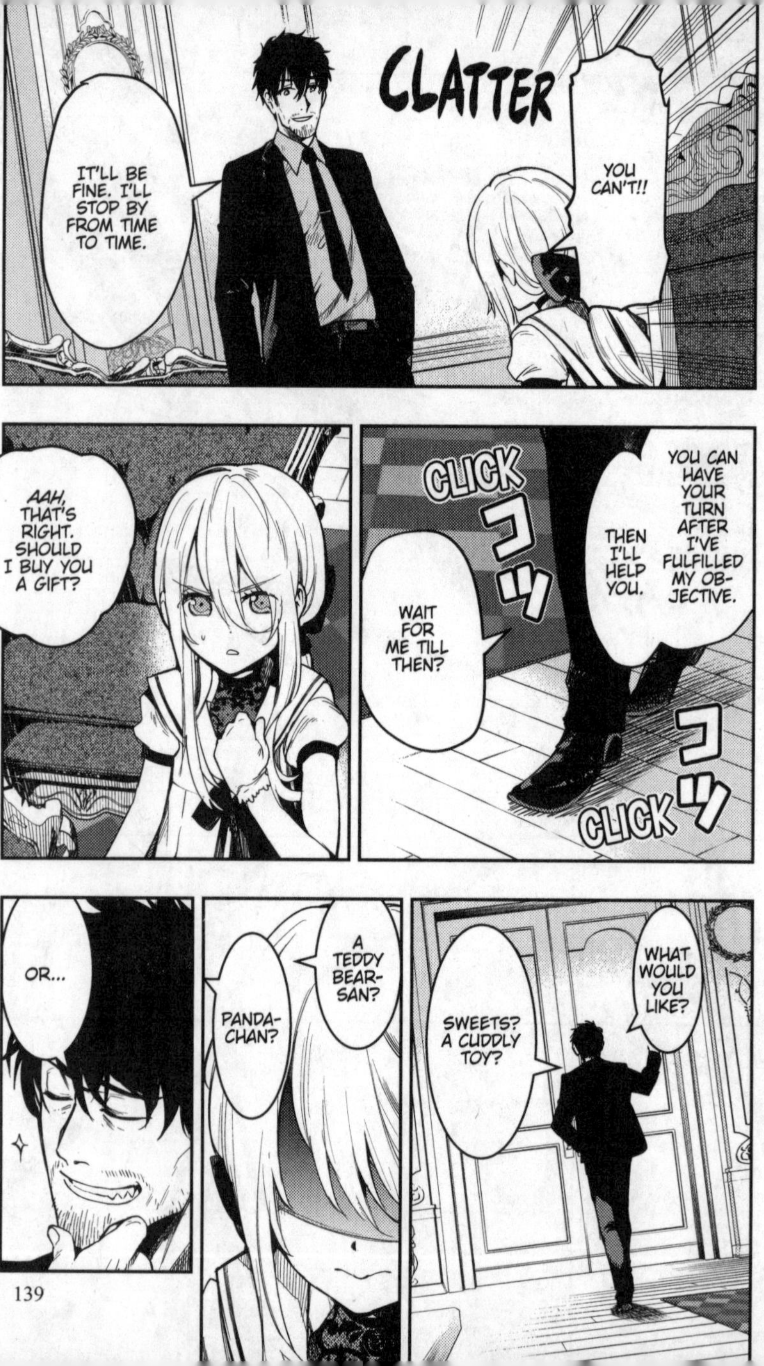
CLATTER
YOU CAN'T!!
IT'LL BE FINE. I'LL STOP BY FROM TIME TO TIME.
YOU CAN HAVE YOUR TURN AFTER I'VE FULFILLED MY OB-JECTIVE.
THEN I'LL HELP YOU.
CLICK
コッ
WAIT FOR ME TILL THEN?
コッ
CLICK
AAH, THAT'S RIGHT. SHOULD I BUY YOU A GIFT?
WHAT WOULD YOU LIKE?
SWEETS? A CUDDLY TOY?
A TEDDY BEAR-SAN?
PANDA-CHAN?
OR...

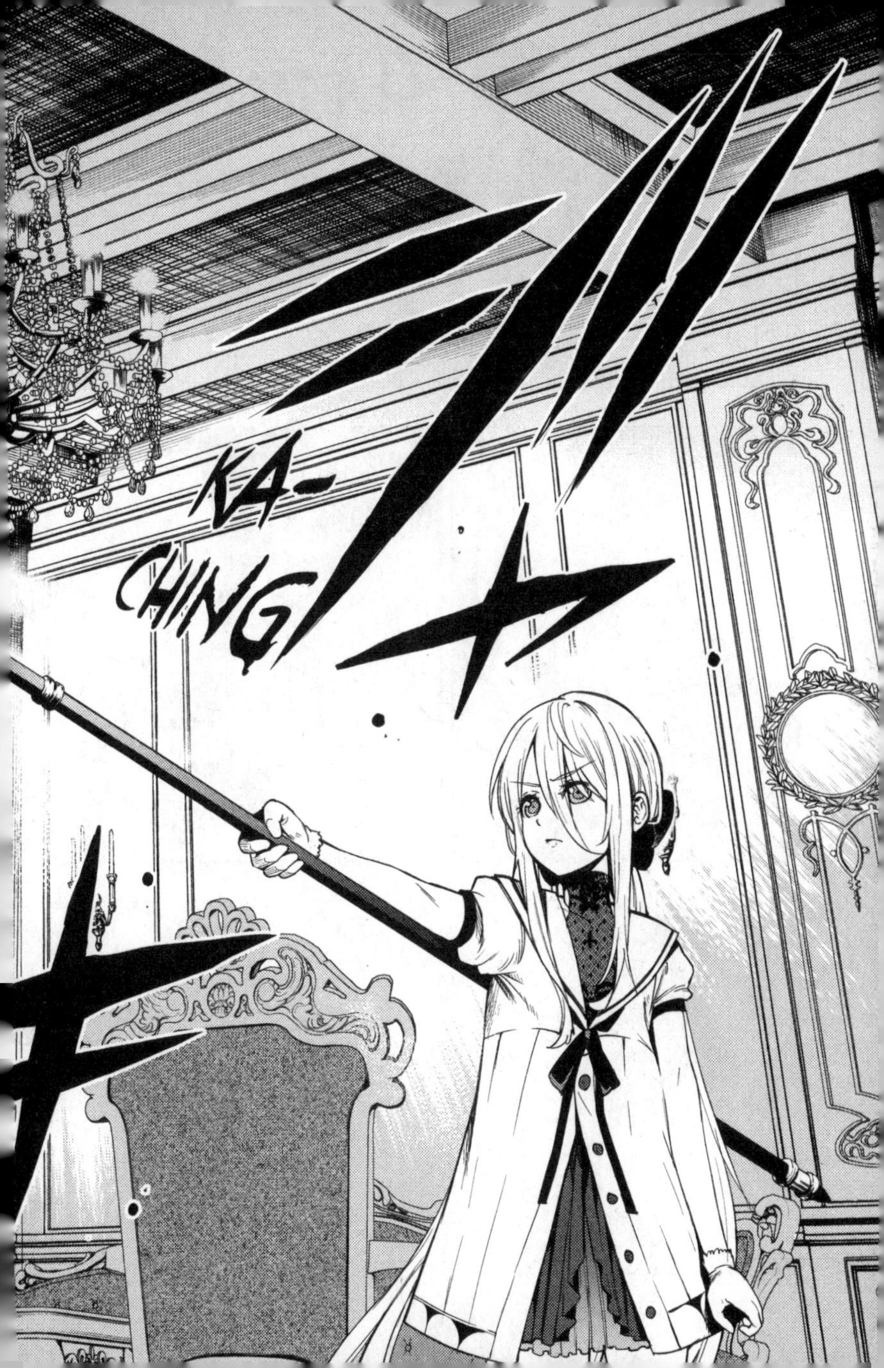
KA-
CHING

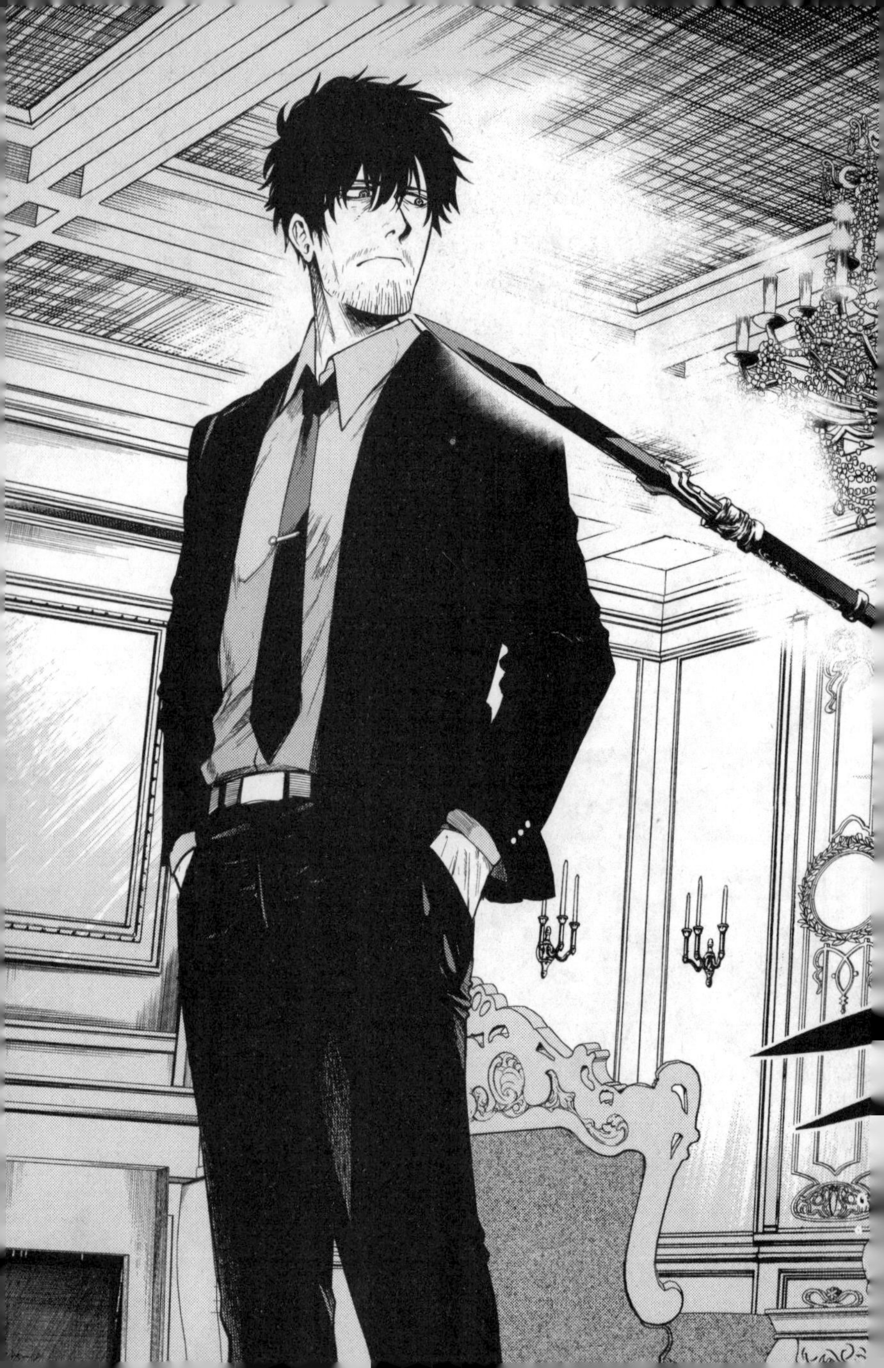

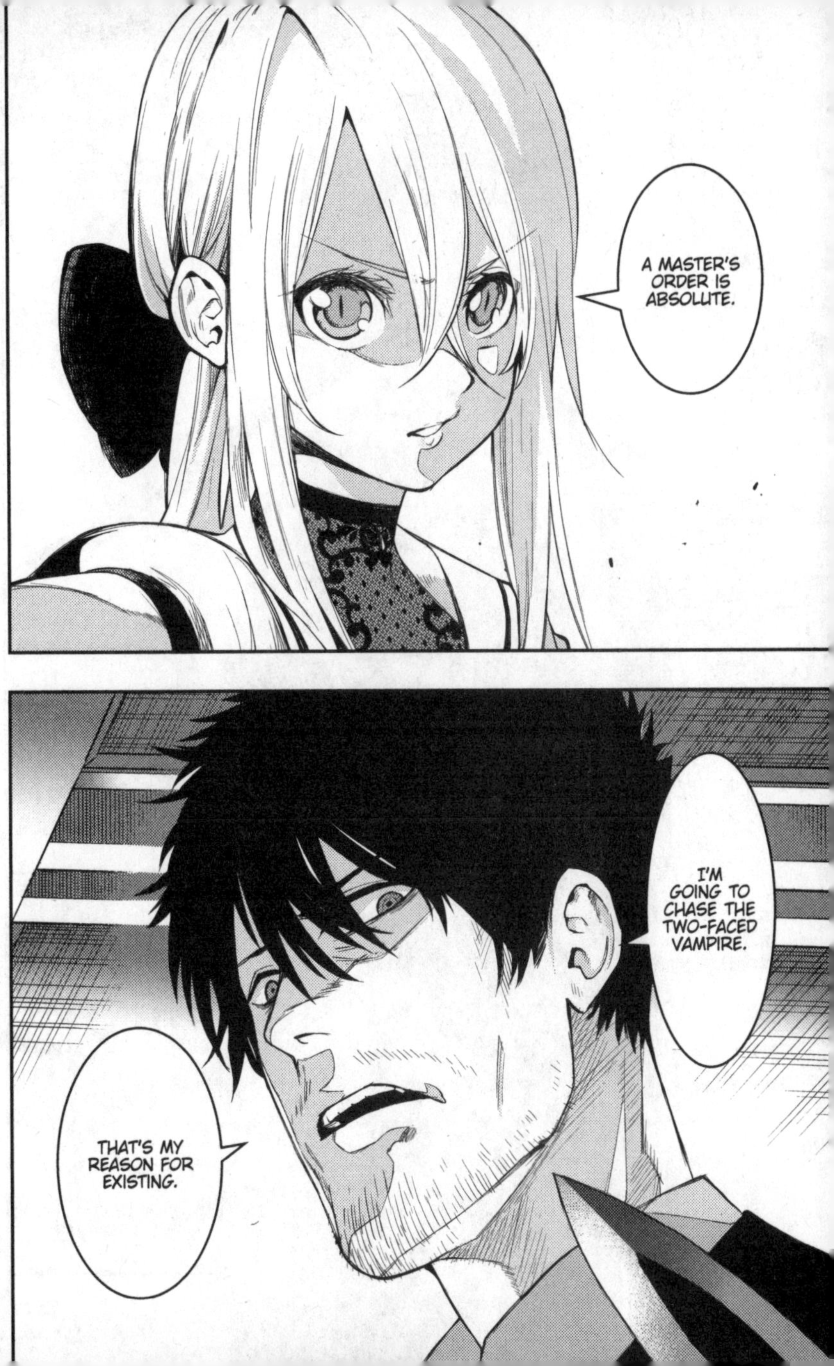
A MASTER'S ORDER IS ABSOLUTE.
I'M GOING TO CHASE THE TWO-FACED VAMPIRE.
THAT'S MY REASON FOR EXISTING.

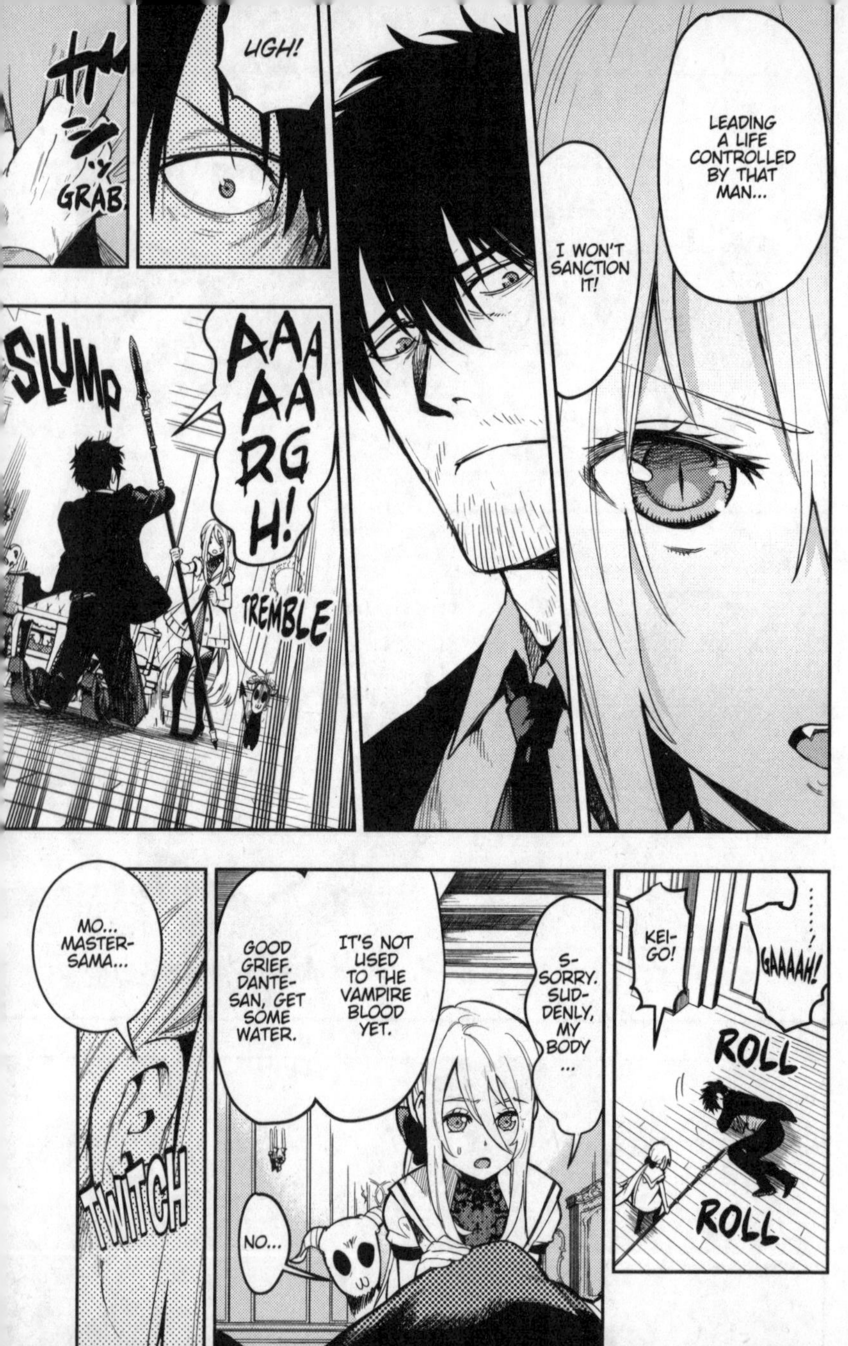

LEADING A LIFE CONTROLLED BY THAT MAN...
I WON'T SANCTION IT!
UGH!
GRAB
AAAAARGH!
SLUMP
TREMBLE
......!
KEI-GO!
GAAAAH!
ROLL
ROLL
S-SORRY. SUDDENLY, MY BODY ...
IT'S NOT USED TO THE VAMPIRE BLOOD YET.
GOOD GRIEF. DANTE-SAN, GET SOME WATER.
NO...
MO... MASTER-SAMA...
TWITCH

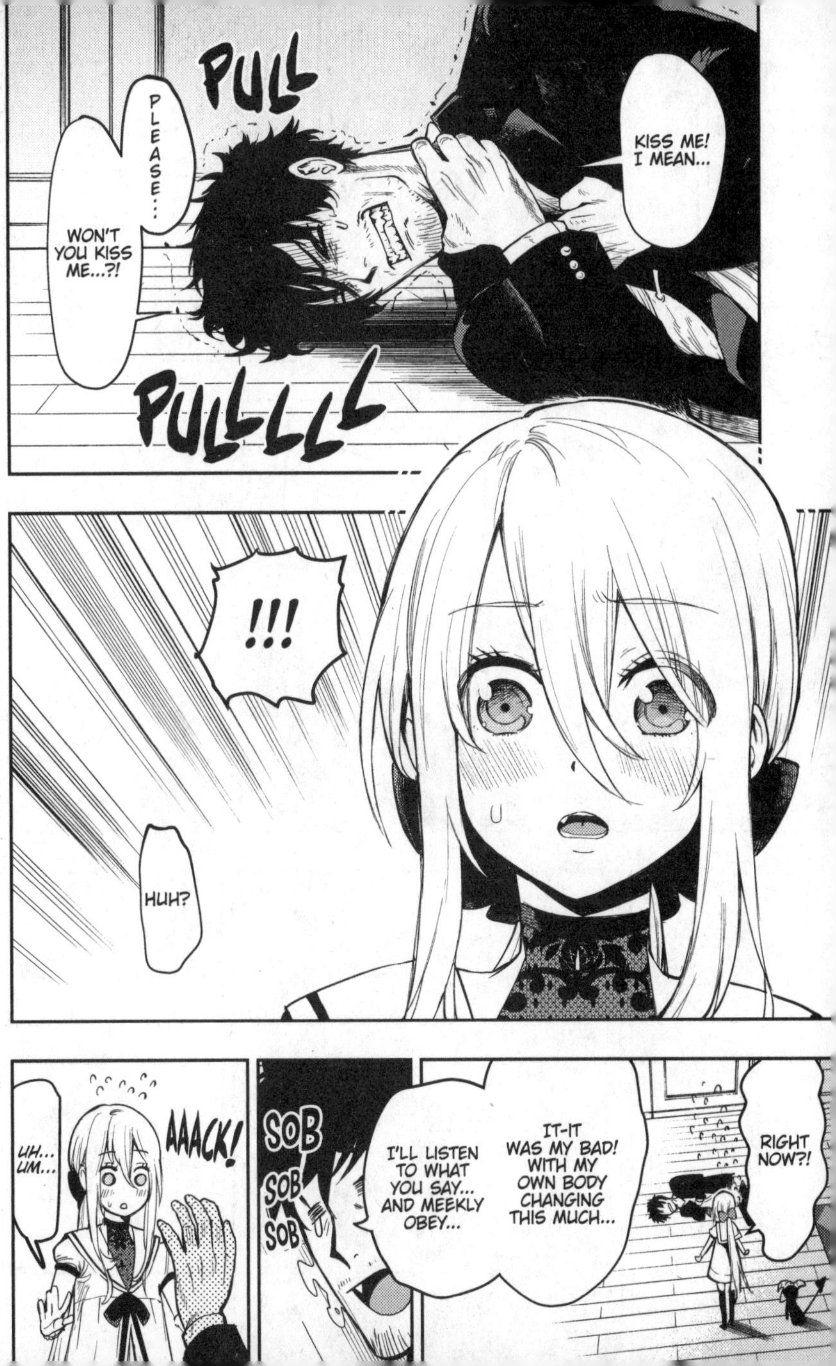
KISS ME! I MEAN...
PULL
PLEASE...
WON'T YOU KISS ME...?!
PULLLLL
!!!
HUH?
RIGHT NOW?!
IT-IT WAS MY BAD! WITH MY OWN BODY CHANGING THIS MUCH...
I'LL LISTEN TO WHAT YOU SAY... AND MEEKLY OBEY...
SOB SOB SOB
AAACK!
UH... UM...

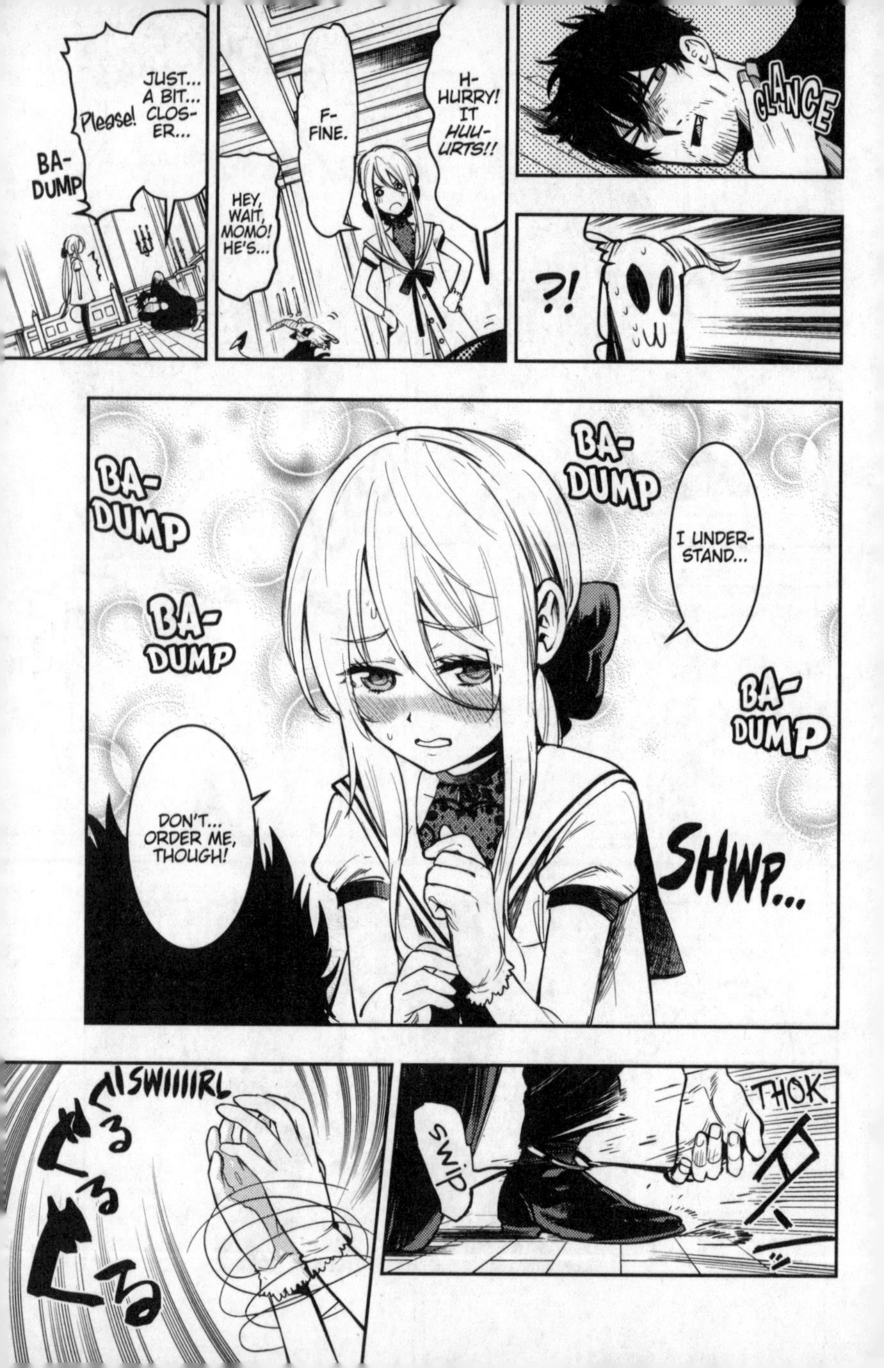
GLANCE
?!
H-HURRY! IT HUUURTS!!
F-FINE.
HEY, WAIT, MOMO! HE'S...
JUST... A BIT... CLOSER...
Please!
BA-DUMP
BA-DUMP
I UNDERSTAND...
BA-DUMP
SHWP...
BA-DUMP
BA-DUMP
DON'T... ORDER ME, THOUGH!
THOK
SWIP
SWIIIIRL

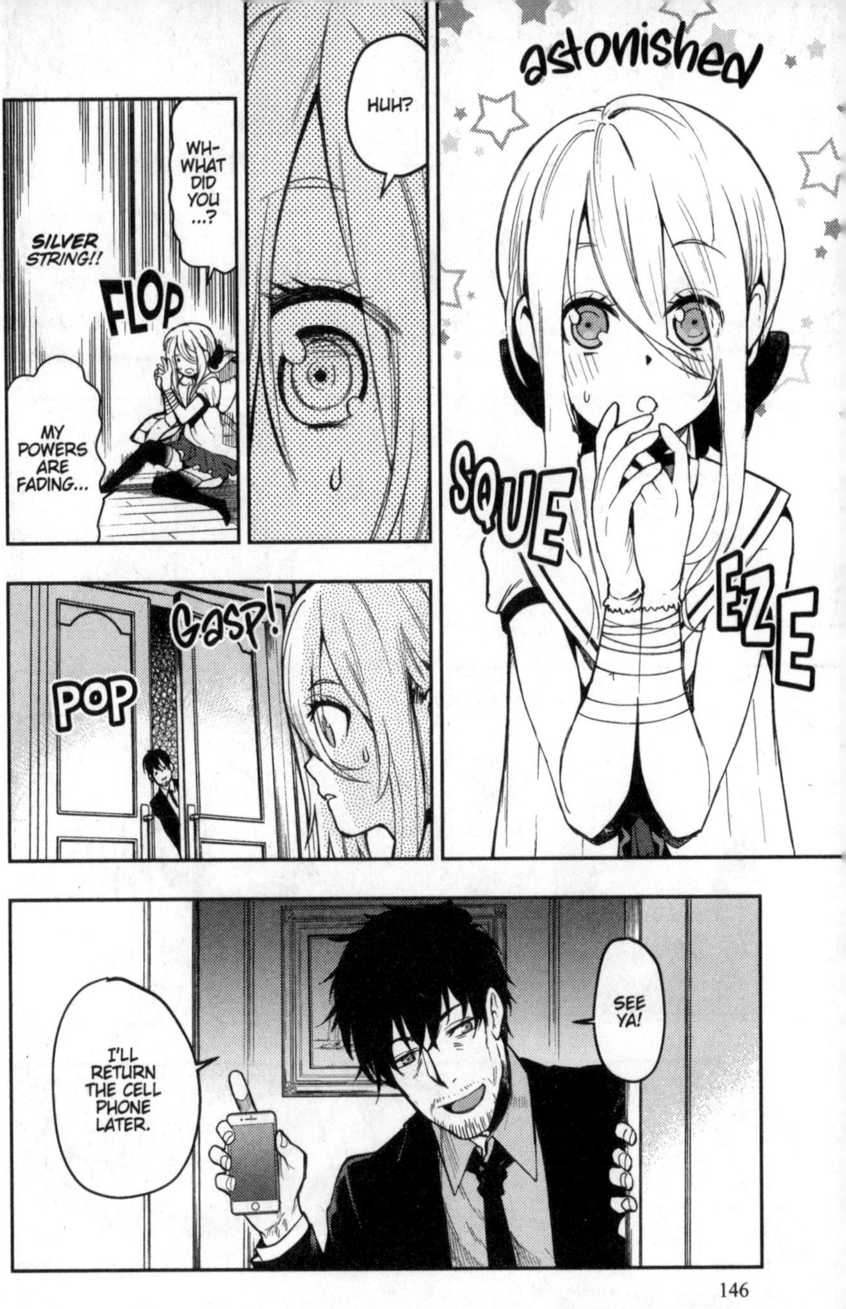
astonished
SQUE EZE
HUH?
WH-WHAT DID YOU ...?
SILVER STRING!!
FLOP
MY POWERS ARE FADING...
Gasp!
POP
SEE YA!
I'LL RETURN THE CELL PHONE LATER.

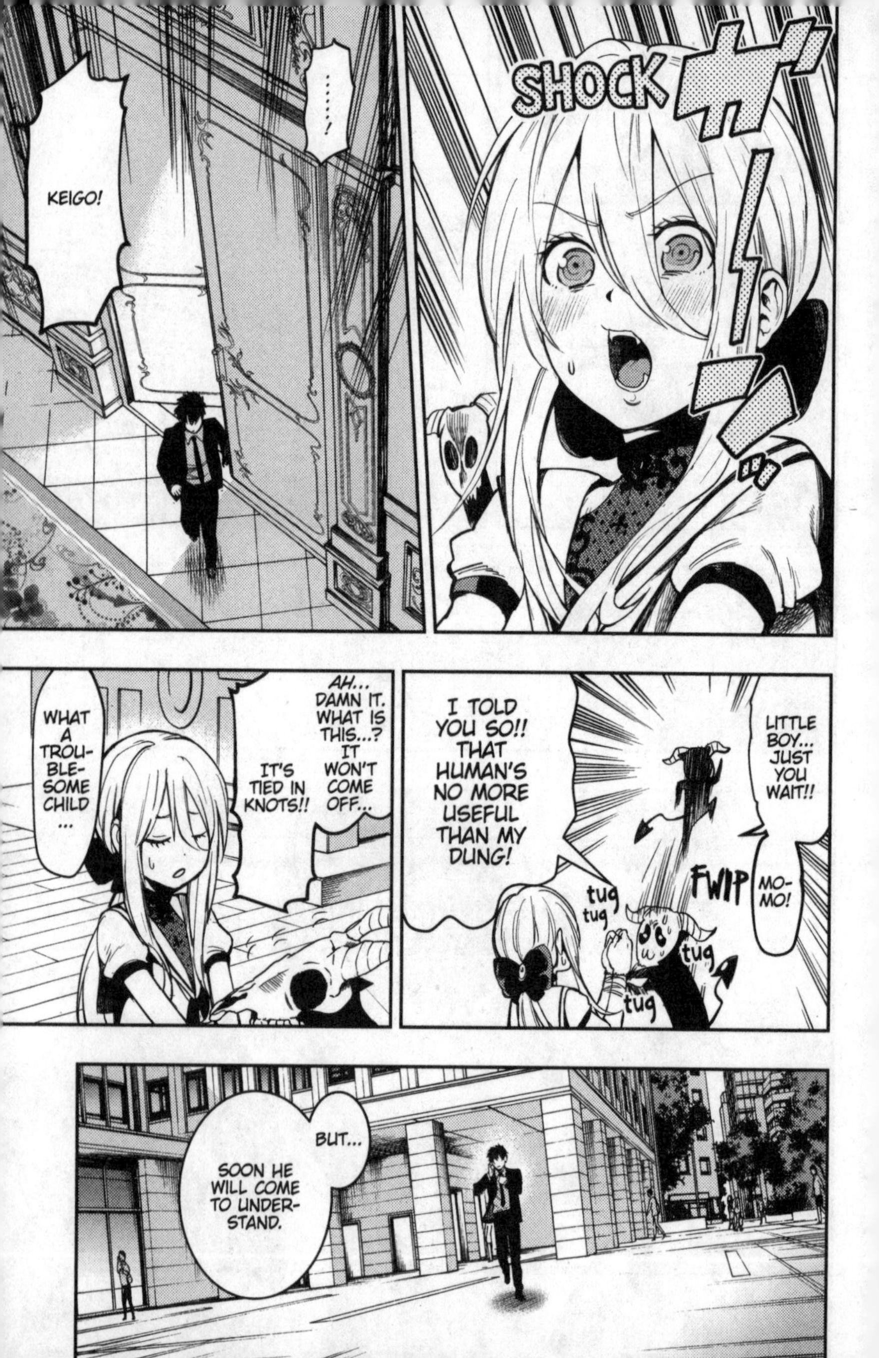
SHOCK
!!
......!
KEIGO!
LITTLE BOY... JUST YOU WAIT!!
I TOLD YOU SO!! THAT HUMAN'S NO MORE USEFUL THAN MY DUNG!
MO-MO!
FWIP
tug tug
tug
tug
AH... DAMN IT. WHAT IS THIS...? IT WON'T COME OFF...
IT'S TIED IN KNOTS!!
WHAT A TROUBLE-SOME CHILD...
BUT...
SOON HE WILL COME TO UNDER-STAND.

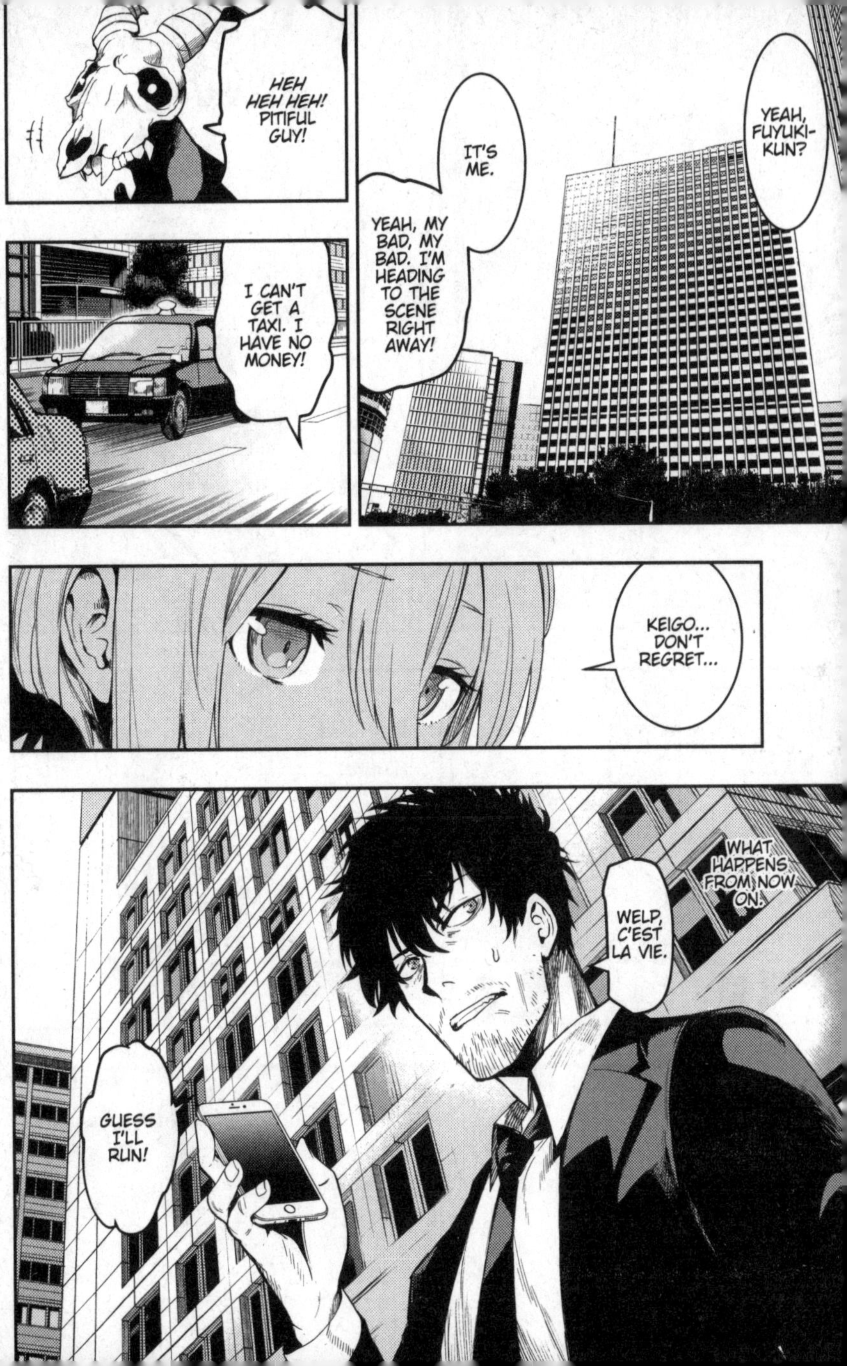
YEAH, FUYUKI-KUN?
IT'S ME.
YEAH, MY BAD, MY BAD. I'M HEADING TO THE SCENE RIGHT AWAY!
HEH HEH HEH! PITIFUL GUY!
I CAN'T GET A TAXI. I HAVE NO MONEY!
KEIGO... DON'T REGRET...
WHAT HAPPENS FROM NOW ON.
WELP, C'EST LA VIE.
GUESS I'LL RUN!

MOMO

the blood taker

MOMO

the blood taker

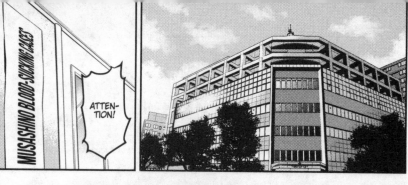

ATTENTION!

MUSASHINO BLOOD-SUCKING CASES

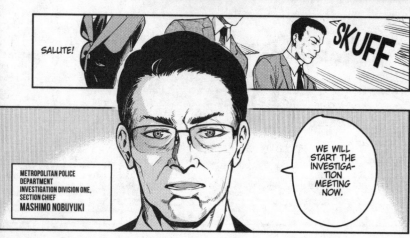

SALUTE!

SKUFF

WE WILL START THE INVESTIGATION MEETING NOW.

METROPOLITAN POLICE DEPARTMENT
INVESTIGATION DIVISION ONE,
SECTION CHIEF
MASHIMO NOBUYUKI

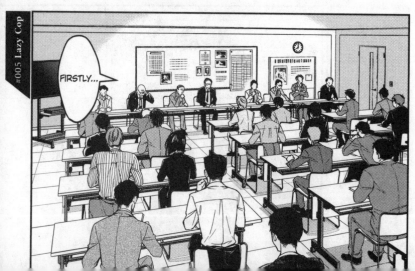

FIRSTLY...

#005 Lazy Cop

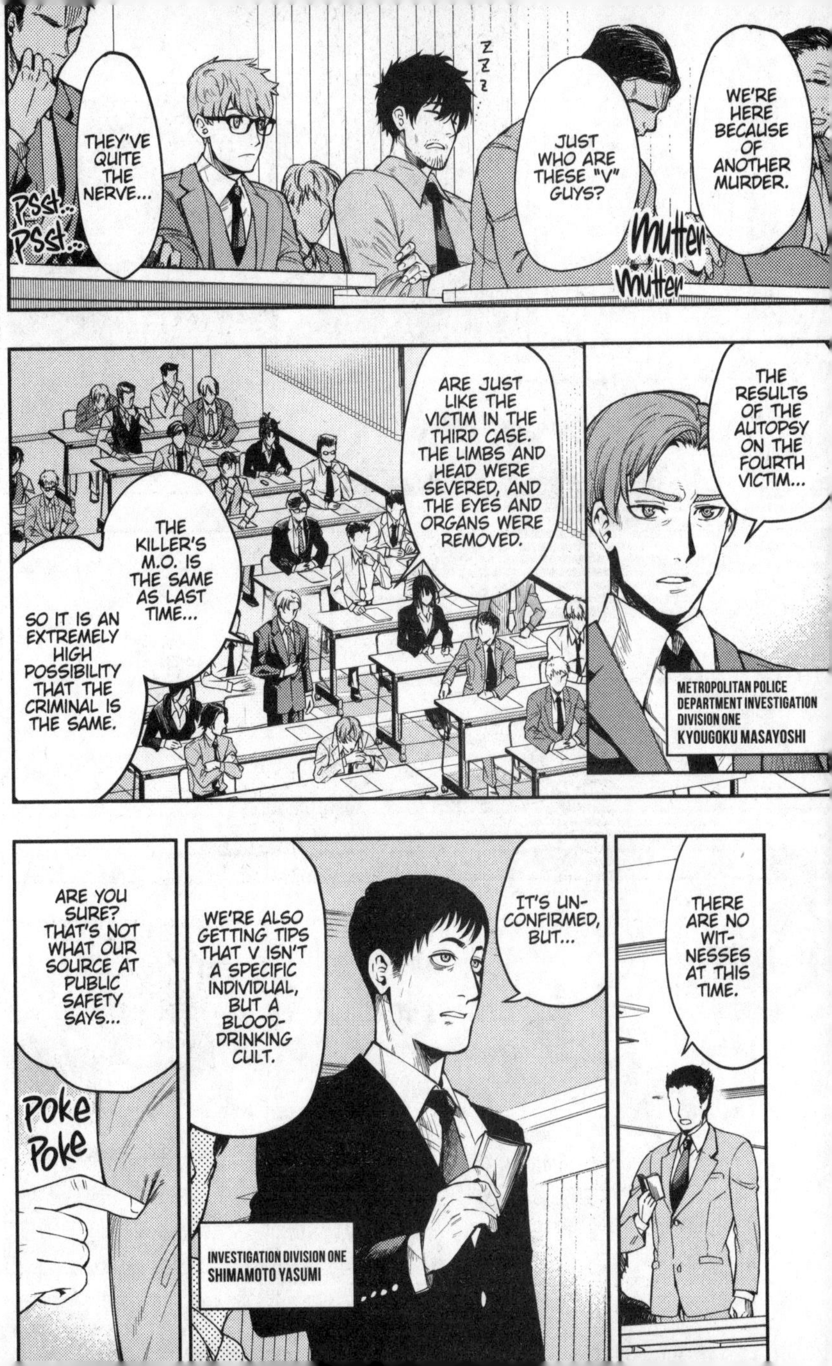
WE'RE HERE BECAUSE OF ANOTHER MURDER.
Mutter mutter
JUST WHO ARE THESE "V" GUYS?
Z Z Z
THEY'VE QUITE THE NERVE...
Psst.. Psst..
THE RESULTS OF THE AUTOPSY ON THE FOURTH VICTIM...
METROPOLITAN POLICE DEPARTMENT INVESTIGATION DIVISION ONE KYOUGOKU MASAYOSHI
ARE JUST LIKE THE VICTIM IN THE THIRD CASE. THE LIMBS AND HEAD WERE SEVERED, AND THE EYES AND ORGANS WERE REMOVED.
THE KILLER'S M.O. IS THE SAME AS LAST TIME...
SO IT IS AN EXTREMELY HIGH POSSIBILITY THAT THE CRIMINAL IS THE SAME.
THERE ARE NO WIT-NESSES AT THIS TIME.
IT'S UN-CONFIRMED, BUT...
WE'RE ALSO GETTING TIPS THAT V ISN'T A SPECIFIC INDIVIDUAL, BUT A BLOOD-DRINKING CULT.
INVESTIGATION DIVISION ONE SHIMAMOTO YASUMI
....
ARE YOU SURE? THAT'S NOT WHAT OUR SOURCE AT PUBLIC SAFETY SAYS...
Poke Poke

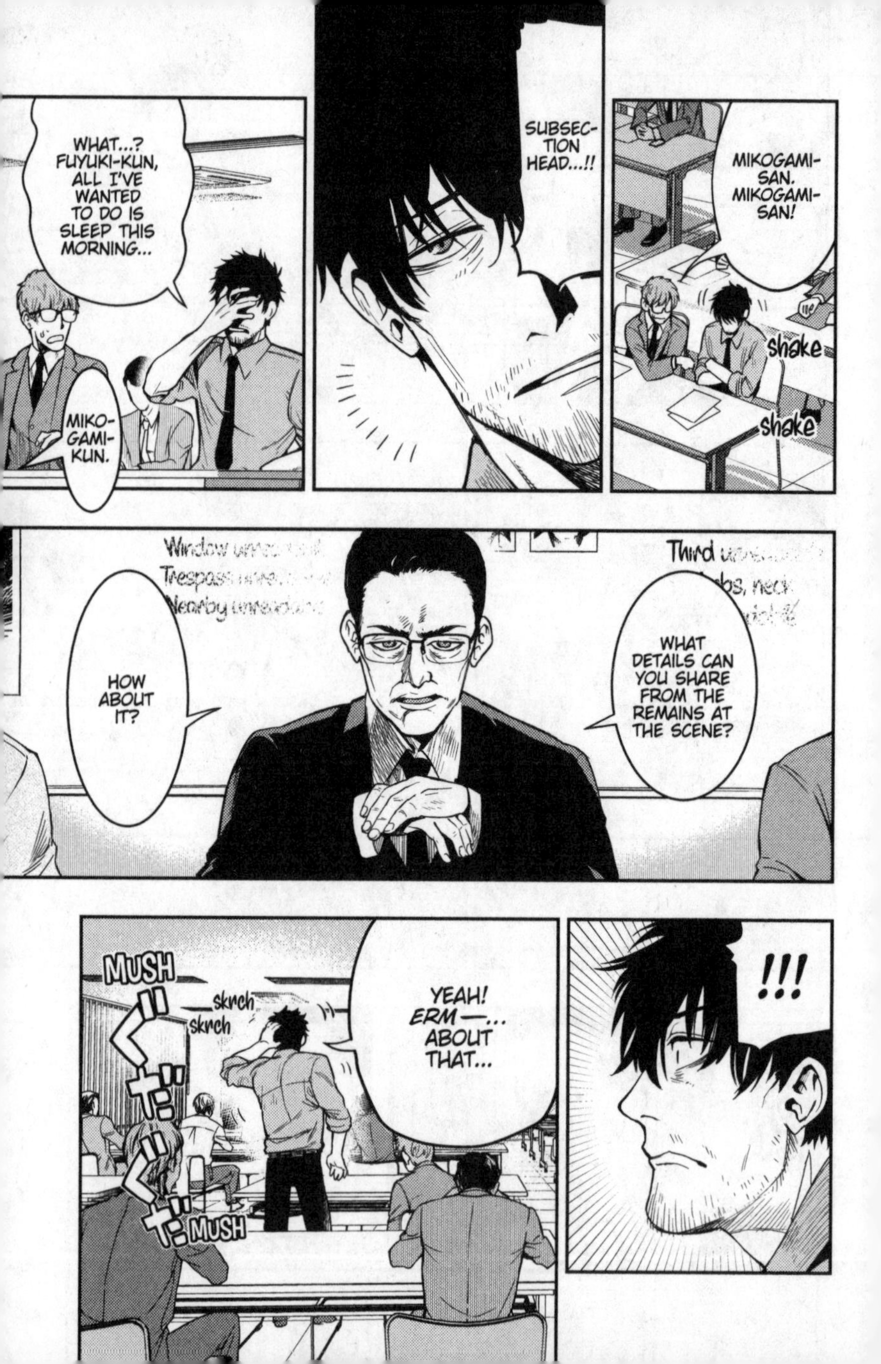
MIKOGAMI-SAN. MIKOGAMI-SAN!
shake
shake
SUBSECTION HEAD...!!
WHAT...? FUYUKI-KUN, ALL I'VE WANTED TO DO IS SLEEP THIS MORNING...
MIKOGAMI-KUN.
WHAT DETAILS CAN YOU SHARE FROM THE REMAINS AT THE SCENE?
HOW ABOUT IT?
!!!
YEAH! ERM—... ABOUT THAT...
skrch
skrch
MUSH
MUSH

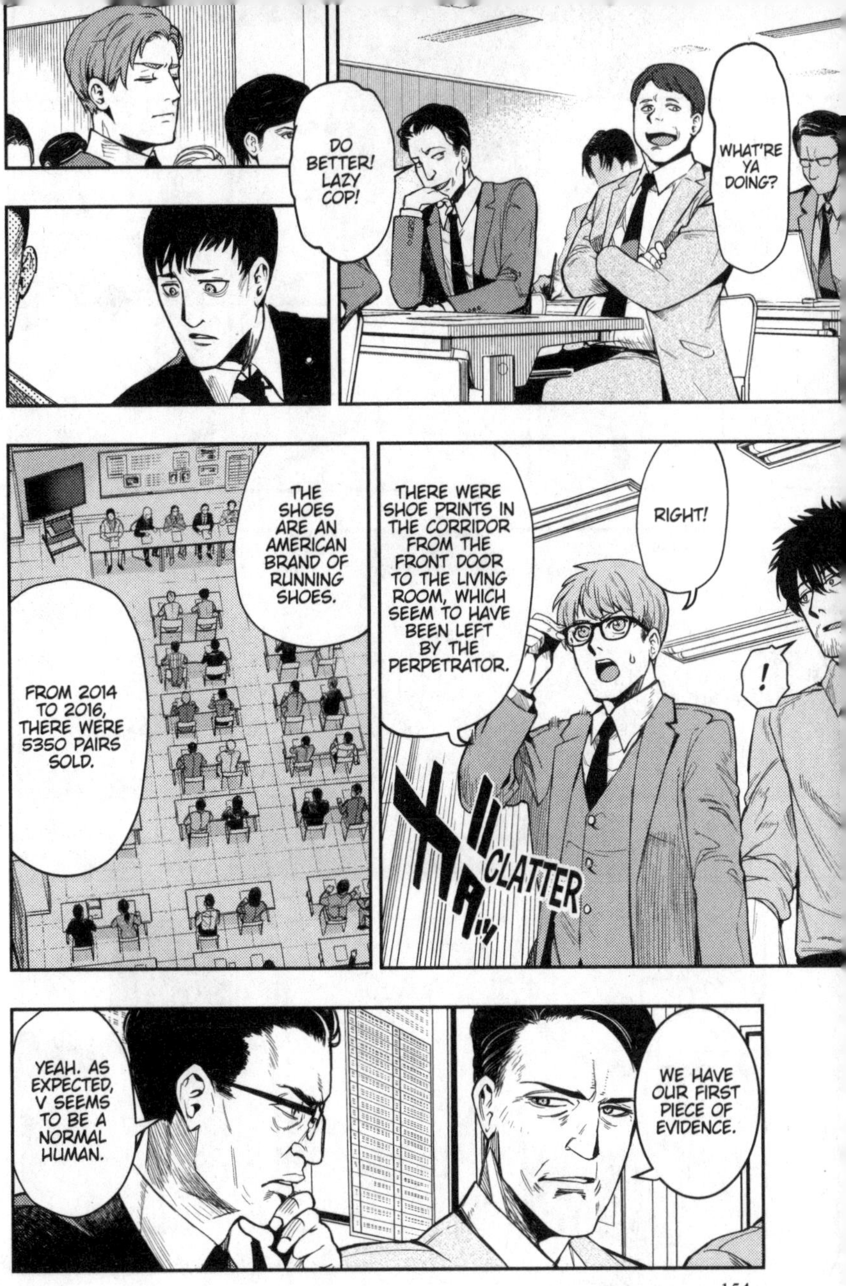
WHAT'RE YA DOING?
DO BETTER! LAZY COP!
RIGHT!
!
THERE WERE SHOE PRINTS IN THE CORRIDOR FROM THE FRONT DOOR TO THE LIVING ROOM, WHICH SEEM TO HAVE BEEN LEFT BY THE PERPETRATOR.
CLATTER
THE SHOES ARE AN AMERICAN BRAND OF RUNNING SHOES.
FROM 2014 TO 2016, THERE WERE 5350 PAIRS SOLD.
WE HAVE OUR FIRST PIECE OF EVIDENCE.
YEAH. AS EXPECTED, V SEEMS TO BE A NORMAL HUMAN.

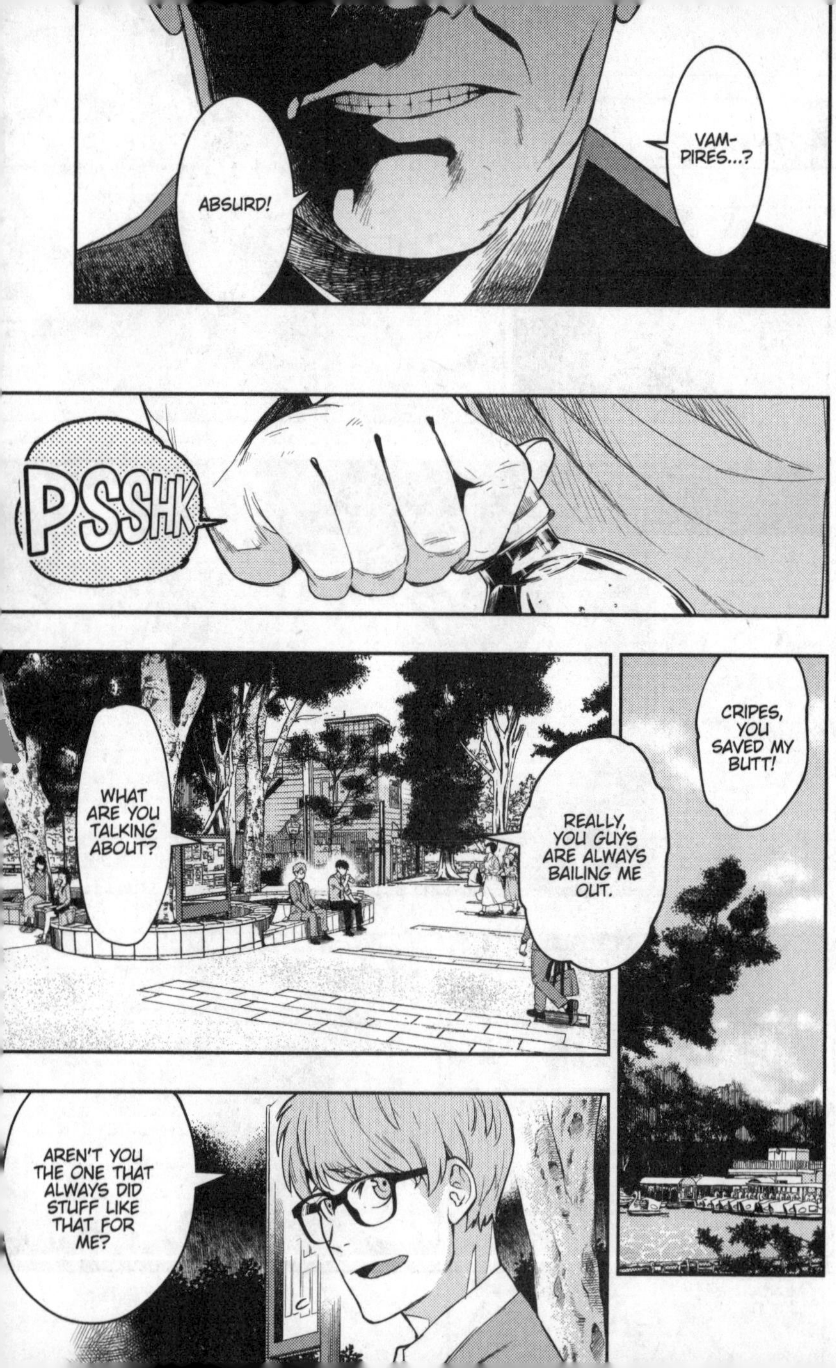
VAM-PIRES...?
ABSURD!
PSSHK
CRIPES, YOU SAVED MY BUTT!
REALLY, YOU GUYS ARE ALWAYS BAILING ME OUT.
WHAT ARE YOU TALKING ABOUT?
AREN'T YOU THE ONE THAT ALWAYS DID STUFF LIKE THAT FOR ME?

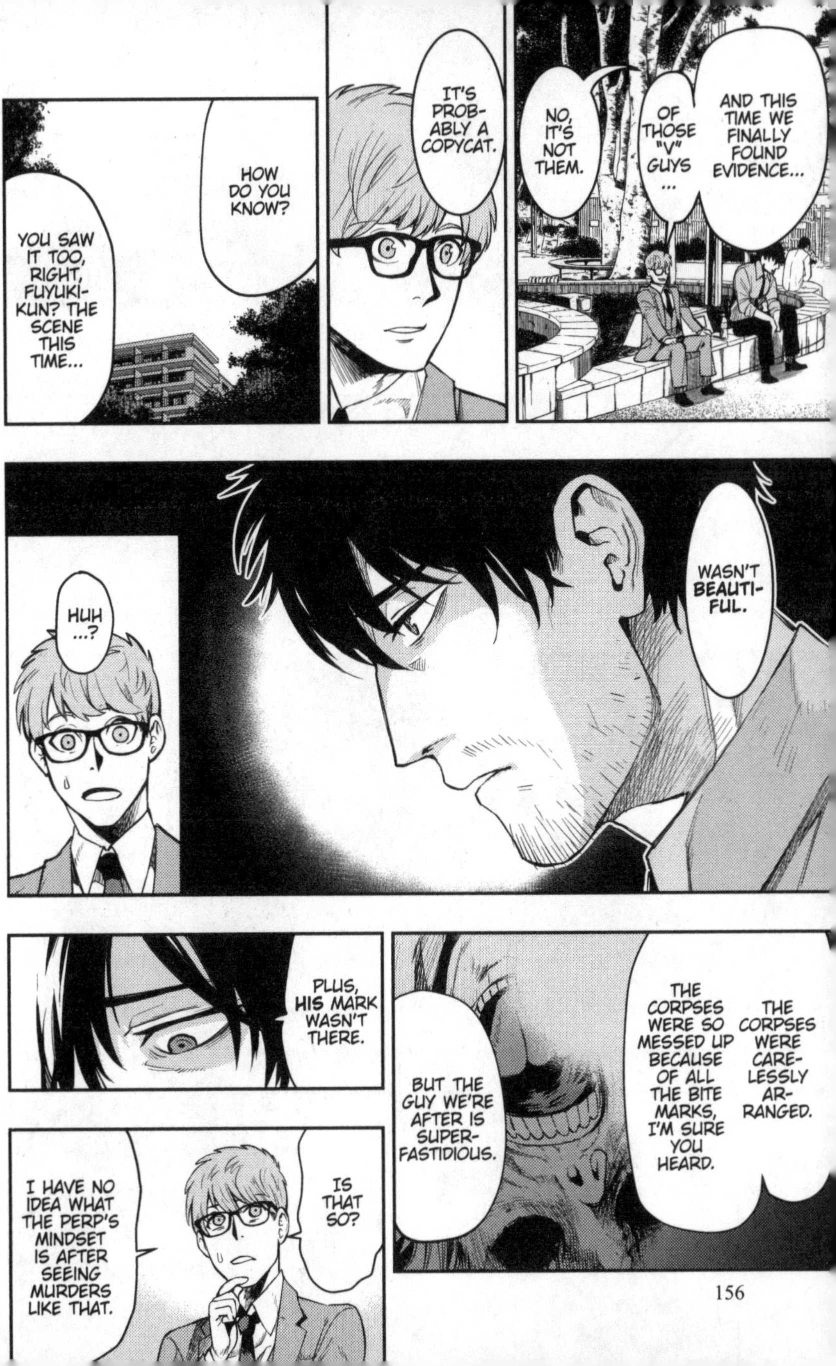
AND THIS TIME WE FINALLY FOUND EVIDENCE...
OF THOSE "V" GUYS ...
NO, IT'S NOT THEM.
IT'S PROBABLY A COPYCAT.
HOW DO YOU KNOW?
YOU SAW IT TOO, RIGHT, FUYUKI-KUN? THE SCENE THIS TIME...
WASN'T BEAUTIFUL.
HUH ...?
THE CORPSES WERE CARELESSLY ARRANGED.
THE CORPSES WERE SO MESSED UP BECAUSE OF ALL THE BITE MARKS, I'M SURE YOU HEARD.
BUT THE GUY WE'RE AFTER IS SUPER-FASTIDIOUS.
PLUS, HIS MARK WASN'T THERE.
IS THAT SO?
I HAVE NO IDEA WHAT THE PERP'S MINDSET IS AFTER SEEING MURDERS LIKE THAT.

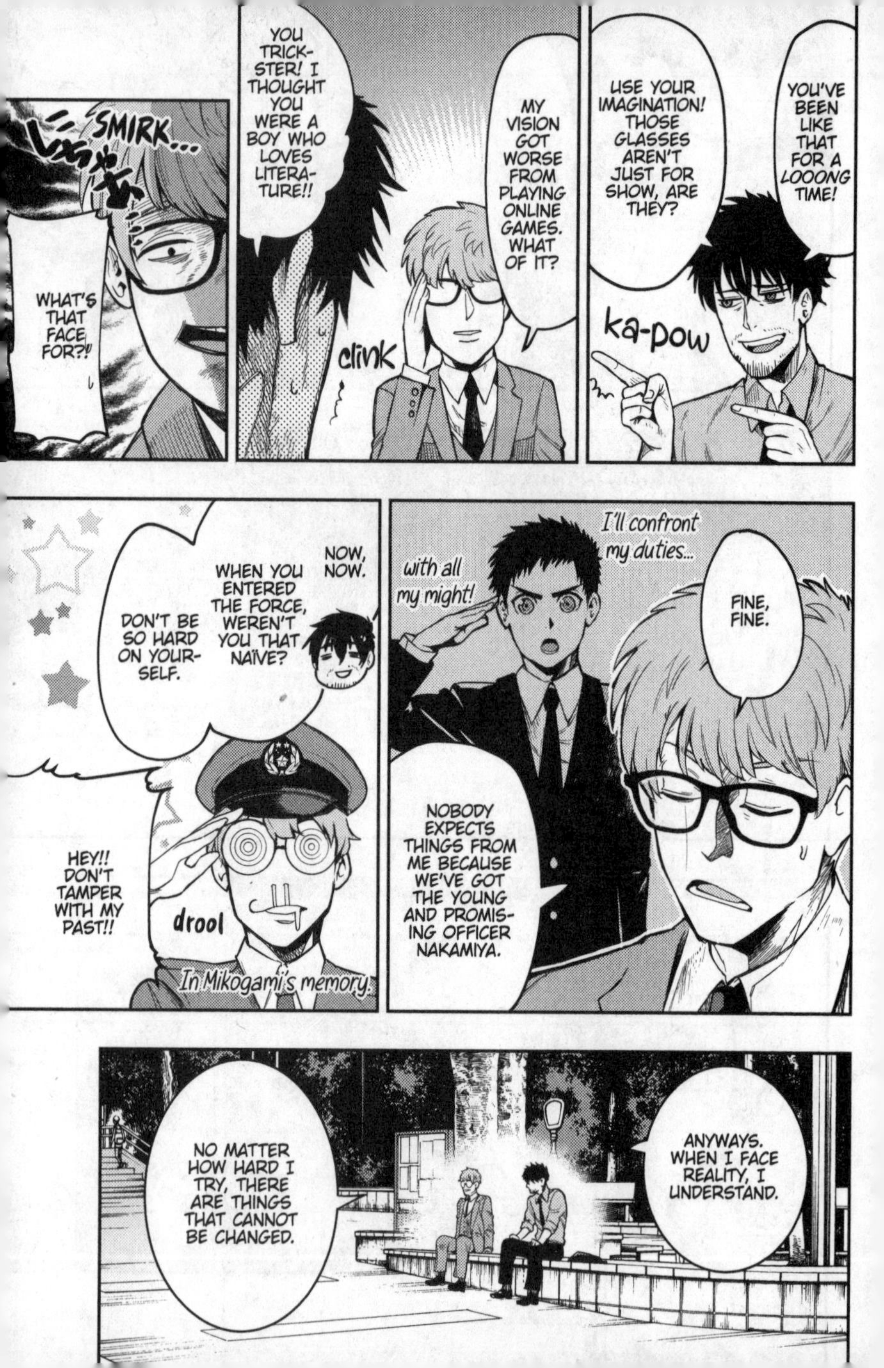
YOU'VE BEEN LIKE THAT FOR A LOOONG TIME!
USE YOUR IMAGINATION! THOSE GLASSES AREN'T JUST FOR SHOW, ARE THEY?
ka-pow
MY VISION GOT WORSE FROM PLAYING ONLINE GAMES. WHAT OF IT?
clink
YOU TRICKSTER! I THOUGHT YOU WERE A BOY WHO LOVES LITERATURE!!
SMIRK...
WHAT'S THAT FACE FOR?!
FINE, FINE.
I'll confront my duties...
with all my might!
NOBODY EXPECTS THINGS FROM ME BECAUSE WE'VE GOT THE YOUNG AND PROMISING OFFICER NAKAMIYA.
NOW, NOW.
WHEN YOU ENTERED THE FORCE, WEREN'T YOU THAT NAÏVE?
DON'T BE SO HARD ON YOURSELF.
HEY!! DON'T TAMPER WITH MY PAST!!
drool
In Mikogami's memory.
ANYWAYS. WHEN I FACE REALITY, I UNDERSTAND.
NO MATTER HOW HARD I TRY, THERE ARE THINGS THAT CANNOT BE CHANGED.

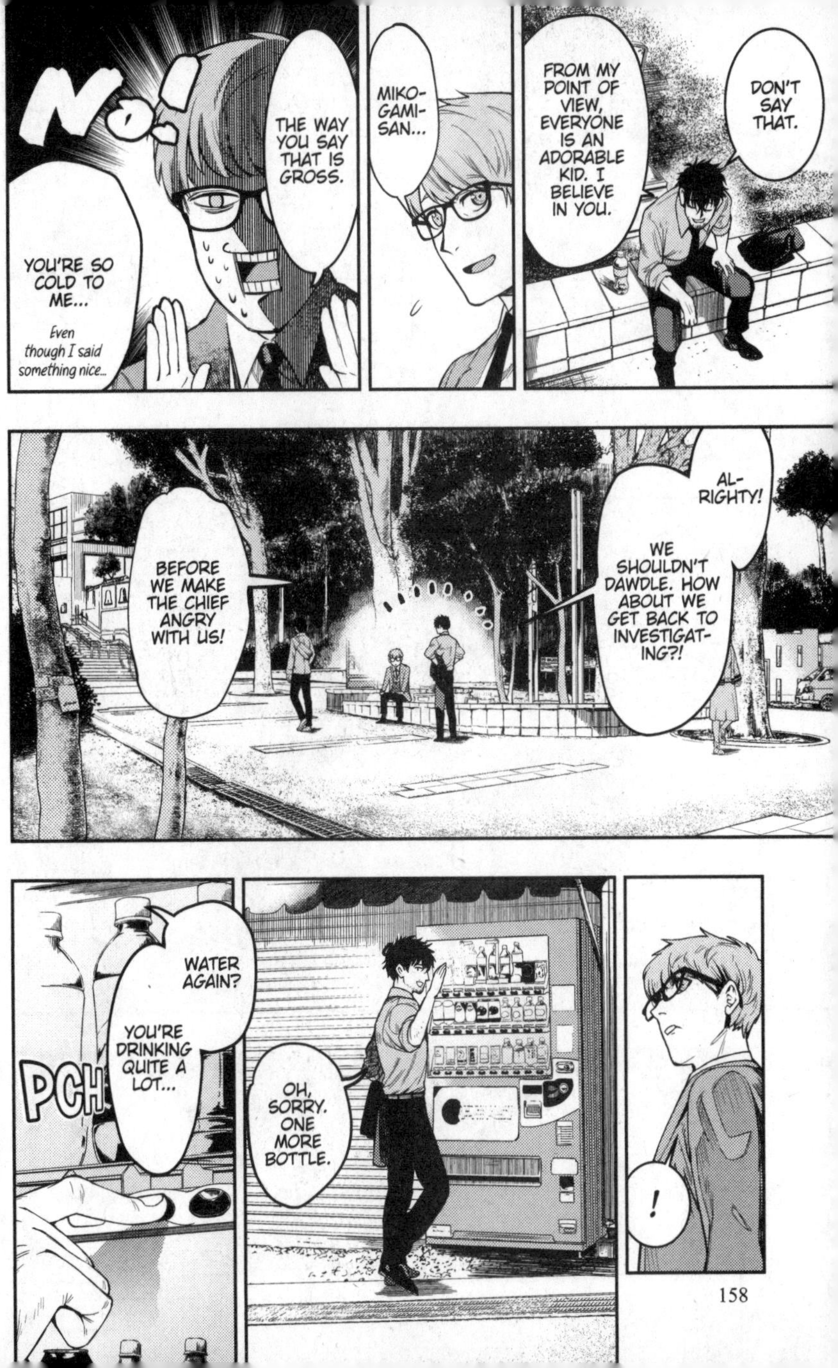
DON'T SAY THAT.
FROM MY POINT OF VIEW, EVERYONE IS AN ADORABLE KID. I BELIEVE IN YOU.
MIKO-GAMI-SAN...
THE WAY YOU SAY THAT IS GROSS.
NO!
YOU'RE SO COLD TO ME...
Even though I said something nice...
AL-RIGHTY!
WE SHOULDN'T DAWDLE. HOW ABOUT WE GET BACK TO INVESTIGAT-ING?!
BEFORE WE MAKE THE CHIEF ANGRY WITH US!
!
WATER AGAIN?
YOU'RE DRINKING QUITE A LOT...
OH, SORRY. ONE MORE BOTTLE.
PCH

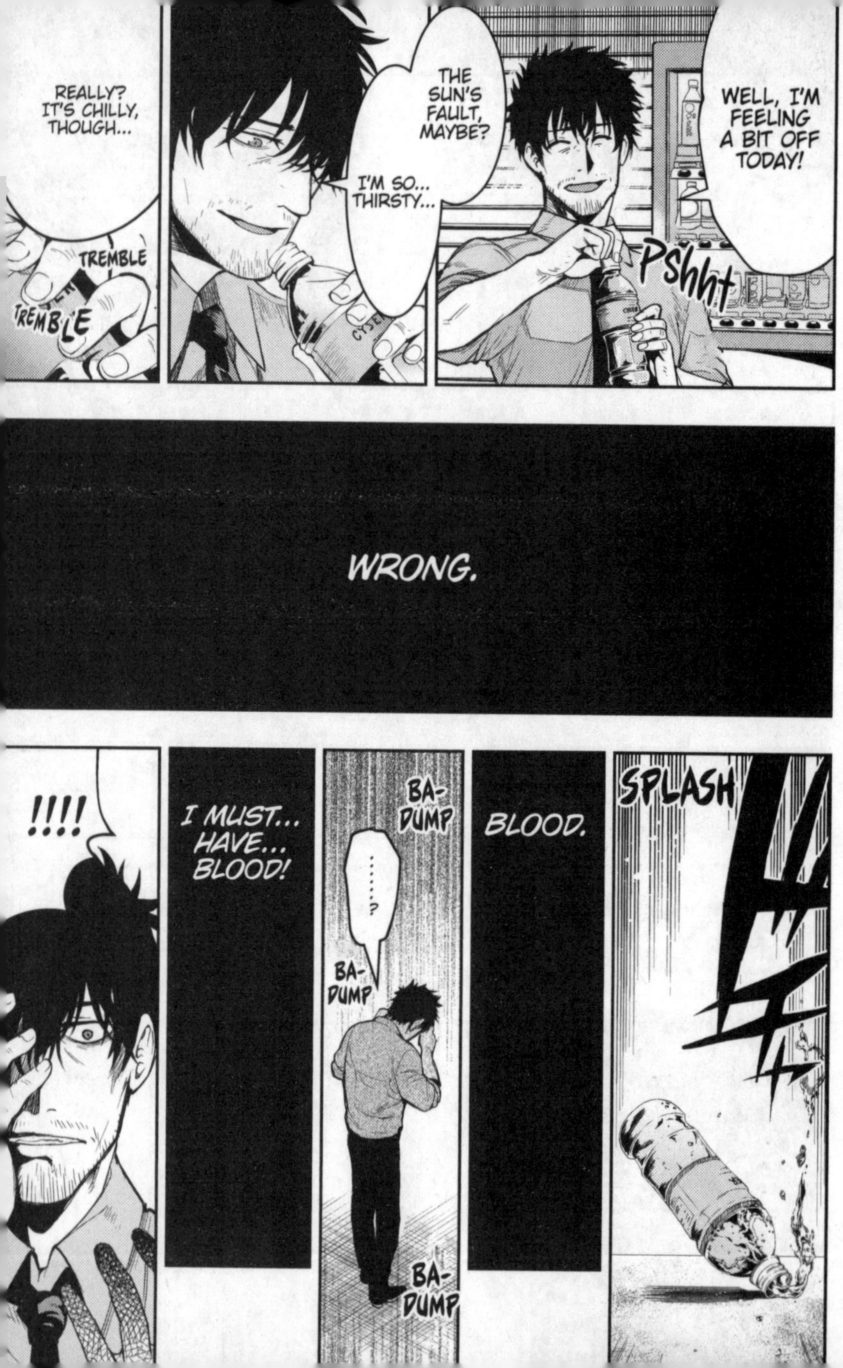
WELL, I'M FEELING A BIT OFF TODAY!
Pshht
THE SUN'S FAULT, MAYBE?
I'M SO... THIRSTY...
REALLY? IT'S CHILLY, THOUGH...
TREMBLE
TREMBLE
WRONG.
SPLASH
BLOOD.
BA-DUMP
......?
BA-DUMP
BA-DUMP
I MUST... HAVE... BLOOD!
!!!!

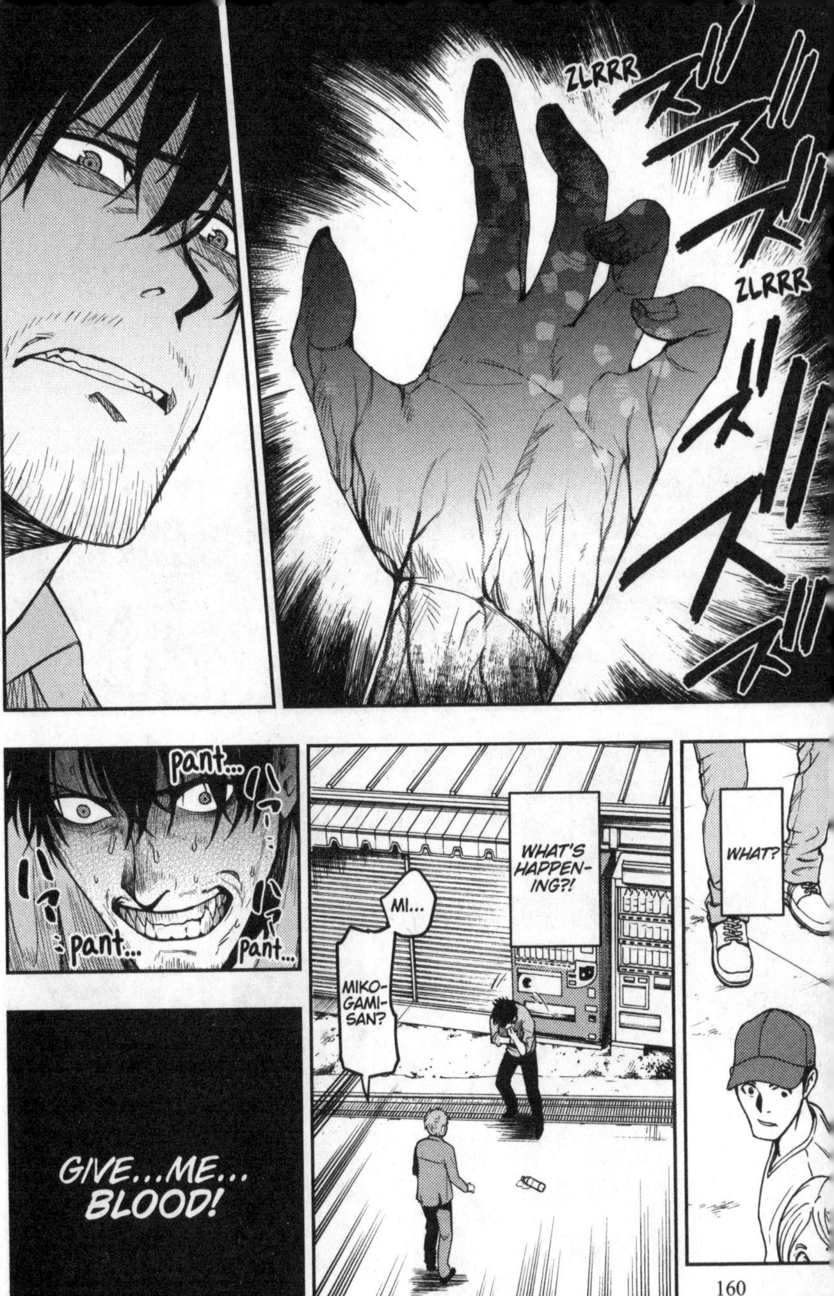
ZLRRR
ZLRRR
WHAT?
WHAT'S HAPPENING?!
MI...
MIKOGAMI-SAN?
pant...
pant...
pant...
GIVE...ME... BLOOD!

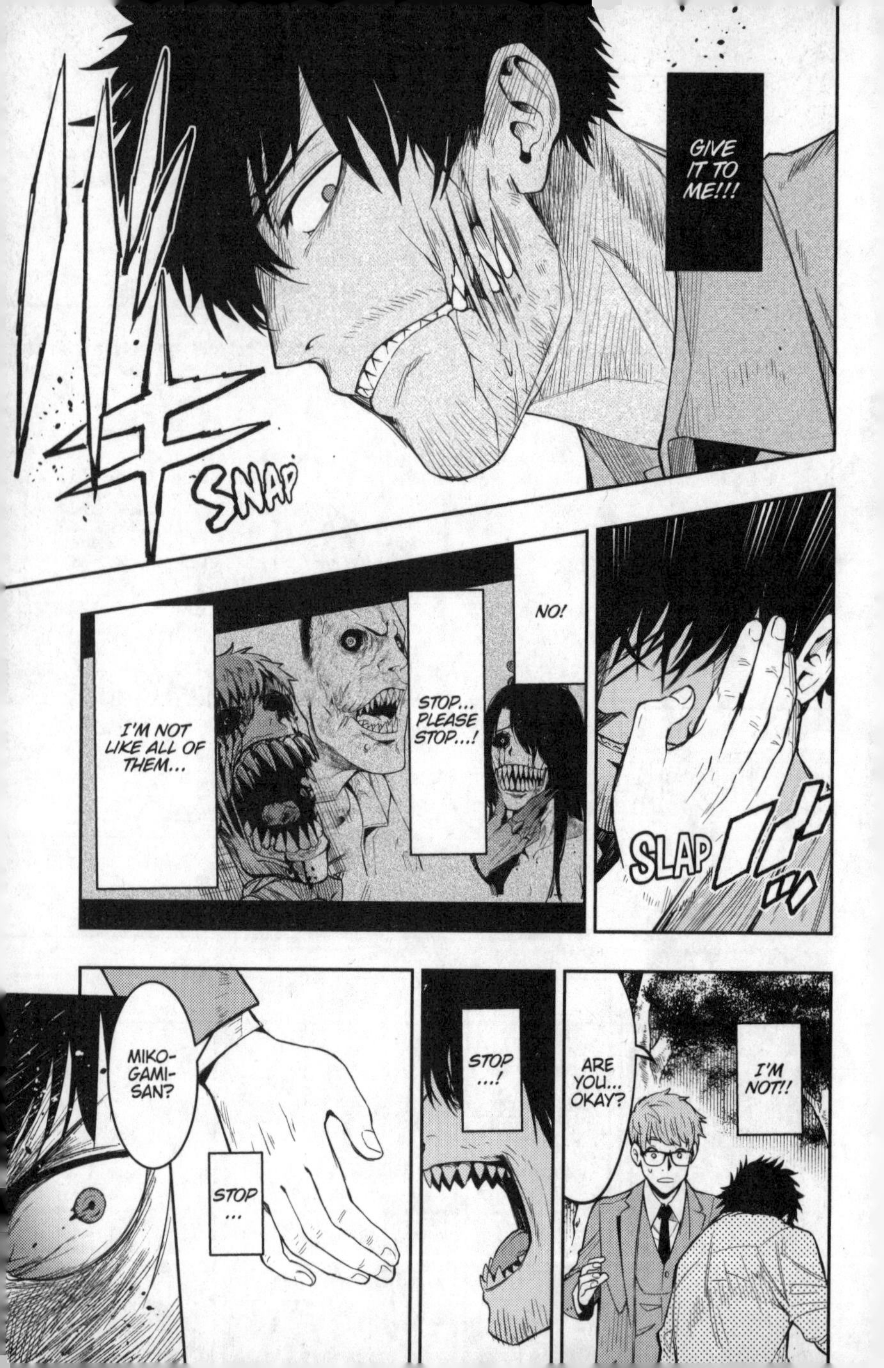
GIVE IT TO ME!!!
SNAP
SLAP
NO!
STOP... PLEASE STOP...!
I'M NOT LIKE ALL OF THEM...
I'M NOT!!
ARE YOU... OKAY?
STOP ...!
MIKO-GAMI-SAN?
STOP ...

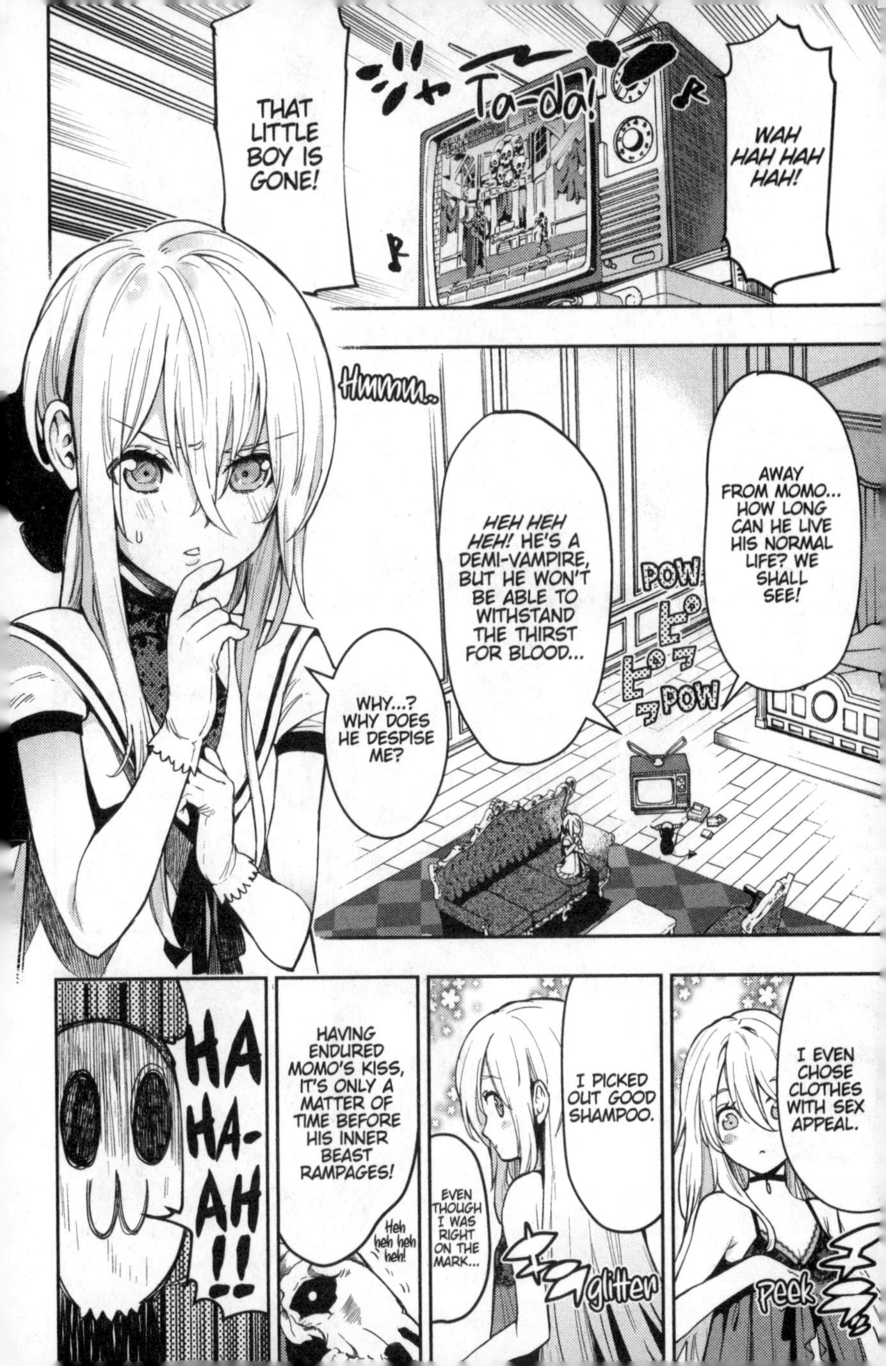
WAH HAH HAH HAH!
Ta-da!
THAT LITTLE BOY IS GONE!
AWAY FROM MOMO... HOW LONG CAN HE LIVE HIS NORMAL LIFE? WE SHALL SEE!
POW POW
HEH HEH HEH! HE'S A DEMI-VAMPIRE, BUT HE WON'T BE ABLE TO WITHSTAND THE THIRST FOR BLOOD...
Hmmm..
WHY...? WHY DOES HE DESPISE ME?
I EVEN CHOSE CLOTHES WITH SEX APPEAL.
Peek
I PICKED OUT GOOD SHAMPOO.
EVEN THOUGH I WAS RIGHT ON THE MARK...
glitter
HAVING ENDURED MOMO'S KISS, IT'S ONLY A MATTER OF TIME BEFORE HIS INNER BEAST RAMPAGES!
Heh heh heh heh!
HA HA-HA AH!!

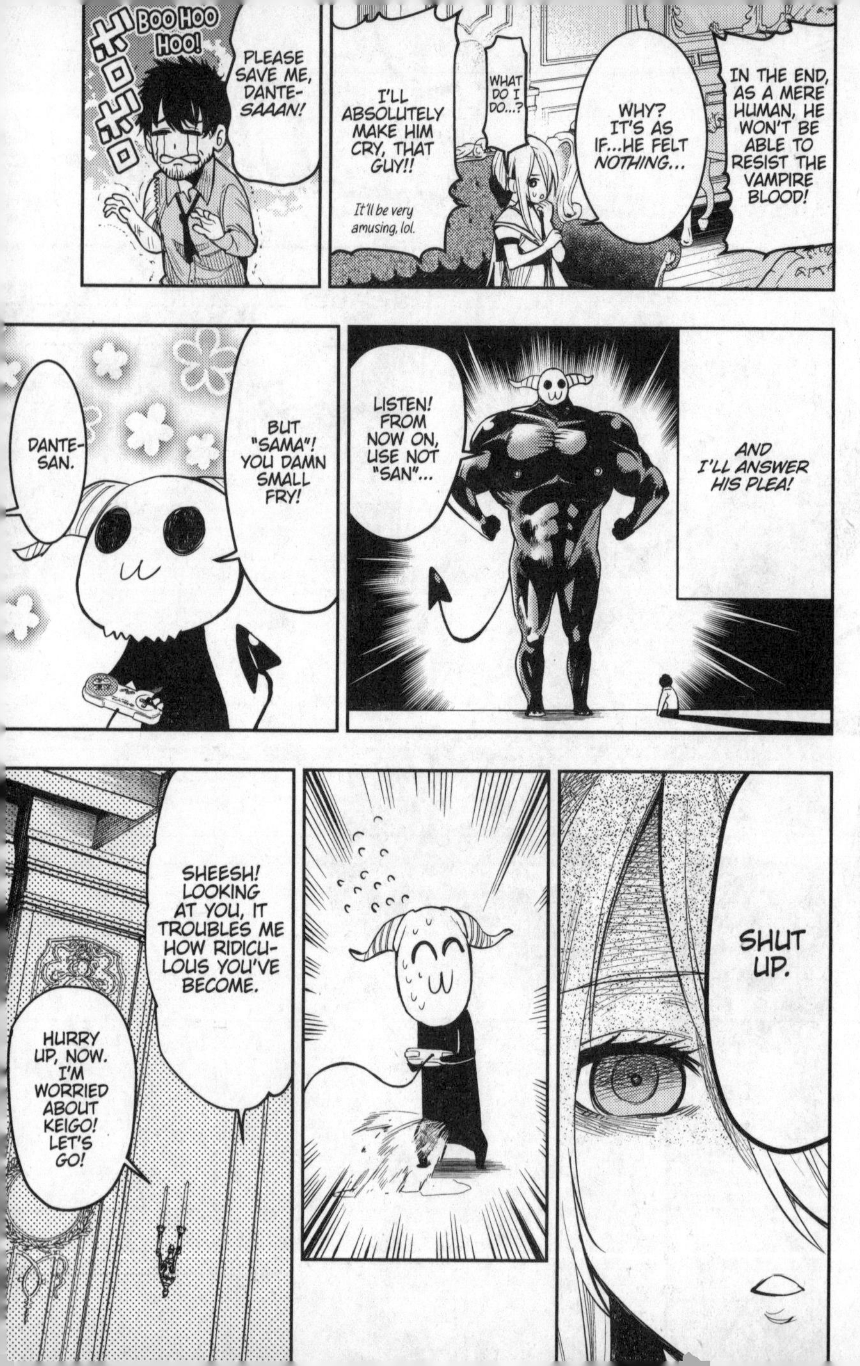

IN THE END, AS A MERE HUMAN, HE WON'T BE ABLE TO RESIST THE VAMPIRE BLOOD!
WHY? IT'S AS IF...HE FELT NOTHING...
WHAT DO I DO...?
I'LL ABSOLUTELY MAKE HIM CRY, THAT GUY!!
It'll be very amusing, lol.
BOO HOO HOO!
PLEASE SAVE ME, DANTE-SAAAN!
AND I'LL ANSWER HIS PLEA!
LISTEN! FROM NOW ON, USE NOT "SAN"...
BUT "SAMA"! YOU DAMN SMALL FRY!
DANTE-SAN.
SHUT UP.
SHEESH! LOOKING AT YOU, IT TROUBLES ME HOW RIDICULOUS YOU'VE BECOME.
HURRY UP, NOW. I'M WORRIED ABOUT KEIGO! LET'S GO!

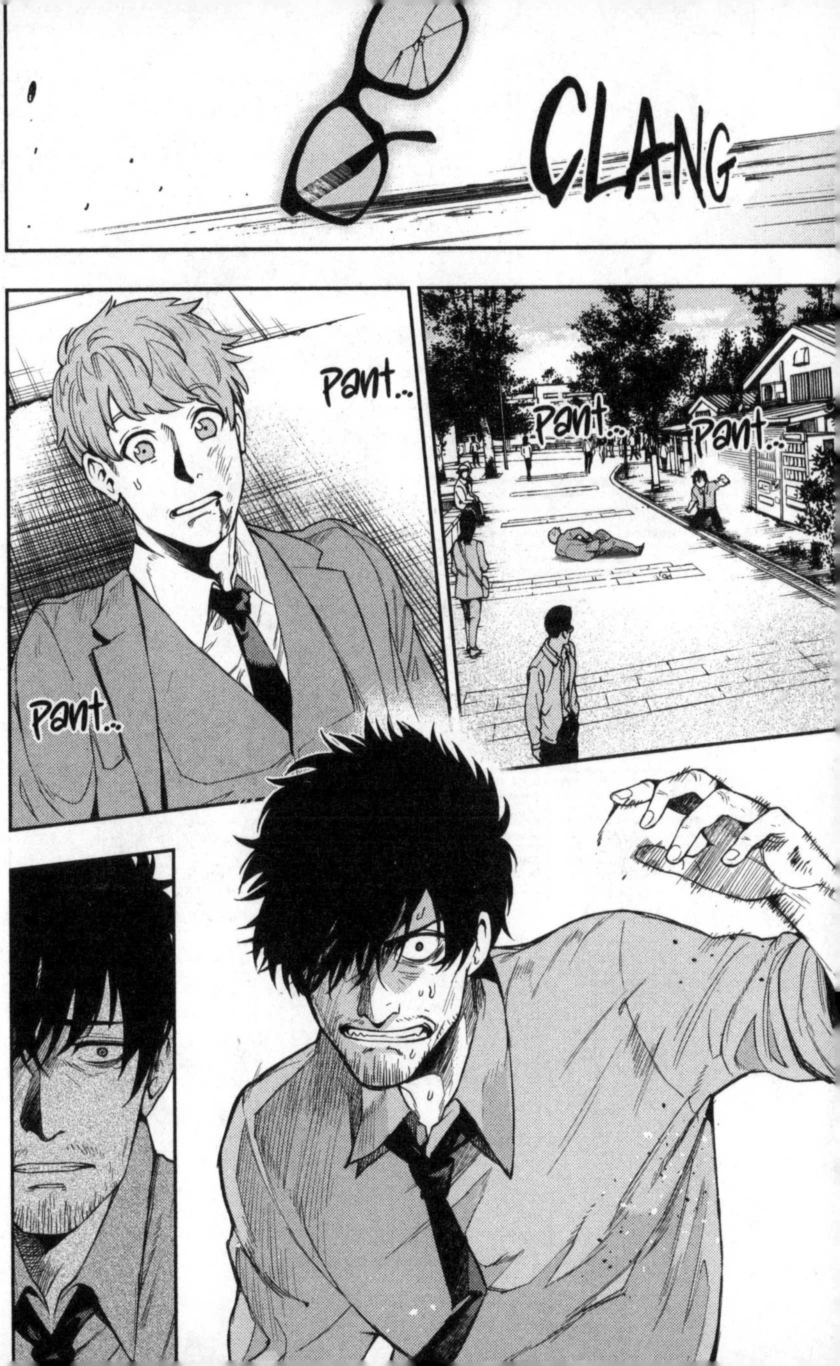
CLANG
Pant...
Pant...
Pant...
Pant...

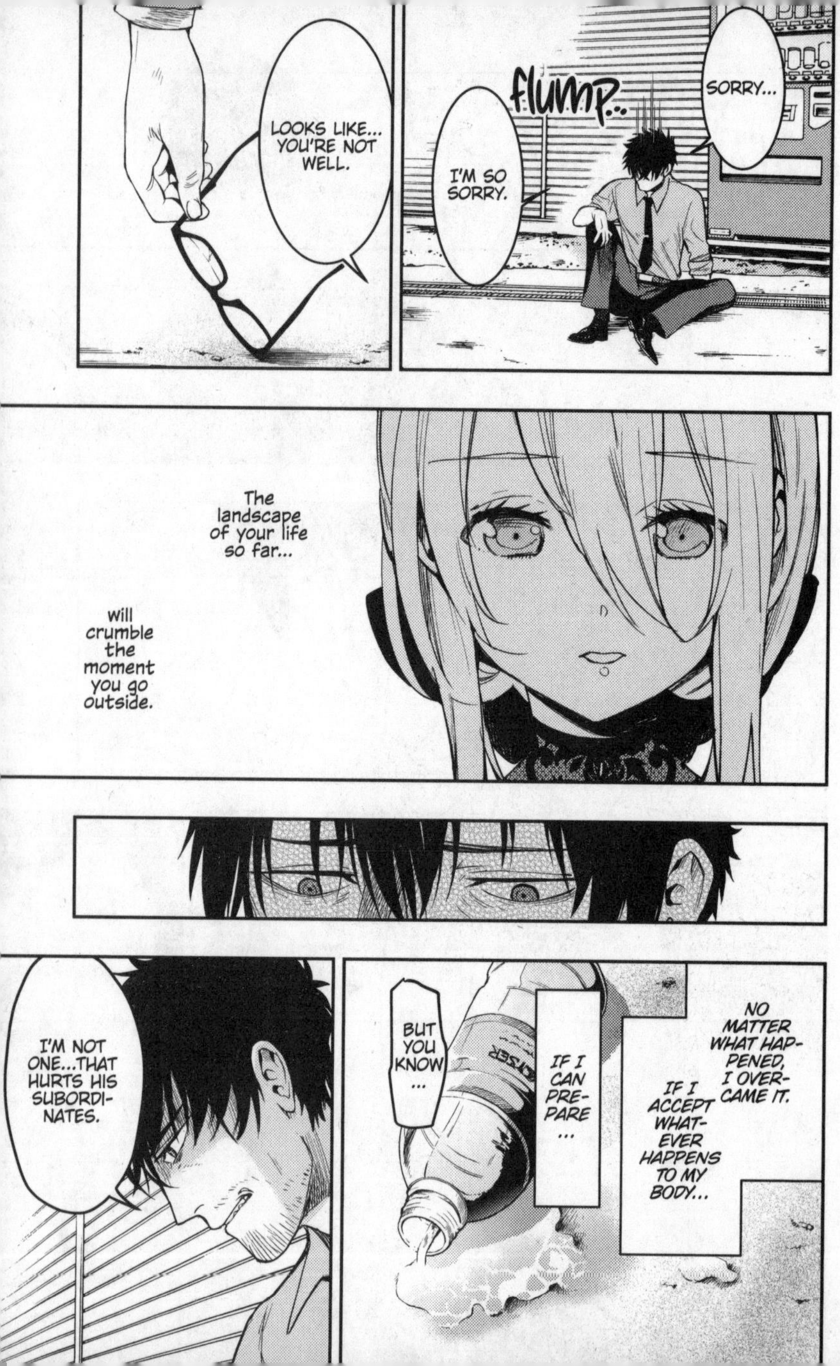
SORRY...
flump...
I'M SO SORRY.
LOOKS LIKE... YOU'RE NOT WELL.
The landscape of your life so far...
will crumble the moment you go outside.
NO MATTER WHAT HAPPENED, I OVERCAME IT.
IF I ACCEPT WHATEVER HAPPENS TO MY BODY...
IF I CAN PREPARE...
BUT YOU KNOW...
I'M NOT ONE...THAT HURTS HIS SUBORDINATES.

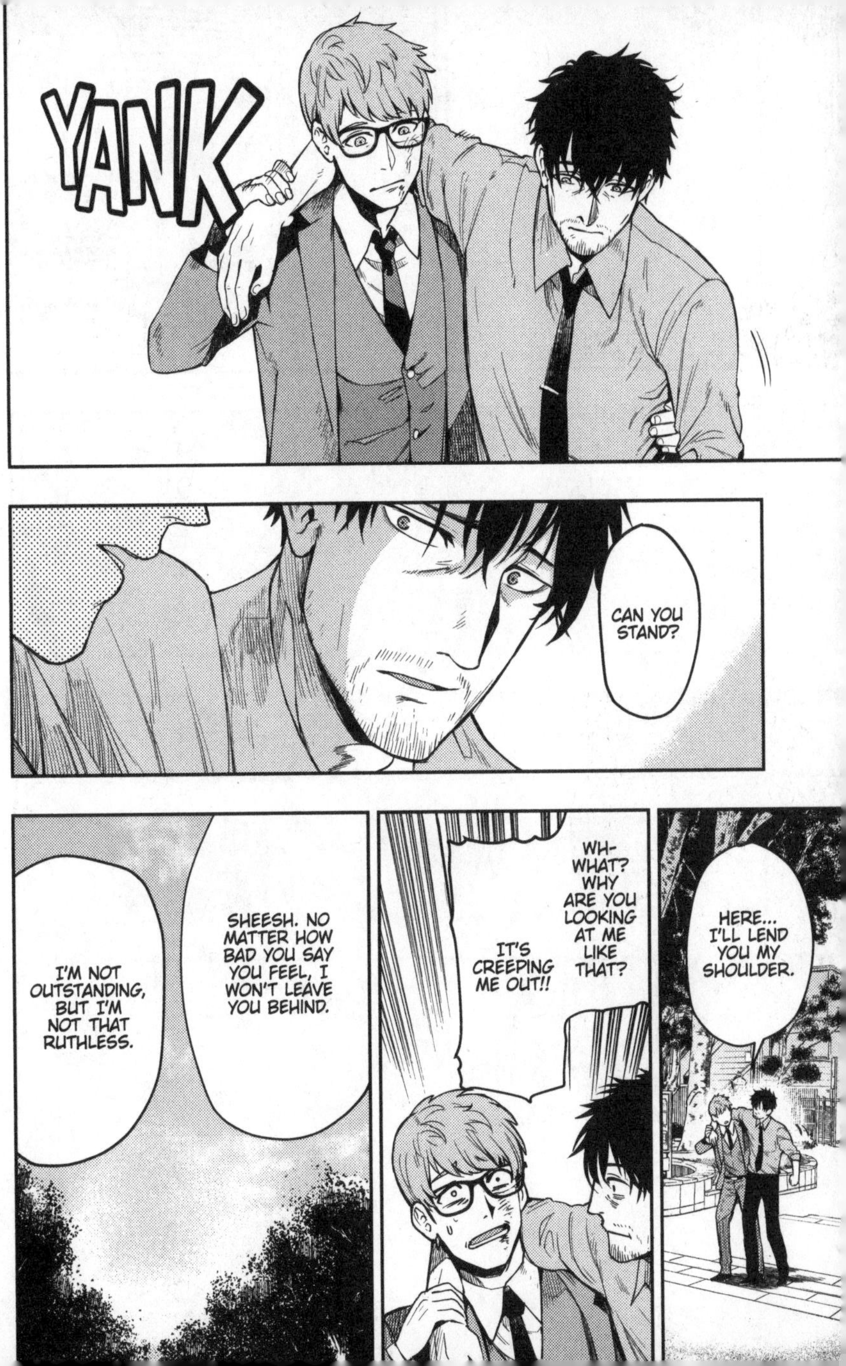
YANK
CAN YOU STAND?
HERE... I'LL LEND YOU MY SHOULDER.
WH-WHAT? WHY ARE YOU LOOKING AT ME LIKE THAT?
IT'S CREEPING ME OUT!!
SHEESH. NO MATTER HOW BAD YOU SAY YOU FEEL, I WON'T LEAVE YOU BEHIND.
I'M NOT OUTSTANDING, BUT I'M NOT THAT RUTHLESS.

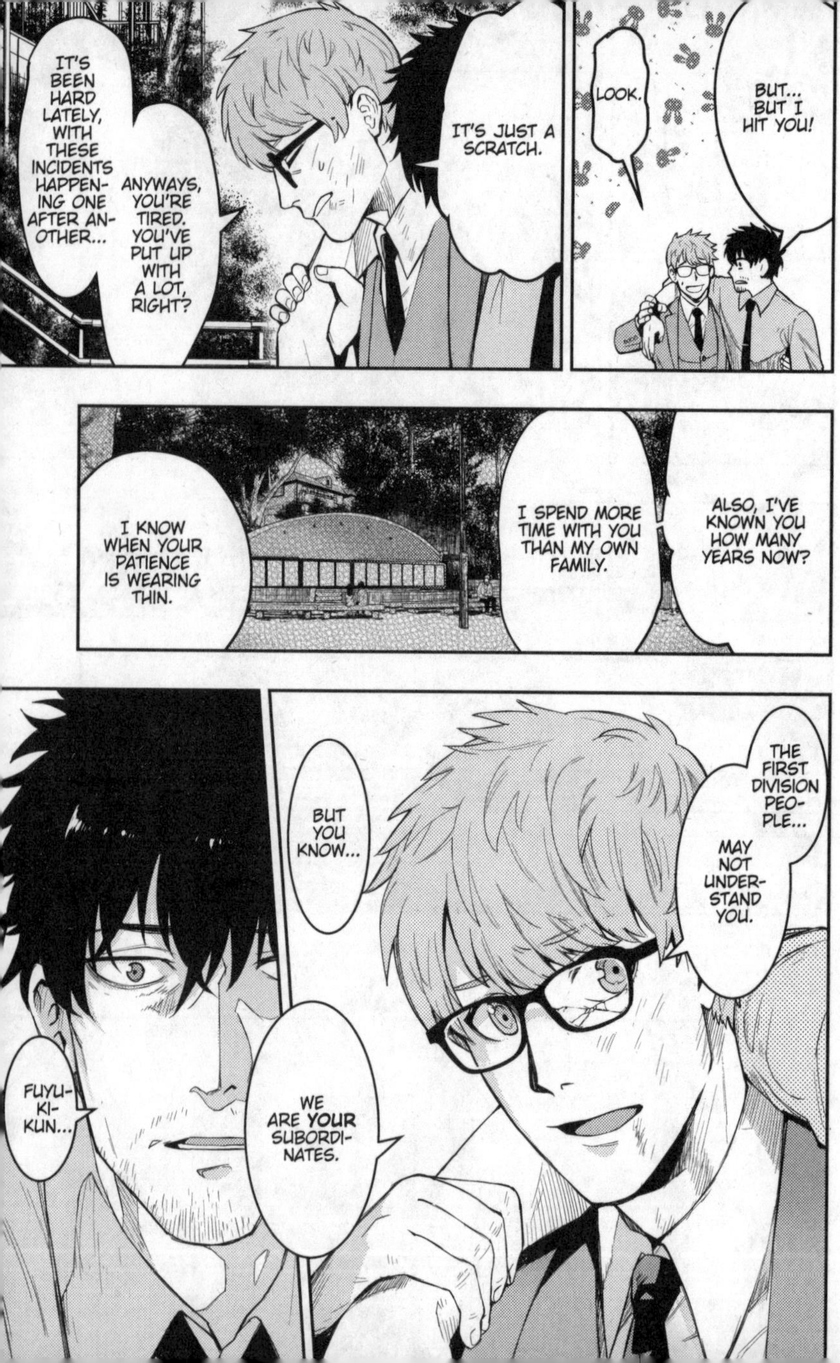
BUT... BUT I HIT YOU!
LOOK.
IT'S JUST A SCRATCH.
ANYWAYS, YOU'RE TIRED. YOU'VE PUT UP WITH A LOT, RIGHT?
IT'S BEEN HARD LATELY, WITH THESE INCIDENTS HAPPENING ONE AFTER ANOTHER...
ALSO, I'VE KNOWN YOU HOW MANY YEARS NOW?
I SPEND MORE TIME WITH YOU THAN MY OWN FAMILY.
I KNOW WHEN YOUR PATIENCE IS WEARING THIN.
THE FIRST DIVISION PEOPLE...
MAY NOT UNDERSTAND YOU.
BUT YOU KNOW...
WE ARE **YOUR** SUBORDINATES.
FUYUKI-KUN...

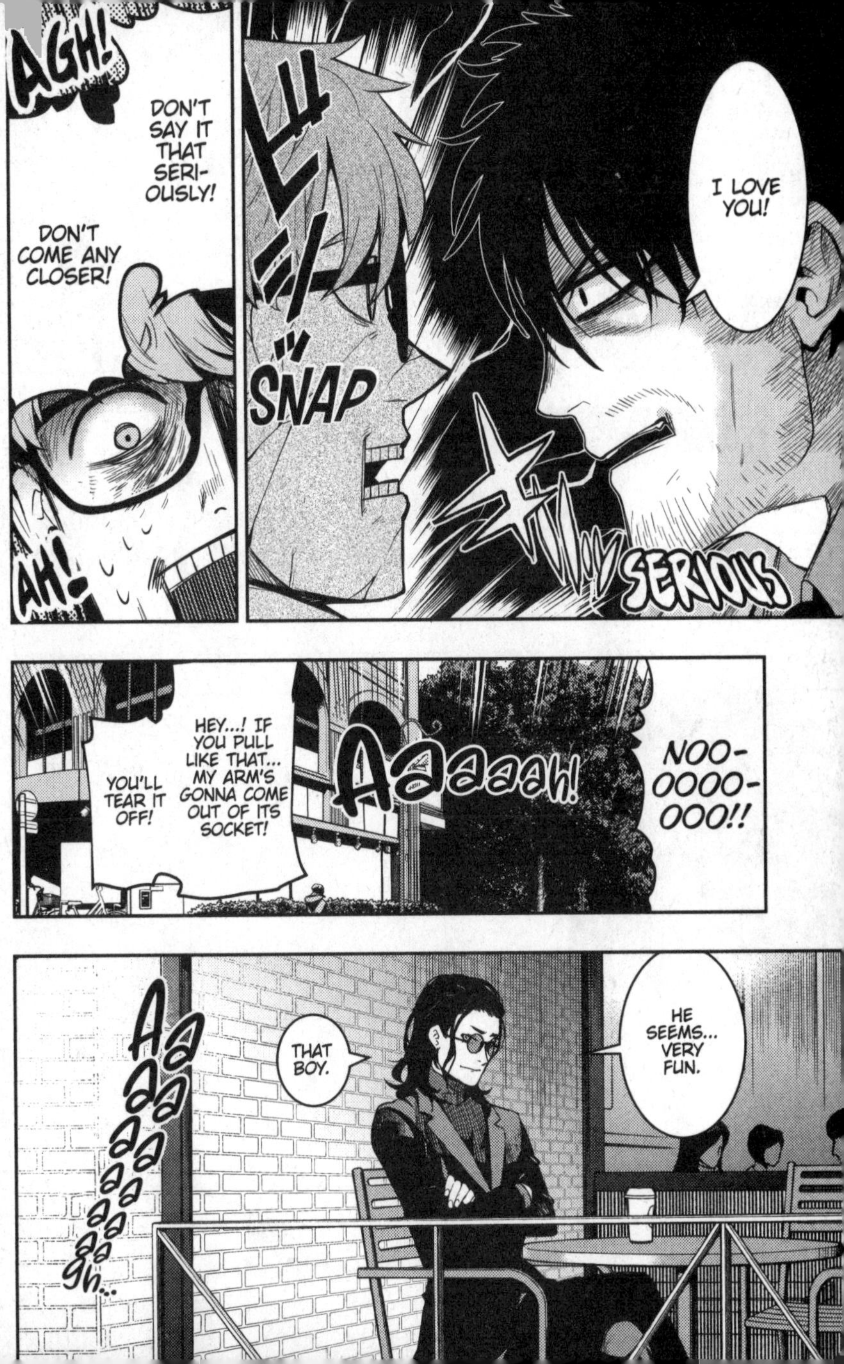
I LOVE YOU!
SERIOUS
SNAP
AGH!
DON'T SAY IT THAT SERI-OUSLY!
DON'T COME ANY CLOSER!
AH!
NOO-OOOO-OOO!!
Aaaaaah!
HEY...! IF YOU PULL LIKE THAT... MY ARM'S GONNA COME OUT OF ITS SOCKET!
YOU'LL TEAR IT OFF!
HE SEEMS... VERY FUN.
THAT BOY.
Aaaaaaaaaaaaaaaagh..

MoMo
the blood taker

MOMO

the blood taker

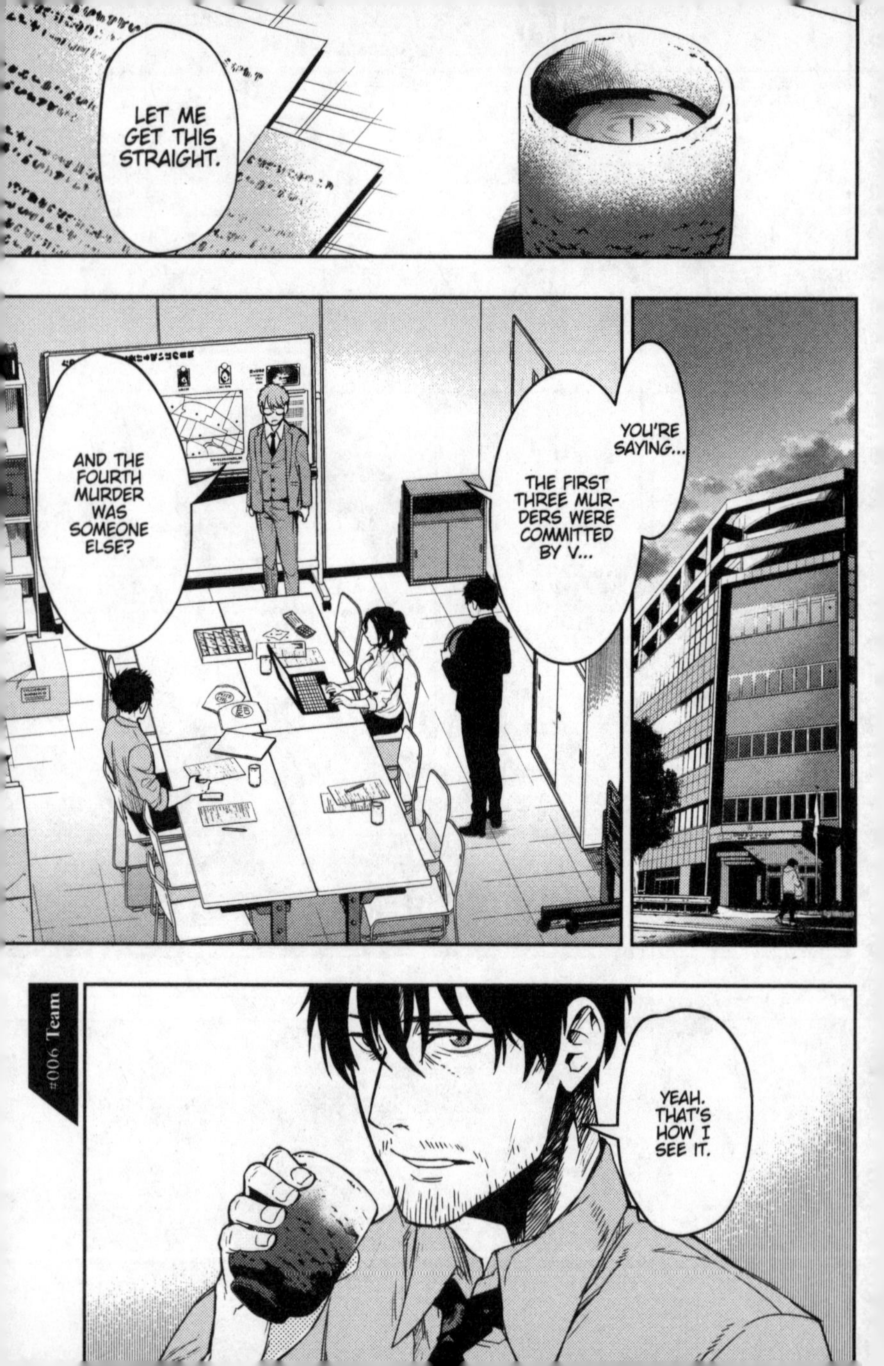
LET ME GET THIS STRAIGHT.
YOU'RE SAYING...
THE FIRST THREE MURDERS WERE COMMITTED BY V...
AND THE FOURTH MURDER WAS SOMEONE ELSE?
#006 Team
YEAH. THAT'S HOW I SEE IT.

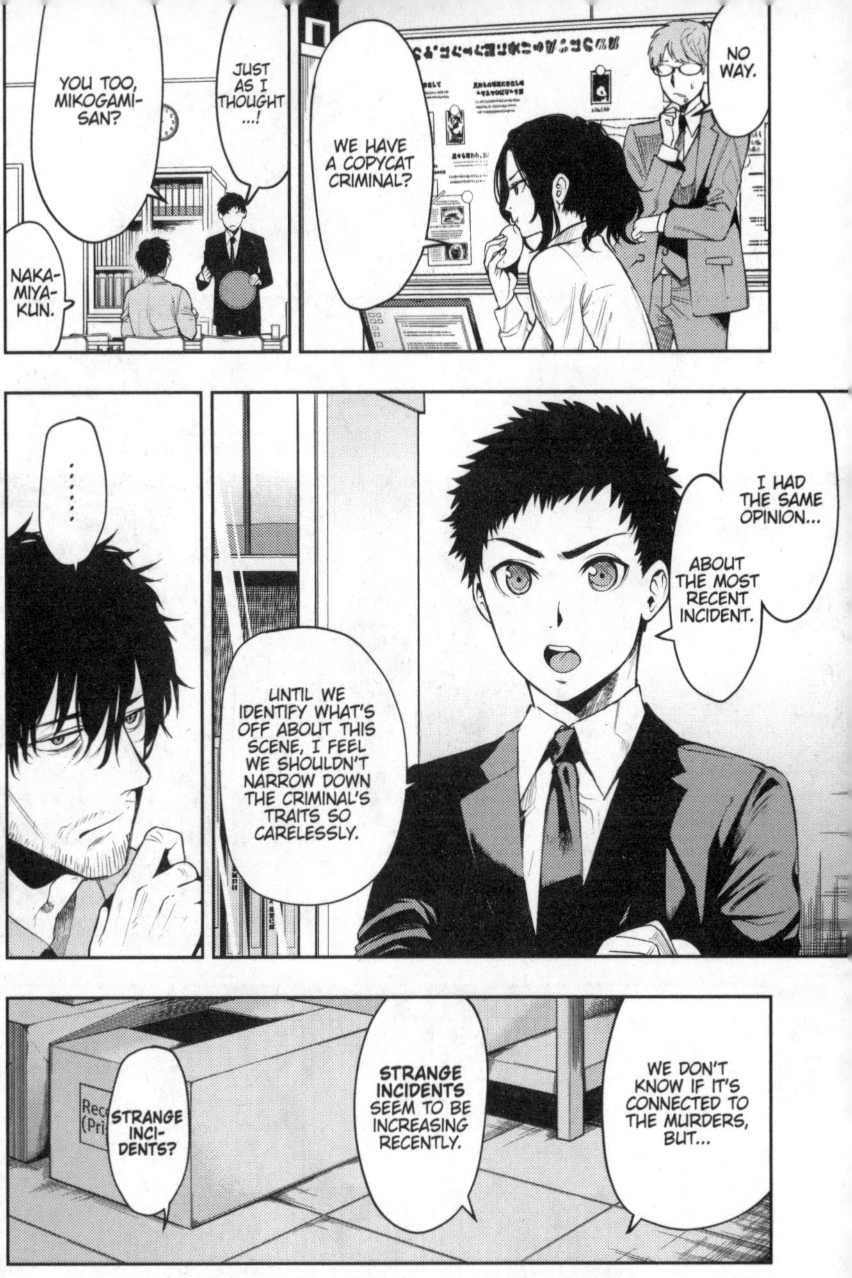
NO WAY.
WE HAVE A COPYCAT CRIMINAL?
JUST AS I THOUGHT ...!
YOU TOO, MIKOGAMI-SAN?
NAKA-MIYA-KUN.
I HAD THE SAME OPINION...
ABOUT THE MOST RECENT INCIDENT.
UNTIL WE IDENTIFY WHAT'S OFF ABOUT THIS SCENE, I FEEL WE SHOULDN'T NARROW DOWN THE CRIMINAL'S TRAITS SO CARELESSLY.
......
WE DON'T KNOW IF IT'S CONNECTED TO THE MURDERS, BUT...
STRANGE INCIDENTS SEEM TO BE INCREASING RECENTLY.
STRANGE INCI-DENTS?

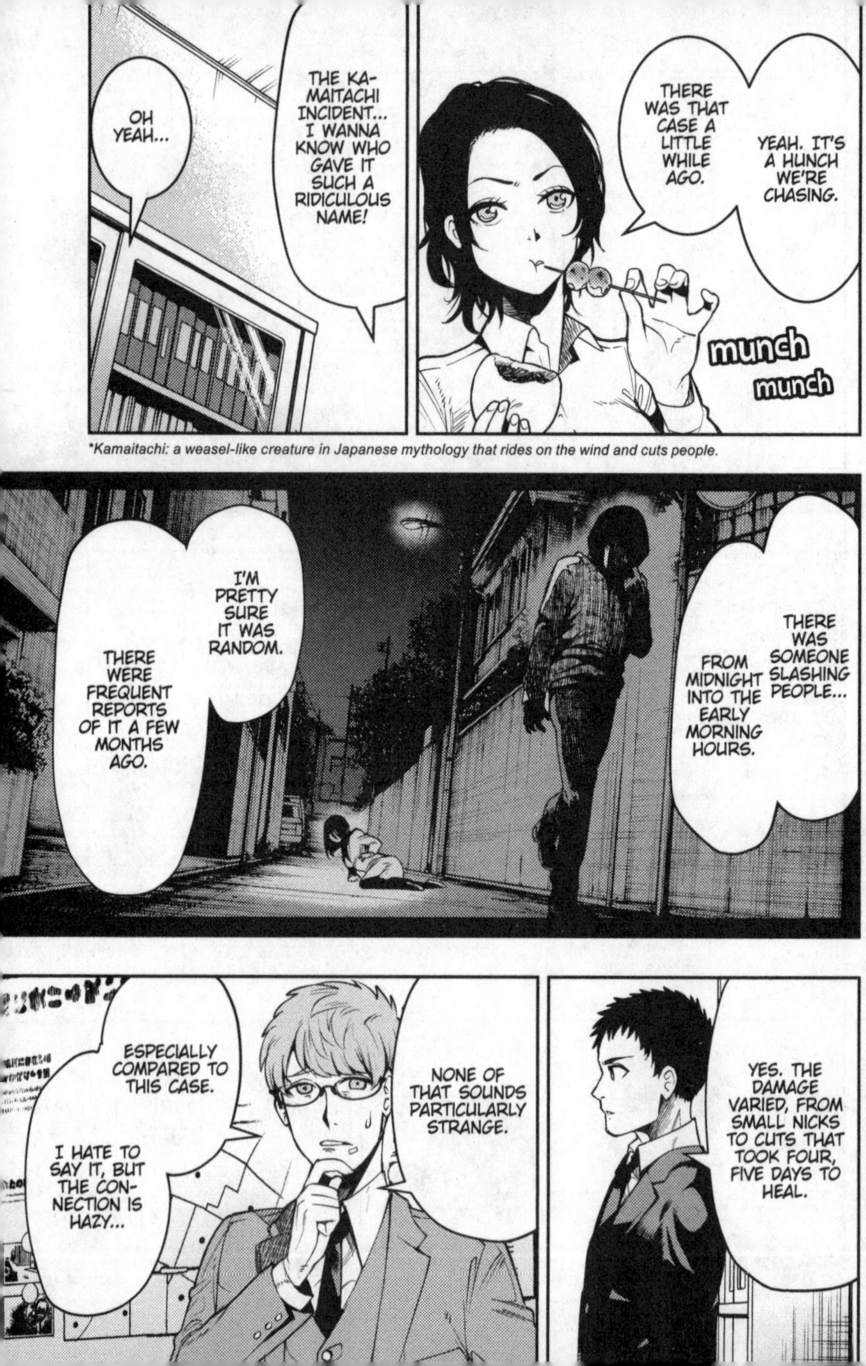
YEAH. IT'S A HUNCH WE'RE CHASING.
THERE WAS THAT CASE A LITTLE WHILE AGO.
munch
munch
THE KA-MAITACHI INCIDENT... I WANNA KNOW WHO GAVE IT SUCH A RIDICULOUS NAME!
OH YEAH...
THERE WAS SOMEONE SLASHING PEOPLE...
FROM MIDNIGHT INTO THE EARLY MORNING HOURS.
I'M PRETTY SURE IT WAS RANDOM.
THERE WERE FREQUENT REPORTS OF IT A FEW MONTHS AGO.
YES. THE DAMAGE VARIED, FROM SMALL NICKS TO CUTS THAT TOOK FOUR, FIVE DAYS TO HEAL.
NONE OF THAT SOUNDS PARTICULARLY STRANGE.
ESPECIALLY COMPARED TO THIS CASE.
I HATE TO SAY IT, BUT THE CON-NECTION IS HAZY...

*Kamaitachi: a weasel-like creature in Japanese mythology that rides on the wind and cuts people.

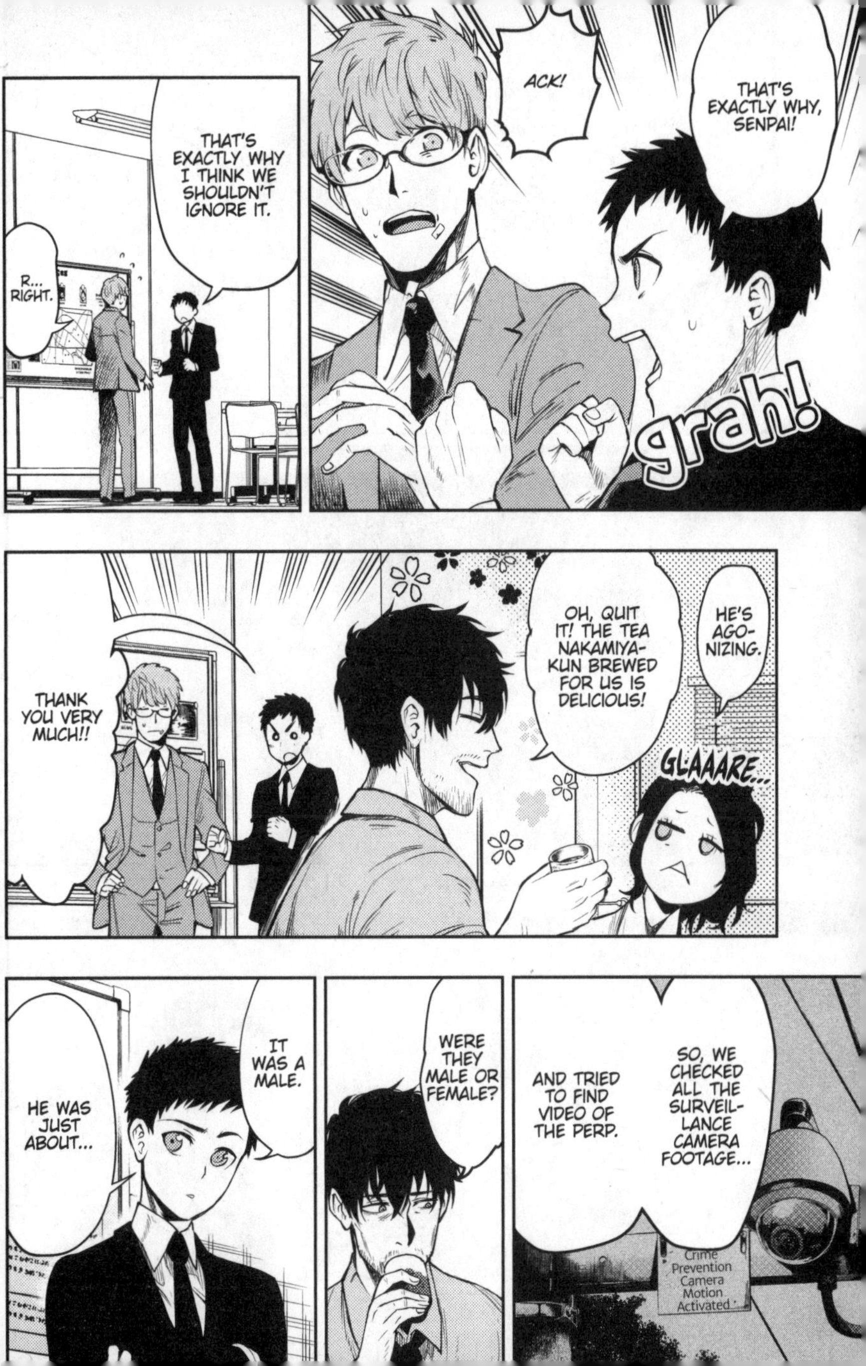
THAT'S EXACTLY WHY, SENPAI!
ACK!
grah!
THAT'S EXACTLY WHY I THINK WE SHOULDN'T IGNORE IT.
R... RIGHT.
HE'S AGO-NIZING.
OH, QUIT IT! THE TEA NAKAMIYA-KUN BREWED FOR US IS DELICIOUS!
GLAAARE...
THANK YOU VERY MUCH!!
SO, WE CHECKED ALL THE SURVEIL-LANCE CAMERA FOOTAGE...
AND TRIED TO FIND VIDEO OF THE PERP.
Crime Prevention Camera Motion Activated
WERE THEY MALE OR FEMALE?
IT WAS A MALE.
HE WAS JUST ABOUT...

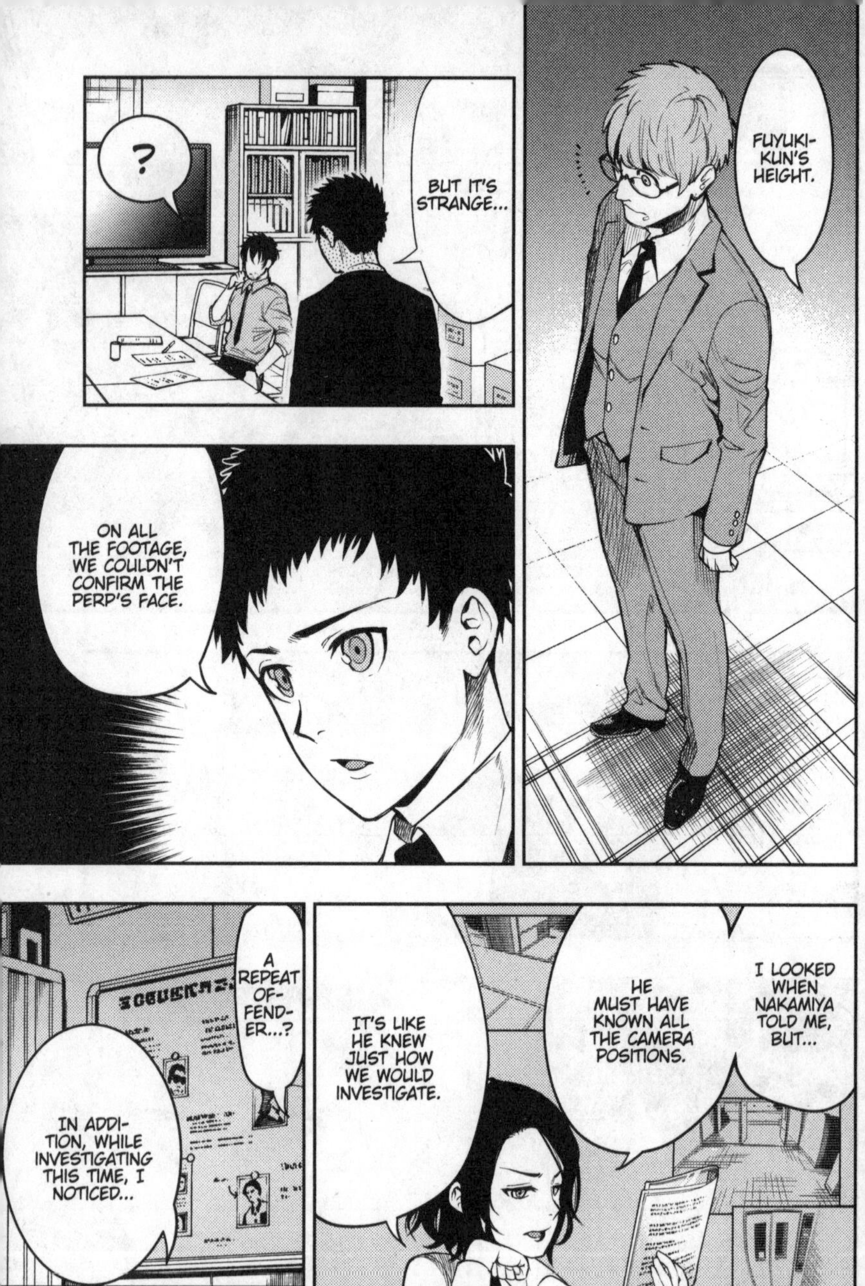
FUYUKI-KUN'S HEIGHT.
BUT IT'S STRANGE...
?
ON ALL THE FOOTAGE, WE COULDN'T CONFIRM THE PERP'S FACE.
I LOOKED WHEN NAKAMIYA TOLD ME, BUT...
HE MUST HAVE KNOWN ALL THE CAMERA POSITIONS.
IT'S LIKE HE KNEW JUST HOW WE WOULD INVESTIGATE.
A REPEAT OF-FENDER...?
IN ADDI-TION, WHILE INVESTIGATING THIS TIME, I NOTICED...

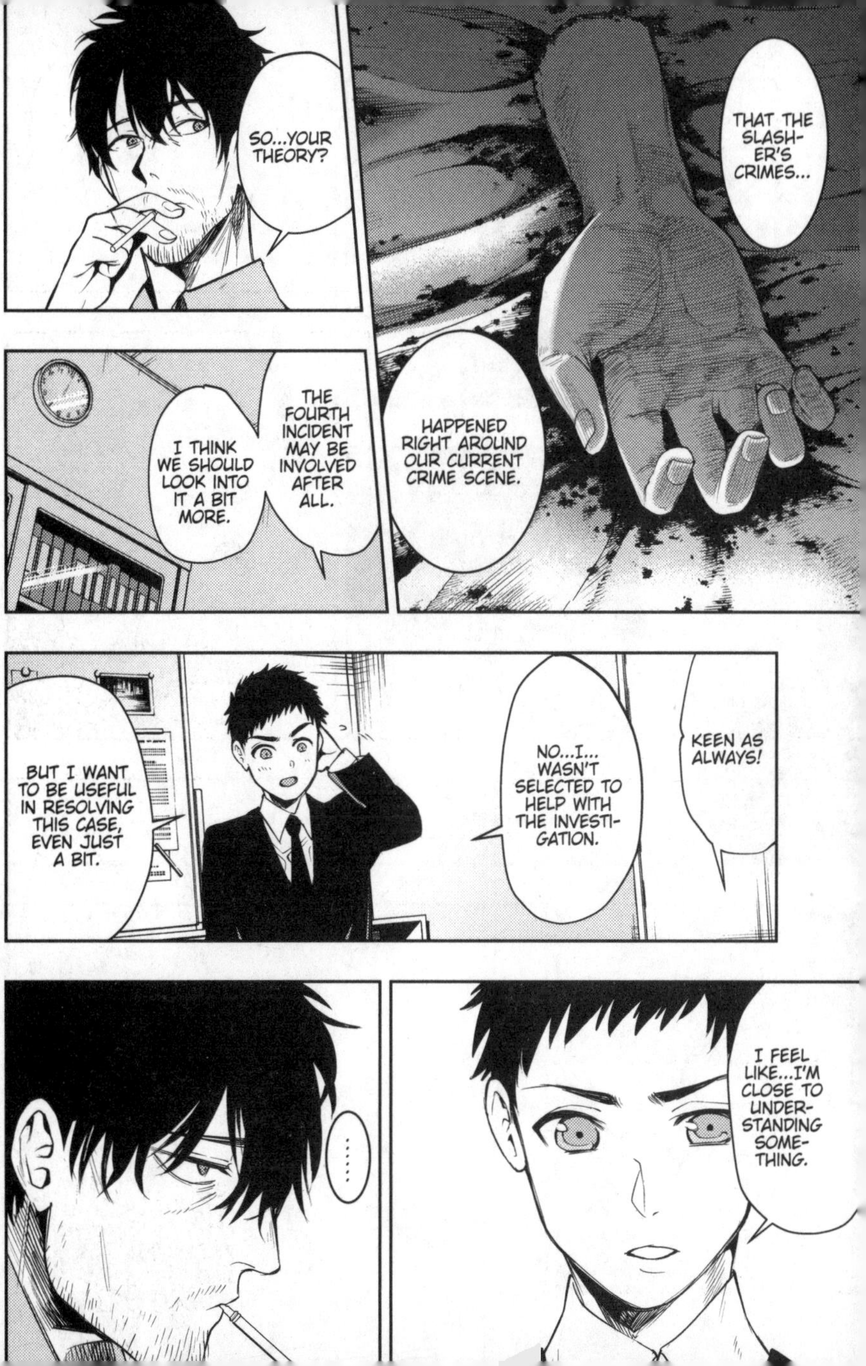
THAT THE SLASHER'S CRIMES...
HAPPENED RIGHT AROUND OUR CURRENT CRIME SCENE.
SO...YOUR THEORY?
THE FOURTH INCIDENT MAY BE INVOLVED AFTER ALL.
I THINK WE SHOULD LOOK INTO IT A BIT MORE.
KEEN AS ALWAYS!
NO...I... WASN'T SELECTED TO HELP WITH THE INVESTIGATION.
BUT I WANT TO BE USEFUL IN RESOLVING THIS CASE, EVEN JUST A BIT.
I FEEL LIKE...I'M CLOSE TO UNDERSTANDING SOMETHING.
......

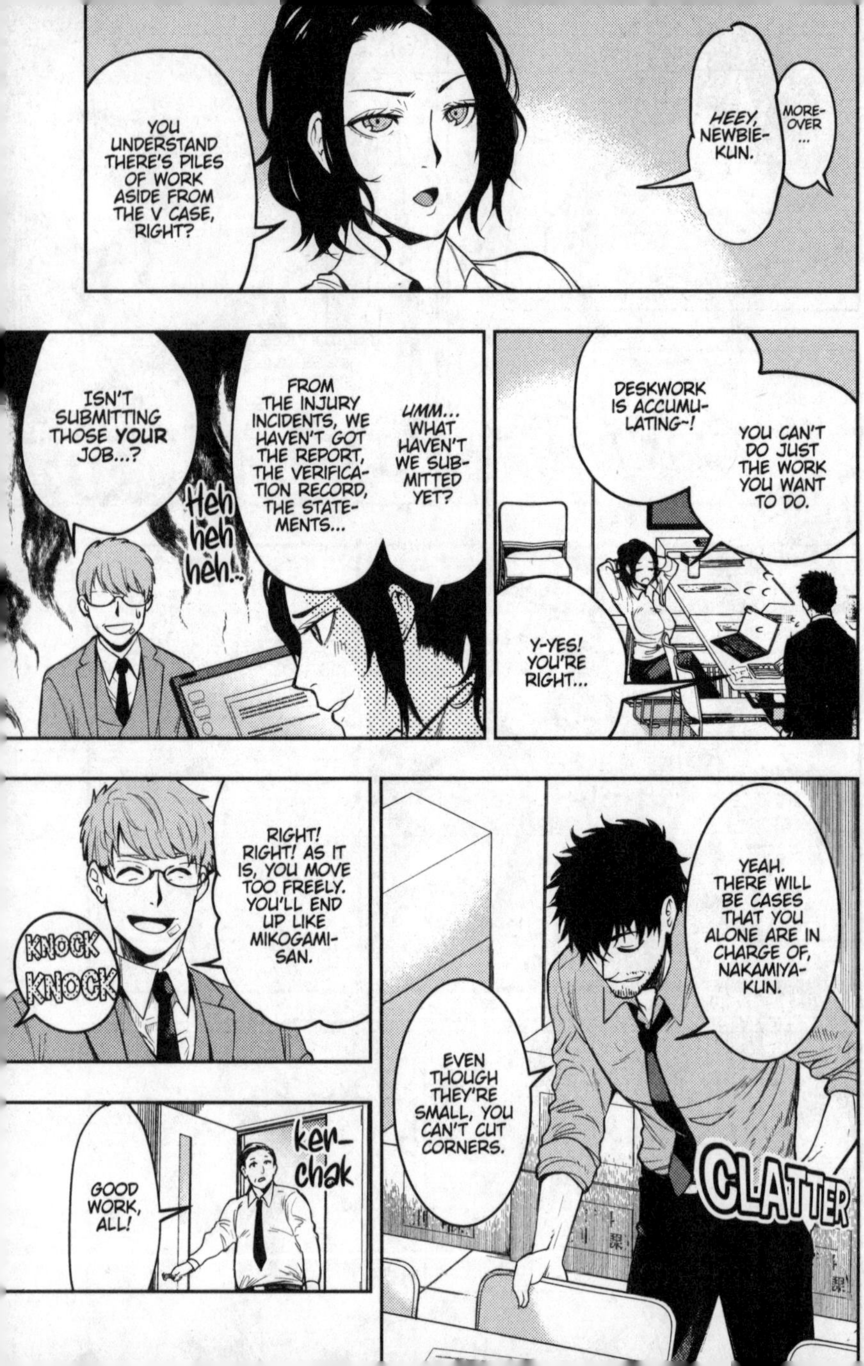
MORE-OVER...
HEEY, NEWBIE-KUN.
YOU UNDERSTAND THERE'S PILES OF WORK ASIDE FROM THE V CASE, RIGHT?
DESKWORK IS ACCUMULATING~!
YOU CAN'T DO JUST THE WORK YOU WANT TO DO.
Y-YES! YOU'RE RIGHT...
UMM... WHAT HAVEN'T WE SUBMITTED YET?
FROM THE INJURY INCIDENTS, WE HAVEN'T GOT THE REPORT, THE VERIFICATION RECORD, THE STATEMENTS...
Heh heh heh...
ISN'T SUBMITTING THOSE YOUR JOB...?
YEAH. THERE WILL BE CASES THAT YOU ALONE ARE IN CHARGE OF, NAKAMIYA-KUN.
EVEN THOUGH THEY'RE SMALL, YOU CAN'T CUT CORNERS.
CLATTER
RIGHT! RIGHT! AS IT IS, YOU MOVE TOO FREELY. YOU'LL END UP LIKE MIKOGAMI-SAN.
KNOCK KNOCK
ker-chak
GOOD WORK, ALL!

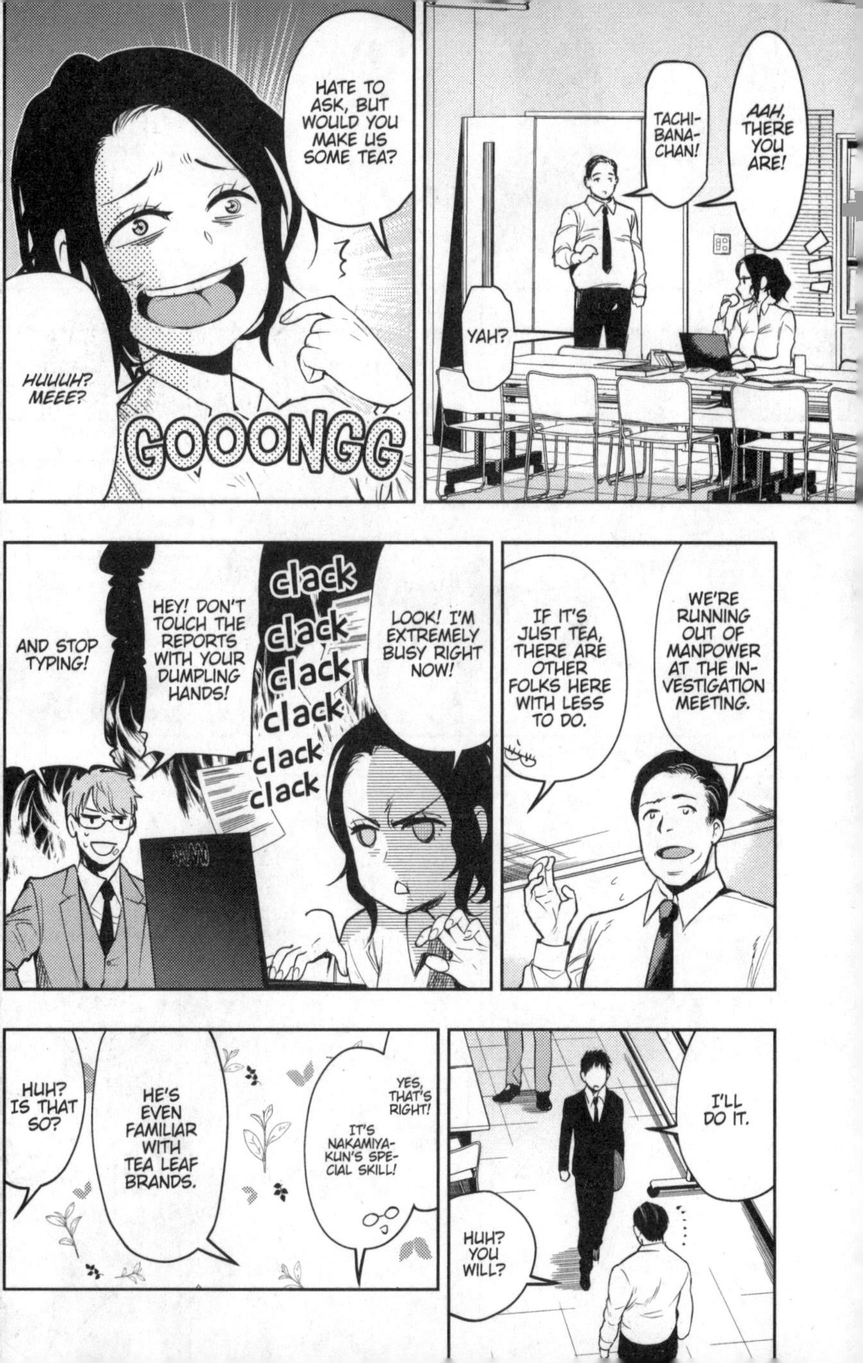
AAH, THERE YOU ARE!
TACHI-BANA-CHAN!
YAH?
HATE TO ASK, BUT WOULD YOU MAKE US SOME TEA?
HUUUH? MEEE?
GOOOONGG
WE'RE RUNNING OUT OF MANPOWER AT THE IN-VESTIGATION MEETING.
IF IT'S JUST TEA, THERE ARE OTHER FOLKS HERE WITH LESS TO DO.
LOOK! I'M EXTREMELY BUSY RIGHT NOW!
clack clack clack clack clack clack
HEY! DON'T TOUCH THE REPORTS WITH YOUR DUMPLING HANDS!
AND STOP TYPING!
I'LL DO IT.
HUH? YOU WILL?
YES, THAT'S RIGHT!
IT'S NAKAMIYA-KUN'S SPE-CIAL SKILL!
HE'S EVEN FAMILIAR WITH TEA LEAF BRANDS.
HUH? IS THAT SO?

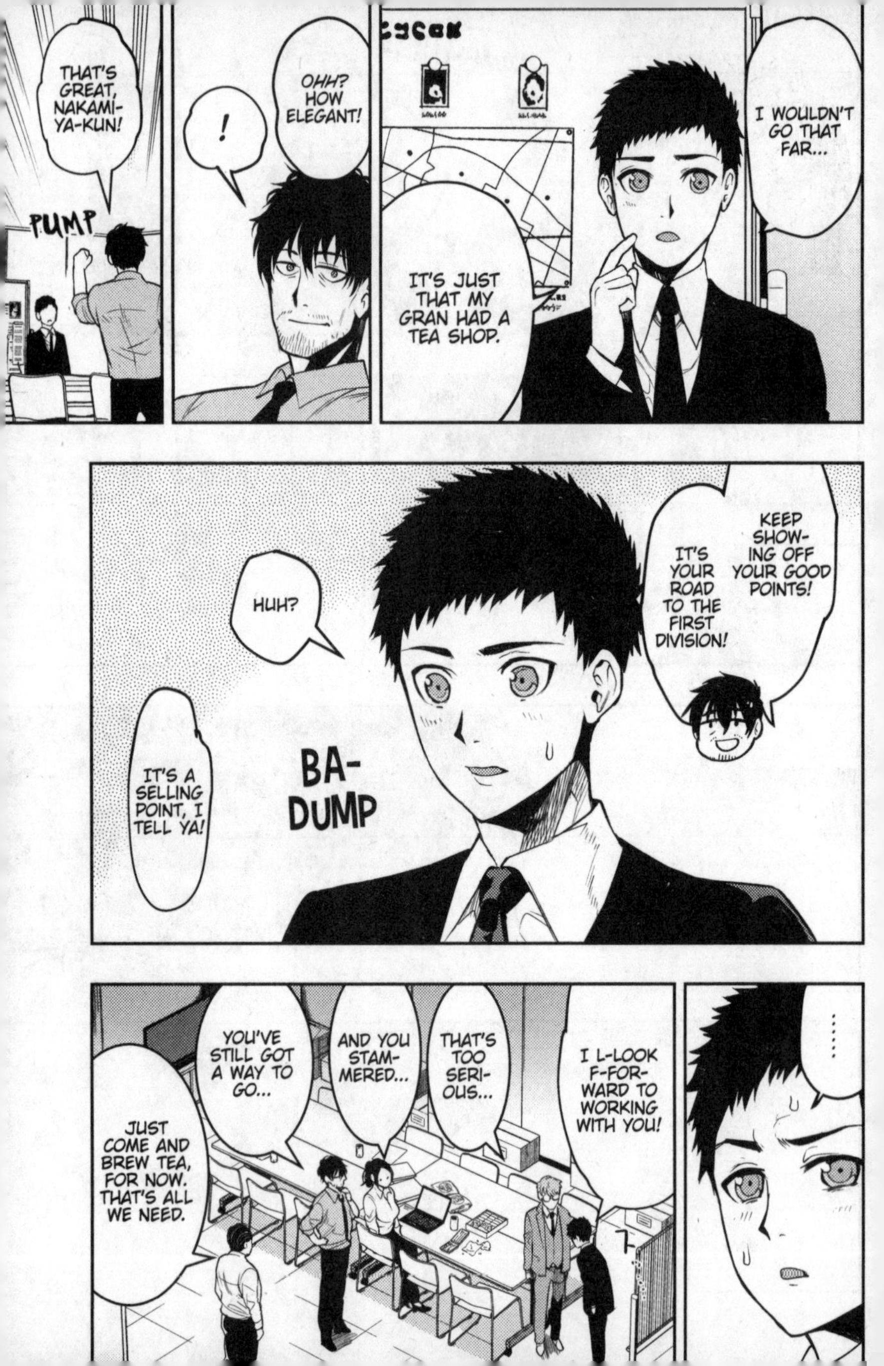
I WOULDN'T GO THAT FAR...
IT'S JUST THAT MY GRAN HAD A TEA SHOP.
OHH? HOW ELEGANT!
!
THAT'S GREAT, NAKAMIYA-KUN!
PUMP
KEEP SHOWING OFF YOUR GOOD POINTS!
IT'S YOUR ROAD TO THE FIRST DIVISION!
HUH?
BA-DUMP
IT'S A SELLING POINT, I TELL YA!
......
I L-LOOK F-FORWARD TO WORKING WITH YOU!
THAT'S TOO SERIOUS...
AND YOU STAMMERED...
YOU'VE STILL GOT A WAY TO GO...
JUST COME AND BREW TEA, FOR NOW. THAT'S ALL WE NEED.

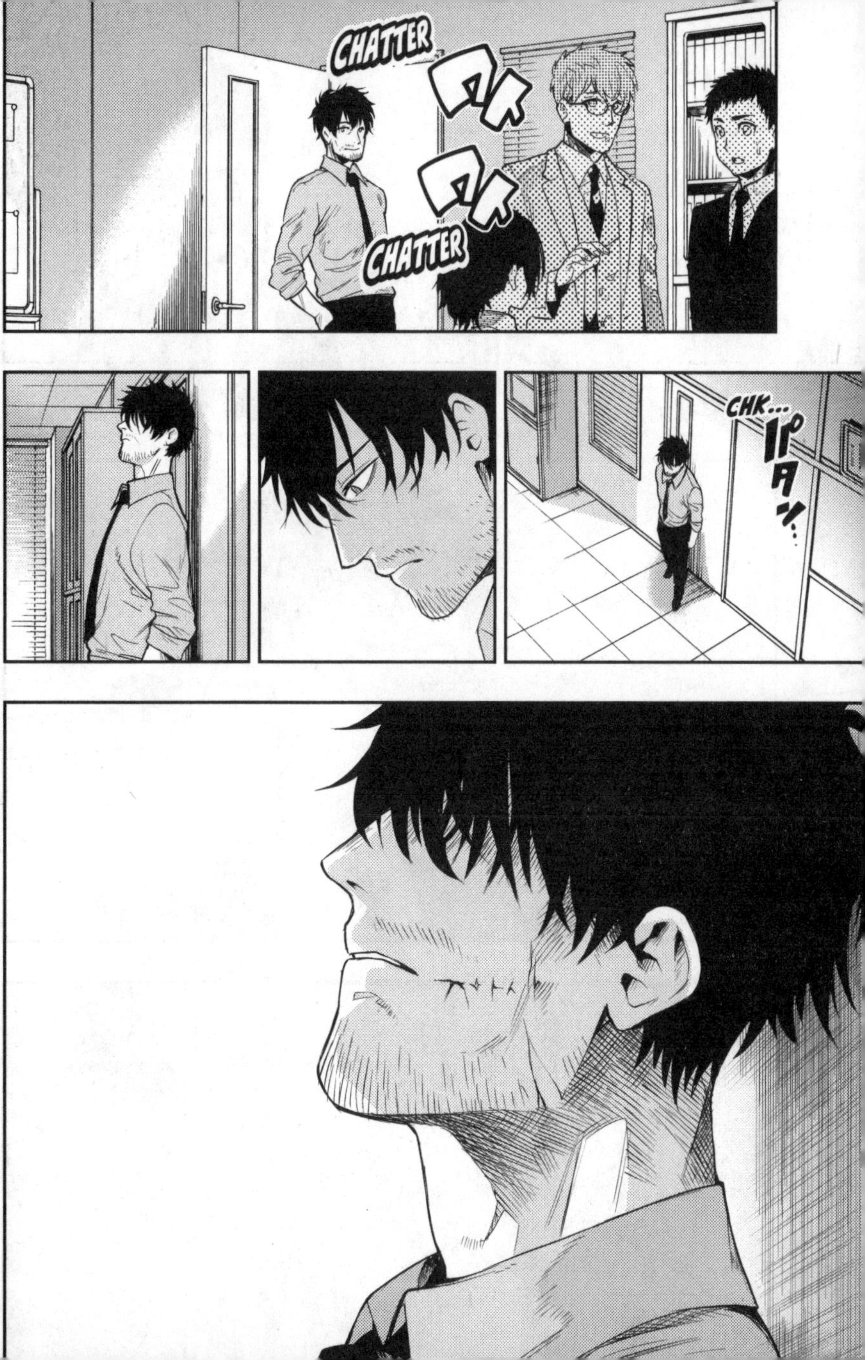
CHATTER
CHATTER
CHK...
パタン…

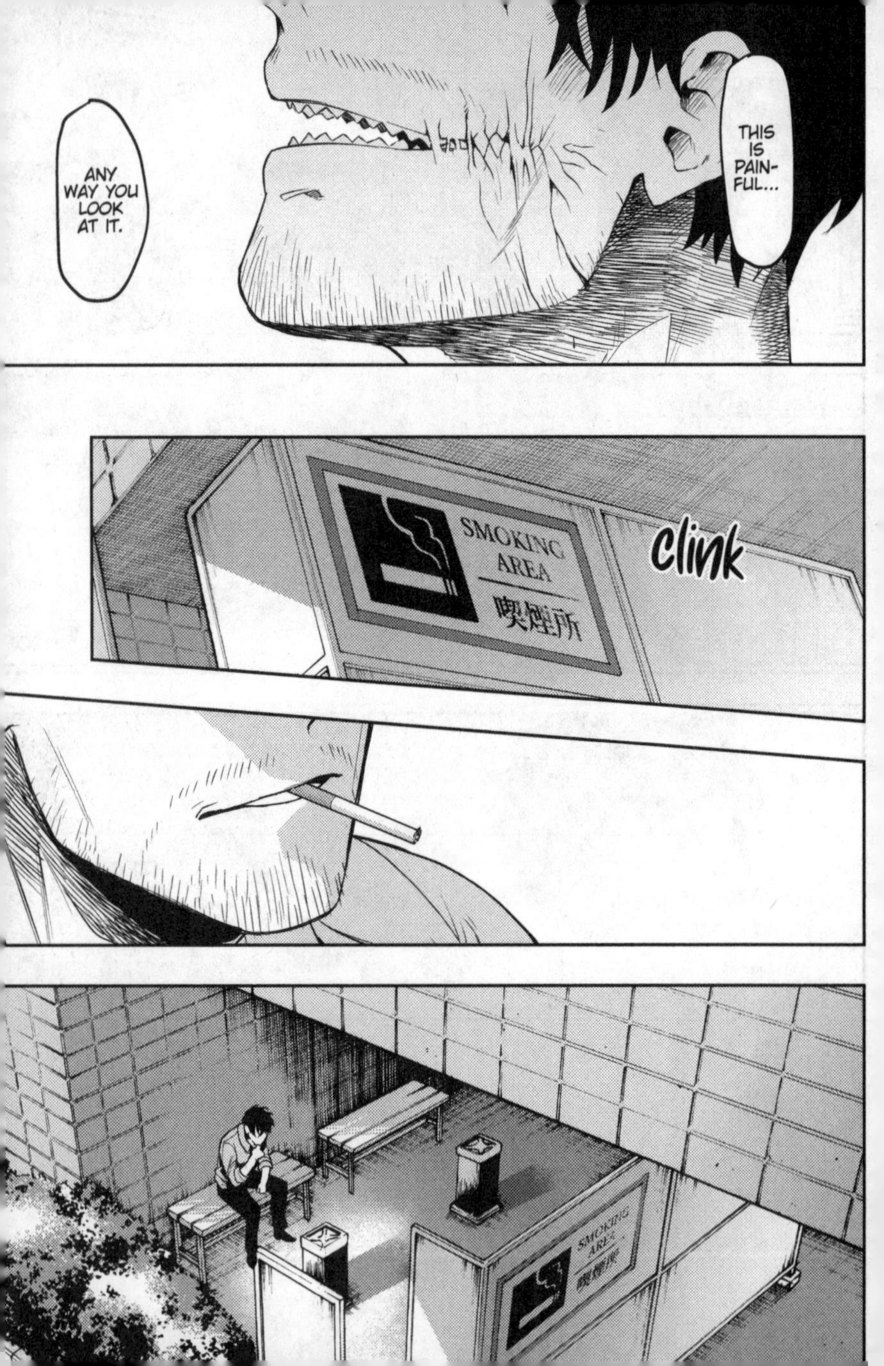
THIS IS PAIN-FUL...
ANY WAY YOU LOOK AT IT.
SMOKING AREA 喫煙所
clink

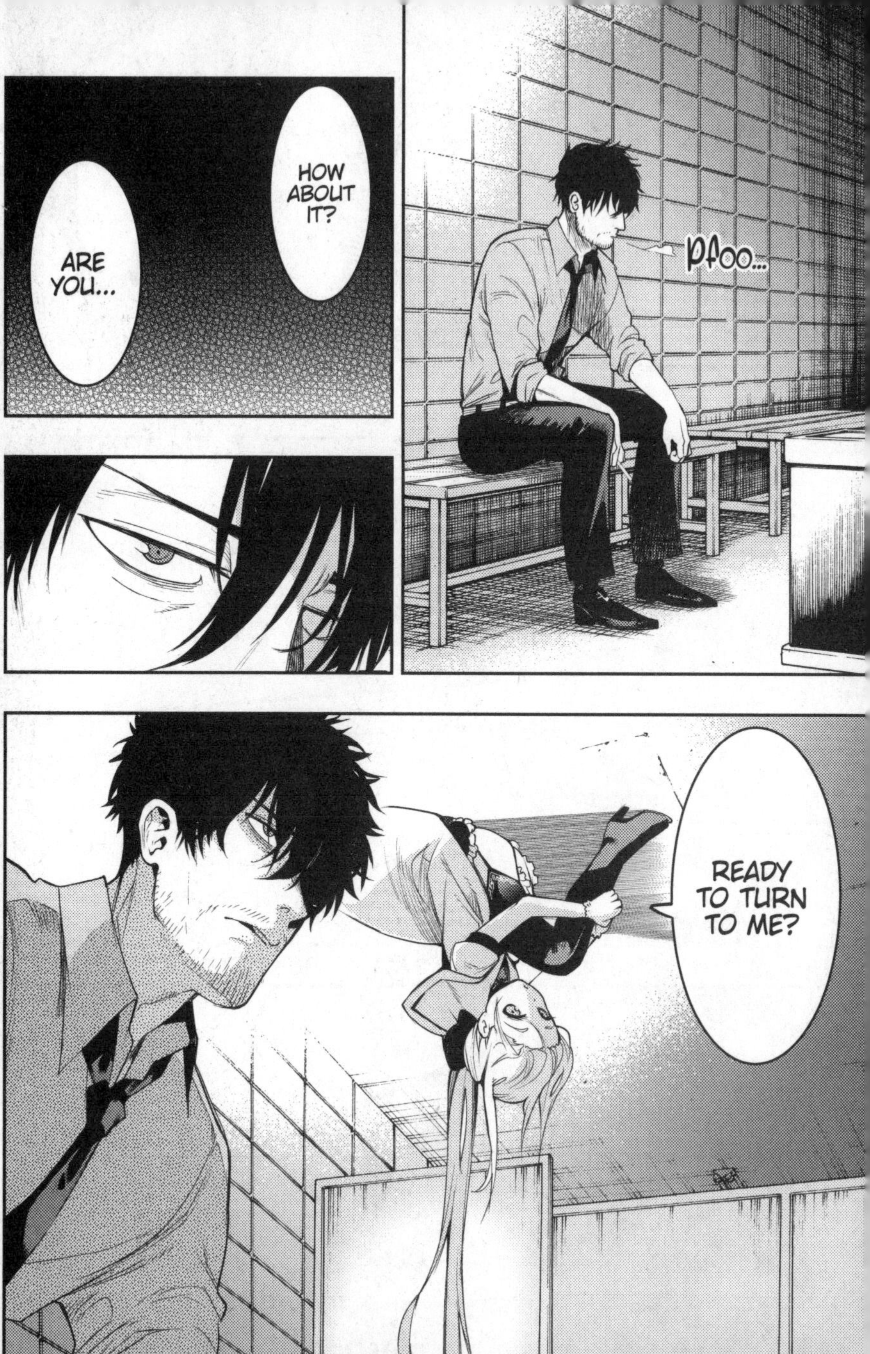
Pfoo...
HOW ABOUT IT?
ARE YOU...
READY TO TURN TO ME?

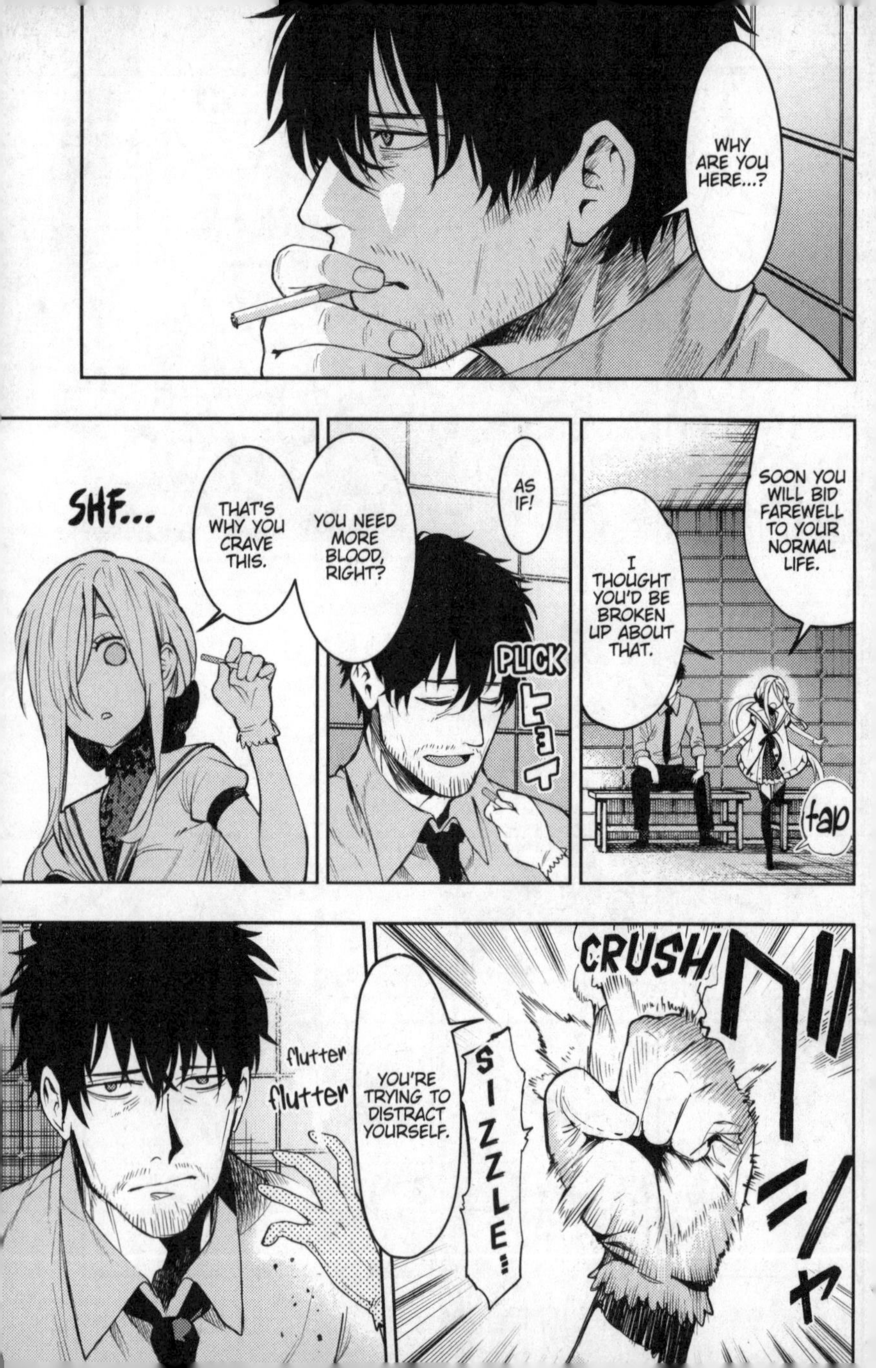
WHY ARE YOU HERE...?
SOON YOU WILL BID FAREWELL TO YOUR NORMAL LIFE.
I THOUGHT YOU'D BE BROKEN UP ABOUT THAT.
tap
AS IF!
PLICK
ヒョイ
YOU NEED MORE BLOOD, RIGHT?
THAT'S WHY YOU CRAVE THIS.
SHF...
CRUSH
SIZZLE...
YOU'RE TRYING TO DISTRACT YOURSELF.
flutter
flutter

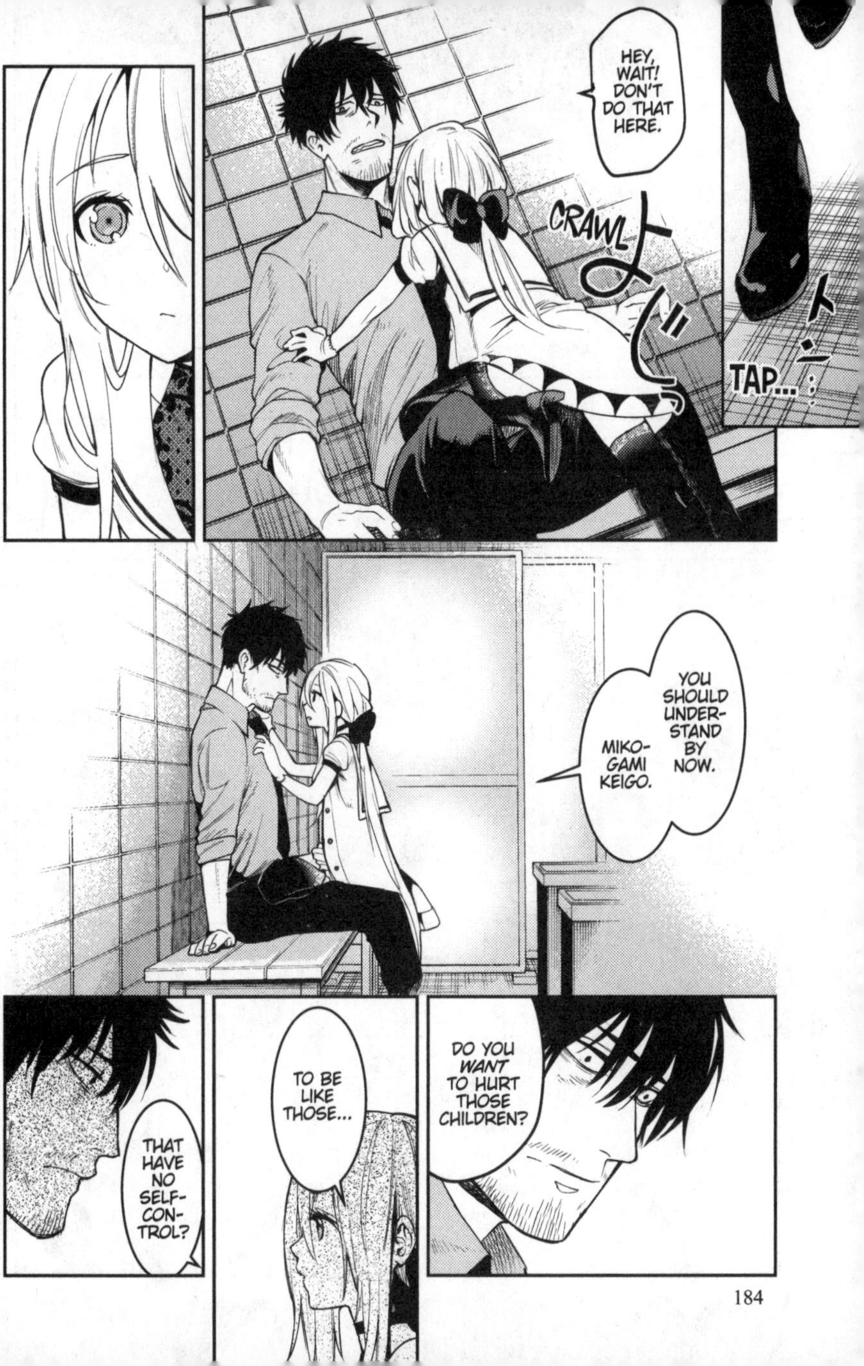
TAP...
HEY, WAIT! DON'T DO THAT HERE.
CRAWL
YOU SHOULD UNDERSTAND BY NOW.
MIKOGAMI KEIGO.
DO YOU *WANT* TO HURT THOSE CHILDREN?
TO BE LIKE THOSE...
THAT HAVE NO SELF-CONTROL?

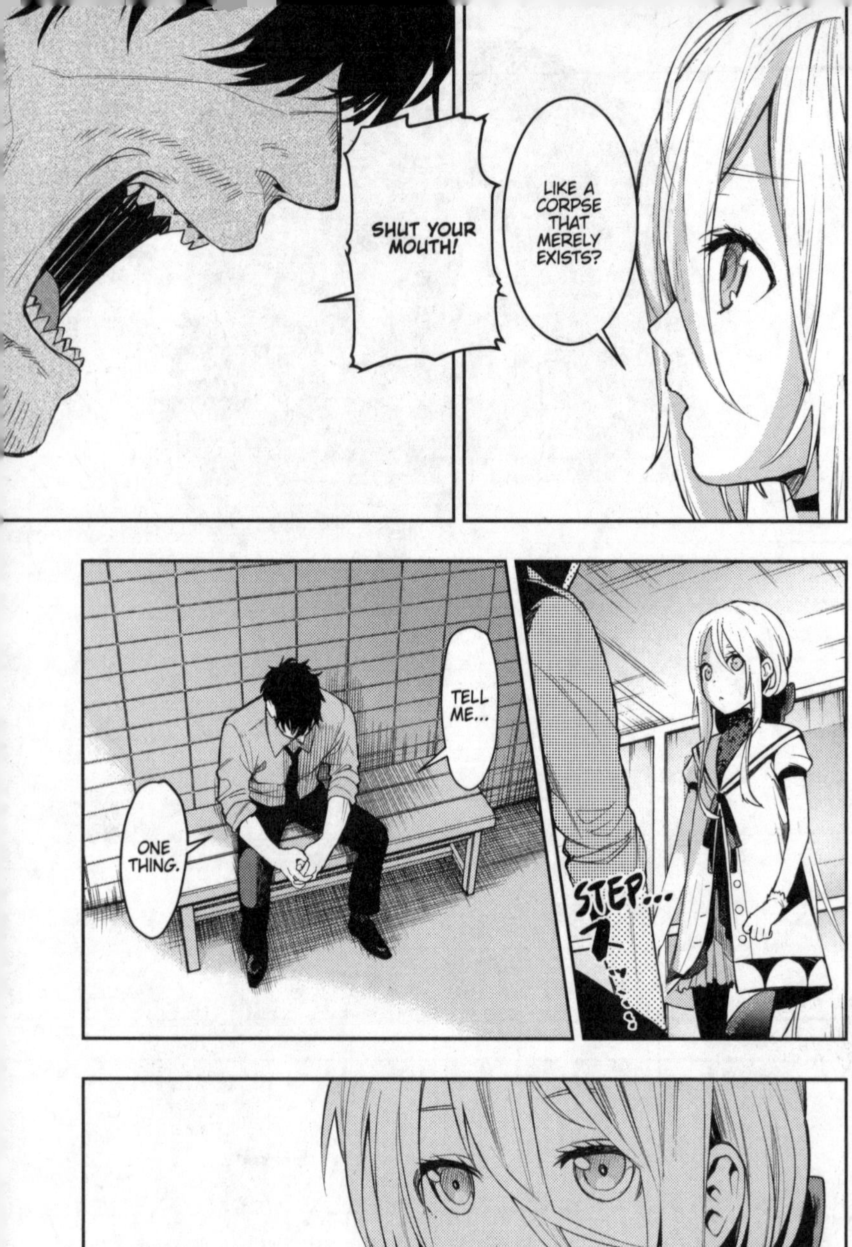
LIKE A CORPSE THAT MERELY EXISTS?
SHUT YOUR MOUTH!
STEP...
TELL ME...
ONE THING.

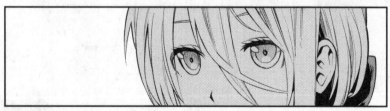

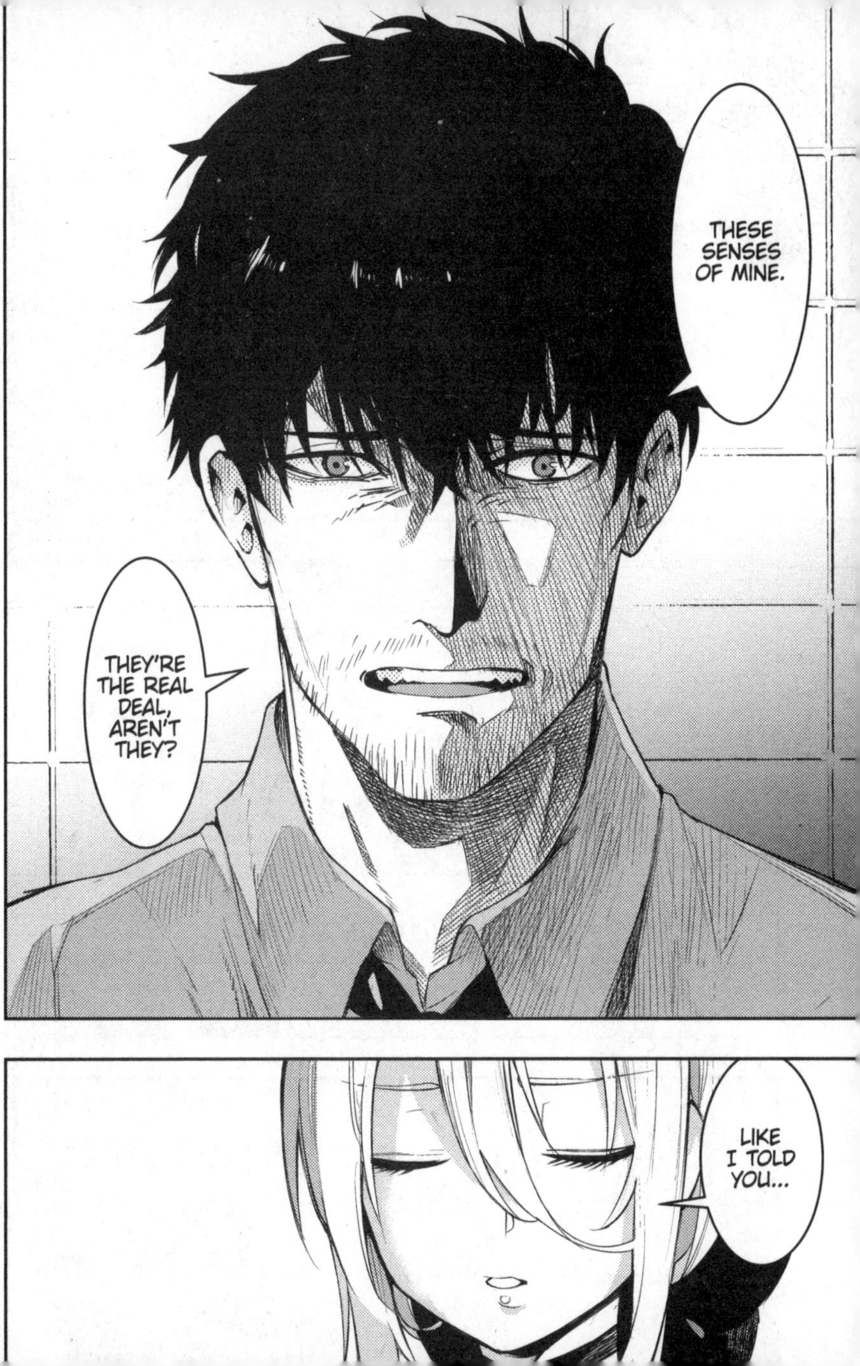
THESE SENSES OF MINE.
THEY'RE THE REAL DEAL, AREN'T THEY?
LIKE I TOLD YOU...

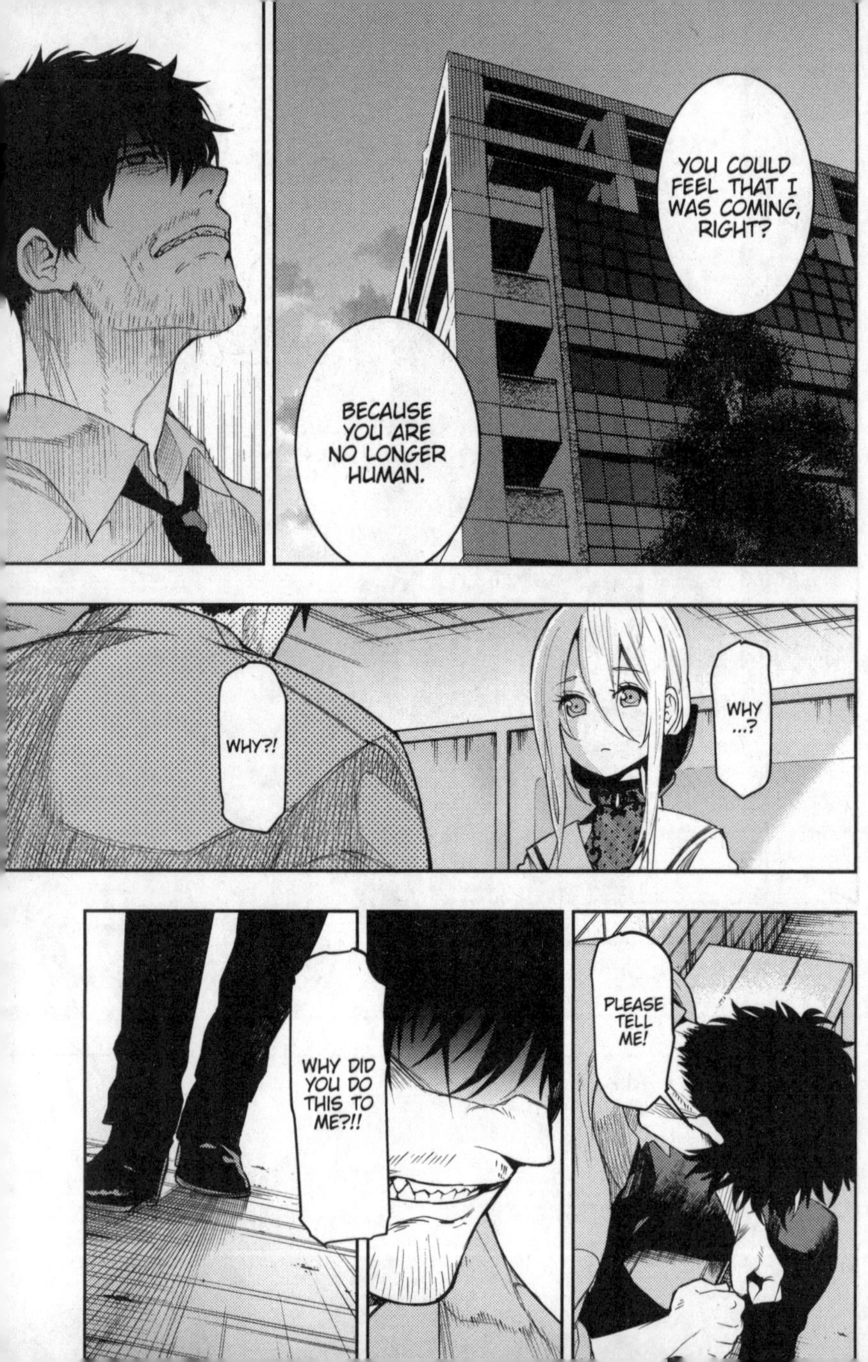
YOU COULD FEEL THAT I WAS COMING, RIGHT?
BECAUSE YOU ARE NO LONGER HUMAN.
WHY ...?
WHY?!
PLEASE TELL ME!
WHY DID YOU DO THIS TO ME?!!

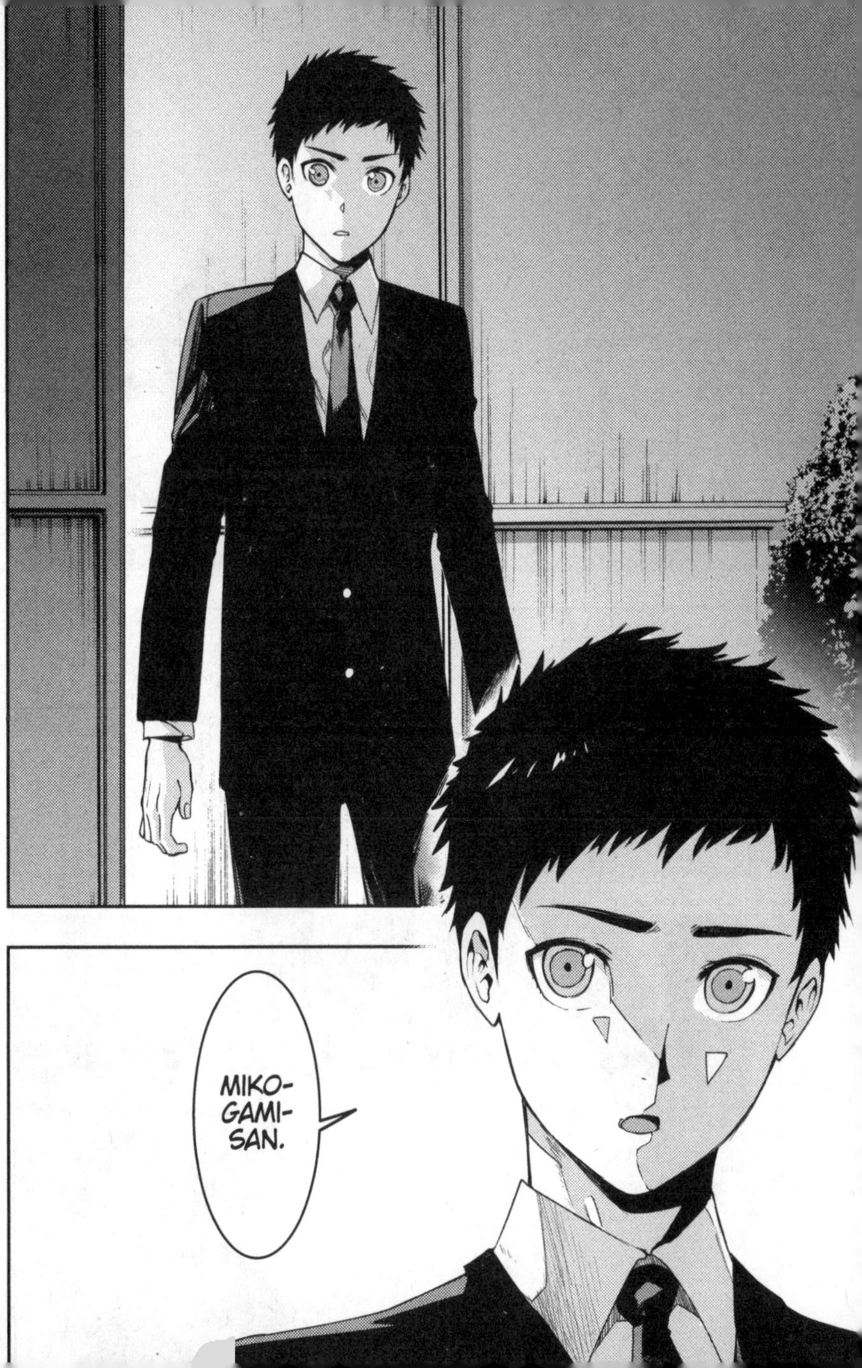
MIKO-
GAMI-
SAN.

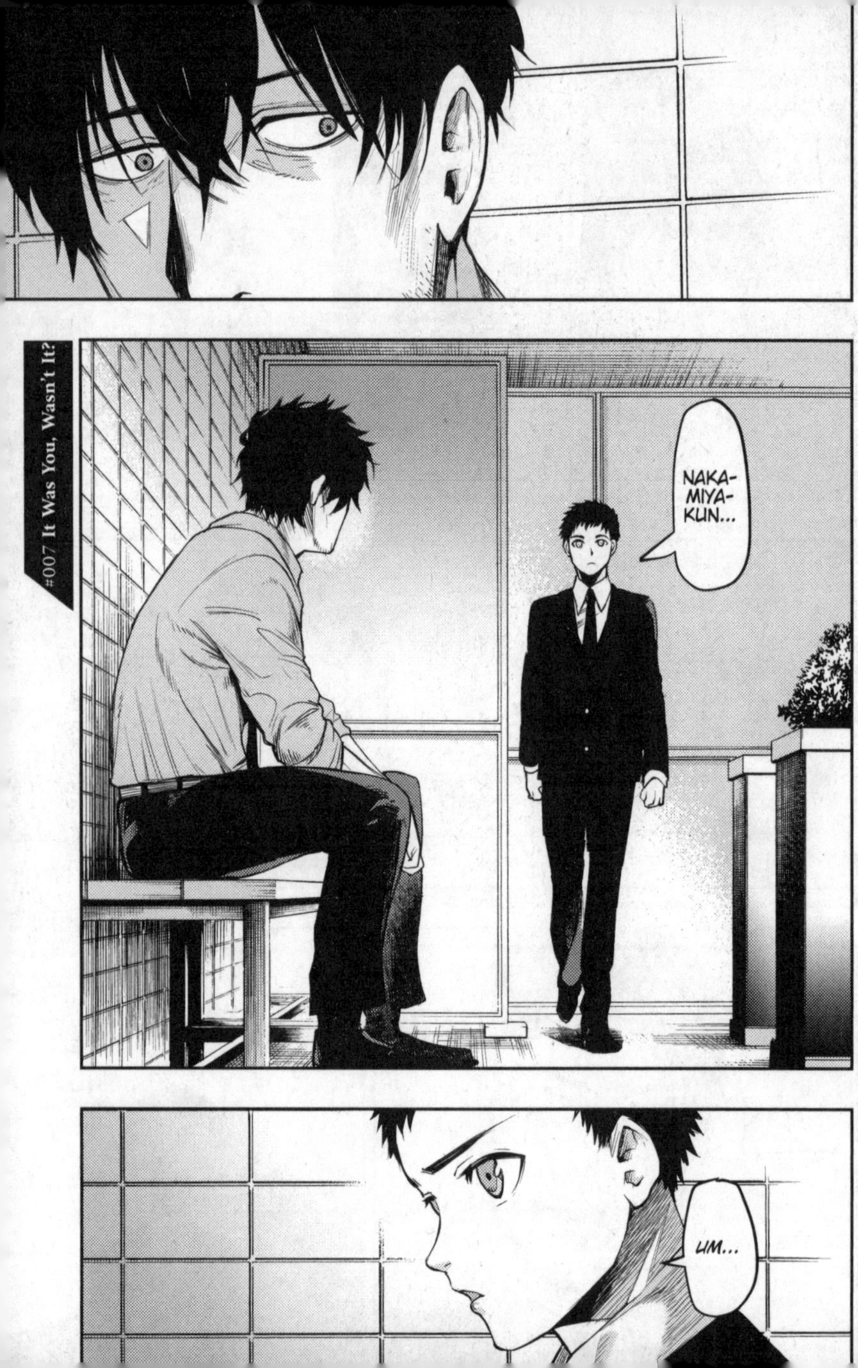
#007 It Was You, Wasn't It?
NAKA-MIYA-KUN...
UM...

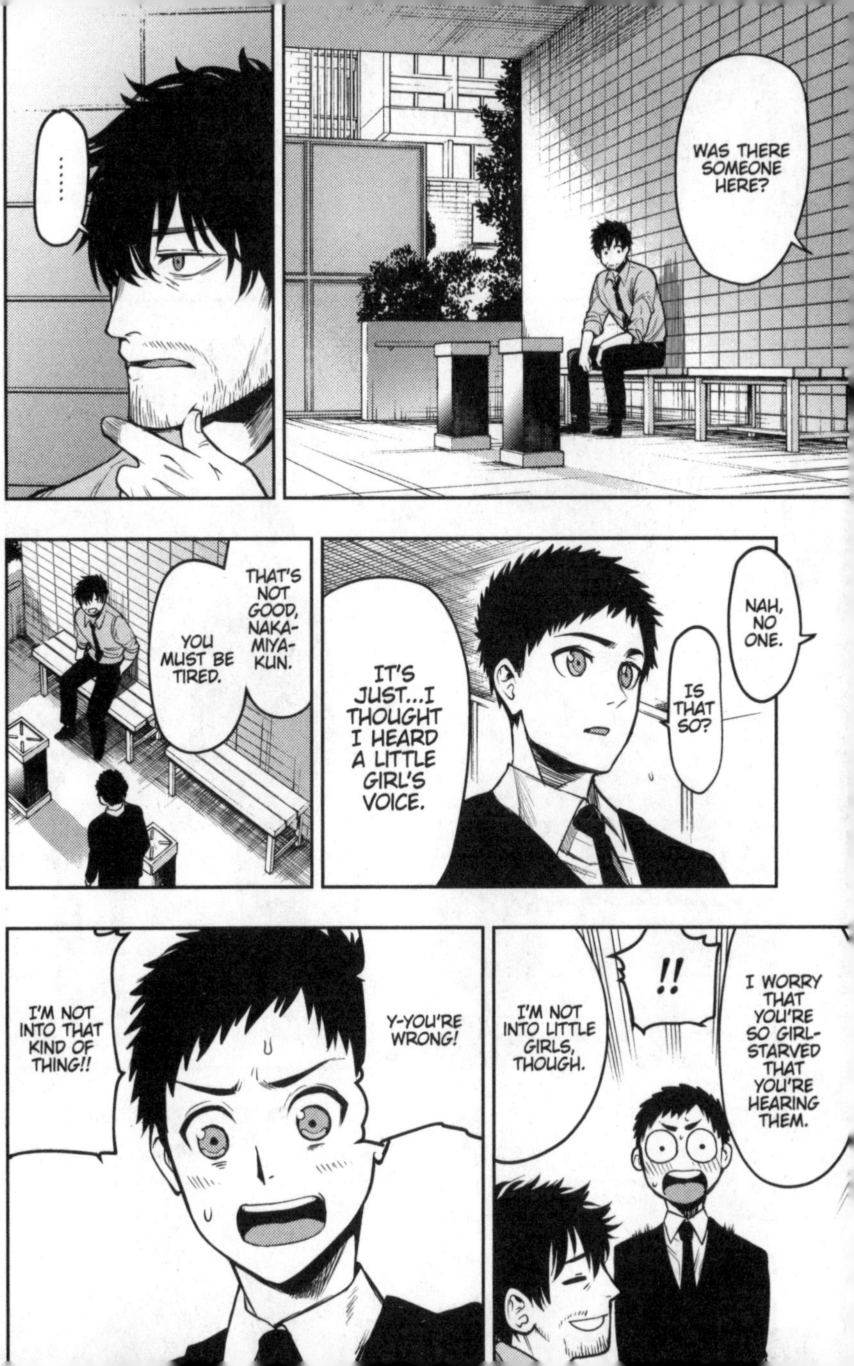
WAS THERE SOMEONE HERE?
......
NAH, NO ONE.
IS THAT SO?
IT'S JUST...I THOUGHT I HEARD A LITTLE GIRL'S VOICE.
THAT'S NOT GOOD, NAKA-MIYA-KUN.
YOU MUST BE TIRED.
I WORRY THAT YOU'RE SO GIRL-STARVED THAT YOU'RE HEARING THEM.
!!
I'M NOT INTO LITTLE GIRLS, THOUGH.
Y-YOU'RE WRONG!
I'M NOT INTO THAT KIND OF THING!!

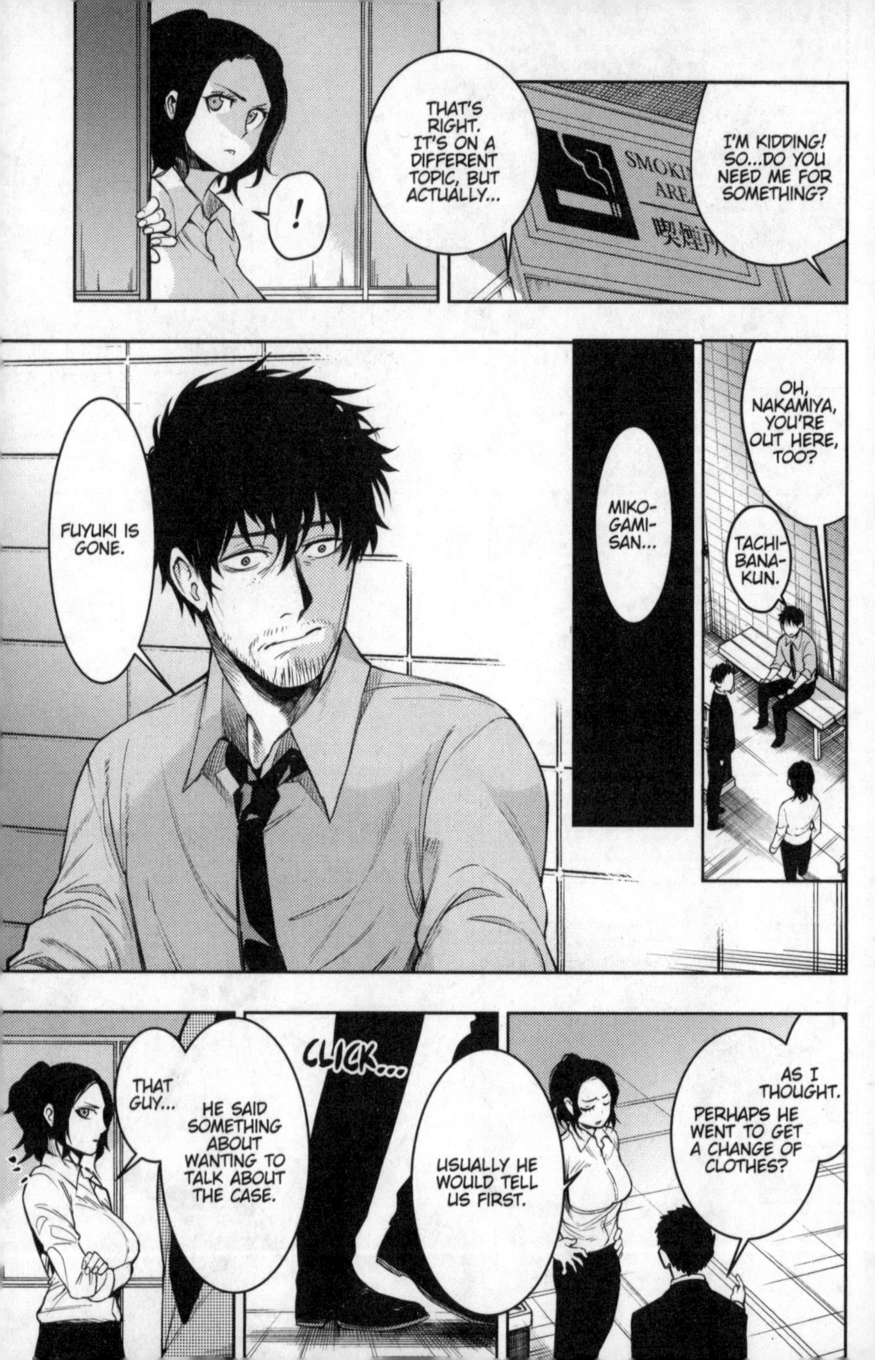
I'M KIDDING! SO...DO YOU NEED ME FOR SOMETHING?
THAT'S RIGHT. IT'S ON A DIFFERENT TOPIC, BUT ACTUALLY...
!
OH, NAKAMIYA, YOU'RE OUT HERE, TOO?
TACHIBANA-KUN.
MIKO-GAMI-SAN...
FUYUKI IS GONE.
AS I THOUGHT.
PERHAPS HE WENT TO GET A CHANGE OF CLOTHES?
USUALLY HE WOULD TELL US FIRST.
CLICK...
THAT GUY...
HE SAID SOMETHING ABOUT WANTING TO TALK ABOUT THE CASE.

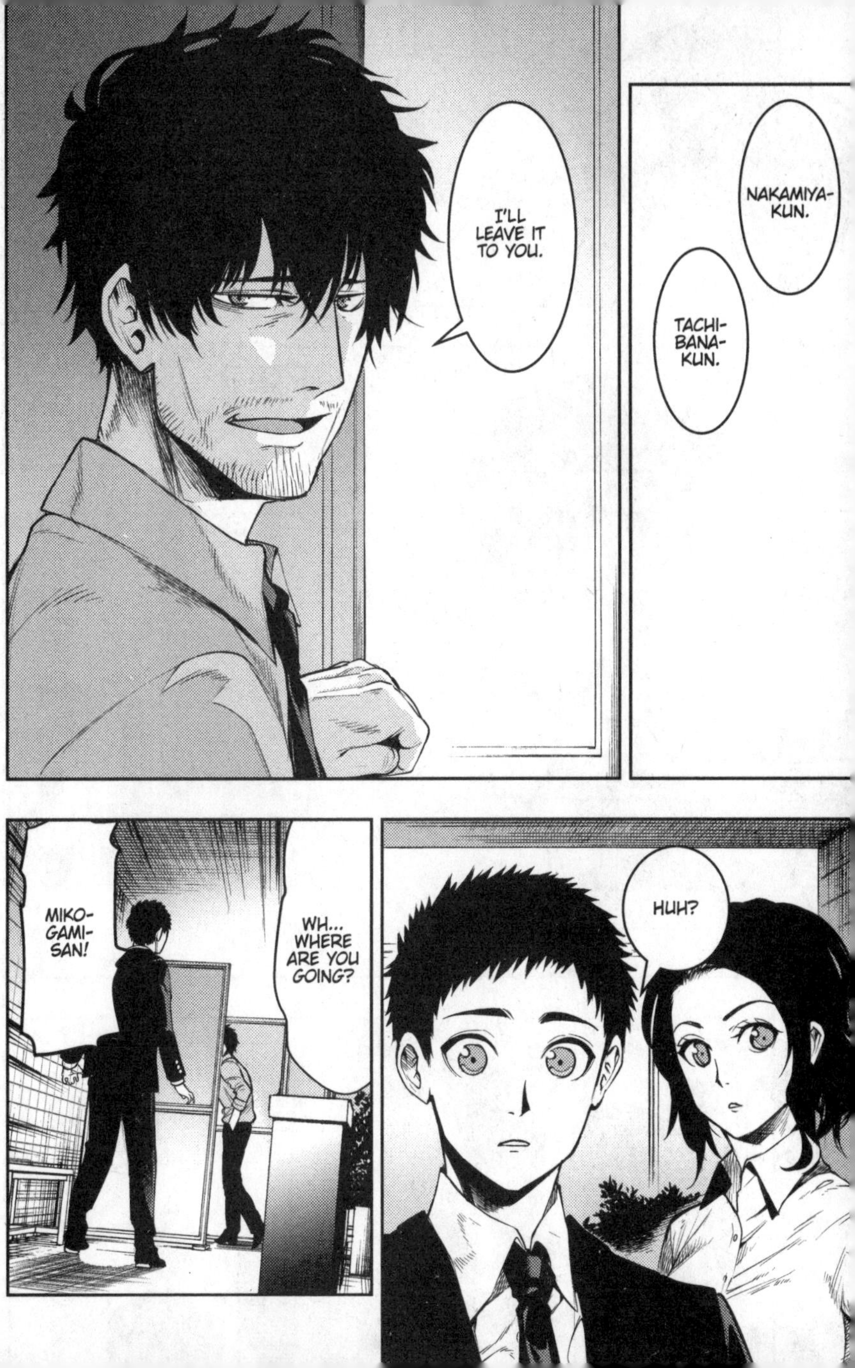
NAKAMIYA-KUN.
TACHI-BANA-KUN.
I'LL LEAVE IT TO YOU.
HUH?
WH... WHERE ARE YOU GOING?
MIKO-GAMI-SAN!

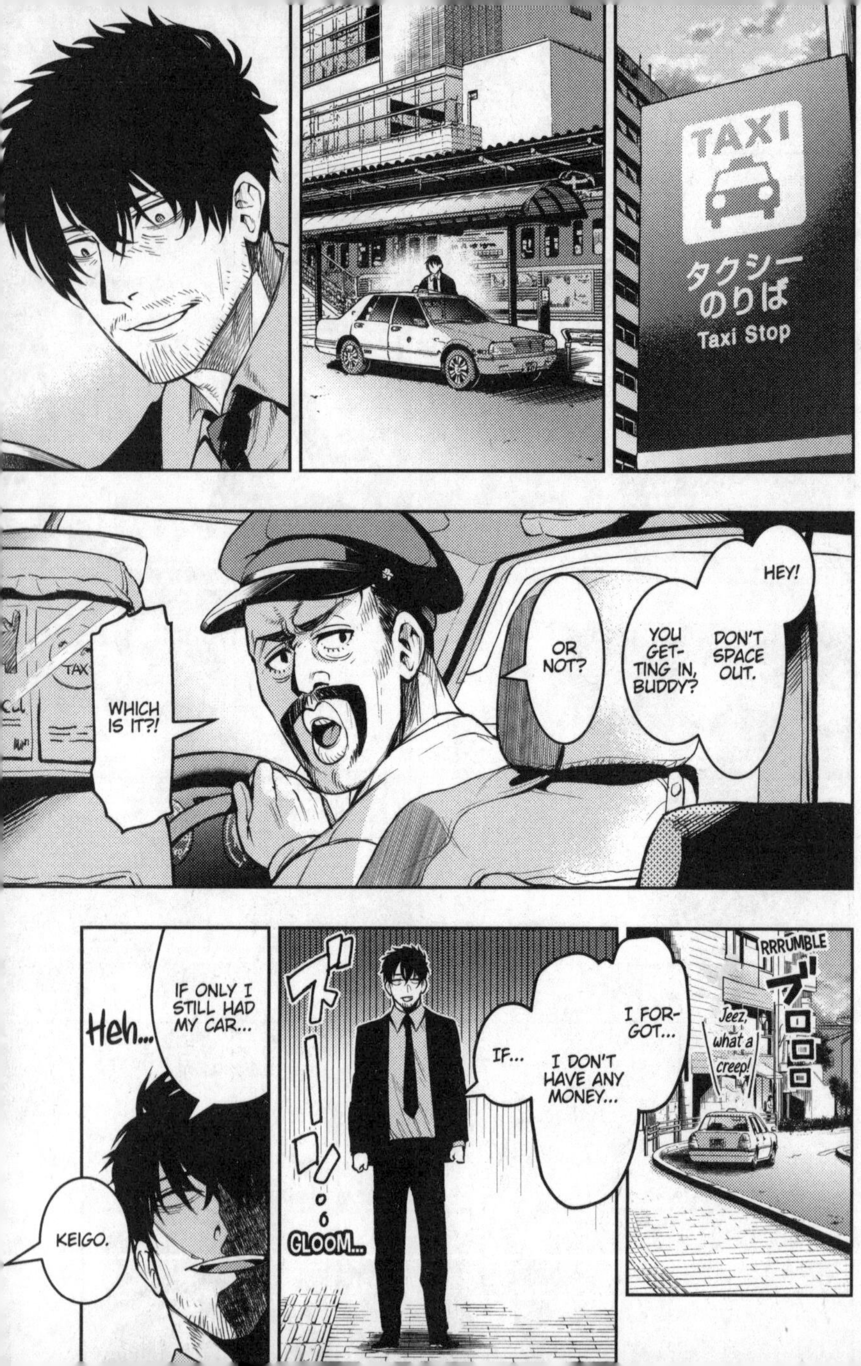
TAXI
タクシーのりば
Taxi Stop
HEY!
DON'T SPACE OUT.
YOU GETTING IN, BUDDY?
OR NOT?
WHICH IS IT?!
RRRUMBLE
ブロロロ
Jeez, what a creep!
I FORGOT...
I DON'T HAVE ANY MONEY...
IF...
ズーン
GLOOM...
IF ONLY I STILL HAD MY CAR...
Heh...
KEIGO.

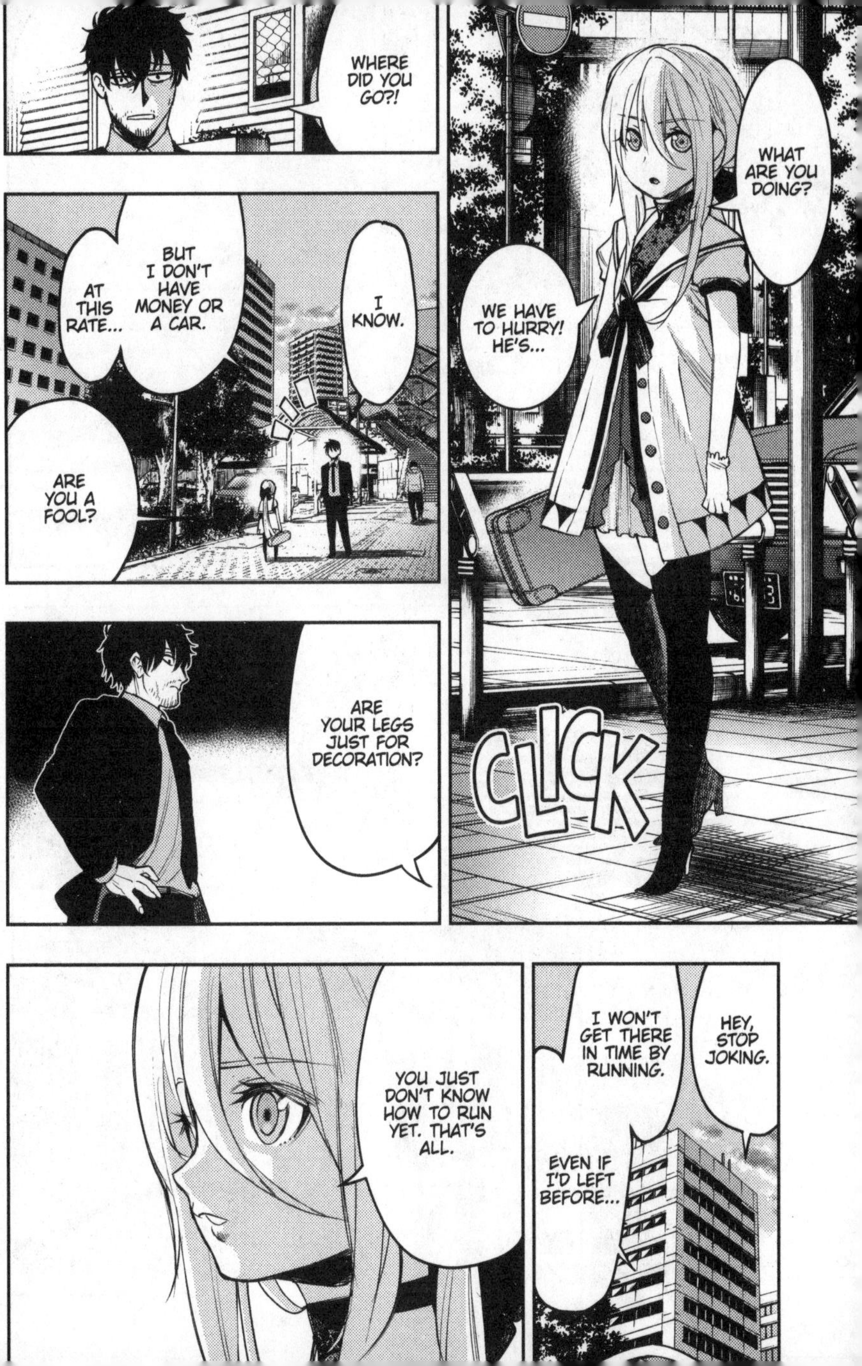
WHAT ARE YOU DOING?
WE HAVE TO HURRY! HE'S...
CLICK
WHERE DID YOU GO?!
I KNOW.
BUT I DON'T HAVE MONEY OR A CAR.
AT THIS RATE...
ARE YOU A FOOL?
ARE YOUR LEGS JUST FOR DECORATION?
HEY, STOP JOKING.
I WON'T GET THERE IN TIME BY RUNNING.
EVEN IF I'D LEFT BEFORE...
YOU JUST DON'T KNOW HOW TO RUN YET. THAT'S ALL.

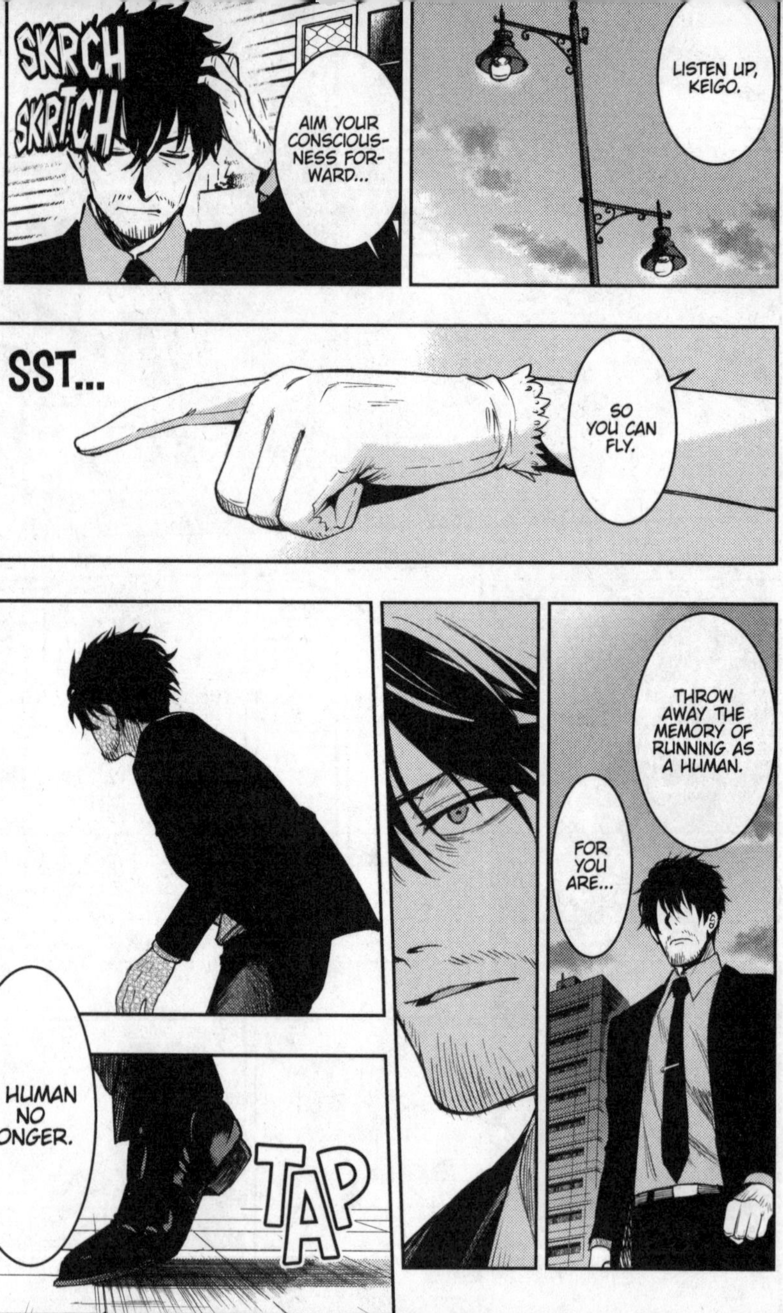
LISTEN UP, KEIGO.
AIM YOUR CONSCIOUSNESS FORWARD...
SKRCH SKRTCH
SO YOU CAN FLY.
SST...
THROW AWAY THE MEMORY OF RUNNING AS A HUMAN.
FOR YOU ARE...
A HUMAN NO LONGER.
TAP

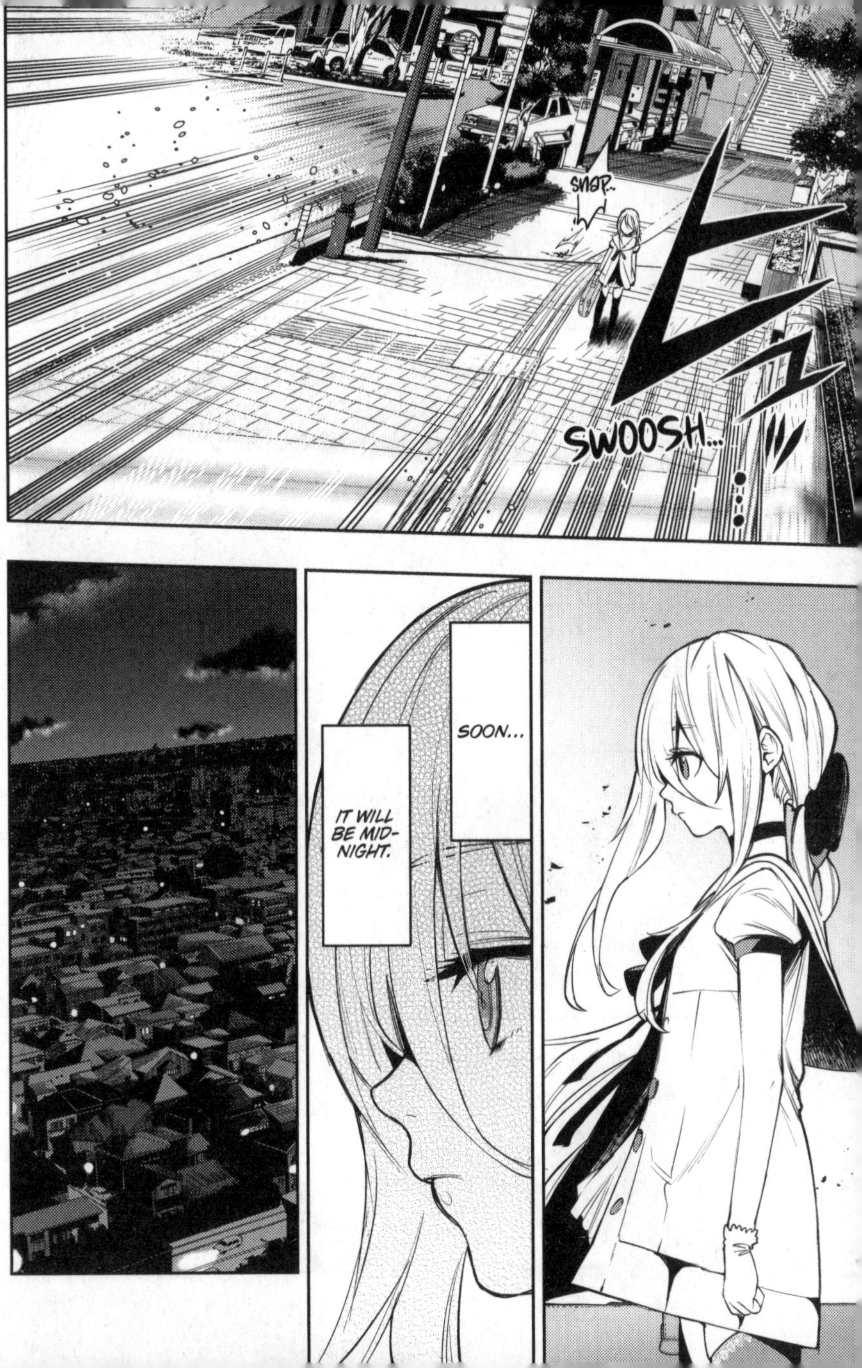
snap..
SWOOSH...
SOON...
IT WILL BE MID-NIGHT.

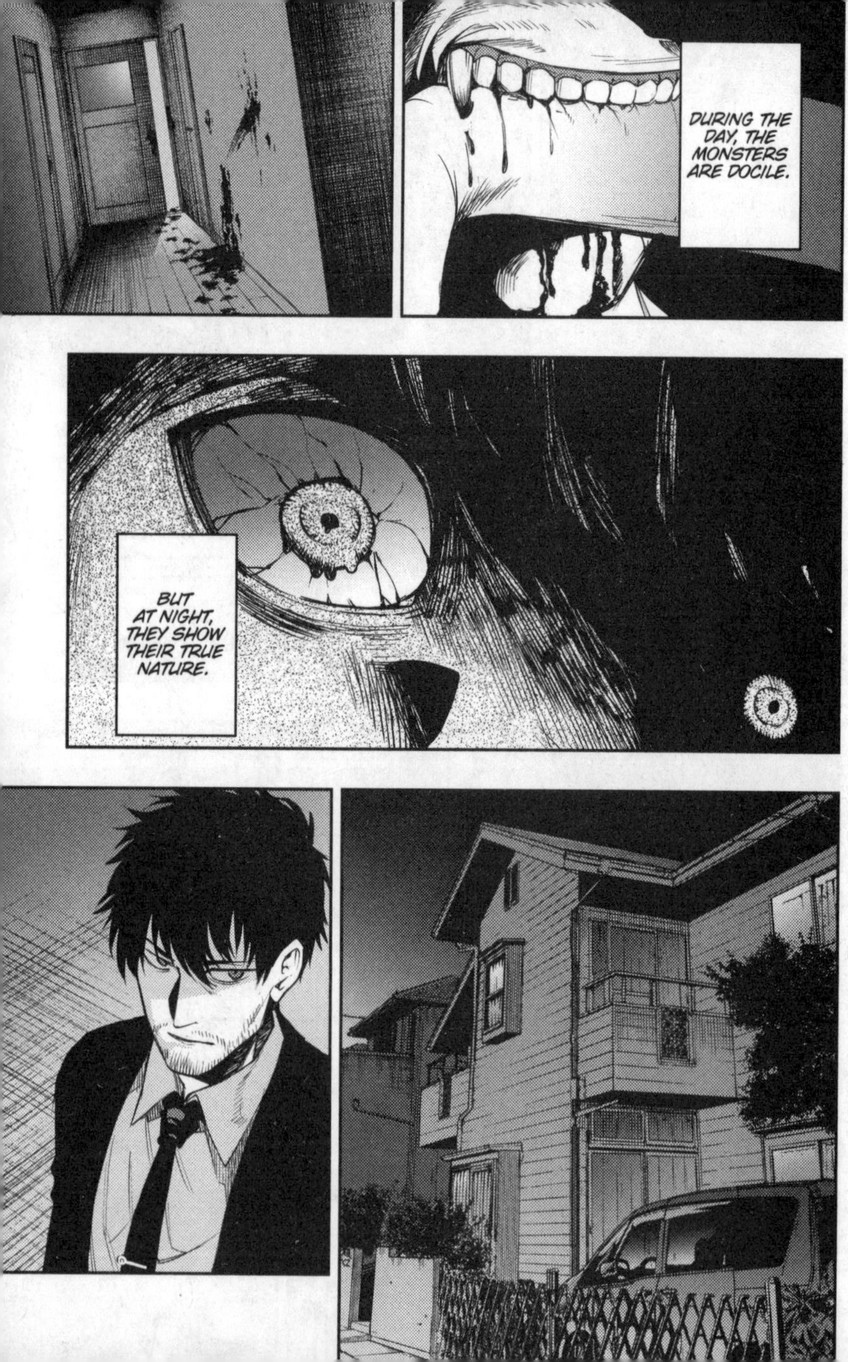
DURING THE DAY, THE MONSTERS ARE DOCILE.
BUT AT NIGHT, THEY SHOW THEIR TRUE NATURE.

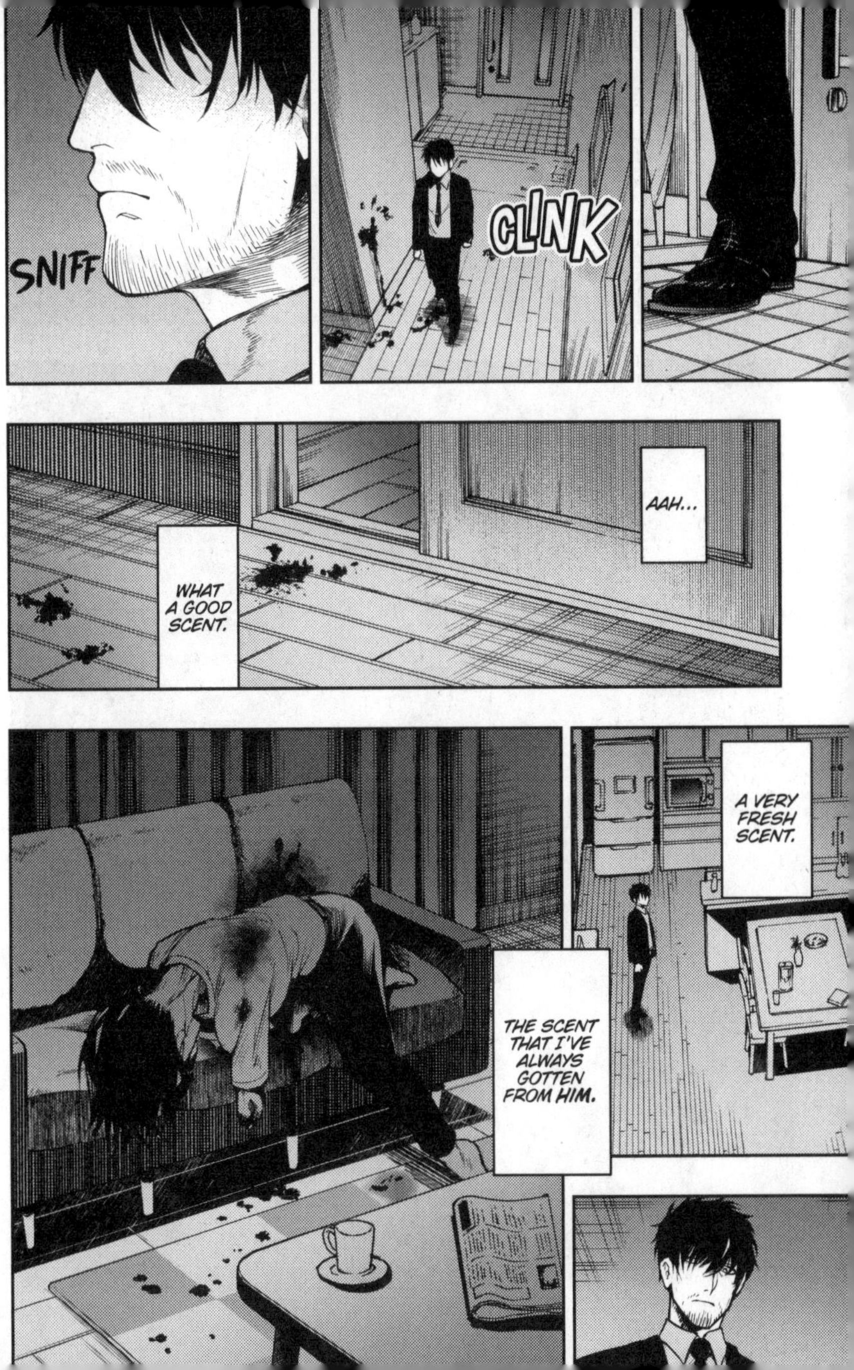
CLINK
SNIFF
AAH...
WHAT A GOOD SCENT.
A VERY FRESH SCENT.
THE SCENT THAT I'VE ALWAYS GOTTEN FROM HIM.

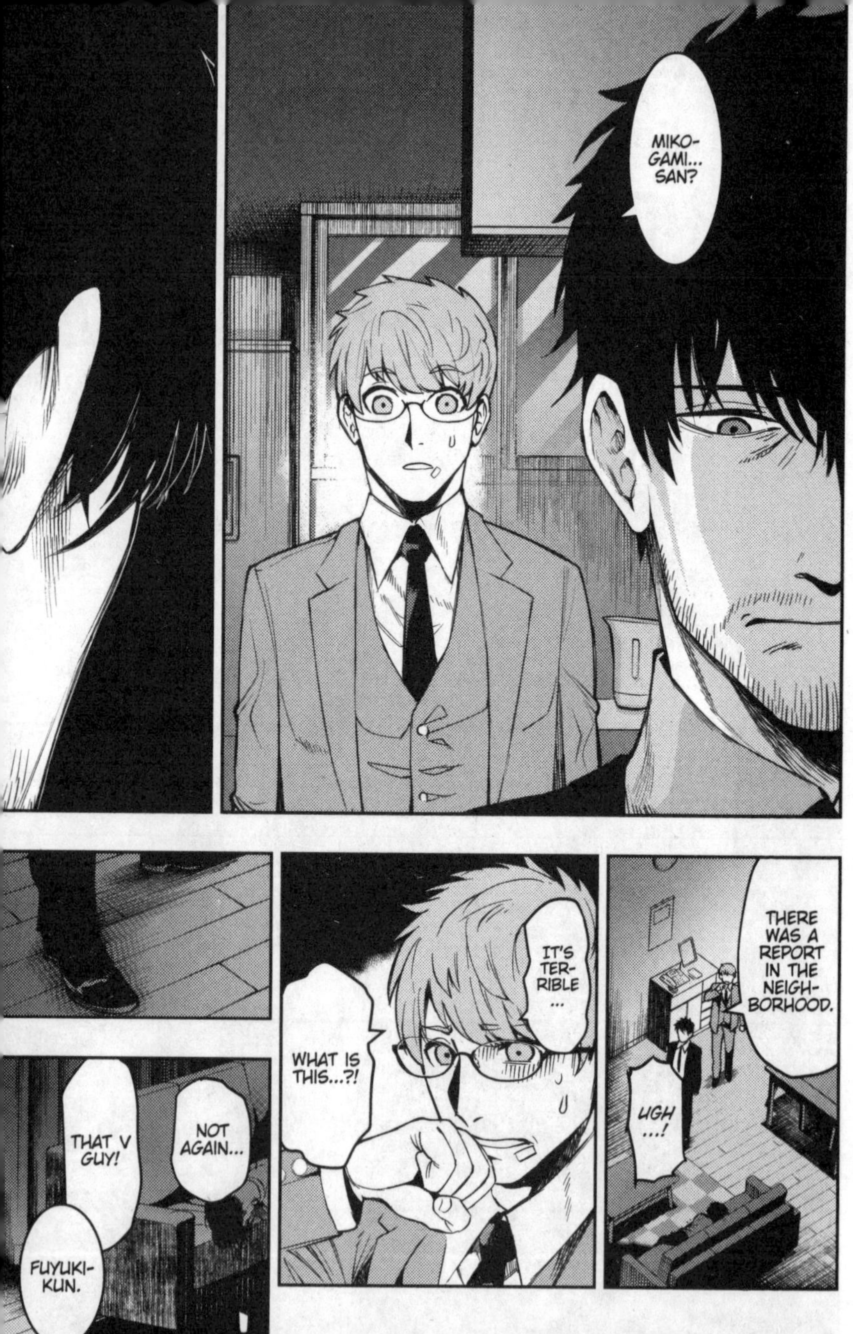
MIKO-GAMI... SAN?
THERE WAS A REPORT IN THE NEIGH-BORHOOD.
UGH...!
IT'S TER-RIBLE...
WHAT IS THIS...?!
NOT AGAIN...
THAT V GUY!
FUYUKI-KUN.

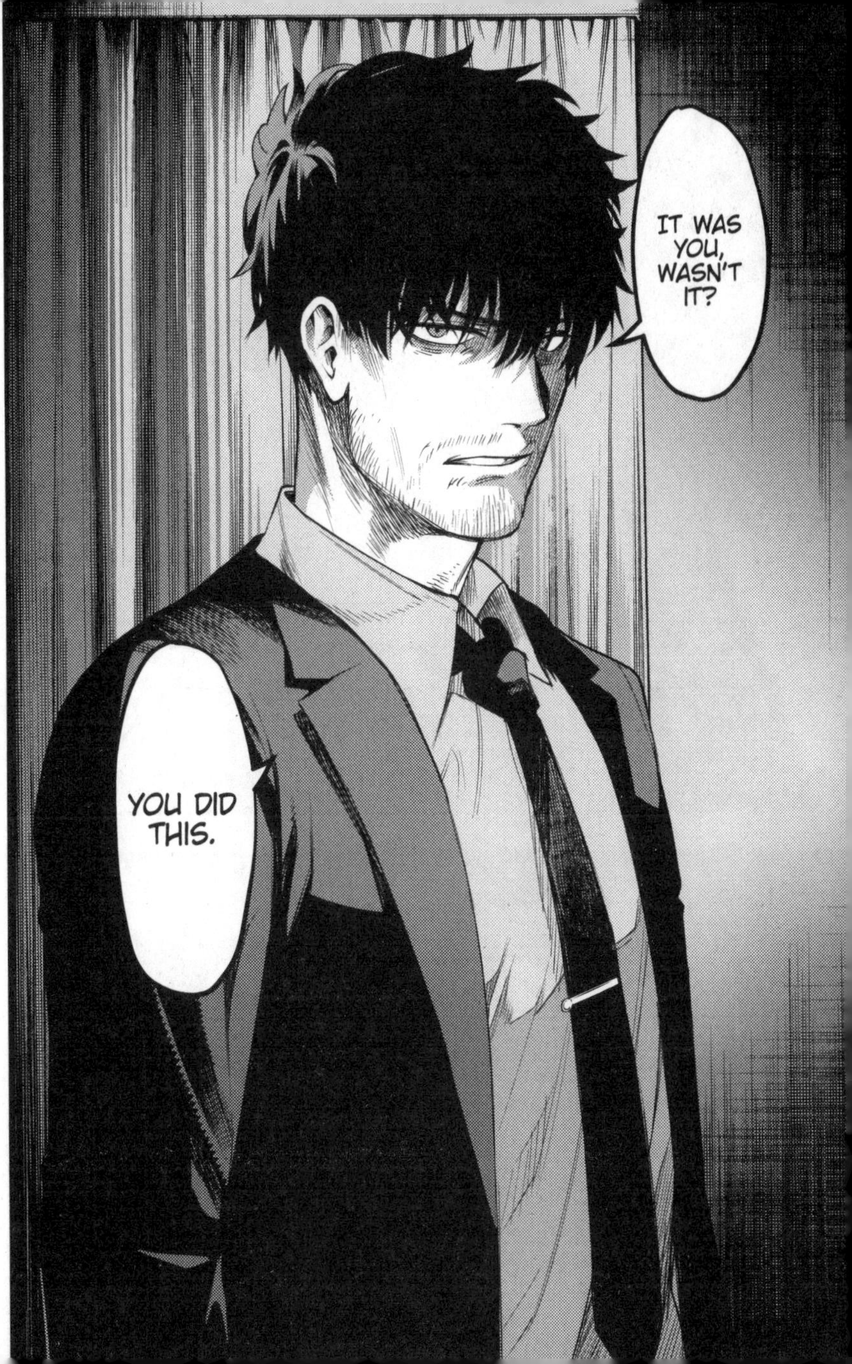
IT WAS YOU, WASN'T IT?
YOU DID THIS.

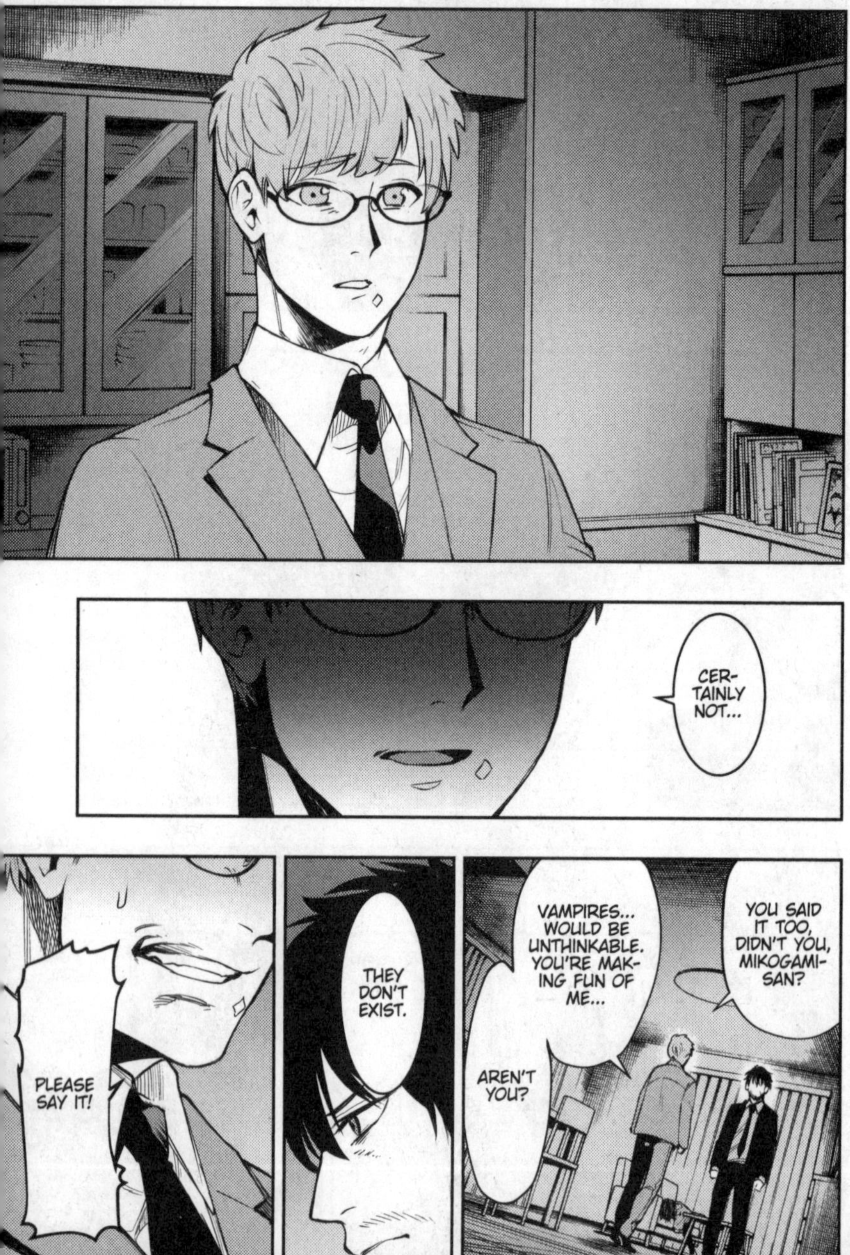
CER-
TAINLY
NOT...
YOU SAID IT TOO, DIDN'T YOU, MIKOGAMI-SAN?
VAMPIRES... WOULD BE UNTHINKABLE. YOU'RE MAK-ING FUN OF ME...
AREN'T YOU?
THEY DON'T EXIST.
PLEASE SAY IT!

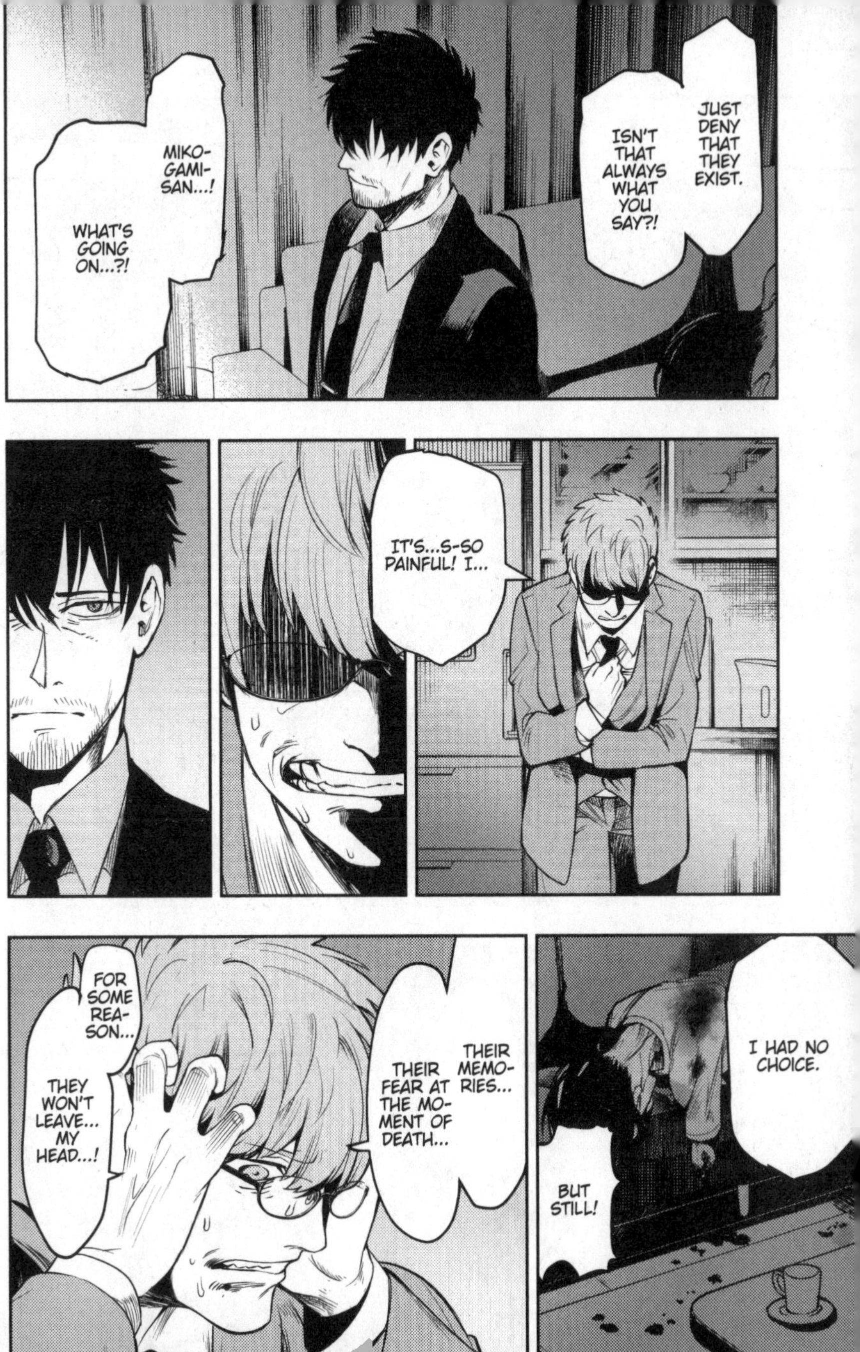
JUST DENY THAT THEY EXIST. ISN'T THAT ALWAYS WHAT YOU SAY?!
MIKO-GAMI-SAN...! WHAT'S GOING ON...?!
IT'S...S-SO PAINFUL! I...
I HAD NO CHOICE.
BUT STILL!
THEIR MEMO-RIES... THEIR FEAR AT THE MO-MENT OF DEATH...
FOR SOME REA-SON... THEY WON'T LEAVE... MY HEAD...!

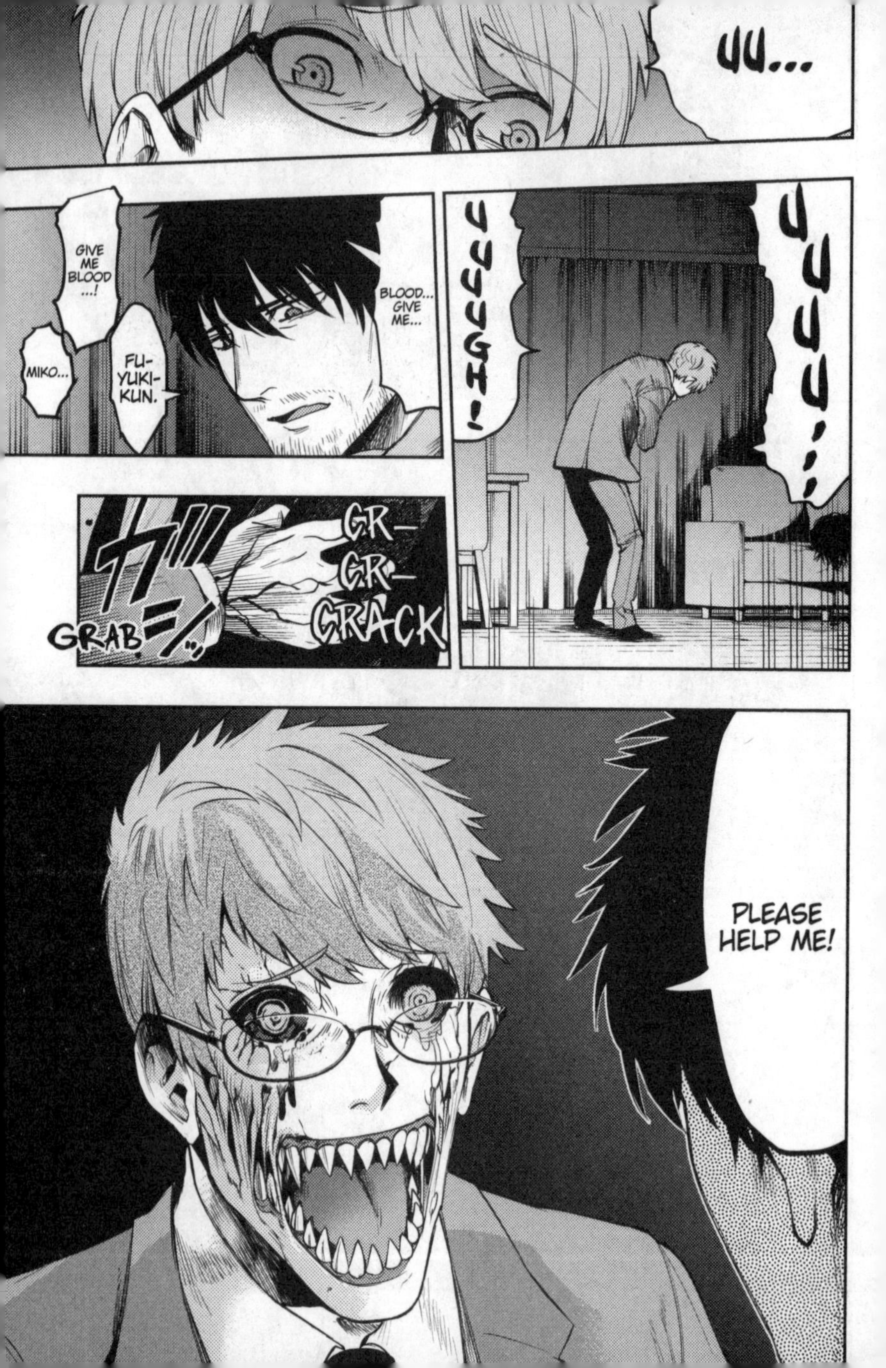
UU...
UUUU...!
UUUUGH!
BLOOD... GIVE ME...
GIVE ME BLOOD...!
FU-YUKI-KUN.
MIKO...
GR-GR-CRACK
GRAB
PLEASE HELP ME!

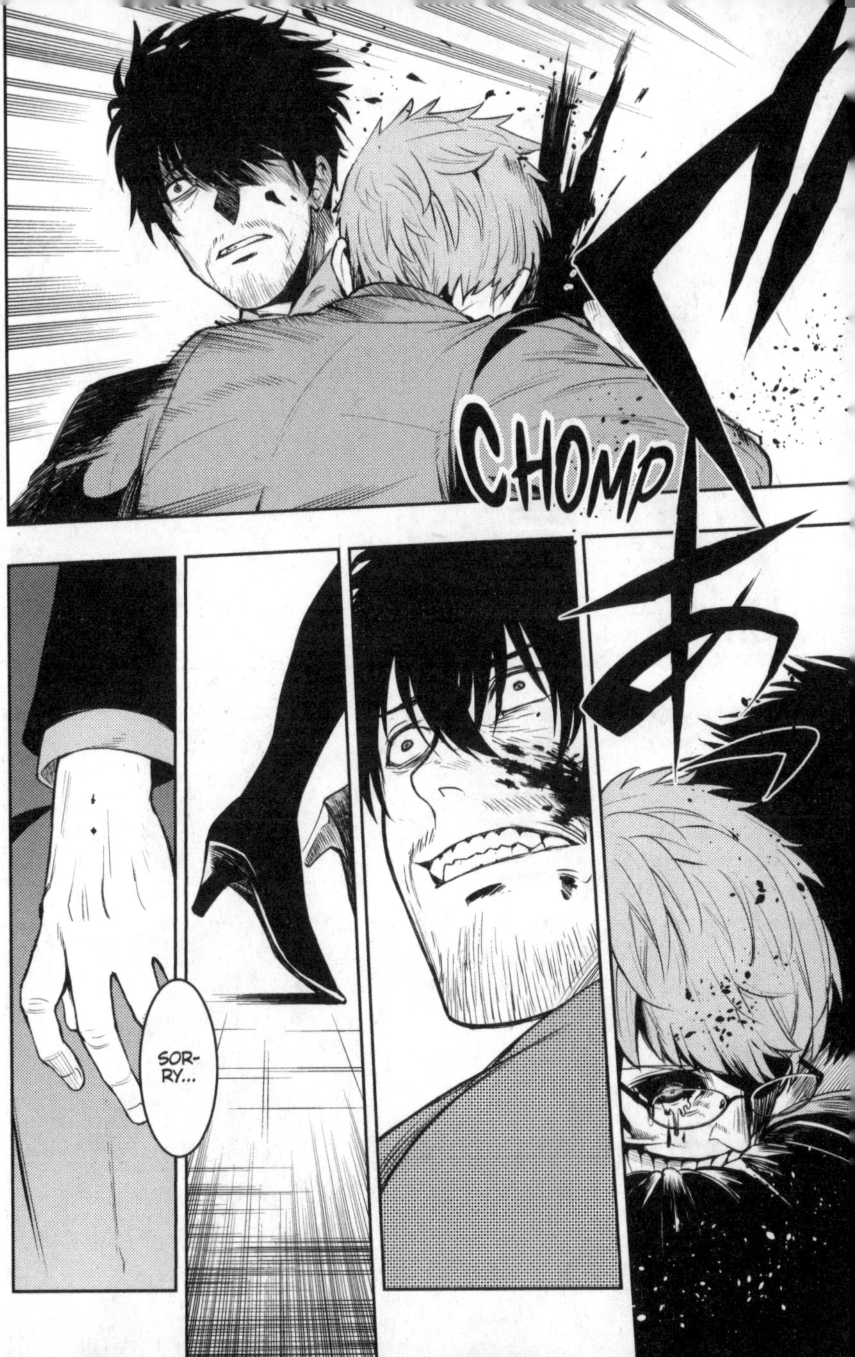
CHOMP
SOR-RY...

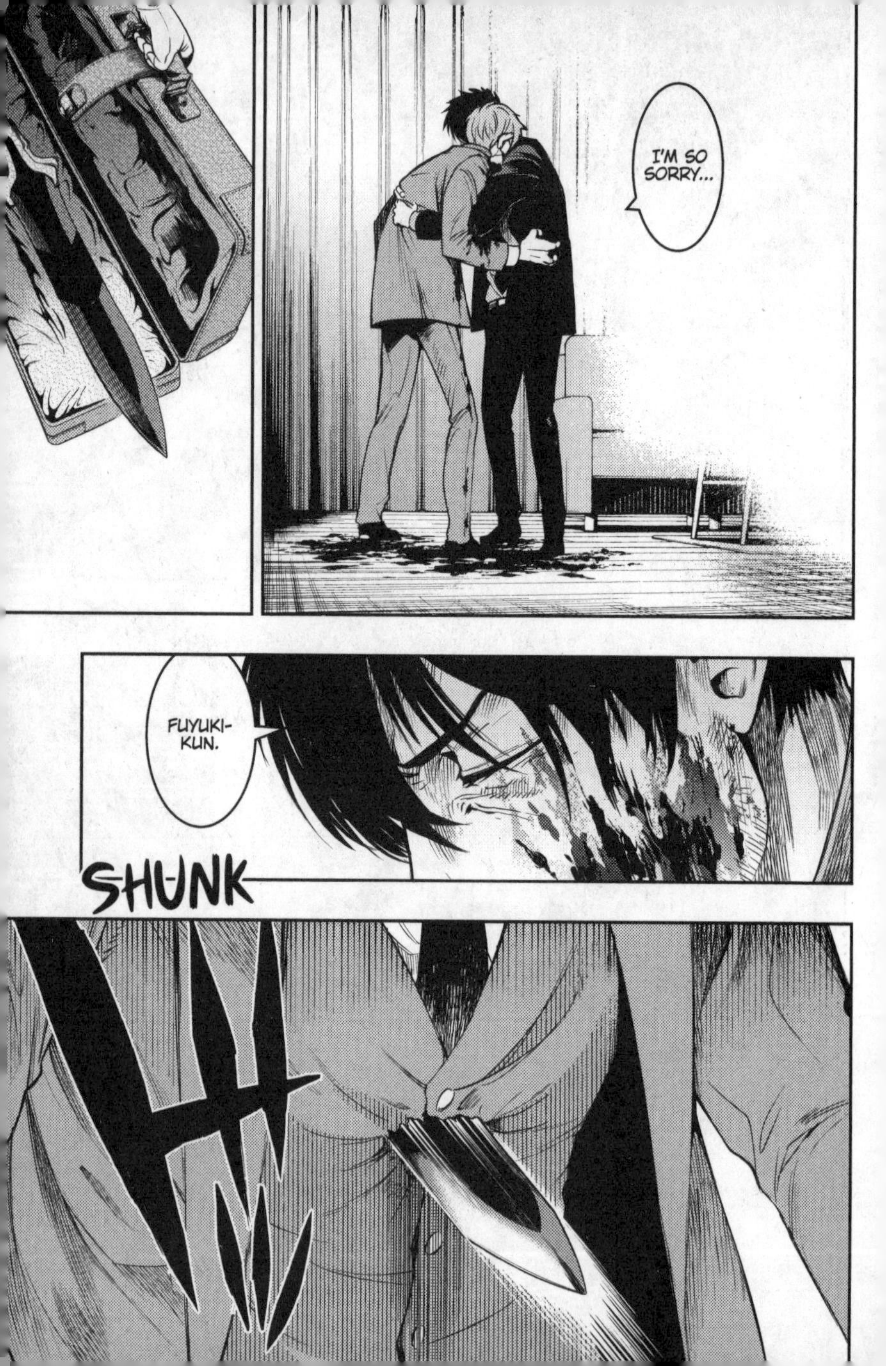
I'M SO SORRY...
FUYUKI-KUN.
SHUNK

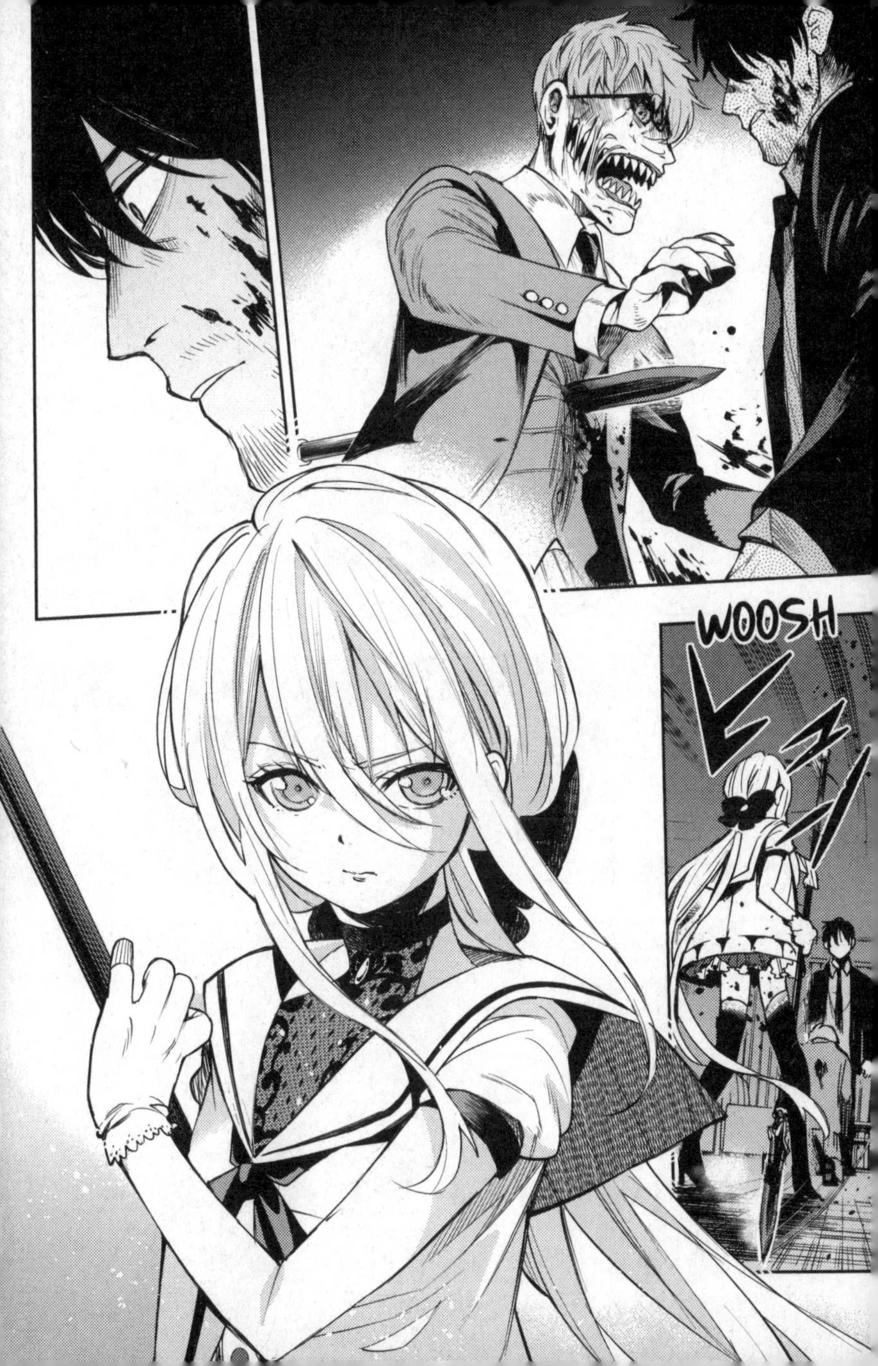
WOOSH

MOMO

the blood taker

MOMO

the blood taker

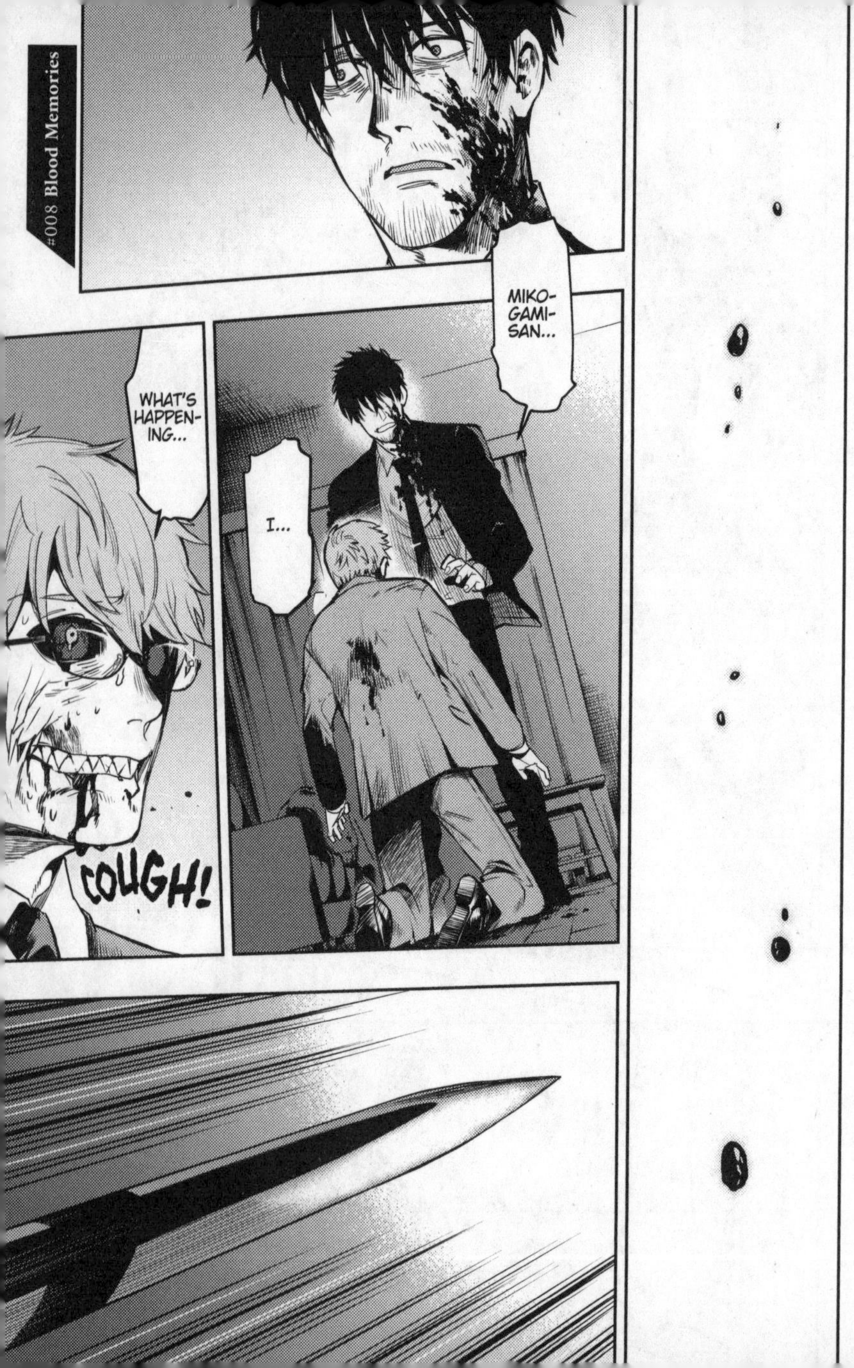
MIKO-GAMI-SAN...
I...
WHAT'S HAPPEN-ING...
COUGH!

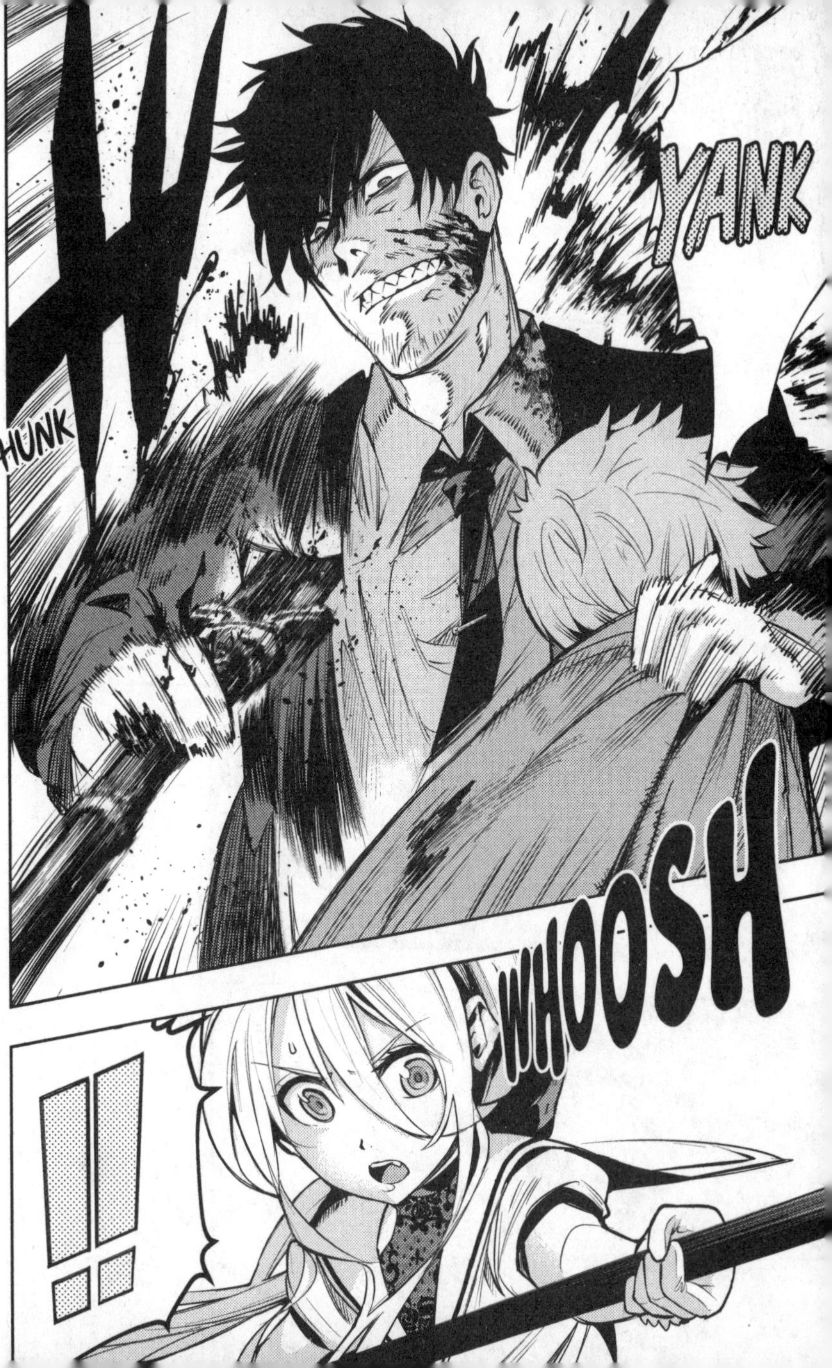
YANK
SHUNK
WHOOSH
!!

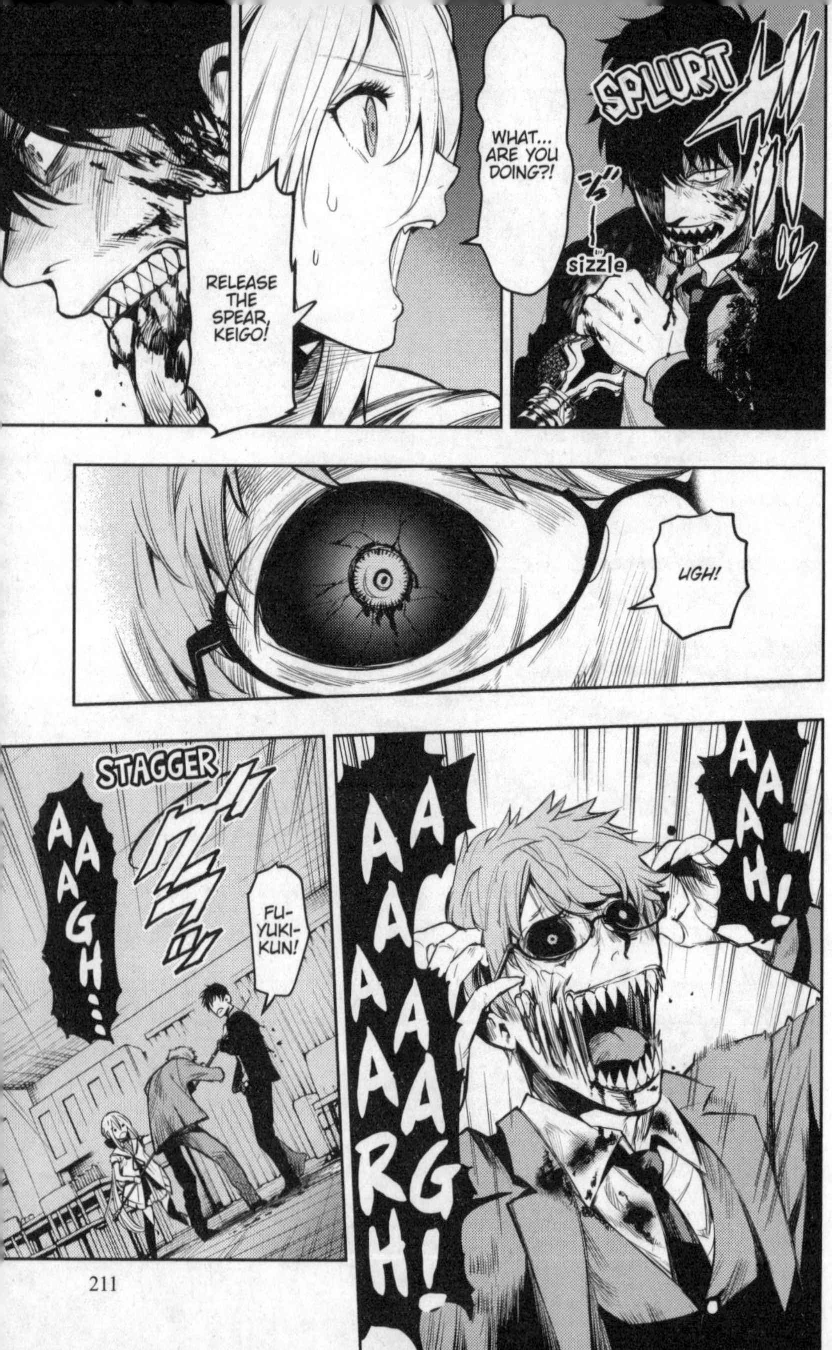
SPLURT
sizzle
WHAT... ARE YOU DOING?!
RELEASE THE SPEAR, KEIGO!
UGH!
AAAH!
AAAAAAAARGH!
STAGGER
FU-YUKI-KUN!
AAAGH...

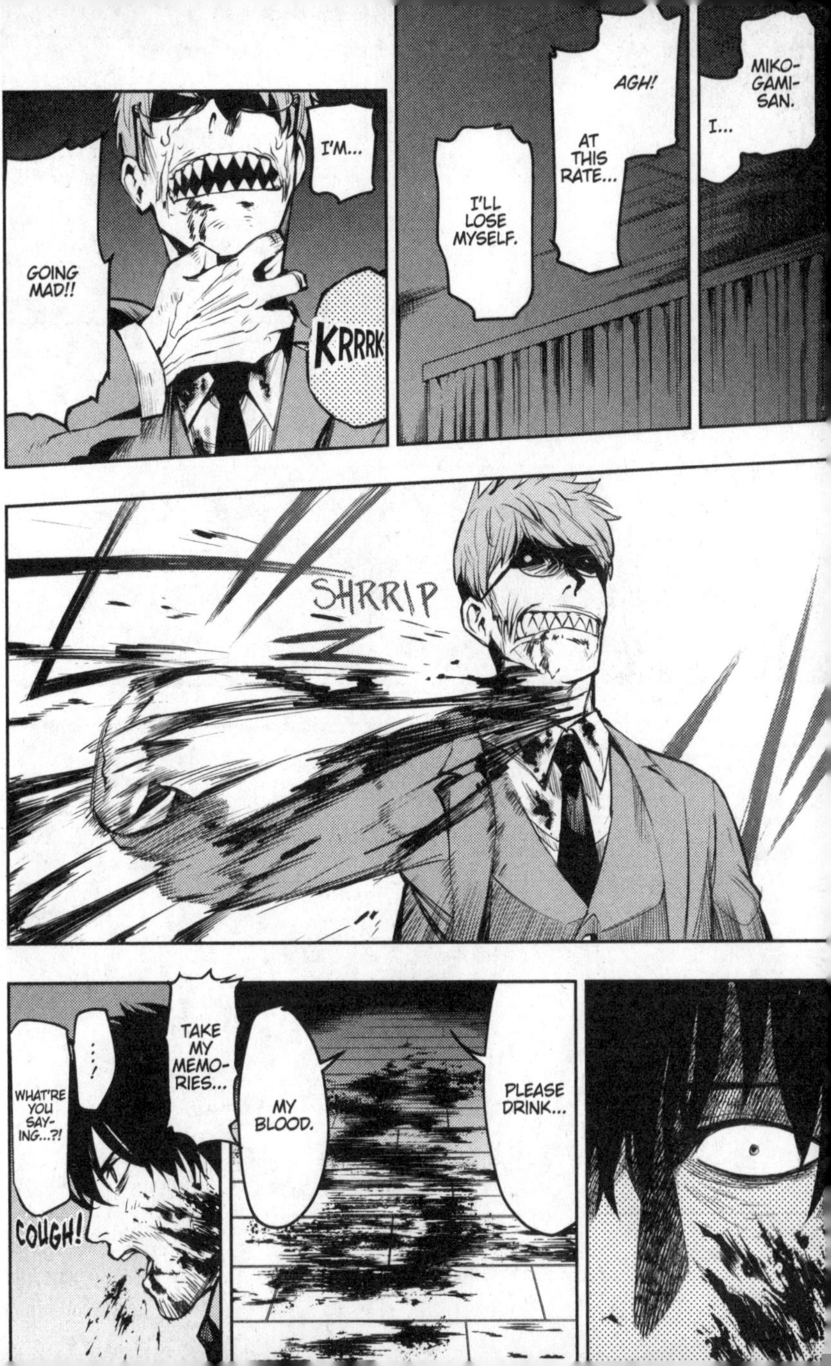
MIKO-GAMI-SAN.
I...
AGH!
AT THIS RATE...
I'LL LOSE MYSELF.
I'M...
GOING MAD!!
KRRRK
SHRRIP
PLEASE DRINK...
MY BLOOD.
TAKE MY MEMO-RIES...
...!
WHAT'RE YOU SAY-ING...?!
COUGH!

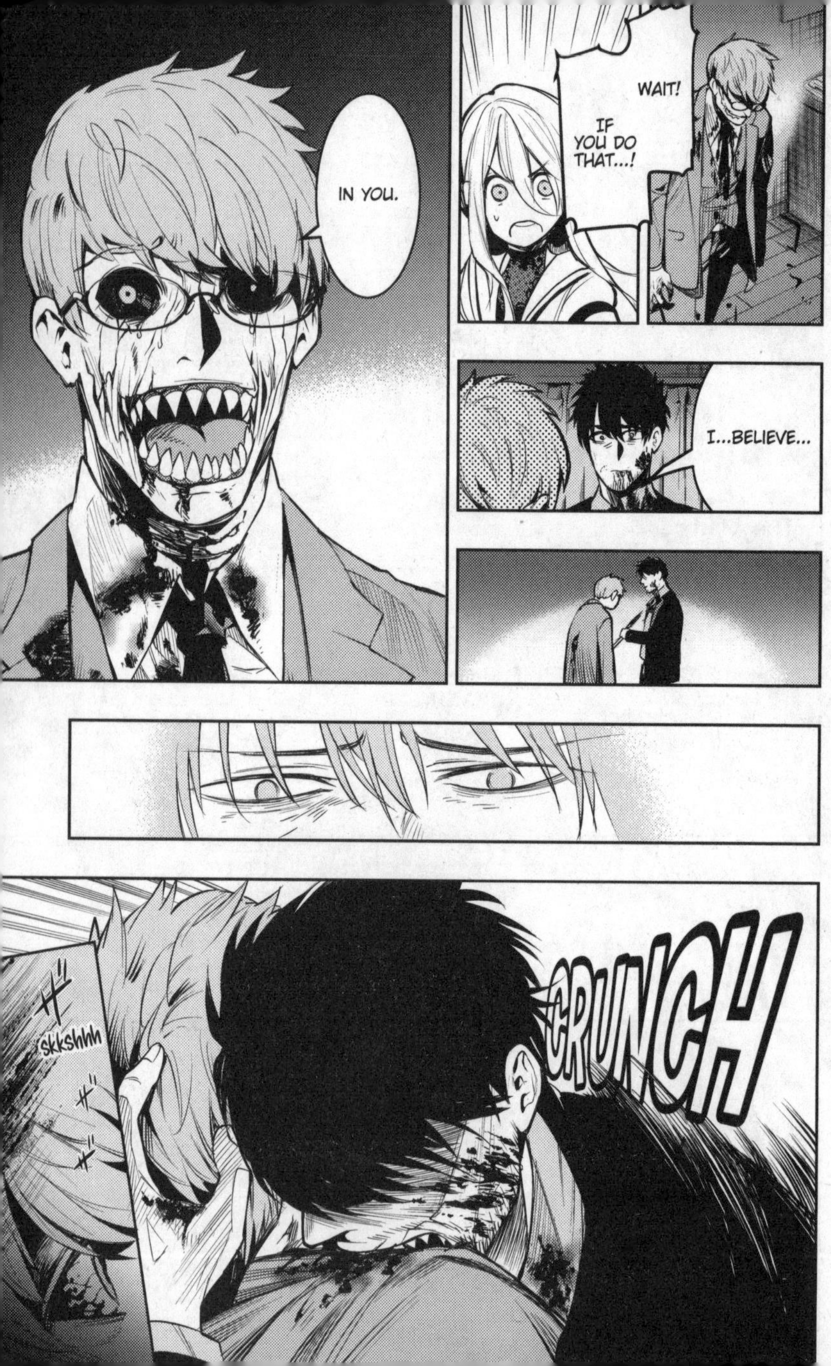
WAIT!
IF YOU DO THAT...!
I...BELIEVE...
IN YOU.
CRUNCH
skkshhh

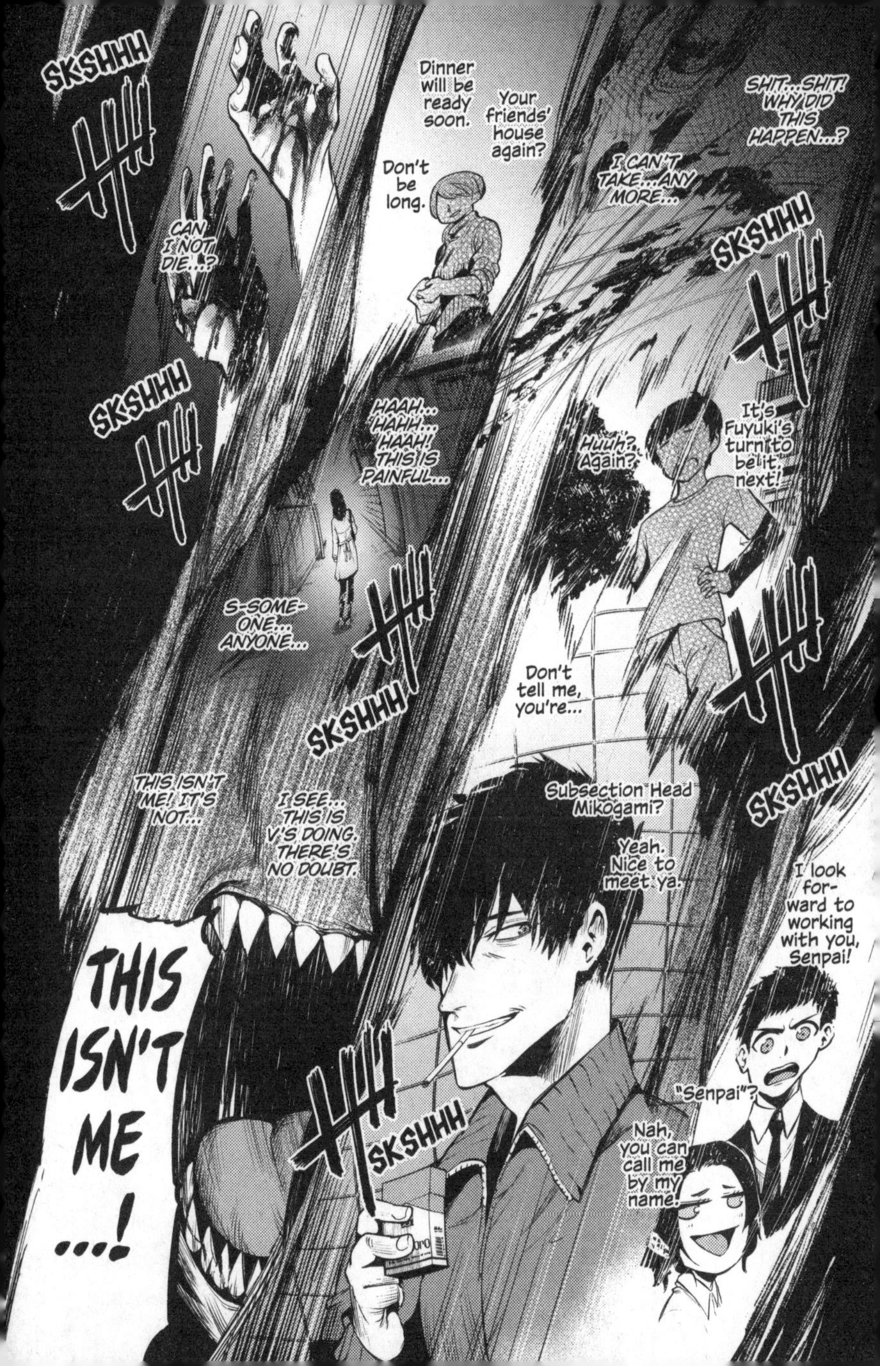
SHIT...SHIT! WHY DID THIS HAPPEN...?
I CAN'T TAKE...ANY MORE...
SKSHHH
It's Fuyuki's turn to be it next!
Huuh? Again?
SKSHHH
Dinner will be ready soon.
Your friends' house again?
Don't be long.
HAAH... HAHH... HAAH! THIS IS PAINFUL...
S-SOME-ONE... ANYONE...
SKSHHH
SKSHHH
CAN I NOT DIE...?
SKSHHH
Don't tell me, you're...
Subsection Head Mikogami?
Yeah. Nice to meet ya.
I look for-ward to working with you, Senpai!
"Senpai"?
Nah, you can call me by my name!
SKSHHH
I SEE... THIS IS V'S DOING. THERE'S NO DOUBT.
THIS ISN'T ME! IT'S NOT...
THIS ISN'T ME ...!

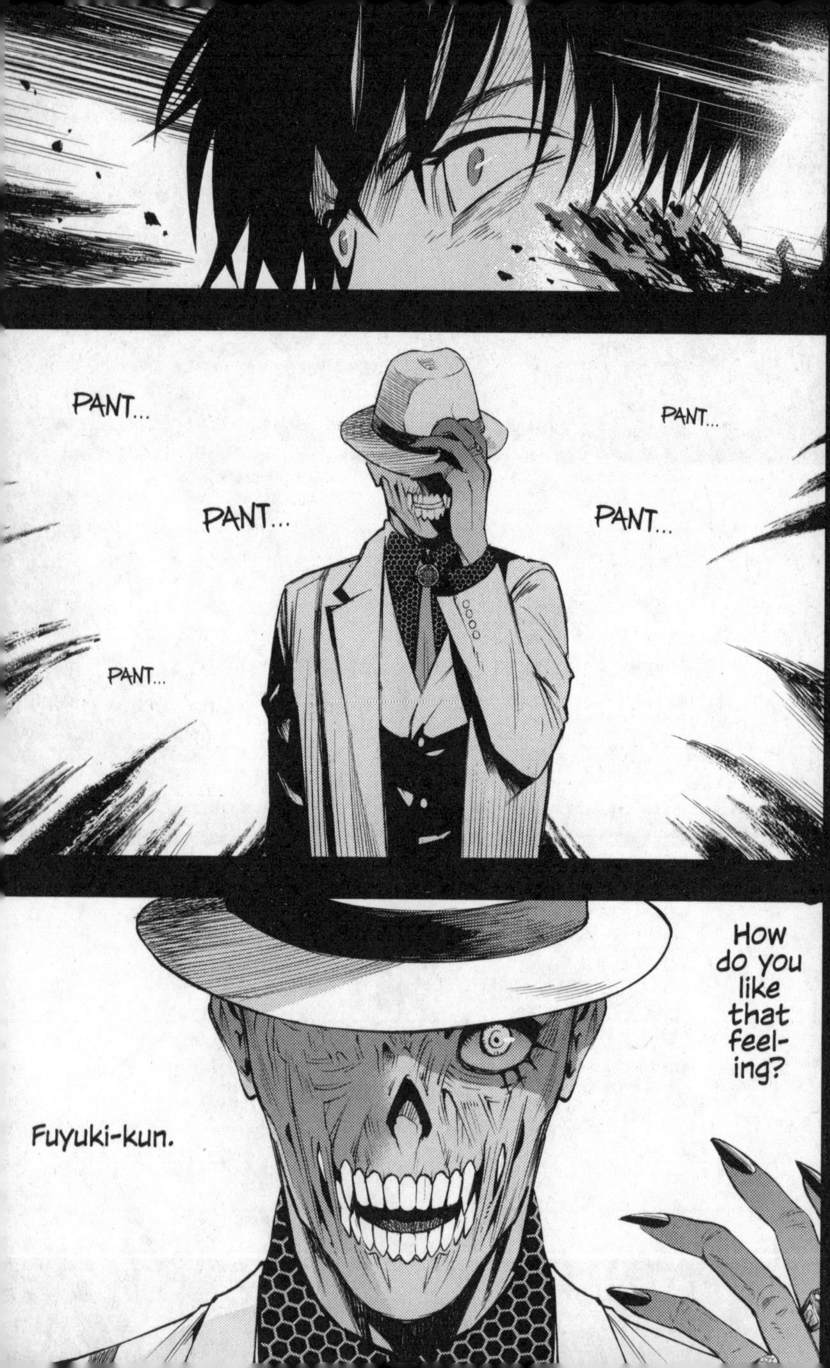
PANT…
PANT…
PANT…
PANT…
PANT…
How do you like that feel-ing?
Fuyuki-kun.

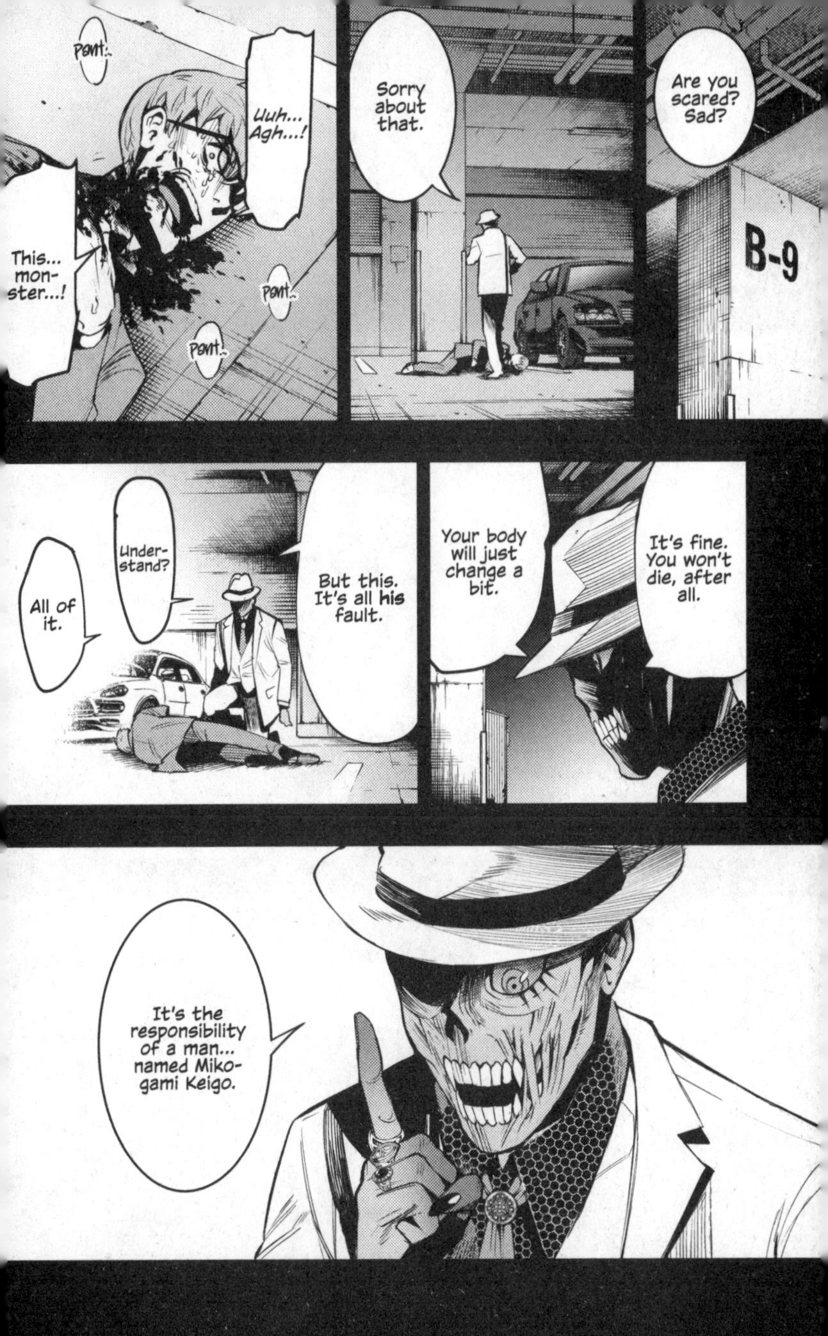
Are you scared? Sad?
B-9
Sorry about that.
Pant..
Uuh... Agh...!
This... mon-ster...!
Pant..
Pant..
It's fine. You won't die, after all.
Your body will just change a bit.
But this. It's all his fault.
Under-stand?
All of it.
It's the responsibility of a man... named Miko-gami Keigo.

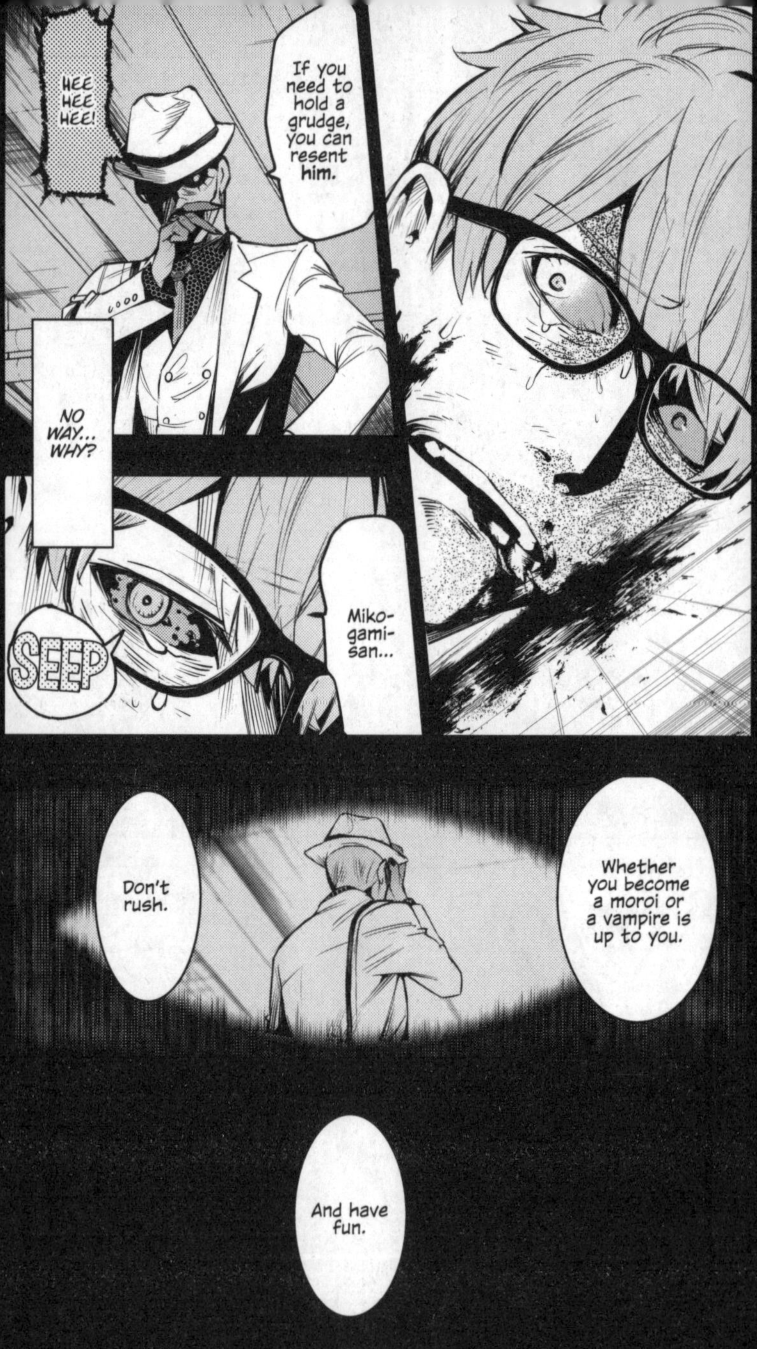
If you need to hold a grudge, you can resent him.
HEE HEE HEE!
NO WAY... WHY?
Miko-gami-san...
SEEP
Whether you become a moroi or a vampire is up to you.
Don't rush.
And have fun.

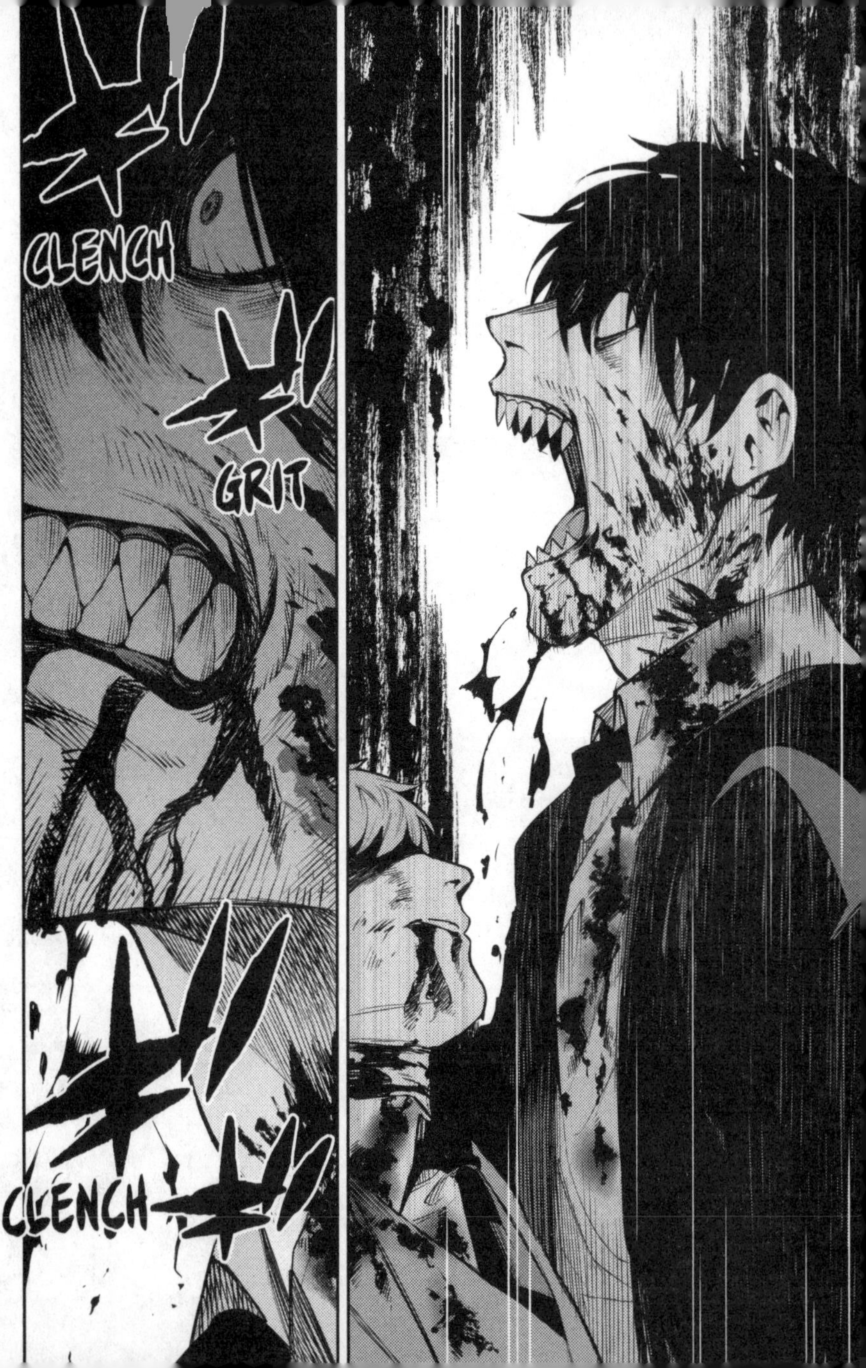
CLENCH
GRIT
CLENCH

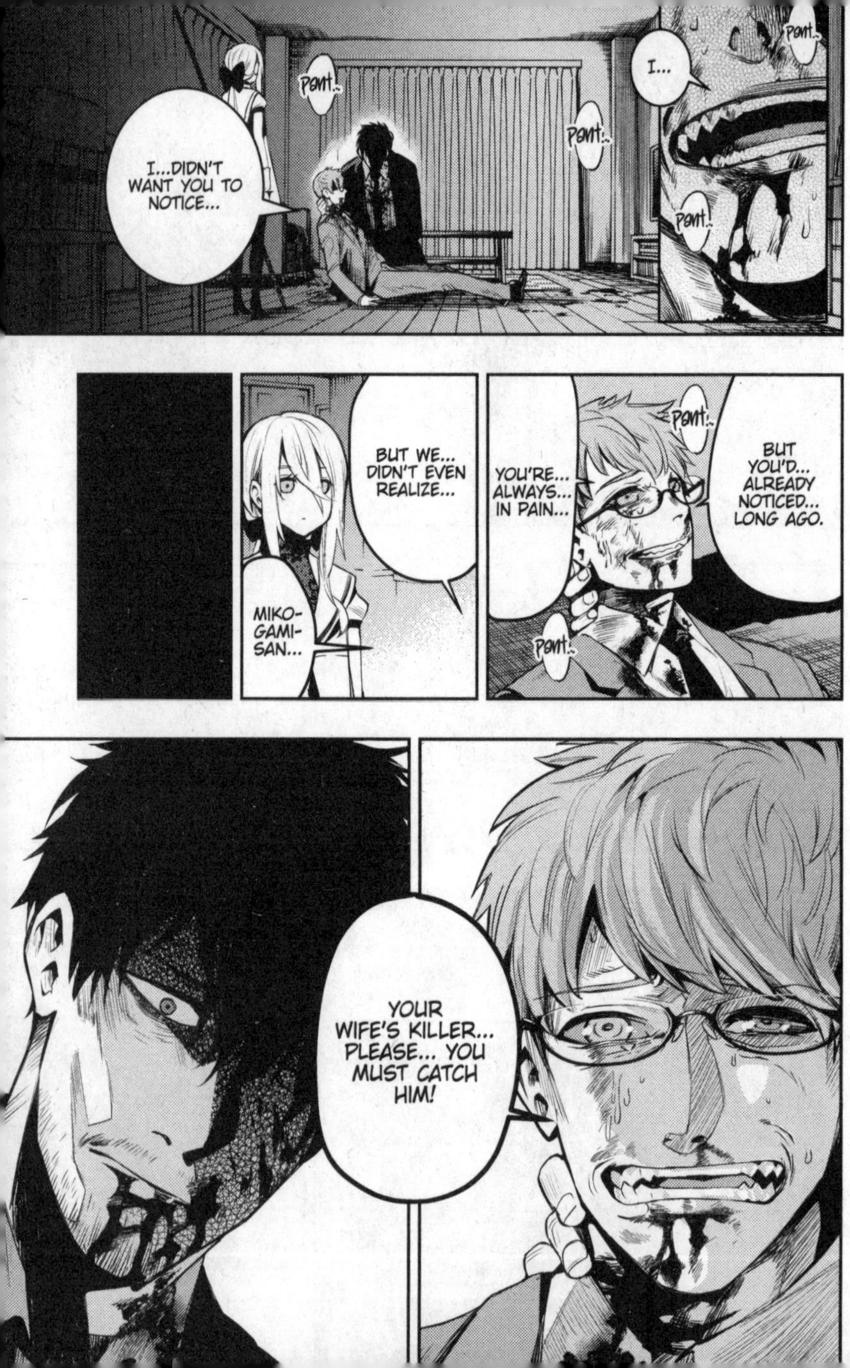
Pant..
I...
Pant..
Pant..
Pant..
I...DIDN'T WANT YOU TO NOTICE...
Pant..
BUT YOU'D... ALREADY NOTICED... LONG AGO.
YOU'RE... ALWAYS... IN PAIN...
Pant..
BUT WE... DIDN'T EVEN REALIZE...
MIKO-GAMI-SAN...
YOUR WIFE'S KILLER... PLEASE... YOU MUST CATCH HIM!

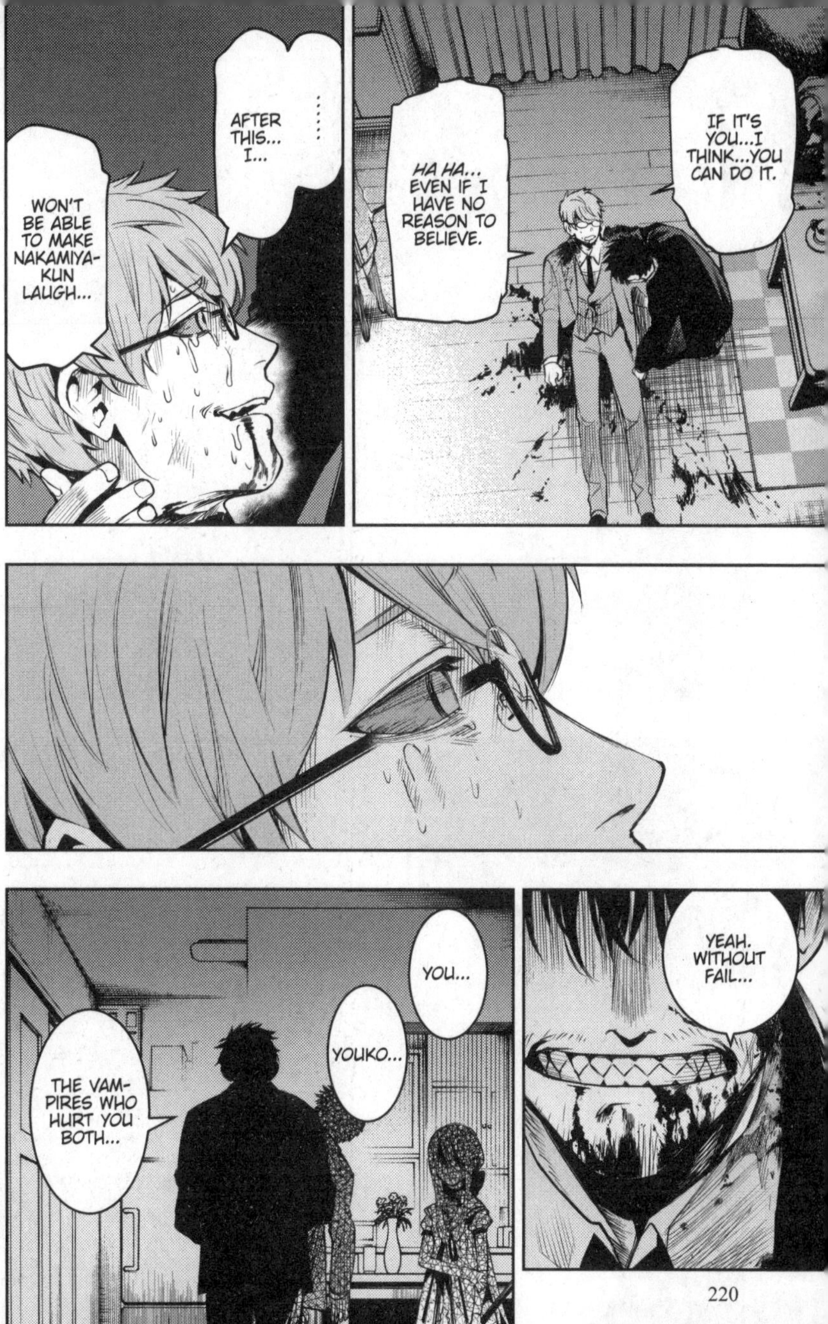
IF IT'S YOU...I THINK...YOU CAN DO IT.
HA HA... EVEN IF I HAVE NO REASON TO BELIEVE.
......
AFTER THIS... I...
WON'T BE ABLE TO MAKE NAKAMIYA-KUN LAUGH...
YEAH. WITHOUT FAIL...
YOU...
YOUKO...
THE VAMPIRES WHO HURT YOU BOTH...

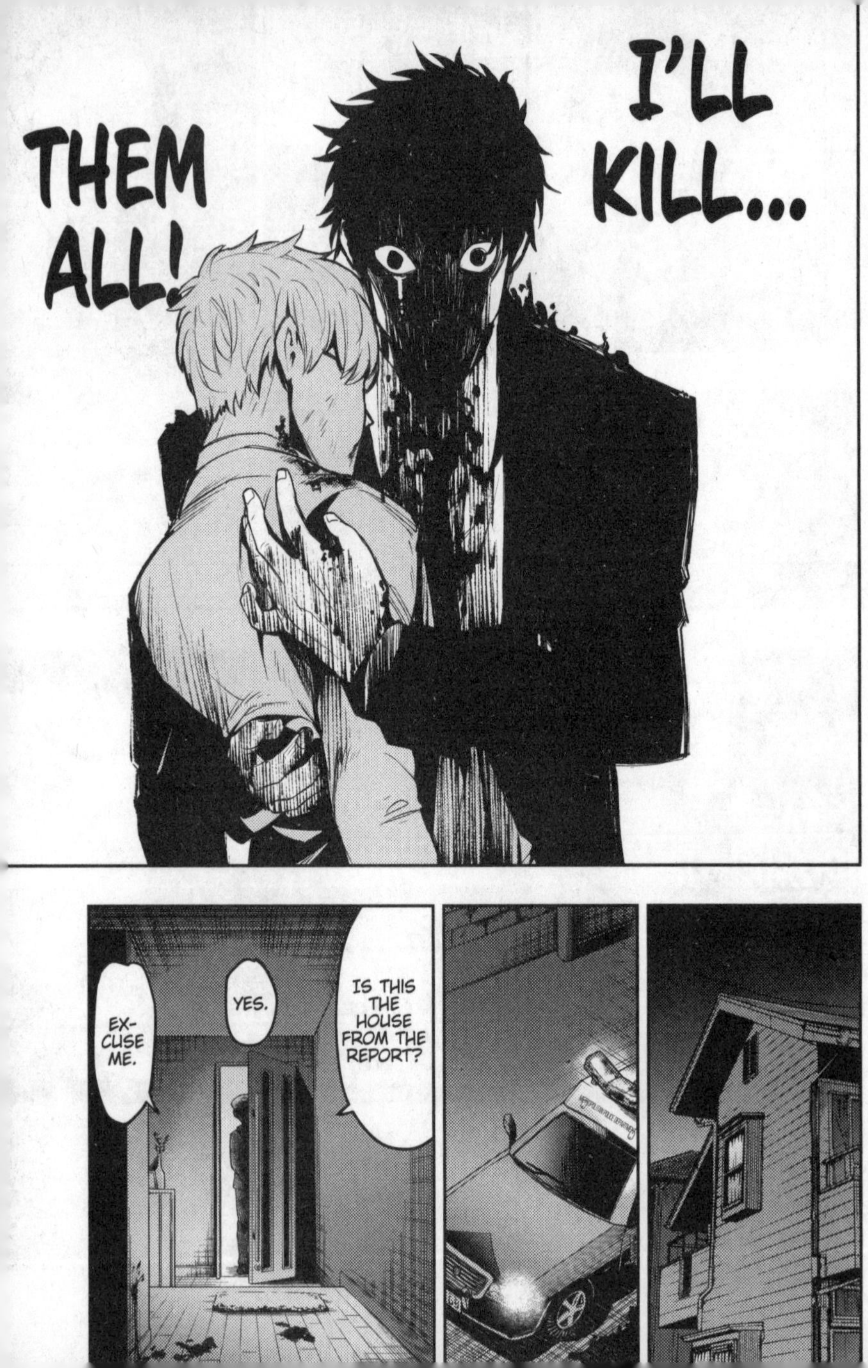
I'LL KILL...
THEM ALL!
IS THIS THE HOUSE FROM THE REPORT?
YES.
EX-CUSE ME.

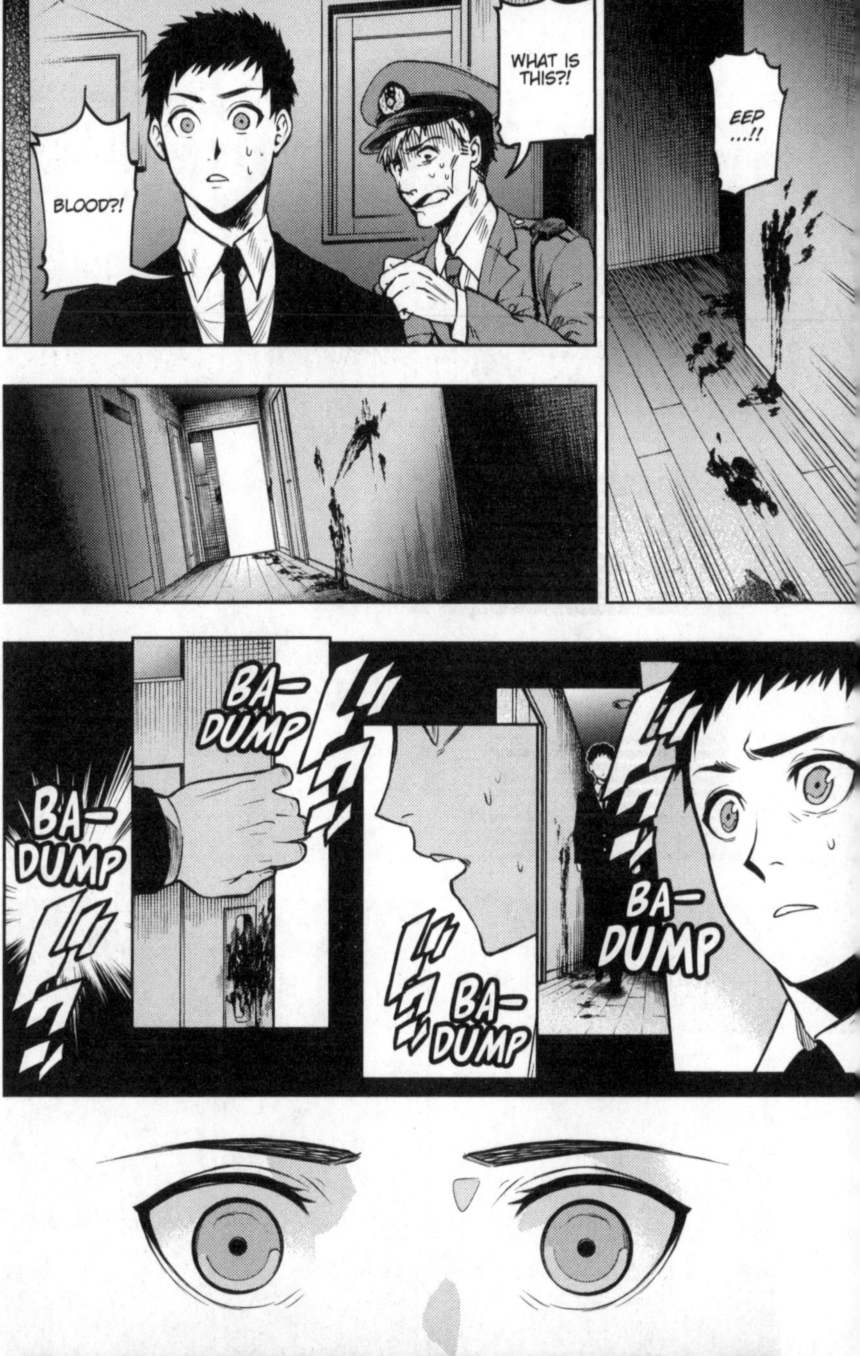
EEP ...!!
WHAT IS THIS?!
BLOOD?!
BA-DUMP
BA-DUMP
BA-DUMP
BA-DUMP

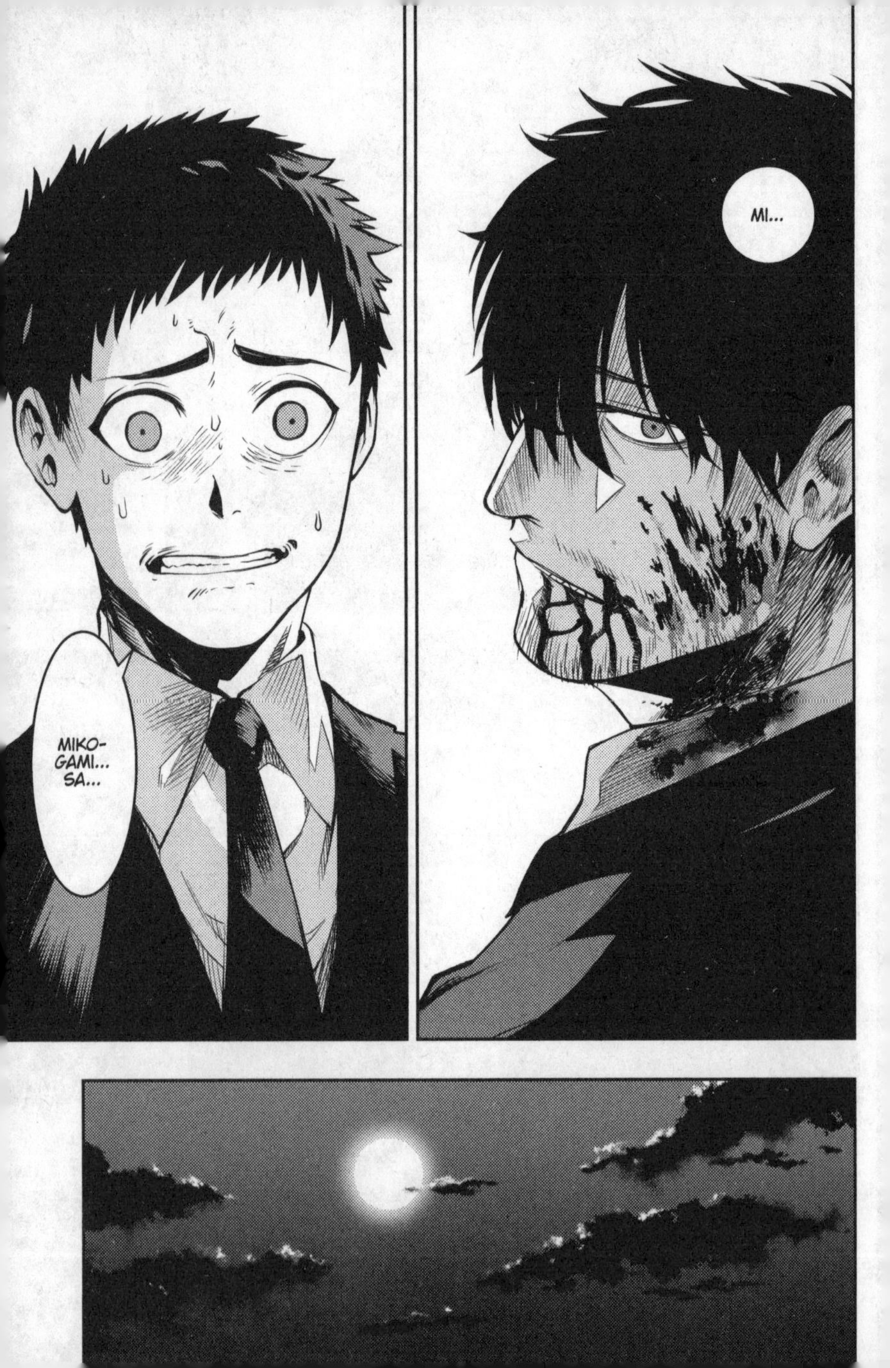
MI...
MIKO-GAMI... SA...

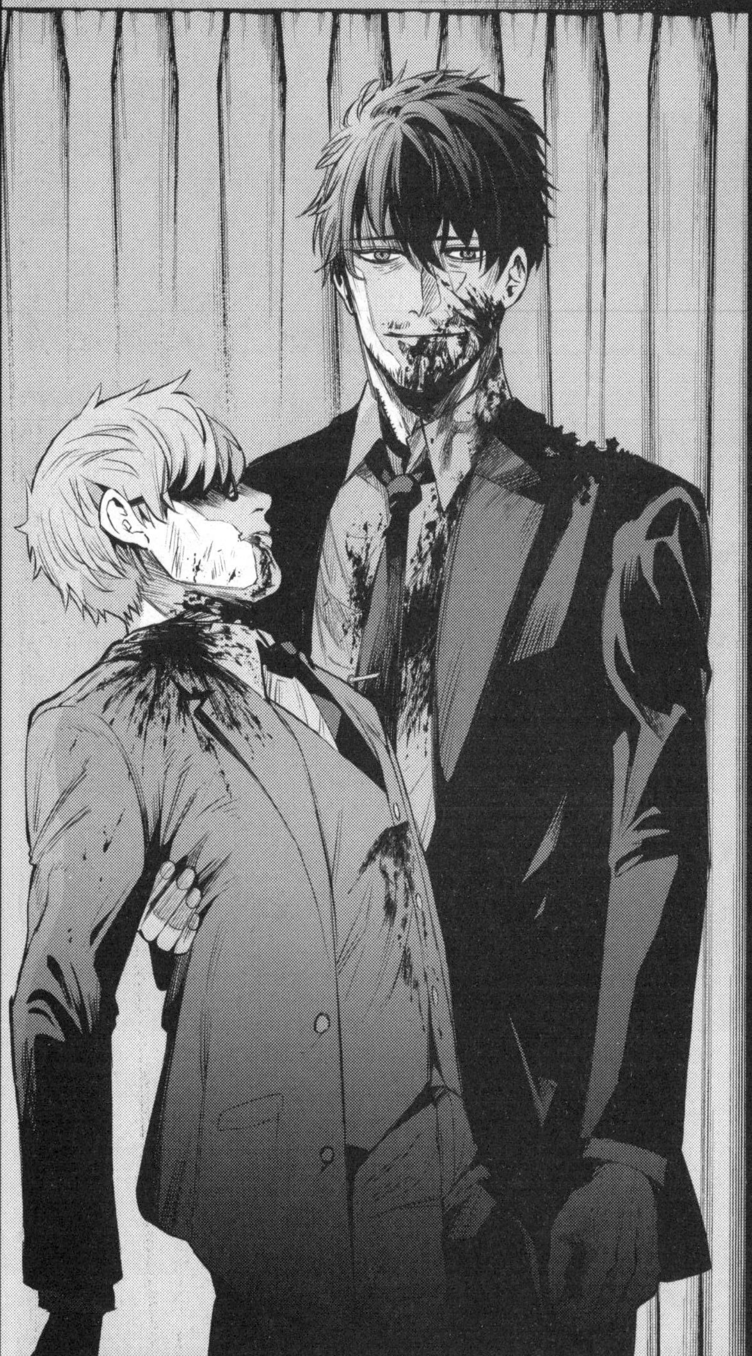

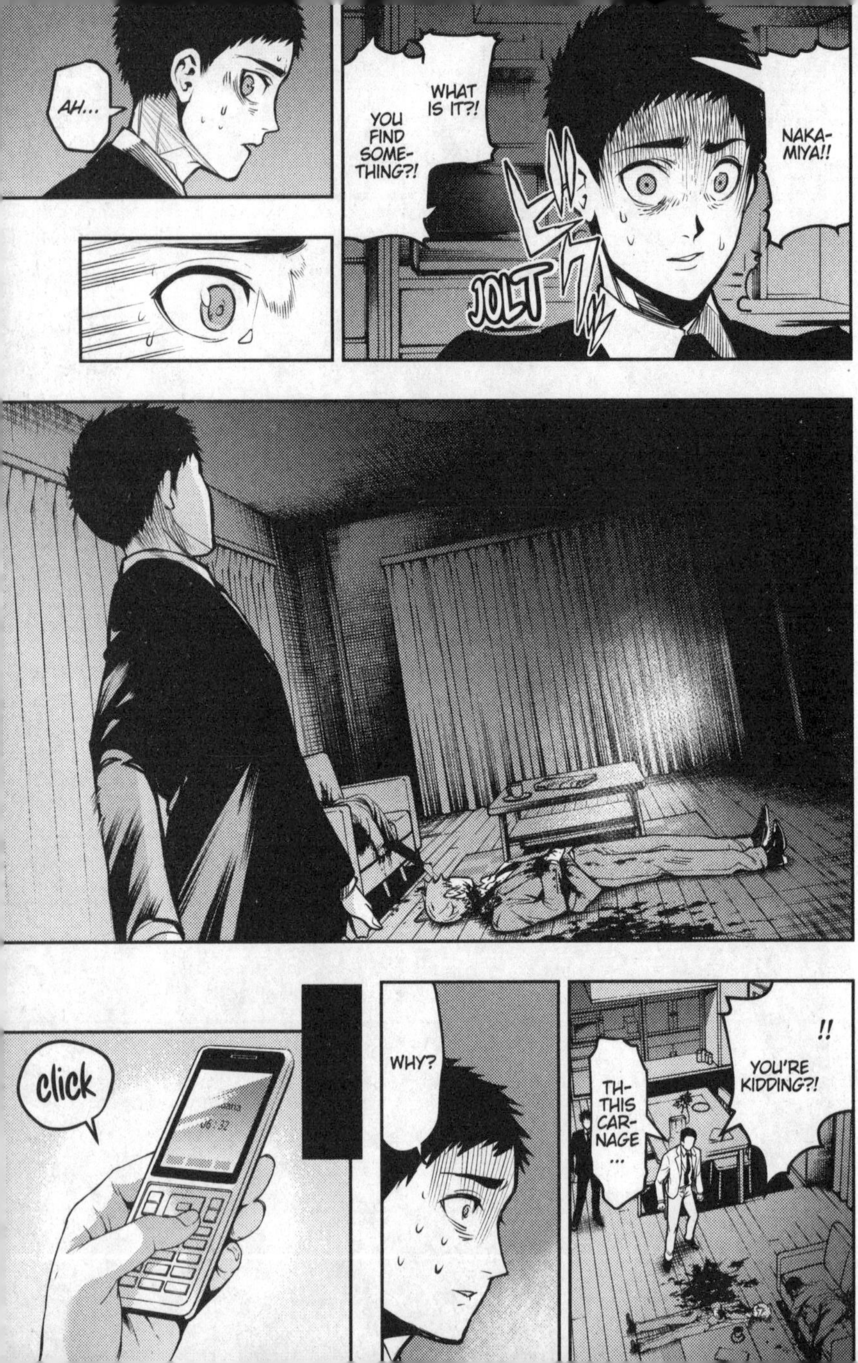
NAKA-MIYA!!
WHAT IS IT?!
YOU FIND SOME-THING?!
JOLT
AH...
!!
YOU'RE KIDDING?!
TH-THIS CARNAGE ...
WHY?
click

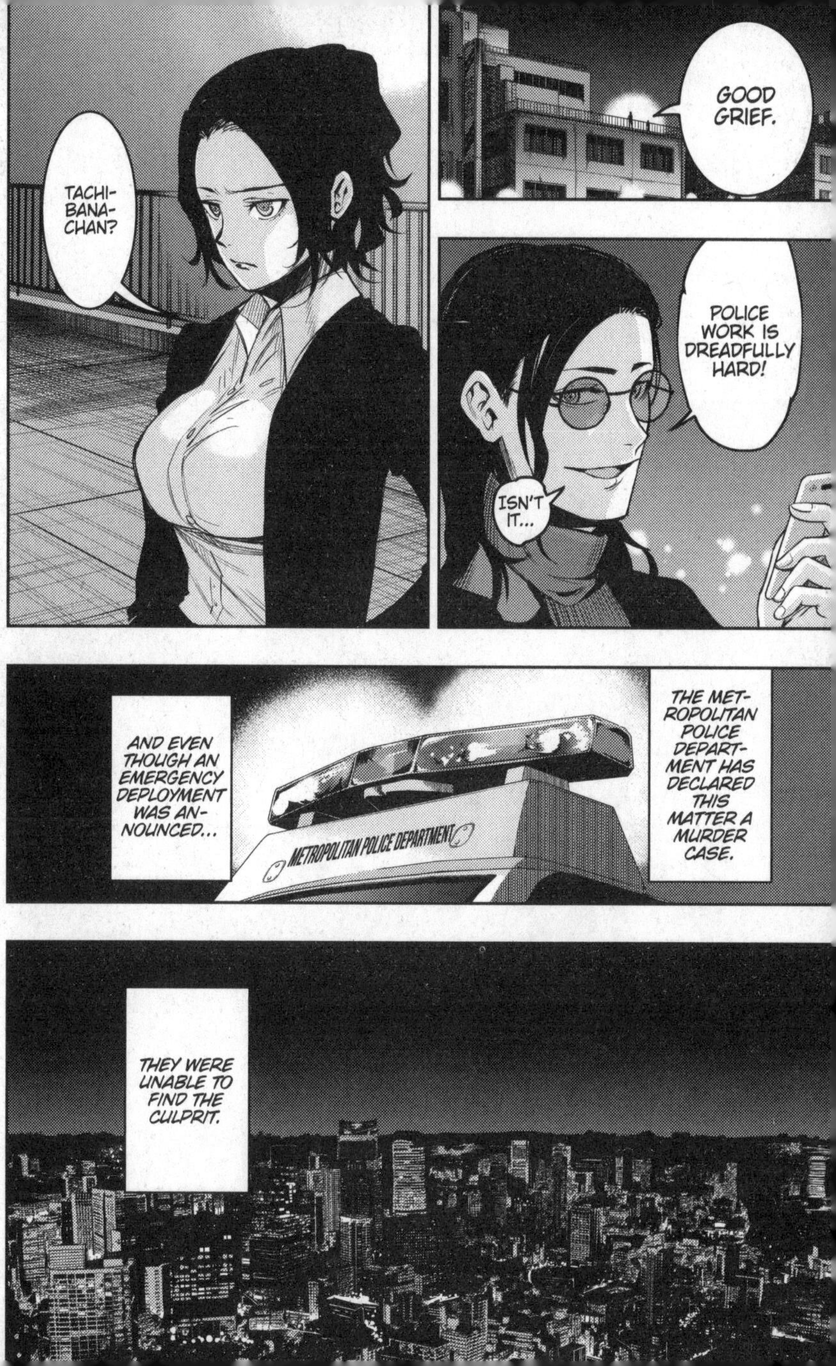
GOOD GRIEF.
POLICE WORK IS DREADFULLY HARD!
ISN'T IT...
TACHIBANA-CHAN?
THE METROPOLITAN POLICE DEPARTMENT HAS DECLARED THIS MATTER A MURDER CASE.
AND EVEN THOUGH AN EMERGENCY DEPLOYMENT WAS ANNOUNCED...
METROPOLITAN POLICE DEPARTMENT
THEY WERE UNABLE TO FIND THE CULPRIT.

STORY & ART

Sugito Akira

STAFF

Hiroki Youichirou
Umino Raku
Nakamura Kousuke
Hoshikawa Aki
Tasuke
Kitabayashi Tetsuya

SPECIAL THANKS

Takematsu Akisa

EDITORS

Ōkuma Hakkō
Matsuo Junpei

DESIGNER

Suehisa Chika (L.S.D.)

COMICS EDITOR

Maehara Masami (Yuki Design)

MoMo
MOMO
-the blood taker-

Afterword

Thank you for picking up *MoMo -the blood taker-*!

I am Akira Sugito.

The direction of my work has changed drastically since my last series, when I drew a slightly lewd comedy manga called *Boku Girl* (all eleven volumes on sale now in Japan). Through trial and error, I drew *MoMo* for you to enjoy this time.

I would be so happy if you did.

Please look forward to the next volume, too!

杉戸
Sugito

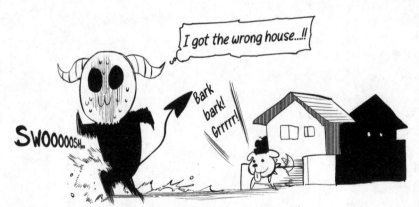

I got the wrong house...!!

Bark bark! Grrrrr!

SWOOOOOSH...

Dante-san around the time of Chapter 7.

Omake: Volume 1 Rough Draft Collection

Storyboards submitted at the serialization meeting.

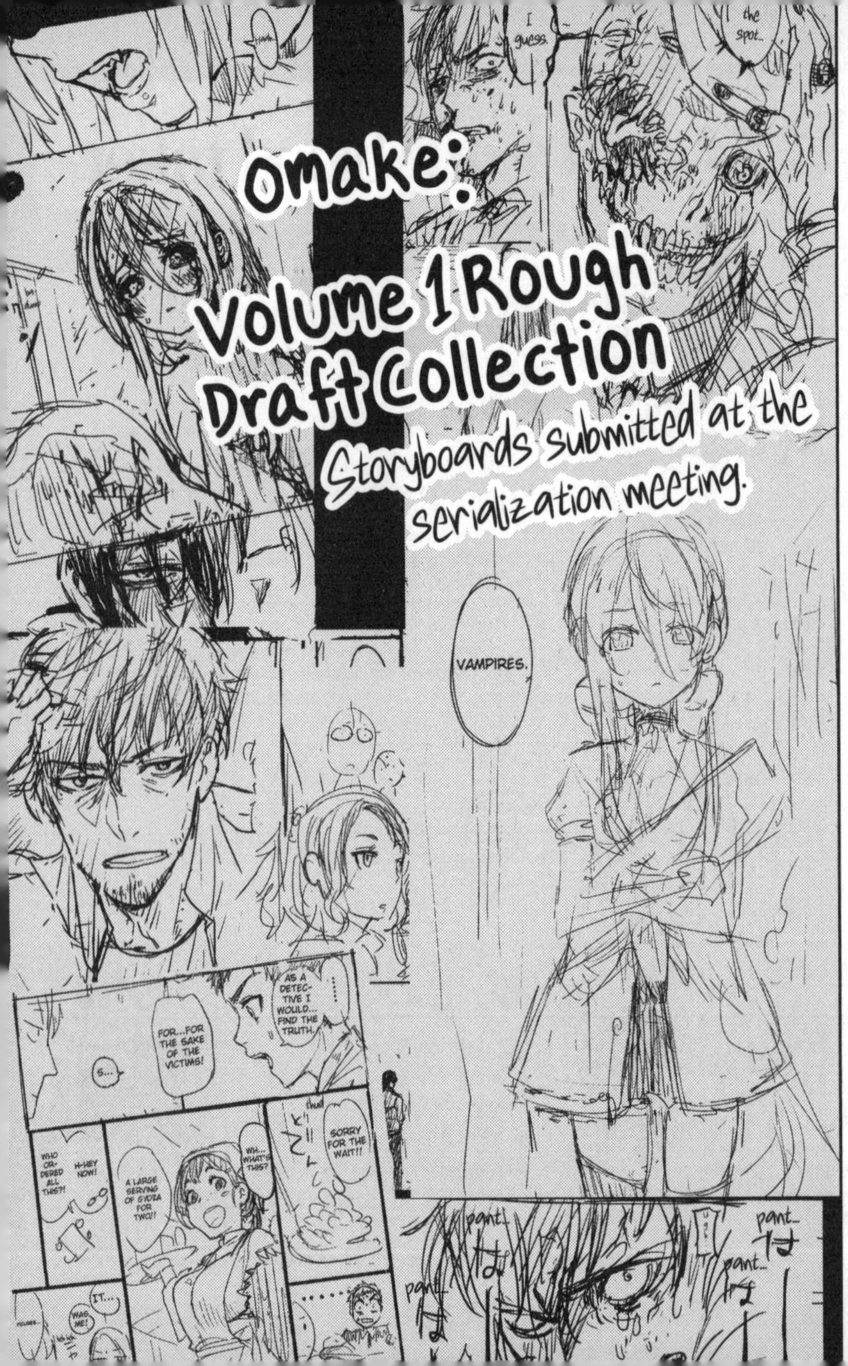

the spot...
I guess.
VAMPIRES.
AS A DETECTIVE I WOULD... FIND THE TRUTH.
......
FOR...FOR THE SAKE OF THE VICTIMS!
S...
SORRY FOR THE WAIT!!
thud
WH... WHAT'S THIS?
A LARGE SERVING OF GYOZA FOR TWO!!
H-HEY NOW!
WHO ORDERED ALL THIS?!
pant...
pant...
pant...
pant...
......
IT...
WAS ME!

SEVEN SEAS ENTERTAIN

MOMO -the

story and art by **AKIRA SUGITO**   **VOLUME ONE**

TRANSLATION
Kathryn Henzler

LETTERING
Viet Phuong Vu

COVER AND LOGO DESIGN
Nicky Lim

PROOFREADER
Krista Grandy

SENIOR COPY EDITOR
Dawn Davis

EDITOR
Jay Edidin

PRODUCTION MANAGER
Lissa Pattillo

PREPRESS TECHNICIAN
Melanie Ujimori

PRINT MANAGER
Rhiannon Rasmussen-Silverstein

EDITOR-IN-CHIEF
Julie Davis

ASSOCIATE PUBLISHER
Adam Arnold

PUBLISHER
Jason DeAngelis

MOMO -THE BLOOD TAKER-
© 2019 by Akira Sugito
All rights reserved.
First published in Japan in 2019 by SHUEISHA Inc., Tokyo.
English translation rights arranged by SHUEISHA Inc.
through TOHAN CORPORATION, Tokyo.

Seven Seas press and purchase enquiries can be sent to Marketing Manager Lianne Sentar at press@gomanga.com. Information regarding the distribution and purchase of digital editions is available from Digital Manager CK Russell at digital@gomanga.com.

Seven Seas and the Seven Seas logo are trademarks of Seven Seas Entertainment. All rights reserved.

ISBN: 978-1-63858-531-2
Printed in Canada
First Printing: August 2022
10 9 8 7 6 5 4 3 2 1

//// READING DIRECTIONS ////

This book reads from *right to left*, Japanese style. If this is your first time reading manga, you start reading from the top right panel on each page and take it from there. If you get lost, just follow the numbered diagram here. It may seem backwards at first, but you'll get the hang of it! Have fun!!

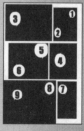

Follow us online: www.SevenSeasEntertainment.com